Foundations of Critical Race Theory in Education

The emergence of Critical Race Theory (CRT) marked an important point in the history of racial politics in the legal academy and the broader conversation about race and racism in the United States. More recently, CRT has proved to be an important analytical tool in the field of education, offering critical perspectives on race and the causes, consequences, and manifestations of race, racism, inequity, and the dynamics of power and privilege in schooling. This groundbreaking anthology is the first to pull together both the foundational writings in the field and more recent scholarship on the cultural and racial politics of schooling. A comprehensive introduction provides an overview of the history and tenets of CRT in education. Each section then seeks to explicate ideological contestation of race in education and to create new, alternative accounts. In so doing, this landmark publication not only documents the progress to date of the CRT movement, it acts to further spur developments in education.

Edward Taylor is Associate Professor in the area of Leadership and Policy Studies and was recently appointed Dean of Undergraduate Academic Affairs at the University of Washington.

David Gillborn is Professor of Education at the Institute of Education, University of London, and editor of the international journal *Race, Ethnicity and Education.*

Gloria Ladson-Billings is the Kellner Family Chair of Urban Education and Professor of Curriculum and Instruction and Educational Policy Studies at the University of Wisconsin-Madison.

THE CRITICAL EDUCATOR

Edited by Richard Delgado and Jean Stefancic

American Indian Education: Counternarratives in Racism, Struggle, and the Law by Matthew L.M. Fletcher

Foundations of Critical Race Theory in Education edited by Edward Taylor, David Gillborn, and Gloria Ladson-Billings

Foundations of Critical Race Theory in Education

Edited by
Edward Taylor, David Gillborn,
and Gloria Ladson-Billings

Routledge
Taylor & Francis Group

NEW YORK AND LONDON

First published 2009
by Routledge
270 Madison Ave, New York, NY 10016

Simultaneously published in the UK
by Routledge
2 Park Square, Milton Park, Abingdon, Oxon OX14 4RN

Routledge is an imprint of the Taylor & Francis Group, an informa business

Transferred to Digital Printing 2011

Typeset in Minion by
RefineCatch Limited, Bungay, Suffolk

Library of Congress Cataloging-in-Publication Data
Foundations of critical race theory in education / edited by Edward Taylor, David Gillborn and
Gloria Ladson-Billings.
     p. cm.—(Critical educator)
    1. Racism in education—United States.   2. Discrimination in education—United States.
3. Critical pedagogy—United States. I. Taylor, Ed (Edward). II. Gillborn, David.
III. Ladson-Billings, Gloria, 1947–
  LC212.2F68 2009
  371.82900973—dc22
  2008038495

ISBN10: 0–415–96143–2 (hbk)
ISBN10: 0–415–96144–0 (pbk)

ISBN13: 978–0–415–96143–1 (hbk)
ISBN13: 978–0–415–96144–8 (pbk)

Contents

Part Eight: Critiques of Critical Race Theory

Foreword

Does the election of Barack Obama as President of the United States prove that critical race theory is not true, or at least has overstated its contrarian claims that racism is permanent? We think this is a fair and balanced question, and consider it cheerfully.

One imagines the progenitors of critical race theory, those who labored in fields, kitchens, laundries, on railroad projects, and in sweatshops not of their choosing, whose yearning for dignity and self determination resulted in small acts of resistance whose sum turned into a social force for justice. Joined by their spiritually elite and politically progressive white brothers and sisters with similar aspirations for democracy and a decent society, the power of such a momentum could surely result, for the hopeful at least, in the opportunity for transformation. We are surrounded by a cloud of witnesses as we march forward, in the words of W. E. B. Du Bois, towards a civilization that is "free, intelligent, healthy, and unafraid" (Du Bois, 1970, 153).

Gloria Ladson-Billings
David Gillborn
Edward Taylor

Reference

Du Bois, W. E. B. (1970). *W. E. B. Du Bois: A reader*. M. Weinberg (Ed.). New York, Harper Torchbooks.

Series Editors' Introduction

This is the second book in a series, *The Critical Educator*, devoted to critical race theory in education. As the reader may know, critical race theory coalesced in law about twenty years ago when progressive lawyers and legal scholars around the nation realized that new approaches were needed to come to terms with latter-day, institutional racism and a court system that increasingly professed itself perversely colorblind. Scholars developed such tools as interest convergence, intersectionality, hate speech, and unconscious racism and applied them to school desegregation, affirmative action, constitutional standards of review, and college and university hate-speech codes.

Recently, critical race analysis has spread to other disciplines, including sociology and education. In education it includes Gloria Ladson-Billings, Larry Parker, William Tate, Dolores Delgado Bernal, Daniel Solórzano, Tara Yosso, and Matthew Fletcher. In England, David Gillborn of University College London is a principal figure.

Critical race education scholars examine such issues as hierarchy in the schools, affirmative action, and white privilege and the Western canon. They analyze school discipline and tracking, high-stakes testing, migrant and bilingual education, school financing, and "acting white." They apply tools like storytelling and narrative analysis, concepts such as white normativity, and critiques of colorblindness in an effort to understand how schools fail.

The following collection addresses many of these issues. Featuring essays by the movement's founding figures as well as many of its rising stars, it offers a rich introduction to critical race theory in education. As the population of the United States and England diversifies, the insights of this promising field of scholarship will increase in pertinence. Teachers, students, and general readers interested in new approaches to education will want to read this volume and its insights. They may, as well, wish to contribute to the burgeoning field and its literature.

Richard Delgado
University Professor of Law
Seattle University

Jean Stefancic
Research Professor of Law
Seattle University

The Foundations of Critical Race Theory in Education: An Introduction

Edward Taylor

This volume offers a selection of some of the key articles that laid the foundation for a form of legal scholarship called critical race theory (CRT) and its subsequent evolution and extension into educational theory, research, policy, and practice. My first goal is to sketch some of the intellectual and academic context in which CRT was born and to detail its central tenets, methodologies, and applications. The second is to describe its interface with education with an eye towards appreciating the rigorous thinking and writing of our lawyerly counterparts. Finally, I want to introduce you to some of the remarkable pieces included in this volume.

CRT comes from a long tradition of resistance to the unequal and unjust distribution of power and resources along political, economic, racial, and gendered lines in America, and across the globe, with the support and legitimacy of the legal system which makes possible the perpetuation of the established power relationships of society. Critical legal thinkers have long resisted this maintenance of the status quo and have worked to identify and eradicate various forms of oppression in the courts, in our classrooms, and throughout society. CRT shares the emancipatory hopes of these forebears whose moral compass led their efforts towards the call for human freedom and equality. This compass continues to guide good teachers, educators, and policy makers still.

Civil Rights Movement and Critical Legal Studies

Resistance to U.S. jurisprudence as an ideology that supports and makes possible economic, political and social injustice has a long and fascinating history. Oliver Wendell Holmes is considered one of the ancestors of this legal scholarship, with his observations in *The Common Law* in 1881. He posited that judicial decisions depended not on the result of a rational system of accumulated wisdom, but largely on the predilections and social situation of the judge. Called Legal Realism, this movement emphasized the social and political context in which judicial judgments were made and peaked in the 1920s and 1930s (Boyle, 1992), influencing, among other things, Roosevelt's New Deal strategy.

In the era of the Civil Rights Movement and the Vietnam War, the principles of Legal Realism re-emerged as a movement known as Critical Legal Studies (CLS). CLS argued that the power and dominion of certain groups (white, male) over an unequal status quo was continuing, and social and political change was needed. Some mark the official start of CLS in 1977 as a conference at the University of Wisconsin, Madison. By 1989, over 700 articles and books had been published. Major figures included Roberto Unger, Duncan Kennedy, and Catherine Mackinnon. CLS charged that the reasoning and logic of the law was in fact based on arbitrary categorizations and decisions that both reflected and advanced established power relationships in society by covering injustices with a mask of legitimacy.

CRT History

Critical race theory can be historically viewed as a sub-division of CLS scholarship about race that grew out of several seminal events. CRT evolved in response to a perceived stalling of traditional civil rights litigation in the United States in arenas such as legislative districting, affirmative action, criminal sentencing, and campus speech codes (Lawrence, Matsuda, Delgado, & Crenshaw, 1993). Following the remarkable advances of the 1950s and 1960s dismantling discrimination in school- ing, hiring, and housing, there arose a backlash against progressive racial reforms. From the Supreme Court to the lower courts unfolded a general hostility towards policies (such as affirmative action) that took race into account in redressing historic and contemporary racial discrimination. The legal requirements to prove illicit prejudice became especially onerous, and the pace of racial reform slowed, and began to reverse. The hiring of faculty of color at leading educational institutions stalled. School integration, as promised by *Brown v. Board of Education*, did not materialize. White flight from newly integrated neighborhoods re-established familiar social and racial separations. Entrenched hiring and lending practices further cemented under- class status for many families of color. Frustrated by this backlash, and the perceived failure of traditional civil rights theories and methods, a group of legal scholars, including Derrick A. Bell, Charles Lawrence, Richard Delgado, Lani Guinier, and Kimberle Crenshaw, began to openly criticize the role of law in the construction and maintenance of racially based social and economic oppression. They also began looking for an explanation of why this seeming retraction occurred, and how to formulate new strategies to effect transformation.

There are many examples of the events and locations that are important to CRT's history. I have chosen to emphasize one at Harvard. Located in a classroom skirmish between students of color and White administrators over the marginalization of race in the classroom and the curriculum, it holds for me, as a college professor, a certain interest. It also illustrates, I believe, CRT's application to some of the leading issues in education, including teacher demographics, classroom racial dynamics, and programs of study.

One founding father, Derrick A. Bell, the first African American to be tenured at Harvard's School of law, did pioneering work in establishing a scholarly agenda that placed race, racism, and colonialism squarely at the center of intellectual legal dialogue.

In 1980, he resigned in protest over the failure of Harvard's law school to hire women of color faculty and moved to Portland to assume the deanship at the University of Oregon. Some of his students, including Kimberle Crenshaw and Mari Matsuda, requested a person of color teach Bell's popular class, "Race, Racism, and American Law." The students' request was denied. Crenshaw later recalled the resulting pain and confusion felt by the Harvard administrators. It appeared difficult for them to understand the students' insistence on a Black professor (which they didn't have available to teach the class) and they assumed that the students would prefer an excellent White professor to a mediocre Black one. It was also unclear to them why a specific class on race would be necessary, since racial topics were already well covered in Harvard's constitutional law and employment discrimination classes. The students boycotted the class. They organized their own alternative course, based on Bell's book, *Race, Racism and American Law*, inviting leading civil rights academicians and practitioners, including Richard Delgado and Charles Lawrence, to teach a chapter each week. This alternative course became a forum for a nascent academic movement aimed at "developing a full account of the legal construction of race and racism in this country" (Crenshaw, Gotanda, Peller & Thomas, 1995). What these embryonic scholars realized was that their objections to the law school's reasoning lacked "an adequate critical vocabulary for articulating exactly what [they] found wrong in [the school's] arguments" (p. xxi). The "Alternative Course" was one of the first institutionalized expressions of critical race theory. Progressive White law professors lent their support and advice, including approving credits for independent study.

Harvard was not the only student-led protest of the stalled hiring of minority faculty. In fact, students of color in major law schools throughout the country organized a boycott of classes in 1989. Most major law schools had no Latino/a professors, or African American, or Asian Americans. The Coalition for a Diverse Faculty at the Boalt Hall School of Law at the University of California at Berkeley sent materials to law school student organizations and, according to an AP story, on April 7, 1989, student-led strikes were held at 25–30 law schools. In response, Boalt Hall administrators brought in Charles Lawrence and Richard Delgado to speak.

Another seminal event was the CLS conference in Los Angeles in 1986, primarily because the Minority Critiques Panel resulted in a special issue of Harvard's *Civil Rights/Civil Liberties Law* review that included influential articles by Richard Delgado, Mari Matsuda, and Patricia Williams. In addition, David Trubek and Kimberle Crenshaw organized the first CRT workshop in 1989 near Madison, Wisconsin in which the early framers, including Derrick Bell, Richard Delgado and 8 or so others, agreed on a name and devised a program of future scholarship (Delgado, 1993).

Separated geographically, and often isolated in their institutions, these early critical race scholars supported each other by phone and met regularly at large law conferences. Within a few years, through study groups, seminars and informal channels, this new intellectual community gradually built a collective identity and began to produce a body of scholarly work.

Suspicious of mainstream definitions of objectivity, methods of empirical verification and claims of colorblindness, the early "Crits" tested non-traditional forms of scholarship, including liberalism, critical legal studies, Marxism, feminism, and postmodernism. For Latinos/Latinas, an important progenitor was Rudolfo Acuna, who published *Occupied America* in 1972 and helped reformulate American history to take into account the colonization of land formerly held by Mexico.

Like other forms of critical inquiry, this scholarship began with recognition of the relationship between knowledge construction, naming, and power. Majoritarian self-interest was identified as an important element in the seeming ebb and flow of civil rights legislation and enforcement. CRT scholars also re-defined racism as not the acts of individuals, but the larger, systemic, structural conventions and customs that uphold and sustain oppressive group relationships, status, income, and educational attainment.

Thus, in CRT scholarship, the terms "White" and "Black" are not meant to signal individuals or even group identity. Rather, they indicate a particular political and legal structure rooted in the ideology of White European supremacy and the global impact of colonialism. "Non-White" is an interchangeable word that can be substituted for "Black."

Critical race theory cannot be understood as an abstract set of ideas or doctrines (Lawrence, Matsuda, Delgado & Crenshaw, 1993). Its scholarship is, however, marked by a number of specific insights and observations, including society's acceptance of racism as ordinary, the phenomenon of white's allowing black progress when it also promotes their interests (interest convergence), the important of understanding the historic effects of European colonialism, and the preference of the experiences of oppressed peoples (narrative) over the "objective" opinions of whites.

Racism as Normal

The first observation is that racism is a normal fact of daily life in U.S. society that is neither aberrant nor rare. The assumptions of White superiority are so ingrained in political, legal, and educational structures that they are almost unrecognizable (Delgado, 1995). Mills (1997) asserts that White supremacy is the unnamed global political system that has profoundly shaped the modern world. Despite its pervasiveness and impact, most standard textbooks about philosophy, political science, history, and education rarely mention this domination. This omission is not accidental. That Whites would have preference over non-Whites throughout the world is generally taken for granted in Europe, the Americas, pre- and post-colonial Africa, Australia, New Zealand, and India. White supremacy is the background against which other systems are defined. According to Mills, "Racism is a global White supremacy and is itself a political system, a particular power structure of formal and informal rule, privilege, socioeconomic advantages, and wealth and power opportunities" (1997, p. 3). Because it is all-encompassing and omnipresent, it cannot be easily recognized by its beneficiaries. Toni Morrison (1992) calls this the difference between looking at the fish and castles and bubbles in a fishbowl versus suddenly seeing the bowl itself, "the structure that transparently (and invisibly) permits the ordered life it contains to exist in the larger world" (p. 17).

The result is ironic. Whites cannot understand the world that they themselves have made. Their political, economic, and educational advantages are invisible to them and many find it difficult to comprehend the non-White experience and perspective that White domination has produced. Mills (1997) states:

> As a general rule, white misunderstanding, misrepresentation, evasion, and self-deception on matters related to race are among the most pervasive mental phenomena of the past few hundred years, a cognitive and moral economy psychically required for conquest, colonization, and enslavement. And these phenomena are in no way accidental, but prescribed, by the terms of the racial contract, which requires a certain schedule of structured blindnesses and opacities in order to establish and maintain the white polity (p. 19).

Even stranger, racial inequality and discrimination in matters such as hiring, housing, criminal sentencing, education, and lending are so widespread as to be uninteresting and unconcerning to most Whites. As a result, most oppression no longer seems like oppression to the perpetrating group (Lawrence, 1987). Contradictory information or events are seen as rare exceptions. CRT insists that the event is connected to the larger, historic and institutional fact of White hegemony.

In stark contrast, non-Whites have a startlingly clear view of the coercion that White supremacy has constructed. From birth, they generally have first-hand knowledge, as well as multigenerational experience, with the political, social, historic, and persistence disadvantages of not being White. It is the expertise of non-Whiteness, then, that forms the data base to challenge and subvert White polity. Statistics, studies, and formal databases, while important, do not, in the view of CRT scholarship, have the moral certitude, proficiency, and knowledge base adequate to name and resist oppression.

Interest Convergence

Another important tenet of CRT is Bell's (1980) theory of interest convergence; that is, the interests of Blacks in gaining racial equality have been accommodated only when they have converged with the interests of powerful Whites. The concept of interest convergence has its roots in the Marxist theory that the bourgeoisie will tolerate advances for the proletariat only if these advances benefit the bourgeoisie even more. Class conflict is therefore intractable and progress is possible only through resistance.

In Bell's parable of "The Space Traders" (1992), he imagines an invasion of aliens that offer to solve the planet's economic and environmental problems in exchange for all persons of African descent. Although many Whites initially argue against it, the majority, like their colonial forebears, are eventually and ultimately willing to exchange the lives, liberty, and happiness of Africans for their own economic and political desires. The final scene is one of shackled lines of millions boarding for unknown shores, leaving the U.S. in much the same condition as when their ancestors had arrived.

Olivas (1990) holds that people respond to the "Space Traders" in largely predictable ways. People of color, including American Indians, Chinese immigrants, Japanese interred during World War II and others whose interests were sacrificed to promote White self interest, are compelled by its explanatory power. Whites are less enthusiastic. Olivas' objection is not that Bell's parable is too farfetched, but that it has happened repeatedly. His summation of the treatment of Cherokees, Hispanic immigrants, and Chinese laborers further confirms Bell's theory.

The desegregation of education in the United States is another such example. *Plessy v. Ferguson* (1896) standardized and legitimized the era of "separate but equal" educational apartheid. Segregation was so deeply woven into the fabric of education that only a few colleges were willing to accept even a token number of exceptionally qualified Black students. "Equal" education in the South produced a record of political deceit and unequal funding that resulted in White schools that were far superior to Black ones (Kujovich, 1987). By modern standards, the accepted discrepancies strain the imagination, even beyond a simple belief by Whites of their superiority. Bell (1987) expresses his bewilderment: "A belief in Black inferiority and even simple greed are insufficient explanation for the relentlessness of the disparities, and mean-spiritedness of the deprivations, and the utter devastation of hopes that the policies wreaked among Blacks wanting only the schooling needed to make their own way" (p. 25).

As a strategy to overturn *Plessy*, Charles Houston and his team, including Thurgood Marshall, reasoned that White judges would be sympathetic to capable students denied access to law schools solely because of race (Humphries, 1994). A number of small cases, decided favorably, could establish enough precedence to overturn the ruling. Indeed, this strategy was a critical component to the favorable *Brown* decision. But it was not the only one.

Dudziak (1988) examined the political context in which *Brown* was argued and found evidence that the desegregation ruling was more likely motivated by foreign policy concerns. It was at the height of the Cold War, and technological advances, television and photography had beamed startling images of racial abuses throughout the world. The Soviet Union, China, and India regularly carried stories about the Ku Klux Klan, including vivid pictures of lynchings, the deplorable living conditions of share-croppers, and chain-gangs. This news coverage sparked an international sensation. Just as the U.S. was attempting to position itself as the leading force of anti-communism, this reporting threatened to undermine America's image as the model of democracy. Thus, the U.S. Justice Department filed an amicus brief asserting that, because of foreign policy concerns, desegregation was in the national interest. The State Department and the Truman administration helped draft the decision in usually clear and simple language and the unanimous decision was broadcast within an hour to Eastern Europe on the Voice of America as a "blow to Communism" (Horne, 1986).

Despite the dramatic heralding of *Brown*'s triumph, and the public relations benefit to the U.S. government, there was no end to segregation in education. There were no enforcement provisions in the ruling and many White schools simply closed for the year. Within a few years, many of the Black schools were shut down, with a significant loss of employment for their Black teachers and staff (Ogletree, 2004).

Fifty years post *Brown*, *de jure* separation has been replaced by *de facto* segregation, as White flight from public schools has created a two-tiered system in many cities and student assignments have shifted from mandatory busing to neighborhood preferences. Most children of color currently attend schools with relatively few Whites; very few White children attend schools where they are the minority (Orfield, Losen, Wald,

& Swanson, 2004). Clarenton, South Carolina, one of the case schools used by civil rights lawyers Thurgood Marshall and Charles Houston, remains as segregated as it was before 1954.

The educational progress of African Americans that has occurred has thus been allowed only if it is perceived by the majority as cost-free, or nearly so. Preferably, these changes have come incrementally, and without social disruptions such as marches, boycotts, or riots. Importantly, for most Whites, advances must come without affirmative action.

Historical Context

Because the U.S. political, legal and educational system is based on Whites having certain unalienable rights to property and capital, CRT insists on grounding itself in a specific historic context. American Indians, Africans and other people have been expected to provide these rights, in the form of land (Indians) and labor (enslaved people, immigrant laborers). Unfortunately, our collective memory around these realities is often dim, especially to the majority.

Julian Bond (1991) contends that our widespread historical illiteracy reveals "an astounding ignorance of our racist past" (p. 222). Few U.S. schoolchildren (or their teachers) know much about U.S. slavery, or the genocide carried out against Native Americans (Takaki, 1993). A common occurrence in discussions about race is a tendency not only to render the complex simply, but to disregard the historic conflict in which it was spawned. This amnesia may not be deliberate but reflects the ordinary narcissism of each generation, or the worry that dwelling on the past may inhibit our ability to move beyond it. The counter-argument is this:

Non-White access to education has never been a *de facto* legal or social right; the Constitution and the courts have been, and continue to be, the gate-keeper. All too often, we avoid discussing the historic reasons that Whites and people of color have had separate and unequal educations. What this gains is a release from the complexities of historical and politic understanding whereby problems such as the academic achievement gap between Whites and children of color, or of immigrants, or the poor, can be rendered as new problems, rather than the expected outcomes of intentional policies and practices. It thus inhibits the formulation of new strategies. According to Stoler (1997), one way of highlighting histories of racism and our accounts of these histories is to pay closer attention to the disparities in both our own stories of origin and those of the majority. She encourages us to take them as telling signs of the tension between fluidity and fixity in racial discourse and between that which is seen and unseen. Our scholarly (and personal) interpretations of history must be attended to carefully.

Narrative

Because Whites thus live in a world they do not understand, their exposure to the viewpoints of people of color can trigger powerful emotions, ranging from denial, anger, and defensiveness to shock, surprise, and sadness. Admittedly, this world was created, crafted, and globally institutionalized by their forebears and they unwittingly, unknowingly, and without express permission, benefit politically, economically, and educationally. One purpose of narrative is to redirect the dominant gaze, to make it see from a new point of view what has been there all along.

The importance of narrative is described by Banks' conception of knowledge itself (1993). He defines knowledge as the way reality is interpreted or explained, and asserts that the knowledge that people create is "heavily influenced by their interpretations of their experiences and their positions within particular social, economic, and political systems and structures of a society" (1993, p. 5). Positionality then becomes a perspective that must be disclosed; it identifies the frame of reference from which researchers, practitioners, and policy makers present their data, interpretations, and analysis. Positionality is a core principle of multiculturalism and is, in a similar way, a central tenet of critical race theory.

Critical race theory scholarship is grounded in a sense of reality that reflects the distinctive experiences of people of color. It recognizes, as Patricia Williams (1991) says, that "the simple matter of the color of one's skin so profoundly affects the way one is treated, so radically shapes what one is allowed to think and feel about this society, that the decision to generalize from this division is valid" (p. 256). CRT challenges the experiences of Whites as the standard (Calmore, 1995) and refutes traditional racial paradigms by claiming a distinctive minority voice. According to Delgado (1994, p. 161), "Most critical race theorists consider the majoritarian mindset—the bundle of presuppositions, received wisdom, and shared cultural understandings of persons in the dominant group—to be a principal obstacle to racial reform." This "call to context" insists that the social/experiential circumstances, situations, and perspectives of racial oppression are crucial for understanding racial dynamics (Delgado, 1995) and connects current social, legal, and educational inequalities to earlier, more overt customs and practices of racial exclusion. CRT scholars often use storytelling, narrative, autobiography, and parable as a way to expose and challenge social constructions of race. It makes use of the experience of people negatively affected by racism as a central, validating data point, in what Crenshaw (1988) calls a condition for a development of a distinct political strategy informed by "the actual conditions of Black people" (p. 1397). CRT thus embraces this subjectivity of perspective and openly acknowledges that perceptions of truth, fairness, and justice reflect the mindset of the knower. Delgado (1995) points out an important distinction between the viewpoints of Whites and people of color: Whites don't see it as their perspective, but the truth.

Narrative serves another important purpose: refuting notions of merit and colorblindness. Merit and colorblindness claims have an insidious effect that has been difficult to counter with traditional forms of research, statistics, and legal procedures. By insisting on a rhetoric that disallows reference to race, groups affected by racism cannot name their reality or point out racism without invoking denial and offense. Colorblindness also has the perilous effect of rendering White privilege invisible, and thus reinforcing its preeminence (Schofield, 1986).

Classroom Beginnings: CRT in Education

It is thus fitting that the genesis of critical race theory would be in classrooms and among academicians and subsequently spread to impact the endeavor of education, both in the U.S. and abroad. CRT has a relatively short history in education, but it came from the same frustrations experienced by the Harvard law students. Educators of color of my generation, like our legal counterparts, were eager for a form of scholarly dialogue, research methodology, and pedagogical framework in which to challenge the stalled civil rights movement and the myth that we were going to soon be living in a colorblind society. We came of age in a time we were led to believe that progressive liberal policies, starting with *Brown*, would eventually prevail and that ultimately, no one would be judged by the color of their skin, but by the content of their character. But events in the 1980s, including the abandonment of affirmative action, the re-segregation of most schools, and the growing racial achievement gap, left many of us disaffected.

For those of us increasingly worried about the backsliding of the gains of the civil rights era, critical race theory was a lifeline, a source of an explanatory model, and a wellspring of tools for action. William Tate and Gloria Ladsen-Billings first published "Towards a critical race theory in education" in 1995. Its growth and application in the field of education has been exponential, with dozens of articles, conferences, classes and seminars addressing issues as disparate (and international) as gender, class, immigration, athletics, and the racial achievement gap. This volume cannot keep pace with the exciting developments of CRT. Rather, our goal is to re-capture and reinvigorate its practitioners in its foundational thinking.

Extending CRT to Educational Theory

U.S. education, in policy and practice, has been accused of lacking a coherent theory of race or the necessary tools to overcome racial inequalities in academic achievement. Like the law students at Harvard, scholars and practitioners seeking to resist and subvert the "natural" order have found themselves without an adequate vocabulary or theoretic framework. It has been sometimes difficult to articulate what exactly is wrong about mainstream beliefs, and often arduous to argue against negative stereotyping and racist practices. There is little agreement on how race is defined or what it means in the training of teachers or classroom practices. We are hobbled by the paradox of a largely White teaching staff whose practices, consciously or not, contribute to the racial achievement gap yet who are unable to see what they are doing. Despite evidence of disproportionate expulsion rates, tracking into vocational or non-academic programs, and limited access to Advanced Placement opportunities, we have yet to agree that these problems exist, much less craft co-racial approaches to fixing them.

CRT scholars believe that racial analysis can be used to deepen understanding of the educational barriers for people of color, as well as exploring how these barriers are resisted and overcome. CRT also focuses on the intersectionality of subordination, including gender, class, and other forms of oppression. Challenging

Eurocentric epistemology and questioning dominant notions of meritocracy, objectivity, and knowledge have particular application to the field of education, and offer a liberatory pedagogy that encourages inquiry, dialogue, and participation from a wide variety of stakeholders. Counterstorytelling and narrative serve as a pedagogical tool that allows educators to better understand the experiences of their students of color through deliberative and mindful listening techniques. Learning to listen to these stories and figuring out how to make them matter in the educational system is potentially invigorating and validating.

Read All About It

In this volume, you will start with the application of critical race theory to education by Gloria Ladson-Billings and David Gillborn. You will also study the original Derrick Bell and Mary Dudziak articles that revealed motivations less than lofty for *Brown*. The collapse of affirmative action as a progressive theory and policy will be analyzed by Mark Tushnet and Richard Delgado. Research methodologists ask the question: Can CRT, with its emphasis on "soft" sources such as narrative and storytelling, be considered legitimate analytical frameworks and useful qualitative research methods? Daniel Solórzano, Tara Yosso, Laurence Parker and Marvin Lynn take seriously issues about CRT's research rigor.

Claude Steele surprised the educational testing world with his evocative studies demonstrating the impact of testing conditions and stereotyping on standardized test results. In a series of experiments conducted at Stanford University, he showed that, depending on what negative stereotype was invoked, standardized test scores could be easily manipulated. Told their results are to be compared to Asian men, White men's math scores went down significantly. Women known to be exceptional at math and science produced depressed test scores when prompted that their results were being compared to men. Older people doing "memory" tests showed similar declines. The racial test gap disappeared when African American students were prompted to take a test merely to judge the merits of the test itself, rather than as a reflection of personal ability.

Amanda Datnow and Robert Cooper challenge the widely popular notion of African American achievement being suppressed by fear of "acting white." It turns out that just about all high schools have an oppositional sub-culture that ridicules kids that get good grades or try to please teachers. Teasing and tormenting "nerds" and "geeks" is a familiar phenomena not unique to African Americans. And when there is a critical mass of high achievers, African American students, like their counterparts, validate and support each other.

Part 6 demonstrates CRT's intersection with a variety of other forms of oppression and its application in challenging gender, class, and culture. In a fascinating piece, Avtar Brah and Ann Phoenix frame critical intersections with feminist critiques of the Iraq war. Writing from a post 9/11 perspective, Zeus Leonardo calls for a discourse on White supremacy as a starting point towards the possibility of resolution of the racial plot that has since unfolded. You will also read about the use of racial identity development theory as a tool to teach white students and teachers about racism in ways that allow them to speak up against systems of oppression. Beverly Daniel Tatum shows that movement beyond the litany of oppression and victimization can be realized in the classroom and, by extension, in the quest towards a more just society.

The last section is devoted to critiques, and counter-critiques. CRT is an important academic movement, and it should be vigorously debated. Douglas Litowitz's 1997 challenge of CRT uses an excellent review of its history and precepts with his "Two Good Points and Five Problems." Adding to this dynamic tension is Daniel Farber and Suzanna Sherry's piece arguing against the use of storytelling rather than established "standards" of legal scholarship. Delgado responds, though, pointing out some curious lapses in their citations in his "On Telling Stories in School: A Reply to Farber and Sherry." He refutes their claims, and notes that all standards are, by definition, arbitrary.

Here is the Chance to Lift up the Banner of Humanity

I'm often asked, as one of the few African American education professors on this Northwest campus, to speak to groups of teachers, administrators, and principals from K-12 schools currently wrestling with segregation, the racial achievement gap, or cultural divides between students and teachers. These front-line educators impress me as good people who are faced with classroom realities that many academicians cannot fully appreciate. Their sincerity and decency humbles me, especially as they fill me in on what is happening in their buildings. There are districts that have, in the course of just a few years, gone from being 98% White to 95% Hispanic, with many of the incoming students speaking English as a second language. There are schools in the city in which I work where children speak 37 different languages. Urban schools have seen their proud history of racial integration fade as middle-class families of all ethnicities seek a more promising future in our area's many private and parochial schools, leaving schools of concentrated poverty, a myriad of social problems and complex inter-group dynamics.

And so I find myself listening to these educators as they express their doubts and worries. There are those who question whether or not they can do the work of dismantling racism in the classroom. There are those who say, "I try to lead, but I'm not sure people here are going to follow." Or, "I've been doing this a long time, and I haven't seen much success yet. I believe so deeply in justice, I believe in closing the achievement gap, but I just haven't seen it happen." And others, "I'm just not sure I have the skill, the knowledge, and on some mornings, even the energy."

If racism is permanent, as CRT asserts, their weariness and despair are predictable and inevitable. Yet I believe that, as Derrick Bell points out, there is something real out there. It is not, he says, a romantic notion of colorblindness nor an idealistic illusion that oppression in all its forms will be eradicated. CRT does not make this promise. In fact, Bell assures his readers: "We must realize, as our slave forebears did, that the struggle for freedom is, at bottom, a manifestation of our humanity which survives and grows stronger through resistance to oppression, even if that oppression is never overcome" (Bell, 1990, 379).

Paradoxically, it is the act of resistance itself that is our triumph. These small and simple decisions to resist domination, added and multiplied, can create significant momentum. Or perhaps they don't do much at all. Perhaps no one listens, and little changes. It is the refusal to remain silent, in and of itself, that gives strength and empowerment in a society determined to cling to established habits of repression. If you remember this, you will understand critical race theory.

CRT holds the promise to inform educational strategies and renew efforts of resistance. Its oppositional character gives voice to otherwise unspoken realities. It can be accused of lacking coherence, since oppressed people are rarely monolithic, and their narratives reflect a wide range of experiences. CRT can rightly be seen as too nihilistic, but that may paradoxically be inspiring. For those engaged in the effort to overcome injustice, this sense of futility may be a source of affirmation. According to Bell (1992), for those who bear the burden of racial insubordination (and their allies), the truth, no matter how dire, may be uplifting.

W. E. B. Du Bois once said, "Here is the chance for young men and women of devotion to lift up the banner of humanity and march towards a civilization that is free, intelligent, healthy and unafraid" (1970, p. 153). This promise is a powerful agenda. When the sunrise wakes me up, and I cross the threshold into the University of Washington, I think about where I am standing right now. I think of those who have resisted, not because they thought they would overturn institutional and idea-logic injustice themselves, or that their actions would lead to a world in which their descendants could achieve this level of education and opportunity. I am grateful to them, and to the many teachers that made it possible for me to be here. I am hopeful that you have students who will benefit from your courage as well.

It may take a dose of racial realism to discover a new vision and the will to pursue it, whether it be the dream of an educational institution that reflects our nation's diversity or the development of a curriculum so authentic and powerful as to eradicate all forms of oppression. The cumulative effect of this may produce a transformation of not only our educational system, but the meaning of American democracy.

References

Banks, J. A. (1993). The canon debate, knowledge construction and multicultural education. *Educational Researcher,* *22*(5), 4–14.

Bell, D. (1980). *Brown v. Board of Education* and the interest convergence dilemma. *Harvard Law Review, 93,* 518.

Bell, D. (1987). *And we are not saved: The elusive quest for racial justice.* New York: Basic Books.

Bell, D. (1990). Racial realism—After we're gone: Prudent speculations on America in a post-racial epoch. *St. Louis Law Journal, 34,* 393.

Bell, D. (1992). *Faces at the bottom of the well: The permanence of racism.* New York: Basic Books.

Bond, J. (1991). Reconstruction and the Southern movement for civil rights—then and now. *Teachers College Record, 93*(2), 221–235.

Boyle, J. (1992). *Critical legal studies.* New York: New York University Press.

Calmore, J. O. (1995). Critical race theory, Archie Shepp, and fire music: Securing an authentic intellectual life in a multicultural world. In K. W. Crenshaw, N. Gotanda, G. Peller, & K. Thomas (Eds.), *Critical Race Theory* (pp. 315–329). New York: The New Press.

Crenshaw, K. W. (1988). Race, reform, and retrenchment: Transformation and legitimation in antidiscrimination law. *Harvard Law Review, 101*(7), 1331–1387.

Crenshaw, K. W., Gotanda, N., Peller, G., & Thomas, K. (1995). *Critical race theory: The key writings that formed the movement.* New York: The New Press.

Delgado, R. (Ed.) (1995). *Critical Race Theory: The cutting edge*. Philadelphia: Temple University Press.

Delgado, R. & Stefancic, J. (1994). Critical race theory: An annotated bibliography 1993, a year of transition. *University of Colorado Law Review, 66*, 159–193.

Du Bois, W. E. B. (1970). *W. E. B. Du Bois: A reader*. M. Weinberg (Ed.). New York: Harper Torchbooks.

Franklin, J. H. & Moss, A. A. (1947/1988). *From slavery to freedom: A history of Negro Americans*. New York: McGraw-Hill.

Fordham, S. & Ogbu, J. U. (1986). Black students' school success: Coping with the burden of "acting white". *The Urban Review, 18*(3), 176–206.

Gay, G. (1983). Multiethnic education: Historical developments and future prospects. *Phi Beta Kappan, 64*, 560–563.

Horne, G. (1986). *Black and red: W.E.B. DuBois and the Afro-American response to the Cold War, 1944–1963*.

Humphries, F. S. (1994). A short history of Blacks in higher education. *The Journal of Blacks in Higher Education, 6*, 57.

Kujovich, G. (1987). Equal opportunity in higher education and the Black public college: The era of separate but equal. *Minnesota Law Review, 72*, 30–172.

Lawrence, C. R. (1987). The id, the ego, and equal protection: Reckoning with unconscious racism. *Stanford Law Review, 39*, 317–388.

Lawrence, C. R., Matsuda, M. J., Delgado, R., & Crenshaw, K. W. (1993). *Words that wound: Critical race theory, assaultive speech, and the First Amendment*. Boulder, CO: Westview Press.

Mills, C. (1997). *The racial contract*. Ithaca, NY: Cornell University Press.

Morrison, T. (1992). *Playing in the dark: Whiteness in the literary imagination*. Cambridge, MA: Harvard University Press.

Ogletree, C. (2004). The significance of *Brown*. *Harvard BlackLetter Law Journal, 20*, 1–15.

Olivas, M. (1990). The chronicles, my grandfather's stories, and immigration law: The slave traders chronicle and racial history. *St. Louis Law Journal, 34*, 425.

Orfield, G., Losen, D., Wald, J., & Swanson, C. (2004). *Losing our future: How minority youth are being left behind by the graduation rate crisis*. Cambridge, MA: The Civil Rights Project at Harvard University.

Schofield, J. W. (1986). Causes and consequences of the colorblind perspective. In J. F. Dovidio & S. L. Gaertmer (Eds.), *Prejudice, discrimination, and racism*, pp. 231–253. San Diego: Academic Press.

Stoler, A. L. (1997). Racial histories and their regimes of truth. *Political Power and Social Theory, 11*, 183–206.

Takaki, R. (1993). *A different mirror: A history of multicultural America*. Boston: Little, Brown.

Williams, P. J. (1991). *The alchemy of race and rights: Diary of a law professor*. Cambridge, MA: Harvard University Press.

Part One

Critical Race Theory in Education

1

Just What is Critical Race Theory and What's it Doing in a *Nice* Field Like Education?

Gloria Ladson-Billings

Introduction

Almost five years ago a colleague and I began a collaboration in which we grap-pled with the legal scholarship known as "critical race theory" (Delgado, cited in Monaghan, 1993). So tentative were we about this line of inquiry that we pro-ceeded with extreme caution. We were both untenured and relatively new to our institution. We were unsure of how this new line of inquiry would be received both within our university and throughout the educational research/scholarly community. Our initial step was to hold a colloquium in our department. We were pleasantly surprised to meet with a room filled with colleagues and graduate students who seemed eager to hear our ideas and help us in these new theoretical and conceptual formulations.

That initial meeting led to many revisions and iterations. We presented versions of the paper and the ideas surrounding it at conferences and professional meetings. Outside the supportive confines of our own institution, we were met with not only the expected intellectual challenges, but also outright hostility. Why were we focusing only on race? What about gender? Why not class? Are you abandoning multicultural perspectives? By the fall of 1995 our much discussed paper was published (Ladson-Billings & Tate, 1995). We have, however, held our collective intellectual breaths for almost a year because, despite the proliferation of critical race legal scholarship, we have seen scant evidence that this work has made any impact on the educational research/scholarly community. Thus, seeing critical race theory (CRT) as a theme in an educational journal represents our first opportunity to "exhale."

It had been a good day. My talk as a part of the "Distinguished Lecture" Series at a major research university had gone well. The audience was receptive; the questions were challenging, yet respectful. My colleagues were exceptional hosts. I spent the day sharing ideas and exchanging views on various phases of their work and my own. There had even been the not so subtle hint of a job offer. The warm, almost tropical climate of this university stood in stark contrast to the overly long, brutal winters of my own institution. But it also had been a tiring day—all that smiling, listening with rapt interest to everyone's research, recalling minute details of my own, trying to be witty and simultaneously serious had taken its toll. I could not wait to get back to the hotel to relax for a few hours before dinner.

One of the nice perks that comes with these lecture "gigs" is a decent hotel. This one was no exception. My accommodations were on the hotel's VIP floor—equipped with special elevator access key and private lounge on the top floor overlooking the city. As I stepped off the elevator, I decided to go into the VIP lounge, read the newspaper, and have a drink. I arrived early, just before the happy hour, and no one else was in the lounge. I took a seat on one of the couches and began catching up on the day's news. Shortly after I sat down comfortably with my newspaper, a White man peeked his head into the lounge, looked at me sitting there in my best (and conservative) "dress for success" outfit—high heels and all—and said with a pronounced Southern accent, "What time are y'all gonna be servin'?"

I tell this story both because storytelling is a part of critical race theory and because this particular story underscores an important point within the critical race theoretical paradigm, i.e. race [still] matters (West, 1992). Despite the scientific refutation of race as a legitimate biological concept and attempts to marginalize race in much of the public (political) discourse, race continues to be a powerful *social* construct and signifier (Morrison, 1992):

> Race has become metaphorical—a way of referring to and disguising forces, events, classes, and expressions of social decay and economic division far more threatening to the body politic than biological "race" ever was.
>
> Expensively kept, economically unsound, a spurious and useless political asset in election campaigns, racism is as healthy today as it was during the Enlightenment. It seems that it has a utility far beyond economy, beyond the sequestering of classes from one another, and has assumed a metaphorical life so completely embedded in daily discourse that it is perhaps more necessary and more on display than ever before. (p. 63)

I am intrigued by the many faces and permutations race has assumed in contemporary society. Our understanding of race has moved beyond the bio-genetic categories and notions of phenotype. Our "advanced ideas" about race include the racialization of multiple cultural forms. Sociologist Sharon Lee (1993) suggests that "questions of race have been included in all U.S. population censuses since the first one in 1790" (p. 86). Although racial categories in the U.S. census have fluctuated over time, two categories have remained stable—Black and White. And, while the creation of the category does not reveal what constitutes within it, it does create for us a sense of polar opposites that posits a cultural ranking designed to tell us who is White or, perhaps more pointedly, who is *not* White!

But determining who is and is not White is not merely a project of individual construction and/or biological designation. For example, in early census data, citizens of Mexican descent were considered White, though over time, political, economic, social, and cultural shifts have forced Mexican Americans out of the White category. Conversely, Haney Lopez (1995) pointed out that some groups came to the USA and brought suit in the courts to be declared White. Omi and Winant (1993) argue, however, that the polar notions of race as either an ideological construct or as an objective condition both have shortcomings. That is, thinking of race strictly as an ideological concept denies the reality of a racialized society and its impact on people in their everyday lives. On the other hand, thinking of race solely as an objective condition denies the problematic aspects of race—how to decide who fits into which racial classifications.

Our notions of race (and its use) are so complex that even when it fails to "make sense" we continue to employ and deploy it. I want to argue, then, that our conceptions of race, even in a postmodern and/or postcolonial world, are more embedded and fixed than in a previous age. However, this embeddedness or "fixed-ness" has required new language and constructions of race so that denotations are submerged and hidden in ways that are offensive though without identification. Thus, we develop notions of "conceptual whiteness" and "conceptual blackness" (King, 1995) that both do and do not map neatly on to bio-genetic or cultural allegiances. Conceptual categories like "school achievement," "middle classness," "maleness," "beauty," "intelligence," and "science" become normative categories of whiteness, while categories like "gangs," "welfare recipients," "basketball players," and "the underclass" become the marginalized and de-legitimated categories of blackness.

The creation of these conceptual categories is not designed to reify a binary but rather to suggest how, in a racialized society where whiteness is positioned as norma-tive, *everyone* is ranked and categorized in relation to these points of opposition. These categories fundamentally sculpt the extant terrain of possibilities even when other possibilities exist. And, although there is a fixedness to the notion of these categories, the ways in which they actually operate are fluid and shifting. For example, as an African American female academic, I can be and am sometimes positioned as conceptually White in relation to, perhaps, a Latino, Spanish-speaking gardener. In that instance, my class and social position override my racial identification and for that moment I become "White."

The significance of race need not be overly debated in this paper. But, as Toni Morrison argues, race is always already present in every social configuring or our lives. Roediger (1991) asserts, "Even in an all-white town, race was never absent" (p. 3). However, more significant/problematic than the omnipresence of race is the notion that "whites reach the conclusion that their whiteness is meaning-ful" (Roediger, p. 6). It is because of the meaning and value imputed to whiteness that CRT becomes an important intellectual and social tool for deconstruc-tion, reconstruction, and construction: deconstruction of oppressive structures and discourses, reconstruction of human agency, and construction of equitable and socially just relations of power. In this paper, then, I am attempting to speak to innovative theoretical ways for framing discussions about social justice and democracy and the role of education in reproducing or interrupting current practices.

I hope to provide a brief synopsis of Critical Race Theory[1] and discuss some of its prominent themes. Then I will discuss its importance to our understanding of the citizen in a democracy, its relationship to education and finally some cautionary implications for further research and study. As is true of all texts, this one is incomplete (O'Neill, 1992). It is incomplete on the part of both the writer and the reader. However, given its incompleteness, I implore readers to grapple with how it might advance the debate on race and education.

Most people in the USA first learned of critical race theory (CRT) when Lani Guinier, a University of Pennsylvania Law Professor, became a political casualty of the Clinton administration. Her legal writings were the focus of much scrutiny in the media. Unschooled and unsophisticated about the nature of legal academic writing, the media vilified Guinier and accused her of advocating "un-American" ideas. The primary focus of the scorn shown Guinier was her argument for proportional representation.

Guinier (1991) asserted that in electoral situations where particular racial groups were a clear (and persistent) minority, the only possibility for an equitable chance at social benefits and fair political representation might be for minority votes to count for more than their actual numbers. Guinier first proposed such a strategy as a solution for a postapartheid South Africa. Because Whites are in the obvious minority, the only way for them to participate in the governing of a new South Africa would be to insure them some seats in the newly formed government.

Guinier made a similar argument in favor of African Americans in the USA. She saw this as a legal response to the ongoing lack of representation. Unfortunately, her political opponents attacked her scholarship as an affront to the American tradition of "one person, one vote." The furor over Guinier's work obscured the fact that as an academic, Guinier was expected to write "cutting-edge" scholarship that pushed theoretical boundaries (Guinier, 1994). Her work was not to be literally applied to legal practice. However, in the broad scope of critical race legal studies, Guinier may be seen as relatively moderate and nowhere near the radical the press made her out to be. But, her "exposure" placed critical race theory and its proponents in the midst of the public discourse.

According to Delgado (1995, p. xiii), "Critical Race Theory sprang up in the mid-1970s with the early work of Derrick Bell (an African American) and Alan Freeman (a white), both of whom were deeply distressed over the slow pace of racial reform in the United States. They argued that the traditional approaches of filing *amicus* briefs, conducting protests and marches, and appealing to the moral sensibilities of decent citizens produced smaller and fewer gains than in previous times. Before long they were being joined by other legal scholars who shared their frustration with traditional civil rights strategies.

Critical race theory is, thus, both an outgrowth of and a separate entity from an earlier legal movement called critical legal studies (CLS). Critical legal studies is a leftist legal movement that challenged the traditional legal scholarship that focused on doctrinal and policy analysis (Gordon, 1990) in favor of a form of law that spoke to the specificity of individuals and groups in social and cultural contexts. Critical legal studies scholars also challenged the notion that "the civil rights struggle represents a long, steady, march toward social transformation" (Crenshaw, 1988, p. 1334).

According to Crenshaw (1988), "Critical [legal] scholars have attempted to analyze legal ideology and discourse as a social artifact which operates to recreate and legitimate American society" (p. 1350). Scholars in the CLS movement decipher legal doctrine to expose both its internal and external inconsistencies and reveal the ways that "legal ideology has helped create, support, and legitimate America's present class structure" (Crenshaw, p. 1350). The contribution of CLS to legal discourse is in its analysis of legitimating structures in the society. Much of the CLS ideology emanates from the work of Gramsci (1971) and depends on the Gramscian notion of "hegemony" to describe the continued legitimacy of oppressive structures in American society. However, CLS fails to provide pragmatic strategies for material social transformation. Cornel West (1993) asserts that:

> . . . critical legal theorists fundamentally question the dominant liberal paradigms prevalent and pervasive in American culture and society. This thorough questioning is not primarily a constructive attempt to put forward a conception of a new legal and social order. Rather, it is a pronounced disclosure of inconsistencies, incoherences, silences, and blindness of legal formalists, legal positivists, and legal realists in the liberal tradition. Critical legal studies is more a concerted attack and assault on the legitimacy and authority of pedagogical strategies in law school than a comprehensive announcement of what a credible and realizable new society and legal system would look like. (p. 196)

CLS scholars critique mainstream legal ideology for its portrayal of U.S. society as a meritocracy but failed to include racism in its critique. Thus, CRT became a logical outgrowth of the discontent of legal scholars of color.

CRT begins with the notion that racism is "normal, not aberrant, in American society" (Delgado, 1995, p. xiv), and, because it is so enmeshed in the fabric of our social order, it appears both normal and natural to people in this culture. Indeed, Bell's major premise in *Faces at the bottom of the well* (1992) is that racism is a permanent fixture of American life. Thus, the strategy becomes one of unmasking and exposing racism in its various permutations.

Second, CRT departs from mainstream legal scholarship by sometimes employing storytelling to "analyze the myths, presuppositions, and received wisdoms that make up the common culture about race and that invariably render blacks and other minorities one-down" (Delgado, 1995, p. xiv). According to Barnes (1990) "Critical race theorists . . . integrate their *experiential knowledge* (emphasis added), drawn from a shared history as 'other' with their ongoing struggles to transform a world deteriorating under the albatross of racial hegemony" (pp. 1864–1865). Thus, the experience of oppressions such as racism or sexism has important aspects for developing a CRT analytical standpoint. To the extent that Whites (or in the case of sexism, men) experience forms of racial oppression, they may develop such a standpoint. For example, the historical figure John Brown suffered aspects of racism by aligning himself closely with the cause of African American liberation.[2] Contemporary examples of such identification may occur when White parents adopt transracially. No longer a White family, by virtue of their child(ren), they become racialized others. A final example was played out in the infamous O. J. Simpson trials. The criminal trial jury was repeatedly identified as the "Black" jury despite the presence of one White and one Latino juror. However, the majority White civil case jury was not given a racial designation. When Whites are exempted from racial designations and become "families," "jurors," "students," "teachers," etc. their ability to apply a CRT analytical rubric is limited. One of the most dramatic examples of the shift from non-raced to CRT perspective occurred when Gregory Williams (1995) moved from Virginia where he was a White boy to Muncie, Indiana, where his family was known to be Black. The changes in his economic and social status were remarkable, and the story he tells underscores the salience of race in life's possibilities. The primary reason, then, that stories, or narratives, are deemed important among CRT scholars is that they add necessary contextual contours to the seeming "objectivity" of positivist perspectives.

Third, CRT insists on a critique of liberalism. Crenshaw (1988) argues that the liberal perspective of the "civil rights crusade as a long, slow, but always upward pull" (p. 1334) is flawed because it fails to understand the limits of current legal paradigms to serve as catalysts for social change and its emphasis on incrementalism. CRT argues that racism requires sweeping changes, but liberalism has no mechanism for such change. Rather, liberal legal practices support the painstakingly slow process of arguing legal precedence to gain citizen rights for people of color.

Fourth, and related to the liberal perspective, is the argument posed by CRT that Whites have been the primary beneficiaries of civil rights legislation. For example, although under attack throughout the nation, the policy of affirmative action has benefited Whites; a contention that is validated by the fact that the actual numbers reveal that the major recipients of affirmative action hiring policies have been White women (Guy-Sheftall, 1993). One might argue, then, that many of these White women have incomes that support households in which other Whites live—men, women, and children. Thus, these women's ability to find work ultimately benefits Whites, in general.

In contrast, let us look at some of the social benefits African Americans have received due to affirmative action policies. Even after 20 years of affirmative action, African Americans constitute only 4.5% of the professorate (Hacker, 1992). In 1991 there were 24721 doctoral degrees awarded to U.S. citizens and noncitizens who intended to remain in the USA, and only 933 or 3.8% of these doctorates went to African American men and women. If every one of those newly minted doctorates went into the academy, it would have a negligible effect on the proportion of African Americans in the professorate. In addition, the majority of the African Americans who earn PhDs earn them in the field of education, and of that group, most of the degrees are in educational administration where the recipients continue as school practitioners (Hacker, 1992).

Thus, CRT theorists cite this kind of empirical evidence to support their contention that civil rights laws continue to serve the interests of Whites. A more fruitful tack, some CRT scholars argue, is to find the place where the interests of Whites and people of color intersect. This notion of "interest-convergence" (Bell, 1980, p. 94) can be seen in what transpired in Arizona over the Martin Luther King, Jr. Holiday commemoration.

Originally, the state of Arizona insisted that the King Holiday was too costly and therefore failed to recognize it for state workers and agencies. Subsequently, a variety of African American groups and their supporters began to boycott business, professional, and social functions in the state of Arizona. When members of the National Basketball Association and the National Football League suggested that neither the NBA All-Star Game nor the Super Bowl would be held in Arizona because of its failure to recognize the King Holiday, the decision was reversed. Hardly anyone is naive enough to believe that the governor of Arizona had a change of heart about the significance of the King Holiday. Rather, when his position on the holiday had the effect of hurting state tourist and sports entertainment revenues, the state's interests (to enhance revenue) converged with that of the African American community (to recognize Dr. King). Thus, converging interests, not support of civil rights, led to the reversal of the state's position.

In a recent compilation of CRT key writings (Crenshaw et al., 1995) it is pointed out that there is no "canonical set of doctrines or methodologies to which [CRT scholars] all subscribe" (p. xiii). But, these scholars are unified by two common interests—to understand how a "regime of white supremacy and its subordination of people of color have been created and maintained in America" (p. xiii) and to change the bond that exists between law and racial power.

In the pursuit of these interests, legal scholars, such as Patricia Williams (1991) and Derrick Bell (1987; 1992), were among the early critical race theorists whose ideas reached the general public. Some might argue that their wide appeal was the result of their abilities to tell compelling stories into which they embedded legal issues.[3] This use of story is of particular interest to educators because of the growing popularity of narrative inquiry in the study of teaching (Carter, 1993; Connelly & Clandinin, 1990). But, just because more people are recognizing and using story as a part of scholarly inquiry does not mean that all stories are judged as legitimate in knowledge construction and the advancement of a discipline.

Lawrence (1995) asserts that there is a tradition of storytelling in law and that litigation is highly formalized storytelling, though the stories of ordinary people, in general, have not been told or recorded in the literature of law (or any other discipline). But this failure to make it into the canons of literature or research does not make the stories of ordinary people less important.

Stories provide the necessary context for understanding, feeling, and interpreting. The ahistorical and acontextual nature of much law and other "science" renders the voices of dispossessed and marginalized group members mute. In response, much of the scholarship of CRT focuses on the role of "voice" in bringing additional power to the legal discourses of racial justice. Indeed, Delgado (1990) argues that people of color speak with experiential knowledge about the fact that our society is deeply structured by racism. That structure gives their stories a common framework warranting the term "voice." Consequently, critical race theorists are attempting to interject minority cultural viewpoints, derived from a common history of oppression, into their efforts to reconstruct a society crumbling under the burden of racial hegemony (Barnes, 1990).

The use of voice or "naming your reality" is a way that CRT links form and substance in scholarship. CRT scholars use parables, chronicles, stories, counterstories, poetry, fiction, and revisionist histories to illustrate the false necessity and irony of much of current civil rights doctrine. Delgado (1989) suggests that there are at least three reasons for "naming one's own reality" in legal discourse:

1. much of "reality" is socially constructed;
2. stories provide members of outgroups a vehicle for psychic self-preservation; and
3. the exchange of stories from teller to listener can help overcome ethnocentrism and the dysconscious (King, 1992) drive or need to view the world in one way.

The first reason for naming one's own reality involves how political and moral analysis is conducted in legal scholarship. Many mainstream legal scholars embrace universalism over particularity. According to Williams (1991), "theoretical legal understanding" is characterized, in Anglo-American jurisprudence, by the acceptance of transcendent, acontextual, universal legal truths or procedures. For instance, some legal scholars might contend that the tort of fraud has always existed and that it is a component belonging to the universal system of right and wrong. This world-view tends to discount anything that is non-transcendent (historical), or contextual (socially constructed), or nonuniversal (specific) with the unscholarly labels of "emotional," "literary," "personal," or false (Williams, 1991).

In contrast, critical race theorists argue that political and moral analysis is situational—"truths only exist for this person in this predicament at this time in history" (Delgado, 1991, p. 11). For the critical race theorist, social reality is constructed by the formulation and the exchange of stories about individual situations (see, for example, Matsuda, 1989). These stories serve as interpretive structures by which we impose order on experience and it on us (Delgado, 1989).

A second reason for the naming one's own reality theme of CRT is the psychic preservation of marginalized groups. A factor contributing to the demoralization of marginalized groups is self-condemnation (Delgado, 1989). Members of minority groups internalize the stereotypic images that certain elements of society have constructed in order to maintain their power. Historically, story-telling has been a kind of medicine to heal the wounds of pain caused by racial oppression. The story of one's condition leads to the realization of how one came to be oppressed and subjugated, thus allowing one to stop inflicting mental violence on oneself.

Finally, naming one's own reality with stories can affect the oppressor. Most oppression, as was discussed earlier, does not seem like oppression to the perpetrator (Lawrence, 1987). Delgado (1989) argues that the dominant group justifies its power with stories, stock explanations, that construct reality in ways that maintain their privilege. Thus, oppression is rationalized, causing little self-examination by the oppressor. Stories by people of color can catalyze the necessary cognitive conflict to jar dysconscious racism.

The "voice" component of CRT provides a way to communicate the experience and realities of the oppressed, a first step in understanding the complexities of racism and beginning a process of judicial redress. For example, the voice of people of color is required for a deep understanding of the educational system. Delpit (1988) argues one of the tragedies of the field of education is how the dialogue of people of color has been silenced. Delpit begins her analysis of the process-oriented versus the skills-oriented writing debate with a statement (or story) from an African American male graduate student at a predominantly white university who is also a special education teacher in an African American community:

> There comes a moment in every class where we have to discuss "The Black Issue" and what's appropriate education for Black children. I tell you, I'm tired of arguing with those White people, because they won't listen. Well, I don't know if they really don't listen or if they just

don't believe you. It seems like if you can't quote Vygotsky or something, then you don't have any validity to speak about your own kids. Anyway, I'm not bothering with it anymore, now I'm just in it for a grade. (p. 280)

The above comment and numerous other statements found in Delpit's analysis illustrate the frustration of teachers of color that is caused by being left out of the dialogue about how best to educate children of color. Further, Delpit raises several very important questions:

> How can such complete communication blocks exist when both parties [Black and Whites] truly believe they have the same aims? How can the bitterness and resentment expressed by educators of color be drained so that all sores can heal? What can be done? (p. 282)

Critical Race Theory and Citizenship

One of the places to begin understanding CRT is to examine how conceptions of citizenship and race interact. Although connections of CRT and citizenship are numerous and complex, in this paper I will attempt to detail only one of the central connections that is important in understanding the relationship of this scholarship to educational issues. That central connection is the "property issue" (Ladson-Billings & Tate, 1995). CRT scholars assert that the USA is a nation conceived and built on property rights (Bell, 1987; Harris, 1993). In the early history of the nation only propertied White males enjoyed the franchise. The significance of property ownership as a prerequisite to citizenship was tied to the British notion that only people who *owned* the country, not merely those who *lived* in it, were eligible to make decisions about it.[4]

The salience of property often is missed in our understanding of the USA as a nation. Conflated with democracy, capitalism slides into the background of our understanding of the way in which U.S. political and economic ideology are entangled and read as synonymous. But it is this foundation of property rights that make civil rights legislation so painfully slow and sometimes ineffective. Civil rights are wedded to the construction of the rights of the individual. Bell (1987) argues that "the concept of individual rights, unconnected to property rights, was totally foreign to these men of property," (p. 239) in his explanation of how men who expressed a commitment to liberty and justice could uphold the repression of African Americans, the indigenous peoples who inhabited the land, and women.

African Americans represented a particular conundrum because not only were they not accorded individual civil rights because they were not White and owned no property, but they were constructed *as* property! However, that construction was only in the sense that they could be owned by others. They possessed no rights of property ownership. Whites, on the other hand, according to Harris (1993), benefited from the construction of whiteness as the ultimate property. "Possession—the act necessary to lay basis for rights in property—was defined to include only the cultural practices of Whites. This definition laid the foundation for the idea that whiteness—that which Whites alone possess—is valuable and is property" (p. 1721).

This thematic strand of whiteness as property in the USA is not confined to the nation's early history. Indeed, Andrew Hacker's (1992) exercise with his college students illustrates the material and social value the students place on their possession of whiteness. Hacker uses a parable to illustrate that although the students insist that "in this day and age, things are better for Blacks" (p. 31), none of them would want to change places with African Americans. When asked what amount of compensation they would seek if they were forced to "become Black," the students "seemed to feel that it would not be out of place to ask for $50 million, or $1 million for each coming Black year" (p. 32). According to Hacker:

> And this calculation conveys, as well as anything, the value that white people place on their own skins. Indeed, to be white is to possess a gift whose value can be appreciated only after it has been taken away. And why ask so large a sum?.... The money would be used, as best it could, to buy protection from the discriminations and dangers white people know they would face once they were perceived to be black. (p. 32)

Thus, even without the use of a sophisticated legal rhetorical argument, Whites know they possess a property that people of color do not and that to possess it confers aspects of citizenship not available to others. Harris's (1993) argument is that the "property functions of whiteness" (p. 1731)—rights of disposition, rights to use and enjoyment, reputation and status property, and the absolute right to exclude—make the American dream of "life, liberty, and the pursuit of happiness" a more likely and attainable reality for Whites as citizens. This reality also is more likely to engender feelings of loyalty and commitment to a nation that works in the interests of Whites. Conversely, Blacks, aware that they will never possess this ultimate property, are less sanguine about U.S. citizenship.

Patricia Williams (1995) explains these differential notions of citizenship as being grounded in differential experiences of rights because "one's sense of empowerment defines one's relation to law, in terms of trust–distrust, formality–informality, or right–no rights (or 'needs')" (pp. 87–88). An example of this differing relation (in this case to commerce) was shared in one of my classes. We were discussing McIntosh's (1990) article on "White privilege." One White woman shared a personal experience of going into a neighborhood supermarket, having her items rung up by the cashier, and discovering that she did not have her checkbook. The cashier told her she could take her groceries and bring the check back later. When she related this story to an African American male friend, he told her that was an example of the privilege she enjoyed because she was White. Her White property was collateral against the cart full of groceries. She insisted that this was the store's good neighbor policy, and the same thing would have happened to him. Determined to show his friend that their life experiences were qualitative different, the young man went shopping a few days later and pretended to have left his checkbook. The young woman was standing off to the side observing the interaction. The same cashier, who had been pointed out by the woman as the "neighborly one," told the young African American man that he could push the grocery items to the side while he went home to get his checkbook. The White woman was shocked as the African American male gave her a knowing look.

These daily indignities take their toll on people of color. When these indignities are skimmed over in the classrooms that purport to develop students into citizens, it is no wonder students "blow off" classroom discourse. How can students be expected to deconstruct rights, "in a world of no rights" (Williams, 1995, p. 98) and construct statements of need "in a world of abundantly apparent need?" (p. 89)

African Americans, thus, represent a unique form of citizen in the USA—property transformed into citizen. This process has not been a smooth one. When Chief Justice Taney concluded in the *Dred Scott* decision that African Americans had no rights that Whites were required to respect, he reinscribed the person-as-property status of African Americans. Later in *Plessy v. Ferguson* the high court once again denied full citizenship rights to African Americans as a way to assert White property rights—rights to use and enjoy and the absolute right to exclude.

Even the laudable decision of *Brown v. Board of Education* comes under scrutiny in the CRT paradigm. Lest we misread *Brown v. Board of Education* as merely a pang of conscience and the triumph of right over wrong, it is important to set *Brown* in context. First, historically the *Brown* decision helped the USA in its struggle to minimize the spread of communism to so-called Third World nations. In many countries, the credibility of the USA had been damaged by the widely broadcast inequitable social conditions that existed in the USA in the 1950s. Both the government and the NAACP lawyers argued the *Brown* decision would help legitimize the political and economic philosophies of the USA with these developing nations (Bell, 1980).

Second, *Brown* provided reassurance to African Americans that the struggle for freedom and equality fought for during World War II might become a reality at home. Black veterans faced not only racial inequality, but also physical harm in many parts of the South. And, the treatment of African Americans after the war in concert with the voice of African American leaders such as Paul Robeson may have greatly influenced the *Brown* decision. Robeson argued:

> It is unthinkable . . . that American Negroes [*sic*] would go to war on behalf of those who have oppressed us for generations . . . against a country [the Soviet Union] which in one generation has raised our people to the full human dignity of mankind.
>
> (in Foner, 1978, pp. 17–18)

According to Bell (1980), it is not unreasonable to assume that those in positions of power would recognize the importance of neutralizing Robeson and others who held similar views. Robeson's comments were an affront to the "national interests." Thus, racial decisions by the courts were pivotal in softening the criticism about the contradiction of a free and just nation that maintained a segment of its citizenry in second-class status based on race. Finally, there were White capitalists who understood that the South could be transformed from an Agrarian society to an industrialized sunbelt only when it ended the divisive battle over state-supported segregation. Here, segregation was read as a barrier obstructing the economic self-interest of U.S. profit makers.

At this writing, the electorate of California have passed Proposition 209, calling for an end to "preferential treatment" in state employment and state university admission policies based on race or gender. The trope of preferential treatment has help create a perception that ending affirmative action will lead to a more fair and equitable society, while, in reality, the proposition will be used to instantiate the hierarchical relations of power that once again privilege whiteness as the most valued property. Citizenship for people of color remains elusive.

Critical Race Theoretical Approaches to Education

Thus far in this paper I have attempted to explain the meaning and historical background of critical race theory in legal scholarship and the role of property rights in understanding citizenship. However, educators and researchers in the field of education will want to know what relevance CRT has to education. The connections between law and education are relatively simple to establish. Since education in the USA is not outlined explicitly in the nation's constitution, it is one of the social functions relegated to individual states. Consequently, states generate legislation and enact laws designed to proscribe the contours of education.

One of the earliest legislative attempts was Massachusetts' "old deluder Satan" act that required citizens of the state to provide education for its children to insure they received moral and religious instruction. In the modern era the intersection of school and law provided fertile ground for testing and enacting civil rights legislation. Thus, the landmark *Brown* decision generated a spate of school desegregation of Central High School in Little Rock, Arkansas, the New Orleans Public Schools, the University of Mississippi, the University of Alabama, and the University of Georgia. By the 1970s, school desegregation/civil rights battles were being fought in northern cities. The fight for school desegregation in Boston schools was among the most vicious in civil rights annals.

One recurring theme that characterized the school/civil rights legal battles was "equal opportunity." This notion of equal opportunity was associated with the idea that students of color should have access to the same school opportunities, i.e. curriculum, instruction, funding, facilities. as White students. This emphasis on "sameness" was important because it helped boost the arguments for "equal treatment under the law" that were important for moving African Americans from their second-class status.

But what was necessary to help African Americans to "catch up" with their White counterparts? Beyond equal treatment was the need to redress past inequities. Thus, there was a move toward affirmative action and the creation of African Americans and other marginalized groups as "protected classes" to insure that they were not systematically screened out of opportunities in employment, college admission, and housing. If we look at the way that public education is currently configured, it is possible to see the ways that CRT can be a powerful explanatory tool for the sustained inequity that people of color experience. I will use the areas of curriculum, instruction, assessment, school funding, and desegregation as exemplars of the relationship that can exist between CRT and education.

Curriculum

Critical race theory sees the official school curriculum as a culturally specific artifact designed to maintain a White supremacist master script. As Swartz (1992) contends:

> Master scripting silences multiple voices and perspectives, primarily legitimizing dominant, white, upper-class, male voicings as the "standard" knowledge students need to know. All other accounts and perspectives are omitted from the master script unless they can be disempowered through misrepresentation. Thus, content that does not reflect the dominant voice must be brought under control, *mastered*, and then reshaped before it can become a part of the master script. (p. 341)

This master scripting means stories of African Americans are muted and erased when they challenge dominant culture authority and power. Thus, Rosa Parks is reduced to a tired seamstress instead of a long-time participant in social justice endeavors as evidenced by her work at the Highlander Folk School to prepare for a confrontation with segregationist ideology. Or, Martin Luther King, Jr. becomes a sanitized folk hero who enjoyed the full support of "good Americans" rather than a disdained scholar and activist whose vision extended to social justice causes throughout the world and challenged the USA on issues of economic injustice and aggression in Southeast Asia.

The race-neutral or colorblind perspective, evident in the way the curriculum presents people of color, presumes a homogenized "we" in a celebration of diversity. This perspective embraces a so-called multicultural perspective by "misequating the middle passage with Ellis Island" (King, 1992, p. 327). Thus, students are taught erroneously that "we are all immigrants," and, as a result, African American, Indigenous, and Chicano students are left with the guilt of failing to rise above their immigrant status like "every other group."

But it is not just the distortions, omissions, and stereotypes of school curriculum content that must be considered, it also is the rigor of the curriculum and access to what is deemed "enriched" curriculum via gifted and talented courses and classes. As Jonathan Kozol (1991) describes:

> The curriculum [the white school] follows "emphasizes critical thinking, reasoning and logic." The planetarium, for instance, is employed not simply for the study of the universe as it exists. "Children also are designing their own galaxies," the teacher says. (p. 96)
> In my [Kozol's] notes: "Six girls, four boys. Nine White, one Chinese. I am glad they have this class. But what about the others? Aren't there ten Black children in the school who could *enjoy* this also?"

This restricted access to the curriculum is a good illustration of Harris's (1993) explanation of the function of property in terms of use and enjoyment.

Instruction

CRT suggests that current instructional strategies presume that African American students are deficient. As a consequence, classroom teachers are engaged in a never-ending quest for "*the* right strategy or technique" to deal with (read: control) "at-risk" (read: African American) students. Cast in a language of failure, instructional approaches for African American students typically involve some aspect of remediation.

This race-neutral perspective purports to see deficiency as an individual phenomenon. Thus, instruction is conceived as a generic set of teaching skills that should work for all students. When these strategies or skills fail to achieve desired results, the students, not the techniques, are found to be lacking.

Fortunately, new research efforts are rejecting deficit models and investigating and affirming the integrity of effective teachers of African American students.[5] This scholarship underscores the teachers' understanding of the saliency of race in education and the society, and it underscores the need to make racism explicit so that students can recognize and struggle against this particular form of oppression.

Examples of counterpedagogical moves are found in the work of both Chicago elementary teacher Marva Collins and Los Angeles high school mathematics teacher Jaime Escalante. While neither Collins nor Escalante is acclaimed as a "progressive" teacher, both are recognized for their persistence in believing in the educability of all students. Both remind students that mainstream society expects them to be failures and prod the students to succeed as a form of counterinsurgency. Their insistence on helping students achieve in the "traditional" curriculum represents a twist on Audre Lorde's notion that one cannot dismantle the master's house with the master's tools. Instead, they believe one can only dismantle the master's house with the master's tools.

Assessment

For the critical race theorist, intelligence testing has been a movement to legitimize African American student deficiency under the guise of scientific rationalism (Alienikoff, 1991; Gould, 1981). According to Marable (1983), one purpose of the African American in the racial/capitalist state is to serve as a symbolic index for poor Whites. If the working-class White is "achieving" at a higher level than Blacks, then they feel relatively superior. This allows Whites with real power to exploit both poor Whites and Blacks. Throughout U.S. history, the subordination of Blacks has been built on "scientific" theories (e.g., intelligence testing) that depend on racial stereotypes about Blacks that make their condition appear appropriate. Crenshaw (1988) contends that the point of controversy is no longer that these sterotypes were developed to rationalize the oppression of Blacks, but rather, "[T]he extent to which these stereotypes serve a hegemonic function by perpetuating a mythology about both Blacks and Whites even today, reinforcing an illusion of a White community that cuts across ethnic, gender, and class lines" (p. 1371).

In the classroom, a dysfunctional curriculum coupled with a lack of instructional innovation (or persistence) adds up to poor performance on traditional assessment measures. These assessment measures—crude by most analyses—may tell us that students do not know what is on the test, but fail to tell us what students actually know and are able to do. A telling example of this mismatch between what schools measure and what students know and can do is that of a 10-year-old African American girl who was repeatedly told by the teacher that she was a poor math student. However, the teacher was unaware that the girl was living under incredible stresses where she was assuming responsibilities her drug-addicted mother could not. To ward off child welfare agents the child handled all household responsibilities, including budgeting and paying all the household bills. Her ability to keep the household going made it appear that everything was fine in the household. According to the teacher, she could not do fourth-grade math, but the evidence of her life suggests she was doing just fine at "adult" math!

School Funding

Perhaps no area of schooling underscores inequity and racism better than school funding. CRT argues that inequality in school funding is a function of institutional and structural racism. The inability of African Americans to qualify for educational advancements, jobs, and mortgages creates a cycle of low educational achievement, underemployment and unemployment, and standard housing. Without suffering a single act of personal racism, most African Americans suffer the consequence of systemic and structural racism.[6]

Jonathan Kozol's *Savage inequalities* (1991) created an emotional and ethical stir within and beyond the education community. White colleagues talked of how moved both they and their students were as they read Kozol's descriptions of inequity in school settings. Some talked of being "moved to tears" and "unable to read more than a few pages at a time." Others talked of how difficult it was for their students to read the book. Interestingly, many African American colleagues indicated that although Kozol had been precise and passionate in his documentation, he had not revealed anything new about the differences that exist between African American and White schools. But, Kozol's research did give voice to people of color. His analysis of funding inequities provides insight into the impact of racism and White self-interest on school funding policies.

CRT argues that the import of property provides another way to consider the funding disparity. Schooling, as a function of individual states, is differentially administered by the various state legislatures. But, one of the most common aspects of these 50 different schooling agencies is the way they are funded. Almost every state funds schools based on property taxes. Those areas with property of greater wealth typically have better funded schools. In the appendix of Kozol's book are comparisons showing the disparities within three different areas. In the Chicago area, for the 1988–89 school year, the funding disparity was an almost a $4,000 per pupil difference. Chicago schools were spending $5,265 per pupil, while the sub-urban Niles Township High School District was spending $9,371. In the New Jersey area the differences between Camden Schools and Princeton Schools was about $4,200 in per pupil spending. In the New York City area the difference was almost $6,000 in per pupil spending.

Talking about the disparity between per pupil spending often invites the critique that money doesn't matter. Studies as far back as Coleman et al. (1966) and Jencks et al. (1972) have argued that family and individual effects are far more powerful than schools in determining poor school performance. Whether or not school spending is a determining factor in school achievement, no one from the family and individual effects camp can mount an ethical case for allowing poor children to languish in unheated, overcrowded schools with bathrooms that spew raw sewage while middle-income White students attend school in spacious, technology rich, inviting buildings. If money doesn't matter, then why spend it on the rich?

CRT takes to task school reformers who fail to recognize that property is a powerful determinant of academic advantage. Without a commitment to redesign funding formulas, one of the basic inequities of schooling will remain in place and virtually guarantee the reproduction of the status quo.

Desegregation

Although desegregation is not occurring in every school district, its impact on the national level is important enough to be included with the more common school experiences of curriculum, instruction, assessment, and funding. Despite the recorded history of the fight for school desegregation, CRT scholars argue that rather than serving as a solution to social inequity, school desegregation has been promoted only in ways that advantage Whites (Bell, 1990)

Lomotey and Staley's (1990) examination of Buffalo's "model desegregation" program revealed that African American students continued to be poorly served by the school system. African American student achievement failed to improve, while suspension, expulsion, and dropout rates continued to rise. What, then, made Buffalo a model desegregation program? In short, the answer is the benefits that Whites derived from the program and their seeming support of desegregation. As a result of the school desegregation program, Whites were able to take advantage of special magnet school programs and free extended child care. Thus, the dominant logic is that a model desegregation program is one that insures that Whites are happy (and do not leave the system altogether).

The report of school desegregation in Buffalo is not unlike the allegorical story presented by CRT dean, Derrick Bell (1987). The story, entitled "The sacrificed Black children," illustrates how the failure to accept African American children into their community schools causes a White school district to ultimately end up begging the students to come because their presence was intimately tied to the economic prosperity of the community. It is this realization that civil rights legislation in the USA always has benefited Whites (even if it has not always benefited African Americans) that forms the crux of the CRT argument against traditional liberal civil rights legislation. The CRT argument provides an important segue into the final section of this paper—the need for caution in proceeding with the integration of CRT into educational research.

Words of Caution

It is the pattern in educational research for a new idea or innovation to take hold and proliferate. Sometimes an idea takes a while to take root, but once it does, most likely its creators lose control of the idea. Consider what happened with the notion of cooperative learning. When Cohen and Roper (1972) proposed cooperative classroom structures to equalize the status of White and African American students, their work held great promise for helping teacher to develop curricular and instructional strategies for improving the academic performance of all children in desegregated classrooms. However, somehow their findings got distilled into day-long workshops and five-step lesson plans. School systems throughout the USA were adopting cooperative learning without any thought to improving the performance of children of color.

A similar transmutation of theory is occurring in the area of multicultural education. Although scholars such as James Banks, Carl Grant, and Geneva Gay[7] began on a scholarly path designed to change schools as institutions so that students might be prepared to reconstruct the society, in its current practice iteration, multicultural education is but a shadow of its conceptual self. Rather than engage students in provocative thinking about the contradictions of U.S. ideals and lived realities, teachers often find themselves encouraging students to sing "ethnic" songs, eat ethnic foods, and do ethnic dances. Consistently, manifestations of multicultural education in the classroom are superficial and trivial "celebrations of diversity."

What, then, might happen to CRT in the hands of educational researchers and school personnel? Well, to be honest, like Lani Guinier, I doubt if it will go very far into the mainstream. Rather, CRT in education is likely to become the "darling" of the radical left, continue to generate scholarly papers and debate, and never penetrate the classrooms and daily experiences of students of color. But, students of color, their families, and communities cannot afford the luxury of CRT scholars' ruminations any more than they could afford those of critical and postmodern theorists, where the ideas are laudable but the practice leaves much to be desired.

As excited as I may be about the potential of CRT for illuminating our thinking about school inequity, I believe educational researchers need much more time to study and understand the legal literature in which it is situated. It is very tempting to appropriate CRT as a more powerful explanatory narrative for the persistent problems of race, racism, and social injustice. If we are serious about solving these problems in schools and classrooms, we have to be serious about intense study and careful rethinking of race and education. Adopting and adapting CRT as a framework for educational equity means that we will have to expose racism in education *and* propose radical solutions for addressing it. We will have to take bold and sometimes unpopular positions. We may be pilloried figuratively or, at least, vilified for these stands. Ultimately, we may have to stand, symbolically, before the nation as Lani Guinier and hear our ideas distorted and misrepresented. We may have to defend a radical approach to democracy that seriously undermines the privilege of those who have so skillfully carved that privilege into the foundation of the nation. We will have to adopt a position of consistently swimming against the current. We run the risk of being permanent outsiders, but, as Wynter (1992) suggests, we must operate from a position of *alerity* or *liminality* where we may "call into question the rules of functioning on whose basis the United States conceptualizes itself as a generically 'White' nation, and elaborate its present system of societal self-knowledge" (p. 19). But, I fear we (educational researchers) may never assume the liminal position because of its dangers, its discomfort, and because we insist on thinking of ourselves as permanent residents in a *nice* field like education.

Notes

1. For a richer description of critical race theory, see Tate (1997).
2. Scholars such as Peggy McIntosh (1990) and Ruth Frankenberg (1993) have begun to deconstruct whiteness through their position of otherness as women. Their work suggests possibilities for Whites to deploy a CRT analysis.
3. Williams is known for her Benetton story where she was locked out of the trendy clothing store in New York because of her race. Some doubted the "generalizability" of Williams story until television personality Oprah Winfrey reported a similar incident. Bell's "Space Traders' " story is an allegorical tale that suggests that White America would gladly "give away" African Americans to space aliens if the aliens made a good enough trade.
4. Of course in America the concept of "ownership" of the land has to be contested by the indigenous people's rights to that land. However, that discussion is beyond the scope of this one.
5. See for example, Foster and Newman (1989), Henry (1992), and Ladson-Billings (1995).
6. The impact of racism generally is tied to the everyday lives of poor and underclass people of color. Recently, revelations of major U.S. corporations (e.g., Texaco and Avis) indicate that they systematically perpetuate racism in hiring, promotion, and customer service.
7. Banks, Grant, and Gay are but a few of the notables who were in the forefront of the intellectual genesis of multicultural education. Gwendolyn Baker, Carlos Cortez, and Margaret Gibson are others. Any attempt to name them all would fall short.

References

Alienikoff, T. A. (1991). A case for race-consciousness. *Columbia Law Review, 91*, 1060–1125.

Barnes, R. (1990). Race consciousness: The thematic content of racial distinctiveness in critical race scholarship. *Harvard Law Review, 103*, 1864–1871.

Bell, D. (1980). *Brown* and the interest-convergence dilemma. In D. Bell (Ed.), *Shades of Brown: New perspectives on school desegregation* (pp. 90–106). New York: Teachers College Press.

Bell, D. (1987). *And we are not saved: The elusive quest for racial justice.* New York: Basic Books.

Bell, D. (1990). *Brown* and the interest-convergence dilemma. In D. Bell (Ed.), *Shades of Brown: New perspectives on school desegregation* (pp. 90–106). New York: Teachers College Press.

Bell, D. (1992). *Faces at the bottom of the well.* New York: Basic Books.

Carter, K. (1993). The place of story in the study of teaching and teacher education. *Educational Researcher, 22* (1), 5–12.

Cohen, E. G., & Roper, S. S. (1972). Modification on interracial interaction disability: An application of status characteristics theory. *American Sociological Review, 37*, 643–657.

Coleman, J. S., Campbell, E. G., Hobson, C. J., McPartland, J., Mood, A. M., Weinfeld, F. D. & York, R. L. (1966). *Equality of educational opportunity.* Washington, DC: U.S. Government Printing Office.

Connelly, F. M., & Clandinin, D. J. (1990). Stories of experience and narrative inquiry. *Educational Researcher, 19* (5), 2–14.

Crenshaw, K. (1988). Race, reform, and retrenchment: Transformation and legitimation in anti-discrimination law. *Harvard Law Review, 101* (7), 1331–1387.

Crenshaw, K., Gotanda, N., Peller, G., & Thomas, K. (Eds.) (1995). *Critical race theory: The key writings that formed the movement.* New York: Free Press.

Delgado, R. (1989). Symposium: Legal storytelling. *Michigan Law Review, 87,* 2073.

Delgado, R. (1990). When a story is just a story: Does voice really matter? *Virginia Law Review, 76,* 95–111.

Delgado, R. (1991). Brewer's plea: Critical thoughts on common cause. *Vanderbilt Law Review, 44,* 1–14.

Delgado, R. (Ed.). (1995). *Critical race theory: The cutting edge.* Philadelphia: Temple University Press.

Delpit, L. (1988). The silenced dialogue: Power and pedagogy in educating other people's children. *Harvard Educational Review, 58,* 280–298.

Foner, P. (Ed.). (1978). *Paul Robeson speaks.* New York: Citadel Press.

Foster, M., & Newman, J. (1989). "I don't know nothin' about it:" Black teachers' code-switching strategies in interviews. *Working papers in educational linguistics* (WPEL). Philadelphia: Graduate School of Education, University of Pennsylvania.

Frankeberg, R. (1993). *White women, race matters: The social construction of whiteness.* Minneapolis: University of Minnesota Press.

Gordon, R. (1990). New developments in legal theory. In D. Kairys (Ed.), *The politics of law: A progressive critique* (pp. 413–425). New York: Pantheon Books.

Gould, S. J. (1981). *The mismeasure of man.* New York: W. W. Norton.

Gramsci, A. (1971). Selections from the prison notebooks. Q. Hoare & G. N. Smith (Eds. and Trans.) New York: International Publishers.

Guinier, L. (1991). No two seats: The elusive quest for political equality. *Virginia Law Review, 77,* 1413–1514.

Guinier, L. (1994). *The tyranny of the majority: Fundamental fairness is representative democracy.* New York: Free Press.

Guy-Sheftall, B. (1993 April). *Black feminist perspective on the academy.* Paper presented at the annual meeting of the American Educational Research Association, Atlanta.

Hacker, A. (1992). *Two nations: Black and White, separate, hostile, unequal.* New York: Ballantine Books.

Haney Lopez, I. (1995). White by law. In Delgado, R. (Ed.), *Critical race theory: The cuttingedge* (pp. 542–550). Philadelphia: Temple University Press.

Harris, C. (1993). Whiteness as property. *Harvard Law Review, 106,* 1707–1791.

Henry, A. (1992). African Canadian women teachers' activism: Recreating communities of caring and resistance. *Journal of Negro Education, 61,* 392–404.

Jencks, C., Smith, M., Acland, H., Bane, M. J., Cohen, D., Gintis, H., Heyns, B., & Michelson, S. (1972). *Inequality: A reassessment of the effect of family and schooling in America.* New York: Basic Books.

King, J. (1991). Dysconscious racism: Ideology, identity and the miseducation of teachers, *Journal of Negro Education, 60,* 133–146.

King, J. (1992). Diaspora literacy and consciousness in the struggle against miseducation in the Black community. *Journal of Negro Education, 61,* 317–340.

King, J. (1995). Culture-centered knowledge: Black studies, curriculum transformation, and social action. In J. Banks & C. M. Banks (Eds.), *Handbook of research on multicultural education* (pp. 265–290). New York: Macmillan.

Kozol, J. (1991). *Savage inequalities.* New York: Basic Books.

Ladson-Billings, G. (1995). "But that's just good teaching!" The case for culturally relevant teaching. *Theory Into Practice, 34,* 159–165.

Ladson-Billings, G., & Tate, W. F. (1995). Toward a critical race theory of education. *Teachers College Record, 97,* 47–68.

Lawrence, C. (1987). The id, the ego, and equal protection: Reckoning with unconsciousracism. *Stanford Law Review, 39,* 317–388.

Lawrence, C. (1995). The word and the river: Pedagogy as scholarship and struggle. In Crenshaw, K., Gotanda, N., Peller, G., & Thomas, K. *Critical race theory: The key writings that formed the movement.* (pp. 336–351). New York: Free Press.

Lee, S. M. (1993). Racial classifications in the U.S. census: 1890–1990. *Ethnic and Racial Studies, 16,* 75–94.

Lomotey, K., & Staley, J. (1990, April). *The education of African Americans in Buffalo Public Schools.* Paper presented at the annual meeting of the American Research Association, Boston.

Marable, M. (1983). *How capitalism underdeveloped Black America.* Boston: South End Press.

Matsuda, M. (1989). Public response to racist speech: Considering the victim's story. *Michigan Law Review, 87,* 2320–2381.

McIntosh, P. (1990). White privilege: Unpacking the invisible knapsack. *Independent School,* Winter, 31–36.

Monaghan, P. (1993, June 23). "Critical race theory" questions the role of legal doctrine in racial inequity. *Chronicle of Higher Education,* A7, A9.

Morrison, T. (1992). *Playing in the dark: Whiteness and the literary imagination.* Cambridge, MA: Harvard University Press.

Omi, M., & Winant, H. (1993). *Racial formation in the United States from the 1960s to the 1990s* (2nd ed.). New York: Routledge.

O'Neill, M. (1992). Teaching literature as cultural criticism. *English Quarterly, 25* (1), 19–24.

Roediger, D. (1991). *The wages of whiteness: Race and the making of the American working class.* London: Verso.

Swartz, E. (1992). Emancipatory narratives: Rewriting the master script in the school curriculum. *Journal of Negro Education, 61,* 341–355.

Tate, W. (1997). Critical Race Theory and education: History, theory, and implications. In M. Apple (Ed.), *Review of Research in Education, 2* (pp. 191–243) Washington, DC: American Educational Research Association.

West, C. (1992, Aug. 2). Learning to talk of race. *New York Times Magazine, 24,* 26.

West, C. (1993). *Keeping faith.* New York: Routledge.

Williams, G. H. (1995). *Life on the color line.* New York: Plume.

Williams, P. (1991). *The alchemy of race and rights: Diary of a law professor.* Cambridge, MA: Harvard University Press.

Williams, P. (1995). Alchemical notes: Reconstructingideals from deconstructed rights. In R. Delgado (Ed.), *Critical race theory: The cutting edge* (pp. 84–94). Philadelphia: Temple University Press.

Wynter, S. (1992). *"Do not call us Negros": How multicultural textbooks perpetuate racism.* San Francisco: Aspire.

2

Who's Afraid of Critical Race Theory?[*]

Derrick A. Bell

As I see it, critical race theory recognizes that revolutionizing a culture begins with the radical assessment of it.[1]

I. Introduction

Radical assessment can encompass illustration, anecdote, allegory, and imagination, as well as analysis of applicable doctrine and authorities. At the outset, I want to utilize all of these techniques to comment on a contemporary phenomenon: *The Bell Curve.*[2]

For the past three or four months, a great deal of attention and energy has been devoted to commending and condemning Mr. Charles Murray and the late Dr. Richard Herrnstein, authors of the best-selling book on racial intelligence, *The Bell Curve.* This book suggests great social policy significance in the fact that black people score, on average, fifteen points below whites on I.Q. tests.[3]

This thesis has been criticized as the rehashing of views long-ago rejected by virtually all experts in the field.[4] There is, critics maintain, no basis for a finding that intelligence is inherited and, indeed, no accepted definition of the vague term "intelligence." There is, on the other hand, a depressingly strong and invariant correlation between resources and race in this country, and resources and success—including success in taking I.Q. tests. These are settled facts.

Even so, the book has enjoyed an enormous success that its critics find difficult to explain. Stephen Jay Gould, for example, writes:

> *The Bell Curve,* with its claims and supposed documentation that race and class differences are largely caused by genetic factors and are therefore essentially immutable, contains no new arguments and presents no compelling data to support its anachronistic social Darwinism, so I can only conclude its success in winning attention must reflect the depressing temper of our time—a historical moment of unprecedented ungenerosity, when a mood for slashing social programs can be powerfully abetted by an argument that beneficiaries cannot be helped, owing to inborn cognitive limits expressed as low I.Q. scores.[5]

Criticism of *The Bell Curve* has been so universal among biologists that one must wonder: Why did these two well-known men produce a book filled with rejected theories? Surely they must have known that the book would provide pseudoscientific support for racial hostilities that always worsen during times of economic stress and anxiety.

The all too easy answer is that *The Bell Curve*'s authors saw a market opportunity and they took it. The book has sold over 300,000 copies and has become a major source of discussion in the media. But utilizing the conceptual and experiential tools of critical race theory, I want to suggest another possibility.

It is not difficult to imagine that the authors were aware of the generally accepted findings regarding the lack of any connection between race and intelligence. Suppose, as well, that recognizing the debilitating effects of discrimination and exclusion on African Americans, they devised an "oppression factor" and, adding it to existing data, discovered that there was indeed a discernible racial difference in intelligence measured by I.Q. tests. However, when the I.Q. data playing field was leveled via the "oppression factors," contrary to their own expectations, they discovered that blacks performed fifteen points higher than whites. Quite likely, they disbelieved and thus reviewed painstakingly their data several times. Each time they did so, the conclusion that they (perhaps) did not want became ever more certain. It was beyond denial. There was an answer beyond simple faith that explained why blacks survived two centuries of the world's most destructive slavery and a century of utter subordination under segregation: Black people are simply smarter than whites.[6]

What would they do with this information? Its release would almost certainly throw the country into turmoil. Let me explain. As history indicates all too well, blacks have suffered greatly as a result of discrimination undergirded and often justified by the general belief in black inferiority. But history shows with equal clarity, though it is less frequently acknowledged, that indications of black success and thus possible black superiority result in racist outrage. Most of the many race riots in this nation's history were sparked by white outrage over black success.[7]

In the nineteenth and early twentieth centuries, blacks who were successful at business or farming were targeted by the Ku Klux Klan and other hate groups for death and destruction.[8] While protection of white womanhood is deemed the major motivation for the thousands of blacks lynched during the latter part of the nineteenth century and the early decades of the twentieth, in fact, retaliation against blacks who dared compete successfully with white men was the real source of many, and perhaps most, of these atrocities.

A debate raged in Florida over a bill intended to compensate black victims for losses suffered more than seventy years ago, when the Klan absolutely destroyed a thriving black town called Rosewood—murdering, raping, pillaging, and finally burning all the property in sight. Denial is the usual response to even such well-documented racist rampages.[9] State officials who opposed the measure noted that the statute of limitations had expired, and that "compensation would be 'bad for the county and bad for our state' because it would encourage similar claims."[10]

In more recent times, discrimination aimed at skilled or talented blacks is a well-understood fact of life in the black community. Dozens of able and ambitious blacks were interviewed by journalist Ellis Cose in his book, *The Rage of a Privileged Class*.[11] They complained bitterly:

I have done everything I was supposed to do. I have stayed out of trouble with the law, gone to the right schools, and worked myself nearly to death. *What more do they want?* Why in God's name won't they accept me as a full human being? Why am I pigeonholed in a "Black job"? Why am I constantly treated as if I were a drug addict, a thief, or a thug? Why am I still not allowed to aspire to the same things every white person in America takes as a birthright? Why, when I most want to be seen, am I suddenly rendered invisible?[12]

In the context of law school faculties, my character Geneva Crenshaw describes an experience with which many professors of color can relate:

When I arrived, [the first Black hired], the white faculty members were friendly and support-ive. They smiled at me a lot and offered help and advice. When they saw how much time I spent helping minority students and how I struggled with my first writing, they seemed pleased. It was patronizing, but the general opinion seemed to be that they had done well to hire me. They felt good about having lifted up one of the downtrodden. And they congratulated themselves for their affirmative-action policies.

Then after I became acclimated to academic life, I began receiving invitations to publish in the top law reviews, to serve on important commissions, and to lecture at other schools. At this point, I noticed that some of my once-smiling colleagues now greeted me with frowns. For them, nothing I did was right: my articles were flashy but not deep, rhetorical rather than scholarly. Even when I published an article in a major review, my colleagues gave me little credit; after all, students had selected the piece, and what did they know anyway? My popularity with students was attributed to the likelihood that I was an easy grader. The more successful I appeared, the harsher became the collective judgement of my former friends.[13]

Professor Richard Delgado, a well-known critical race theorist, believes the shift may be caused by "cognitive dissonance":

At first, the white professor feels good about hiring the minority. It shows how liberal the white is, and the minority is assumed to want nothing more than to scrape by in the rarefied world they both inhabit. But the minority does not just scrape by, is not eternally grateful, and indeed starts to surpass the white professor. This is disturbing; things weren't meant to go that way. The strain between former belief and current reality is reduced by reinterpreting the current reality. The minority has a fatal flaw. Pass it on.[14]

Recognizing this strong, though often unconscious, white preference for black mediocrity in even the most elite professional schools, *The Bell Curve*'s authors faced a dilemma that they chose to resolve by intentionally falsifying their data, to spare blacks the reprisals and even bloody retaliation they would have suffered had the real truth regarding superior test performance by blacks come out. Dr. Herrnstein and Mr. Murray may well have foreseen the serious criticism of their work, if published without their new findings, criticism that, in fact, has been heaped on them by social scientists and experts in biology. They may have feared, though, that if they published the new data revealing the superiority of black intelligence, black people would be deemed a threat to many whites and thus placed in far greater danger than if the book served simply as a comfort to whites by repeating the oft-told tale of black inferiority.

The Bell Curve's authors must have known what every professional and skilled black has learned the hard way: that policies of affirnative action are endangered far more by the presence of blacks who are clearly competent than they are by those blacks who are only marginally so. Because it has been difficult for many whites to acknowledge that black people are competent—even superior—at some sports, it would be impossible to gain the same acknowledgement for blacks across the board, particularly if the reluctant recognition required the admission that inferior status is the result of discrimination rather than the old racial rationales of inferior skills, lack of drive, or the unwillingness to compete. The Dodger's official, Al Camparis, lost his job for saying so, but he was far from the only white person who believed that blacks lack "some of the necessities" to become managers in baseball.[15]

Finally, Dr. Herrnstein and Mr. Murray may have feared that, even if they were to convince a reluctant America of blacks' superior intelligence and ability—much of which has been smothered by racial discrimination—that reality may have opened the question for many whites as to whether they had not been similarly disadvantaged on the basis of class. Such a long-overdue revelation could well spark serious political unrest and perhaps a rebellion.

Given the potential for societal mischief at this level, the authors would almost certainly opt for conclusions that conform closely with what most people already believe. Better one more libel of blacks as an inferior people than a truth posing a greater threat that could lead to racial atrocities and class warfare. Thus, while *The Bell Curve*, as published, is condemned as a perversion of truth and a provocation for racial stereotyping, we should view it less harshly for what it is, and more sympathetically for what it might have been.

The moral: To understand the motivation for and the likely intent of racial policies in America, one need only be willing to reverse the racial composition of the major components of those policies. To see things as they really are, you must imagine them for what they might be. In this instance, the effort is intended to delegitimize the illegitimate. *The Bell Curve* captured the nation's fascination precisely because it laid out in scientific jargon what many whites believe, need desperately to believe, but dare not reveal in public or even to their private selves. The critical race theory perspective offers blacks and their white allies insight, spiked with humor, as a balm for this latest insult, and enables them to gird themselves for those certain to follow.

II. The Ongoing Debate over the Legitimacy of Critical Race Theory

At the outset, I asked, "Who's Afraid of Critical Race Theory?" The interrogatory poses indirectly two additional questions that may remain after my *Bell Curve* illustration. First, what *is* critical race theory? And second, what *ought* critical race theory to be? The distinction is useful even though the dividing line between the descriptive (what is) and the prescriptive (what it ought to be) can be quite fine.

The answers to what *is* critical race theory are fairly uniform and quite extensive. As to what critical race theory *ought* to be, the answers are far from uniform and, not coincidentally, tend to be leveled in the form of outsider criticism rather than insider inquiry. As to the *what is*, critical race theory is a body of legal scholarship, now about a decade old, a majority of whose members[16] are both existentially people of color and ideologically committed to the struggle against racism, particularly as institutionalized in and by law. Those critical race theorists who are white are usually cognizant of and committed to the overthrow of their own racial privilege.

Critical race theory writing and lecturing is characterized by frequent use of the first person, storytelling, narrative, allegory, interdisciplinary treatment of law, and the unapologetic use of creativity.[17] The work is often disruptive because its commitment to anti-racism goes well beyond civil rights, integration, affirmative action, and other liberal measures. This is not to say that critical race theory adherents automatically or uniformly "trash" liberal ideology and method (as many adherents of critical legal studies do). Rather, they are highly suspicious of the liberal agenda, distrust its method, and want to retain what they see as a valuable strain of egalitarianism which may exist despite, and not because of, liberalism.

There is, as this description suggests, a good deal of tension in critical race theory scholarship, a tension that Angela Harris characterizes as between its commitment to radical critique of the law (which is normatively deconstructionist) and its commitment to radical emancipation by the law (which is normatively reconstructionist). Harris views this tension—between "modernist" and "postmodernist" narrative—as a source of strength because of critical race theorists' ability to use it in ways that are creative rather than paralyzing.[18] Harris explains:

> CRT is the heir to both CLS [Critical Legal Studies] and traditional civil rights scholarship. CRT inherits from CLS a commitment to being "critical," which in this sense means also to be "radical" [while] . . . [a]t the same time, CRT inherits from traditional civil rights scholarship a commitment to a vision of liberation from racism through right reason. Despite the difficulty of separating legal reasoning and institutions from their racist roots, CRT's ultimate vision is redemptive, not deconstructive.[19]

Consider how the two groups view the law. Duke English Professor Stanley Fish explains the critical legal studies view of legal precedent as not

> a formal mechanism for determining outcomes in a neutral fashion—as traditional legal scholars maintain—but is rather a ramshackle ad hoc affair whose ill-fitting joints are soldered together by suspect rhetorical gestures, leaps of illogic, and special pleading tricked up as general rules, all in the service of a decidedly partisan agenda that wants to wrap itself in the mantle and majesty of law.[20]

Adherents of critical race theory basically agree with this assessment. They depart from their critical legal theory colleagues regarding what is to be done with this tangle of illogic and corrupted jurisprudence. I think Professor Patricia Williams speaks for most practitioners of critical race theory when she concedes that the concept of rights is indeterminate, vague, and disutile. She readily acknowledges as example that the paper-promises of enforcement packages like the Civil Rights Act of 1964 have held out as many illusions as gains. Recognizing further that blacks have never fully believed in constitutional rights as literal mandate, Williams states (in terms that constitute as much creed as response):

> To say that blacks never fully believed in rights is true; yet it is also true that blacks believed in them so much and so hard that we gave them life where there was none before. We held onto them, put the hope of them into our wombs, mothered them—not just the notion of them. We nurtured rights and gave rights life. And this was not the dry process of reification, from which life is drained and reality fades as the cement of conceptual determinism hardens round—but its opposite. [This was the story of Phoenix]; the parthenogenesis of unfertilized hope.[21]

It seems fair to say that most critical race theorists are committed to a program of scholarly resistance, and most hope scholarly resistance will lay the groundwork for wide-scale resistance. Veronica Gentilli puts it this way: "Critical race theorists seem grouped together not by virtue of their theoretical cohesiveness but rather because they are motivated by similar concerns and face similar theoretical (and practical) challenges."[22] To reiterate, the similar concerns referred to here include, most basic-ally, an orientation around race that seeks to attack a legal system which disempowers people of color.

Although critical race theory is not cohesive, it is at least committed. As John Calmore observes, "almost all the critical race theory literature seems to embrace the ideology of antisubordination in some form."[23] It is our hope that scholarly resist-ance will lay the groundwork for wide-scale resistance. We believe that standards and institutions created by and fortifying white power ought to be resisted.[24] Decontextu-alization, in our view, too often masks unregulated—even unrecognized—power. We insist, for example, that abstraction, put forth as "rational" or "objective" truth, smuggles the privileged choice of the privileged to depersonify their claims and then pass them off as the universal authority and the universal good. To counter such assumptions, we try to bring to legal scholarship an experientially grounded, oppositionally expressed, and transformatively aspirational concern with race and other socially constructed hierarchies.[25] John Calmore puts it well:

> [C]ritical race theory can be identified as such not because a random sample of people of color are voicing a position, but rather because certain people of color have deliberately chosen race-conscious orientations and objectives to resolve conflicts of interpretation in acting on the commitment to social justice and antisubordination.[26]

Professor Charles Lawrence speaks for many critical race theory adherents when he disagrees with the notion that laws are or can be written from a neutral perspec-tive. Lawrence asserts that such a neutral perspective does not, and cannot, exist—that we all speak from a particular point of view, from what he calls a "positioned perspective."[27] The problem is that not all positioned perspectives are equally valued, equally heard, or equally included. From the perspective of critical race theory, some positions have historically been oppressed, distorted, ignored, silenced, destroyed, appropriated, commodified, and marginalized—and all of this, not acci-dentally. Conversely, the law simultaneously and systematically privileges subjects who are white.

Critical race theorists strive for a specific, more egalitarian, state of affairs. We seek to empower and include traditionally excluded views and see all-inclusiveness as the ideal because of our belief in collective wisdom. For example, in a recent debate over "hate speech," both Chuck Lawrence and Mari Matsuda made the point that being committed to "free speech" may seem like a neutral principle, but it is not.[28] Thus, proclaiming that "I am committed equally to allowing free speech for the KKK and 2LiveCrew" is a non-neutral value judgment, one that asserts that the freedom to say hateful things is more important than the freedom to be free from the victimization, stigma, and humiliation that hate speech entails.

We emphasize our marginality and try to turn it toward advantageous perspective building and concrete advocacy on behalf of those oppressed by race and other interlocking factors of gender, economic class, and sexual orientation. When I say we are marginalized, it is not because we are victim-mongers seeking sympathy in return for a sacrifice of pride. Rather, we see such identification as one of the only hopes of transformative resistance strategy. However, we remain members of the whole set, as opposed to the large (and growing) number of blacks whose poverty and lack of opportunity have rendered them totally silent. We want to use our perspective as a means of outreach to those similarly situated but who are so caught up in the property perspectives of whiteness that they cannot recognize their subordination.

I am not sure who coined the phrase "critical race theory" to describe this form of writing, and I have received more credit than I deserve for the movement's origins. I rather think that this writing is the response to a need for expressing views that cannot be communicated effectively through existing techniques. In my case, I prefer using stories as a means of communicating views to those who hold very different views on the emotionally charged subject of race. People enjoy stories and will often suspend their beliefs, listen to the story, and then compare their views, not with mine, but with those expressed in the story.

Probably my best known story is *The Space Traders*,[29] which I wrote to convince a resisting class that the patterns of sacrificing black rights to further white interests, so present in American history, pose a continuing threat. In the story, as at least some of you know, aliens from outer space visit this country on New Year's Day in the year 2000. They promise wealth in the form of gold, environmental-cleansing material, and a substitute for fossil fuels. If accepted, their gold and space-age technology will guarantee another century of prosperity for the nation. In return for these wares, the space traders want to take back to their home star all black people. Given two weeks to decide, Americans in a variety of settings debate the trade offer. Finally, in a referendum vote, they opt for the trade by a seventy to thirty percentage. The story ends:

> The last Martin Luther King holiday the nation would ever observe dawned on an extraordinary sight. In the night, the Space Traders had drawn their strange ships right up to the beaches and discharged their cargoes of gold, minerals, and machinery, leaving vast empty holds. Crowded on the beaches were the inductees, some twenty million silent black men, women, and children, including babes in arms. As the sun rose, the Space Traders directed them, first, to strip off all but a single undergarment; then, to line up; and finally, to enter those holds which yawned in the morning light like Milton's "darkness visible." The inductees looked fearfully behind them. But, on the dunes above the beaches, guns at the ready, stood U.S. guards. There was no escape, no alternative. Heads bowed, arms now linked by slender chains, black people left the New World as their forbears [sic] had arrived.[30]

Initially, a number of reviewers criticized *The Space Traders* story as negative and unremittingly despairing. Blacks should be more grateful, critics complained, given the substantial gains made by your people in this great country. Some even condemned me as a racist for daring suggest that white Americans would ever trade away any American lives for profit and well-being. Most black people accepted the story as an all too accurate portrayal of their worst fears. Always, there were a few blacks in my audiences who not only were certain that if offered, Americans would accept the trade, but also indicated their willingness to go voluntarily. "Better the unknown," one man told me, "than the certainty of the disaster that awaits us here."

This is a strong statement, but even criticism of the story has been muted by subsequent events. While some blacks are doing very well—the true beneficiaries of the civil rights era—more than one-third of all black people are mired in poverty that is degrading, dispiriting, and destructive. Those in the middle-class have seen their progress halted and many are sliding back toward the low-income status they worked so hard to escape. The spaceships are looking more like a means of escape rather than vehicles of danger, exile, and death.

Let us further consider another phenomenon. Whites in this society seem so willing to accept their own subordination to other whites because of class and social barriers, yet they portray so much hostility toward blacks. The historian, C. Vann Woodward, put the issue well when he wondered how much racism must exist in the bosom of a white man who feels superior to a black while working at a black man's wages. I have suggested that in this country (which views property ownership as a measure of worth), many whites with relatively little property of the traditional kind—money, securities, and land—see their whiteness as a property right.

Professor Cheryl Harris takes up this challenge[31] and examines how whiteness, initially constructed as a form of racial identity, evolved into a form of property, historically and presently acknowledged and protected in American law. To state this view is to meet resistance. There is no direct support for it in the precedents or in the traditional legal writing on race and rights. Harris sets the stage for her long piece by telling the reader about her grandmother. Harris writes:

In the 1930s, some years after my mother's family became part of the great river of Black migration that flowed north, my Mississippi-born grandmother was confronted with the harsh matter of economic survival for herself and her two daughters. Having separated from my grandfather, who himself was trapped on the fringes of economic marginality, she took one long hard look at her choices and presented herself for employment at a major retail store in Chicago's central business district. This decision would have been unremarkable for a white woman in similar circumstances, but for my grandmother, it was an act of both great daring and self-denial, for in so doing she was presenting herself as a white woman. In the parlance of racist America, she was "passing."

Her fair skin, straight hair, and aquiline features had not spared her from the life of sharecropping into which she had been born in anywhere/nowhere, Mississippi—the outskirts of Yazoo City. But in the burgeoning landscape of urban America, anonymity was possible for a Black person with "white" features. She was transgressing boundaries, crossing borders, spinning on margins, traveling between dualities of Manichean space, rigidly bifurcated into light/dark, good/bad, white/Black. No longer immediately identifiable as "Lula's daughter," she could thus enter the white world, albeit on a false passport, not merely passing, but trespassing.

Every day my grandmother rose from her bed in her house in a Black enclave on the south side of Chicago, sent her children off to a Black school, boarded a bus full of Black passengers, and rode to work. No one at her job ever asked if she was Black; the question was unthinkable. By virtue of the employment practices of the "fine establishment" in which she worked, she could not have been. Catering to the upper-middle class, understated tastes required that Blacks not be allowed.

She quietly went about her clerical tasks, not once revealing her true identity. She listened to the women with whom she worked discuss their worries—their children's illnesses, their husband's disappointments, their boyfriends' infidelities—all of the mundane yet critical things that made up their lives. She came to know them but they did not know her, for my grandmother occupied a completely different place. That place—where white supremacy and economic domination meet—was unknown turf to her white co-workers. They remained oblivious to the worlds within worlds that existed just beyond the edge of their awareness and yet were present in their very midst.

Each evening, my grandmother, tired and worn, retraced her steps home, laid aside her mask, and reentered herself. Day in and day out, she made herself invisible, then visible again, for a price too inconsequential to do more than barely sustain her family and at a cost too precious to conceive. She left the job some years later, finding the strain too much to bear.

From time to time, as I later sat with her, she would recollect that period, and the cloud of some painful memory would pass across her face. Her voice would remain subdued, as if to contain the still remembered tension. On rare occasions she would wince, recalling some particularly racist comment made in her presence because of her presumed, shared group affiliation. Whatever retort might have been called for had been suppressed long before it reached her lips, for the price of her family's well-being was her silence. Accepting the risk of self-annihilation was the only way to survive.

Although she never would have stated it this way, the clear and ringing denunciations of racism she delivered from her chair when advanced arthritis had rendered her unable to work were informed by those experiences. The fact that self-denial had been a logical choice and had made her complicit in her own oppression at times fed the fire in her eyes when she confronted some daily outrage inflicted on Black people. Later, these painful memories forged her total identification with the civil rights movement. Learning about the world at her knee as I did, these experiences also came to inform my outlook and my understanding of the world.[32]

Professor Harris conveys to her white readers what those who are black already know, namely, that her grandmother's story is far from unique. Indeed, there are many who crossed the color line never to return. Passing is well known among black people in the United States and is a feature of race subordination in all societies structured on white supremacy. Notwithstanding the purported benefits of black heritage in an era of affirmative action, passing is not an obsolete phenomenon that has slipped into history.

The persistence of passing is related to the historical and continuing pattern of white racial domination and economic exploitation that has given passing a certain economic logic. It was a given to Harris's grandmother that being white automatically ensured higher economic returns in the short term, as well as greater economic, social, and political security in the long run. Becoming white meant gaining access to a whole set of public and private privileges that materially and permanently guaranteed basic needs and, therefore, survival. Becoming white increased the possibility of controlling critical aspects of one's life rather than being the object of others' domination.

Harris's grandmother's story illustrates the valorization of whiteness as treasured property in a society structured on racial castes. In ways so embedded that they are rarely apparent, the set of assumptions, privileges, and benefits that accompany the status of being white have become a valuable asset that whites sought to protect and that those who passed sought to attain—by fraud if necessary. Whites have come to expect and rely on these benefits, and over time these expectations have been affirmed, legitimated, and protected by the law. Even though the law is neither uniform nor explicit in all instances, in protecting settled expectations based on white privileges, American law has recognized a property interest in whiteness that, although unacknowledged, now forms the background against which legal disputes are framed, argued, and adjudicated.

In a fairly traditional fashion, Professor Harris develops these themes and their effect on racial policies from slavery to affirmative action. But the tragic image of her grandmother provides an almost mystical presence to her piece that informs, validates, and finally renders her conclusions impossible to avoid or deny.

As Harris's article illustrates, critical race theory writing embraces an experientially grounded, oppositionally expressed, and transformatively aspirational concern with race and other socially constructed hierarchies. Indeed, even a critical race theory critic finds that the "clearest unifying theme" of the writing is "a call for a change of perspective, specifically, a demand that racial problems be viewed from the perspective of minority groups, rather than a white perspective."[33] We use a number of different voices, but all recognize that the American social order is maintained and perpetuated by racial subordination. The narrative voice, the teller, is important to critical race theory in a way not understandable by those whose voices are tacitly deemed legitimate and authoritarian. The voice exposes, tells and retells, signals resistance and caring, and reiterates what kind of power is feared most—the power of commitment to change.

Given all of this, you will not be surprised to learn that the legal academy has come to recognize, but is far from ready to embrace, critical race theory, particularly at the faculty level. Indeed, there is now a small but growing body of work that views critical race theory as interesting, but not a "subdiscipline" unto itself and therefore must be amenable to mainstream standards.[34] These writers are not reluctant to tell us what critical race theory *ought* to be. They question the accuracy of the stories, fail to see their relevance, and want more of an analytical dimension to the work—all this while claiming that their critiques will give this writing a much-needed "legitimacy" in the academic world.

In one of the major critiques by Daniel Farber and Suzanna Sherry, the authors urge the storytellers in critical race theory to tell stories that are more "accurate" and "typical," that "articulate the legal relevance of the stories," and that "include an analytic dimension."[35] The authors seem unaware of the bizarre irony in their pronouncement that "[w]e know of no work on critical race theory that discusses psychological or other social science studies supporting the existence of a voice of color."[36]

They do not tell us just what such a study would look like, and why centuries of testimony by people of color regarding their experiences, including individuals like Frederick Douglass, W.E.B. Du Bois, Charles Wright, and Toni Morrison, are not measure enough. But Farber and Sherry "find little support for the general claim that traditional [academic] standards are inherently unfair to work by women and minorities," and contend that "creating literature has little nexus with the specific institutional traits of law schools."[37] They urge critical race theory writers to include more "traditional" scholarship in their approach.[38]

Perhaps critical race theory's most politically damaging critic is Randall Kennedy, whose blackness lends his critique a super legitimacy inversely proportional to the illegitimacy bequeathed to critical race theory. Kennedy notes the "insurgent" quality of minority scholars whose "impatience" has succeeded in making the race question a burning issue as never before in legal academia.[39] But, he says, the writings of critical race theory reveal "significant deficiencies"; they "fail to support persuasively their claims of racial exclusion or their claims that legal academic scholars of color produce a racially distinctive brand of scholarship."[40]

Kennedy adds to his critique by severely criticizing critical race theory's race-conscious perspective. When a black scholar at a prominent law school tells anyone who will listen that other folks of color are deluded about being excluded on the basis of their race; when a black scholar argues against race-conscious legal remedies or hiring policies; when a black scholar contends that there is no hidden "white" normativity or perspective but rather a meritocratic normativity (the companion claim to the claim that there is no minority perspective); when a black scholar says these things, all who rarely listen to scholars of color sit up and take notice. And take notes. And turn those notes into more fuel for the legitimacy debate that has always attended renegade movements. And critical race theory is renegade in the best sense of the word. Having drawn on the experience of the failed Second Reconstruction, how ironic and *scary* it is that the twentieth century draws to a close with racial hostility in full cry just as it was at the end of the nineteenth century.

At a time of crisis, critics serve as reminders that we are being heard, if not always appreciated. For those of us for whom history provides the best guide to contemporary understanding, criticism is a reassurance. The reason for this reassurance is contained in this final observation.

III. Black Art in a White Land

It was in the early years of African slavery, after the point where the nation decided that slaves were essential for the exploitation of the land's natural resources, but before the techniques of enslavement had been perfected. As a part of the subjugation process, newly arrived Africans—those who had survived the dreaded middle-passage—were separated from those of the same tribe. They were barred from using their native language or practicing their customs. While required to learn sufficient English to understand the white masters who would rule their lives, penalties for actually learning to read and write were severe. Despite the dangers, we know that many of the enslaved did acquire basic literacy skills. The Bible was often their primer as well as the primary access to their adopted religion, Christianity.

The Africans were allowed to sing. It is said that many had voices that were pleasant to the ear, and their singing in the evening after a day of hard labor in the fields or in the master's house, seemed an innocent relaxation for the slaves and those who owned them. It was a long time before the masters learned, if they ever did, that the slaves used their songs as a means of communication: giving warning, conveying information about escapes planned and carried out, and simply for uplifting the spirit and fortifying the soul. It was even longer before the Spirituals were recognized as a theology in song, a new interpretation of Christianity, one far closer to the original than that practiced by those who hoped the Bible would serve as a tool of pacification, not enlightenment.

At some point, white scholars must have heard the Spirituals. It is easy to imagine their reaction. Even the most hostile would have had to admit that the sometimes joyous and often plaintive melodies had a surface attraction. The scholars would have concluded, though, that the basically primitive song-chants were not capable of complex development and were certainly too simplistic to convey sophisticated musical ideas. The music, moreover, was not in classical form, likely deemed a fatal defect. Indeed, the slave songs were not even written down by those unknown persons who had composed them. Surely, these simple melodies could not be compared with the lieder of Haydn, Mozart, Schubert, or Brahms.

Whatever they were, the critics would conclude, these songs were not art. There was no potential in the music for intellectual inspiration as opposed to purely emotional satisfaction. Of course, the critics might concede, in the hands of classically trained composers and musicians, the Spirituals might serve as folk melodies from which true art might be rendered. Stephen Foster was said to have done this, and later Antonin Dvorak, and still later, George Gershwin. Many others followed. A few of them credited the genius in the slave songs, but most simply took what they wanted and called it their own without acknowledgement of the sources that, when asked, they deprecated and denied.

Need it be said that fortunes were made through the utilization and often the corruption of the slave melodies? Need it be said that those who originated this music seldom benefitted financially from their creations? There is no surprise here. A nation built on the backs of black labor would have little difficulty profiting from the product of black minds and hearts.

IV. Concluding Thoughts

Comparing critical race theory writing with the Spirituals is an unjustified conceit, but the essence of both is quite similar: to communicate understanding and reassurance to needy souls trapped in a hostile world. Moreover, the use of unorthodox structure, language, and form to make sense of the senseless is another similarity. Quite predictably, critics wedded to the existing legal canons will critique critical race theory, and the comparable work by feminists, with their standards of excellence and find this new work seriously inadequate. Many of these critics are steeped in theory and deathly afraid of experience. They seek meaning by dissecting portions of this writing—the autobiographical quality of some work, and the allegorical, story-telling characteristic in others. But all such criticisms miss the point. Critical race theory cannot be understood by claiming that it is intended to make critical race studies writing more accessible and more effective in conveying arguments of discrimination and disadvantage to the majority. Moreover, it is presumptuous to suggest, as a few critics do, that by their attention, even negative attention, they provide this work with legitimacy so that the world will take it seriously. Even if correct, this view is both paternalistic and a pathetically poor effort to regain a position of dominance.

I hope that those doing critical race theory, when reviewing these critiques, will consider the source. As to a response, a sad smile of sympathy may suffice. For those who press harder for explanations, both Beethoven and Louie Armstrong are available for quotation. When questioned about the meaning of his late quartets, Beethoven dismissed the critics with a prediction: "it was not written for you, but for a later age." And when asked for the meaning of jazz, Armstrong warned, "Man, if you don't know, don't mess with it."

These are wonderful retorts precisely because they do not seek to justify. The work, they say, speaks for itself and is its own legitimation. It was written to record experience and insight that are often unique and prior to this new work, too little heard. There is sufficient satisfaction for those who write in the myriad methods of critical race theory that comes from the work itself.

Notes

* *This essay was originally presented on February 23, 1995, as the second lecture of the David C. Baum Memorial Lectures on Civil Liberties and Civil Rights at the University of Illinois College of Law.*

1. John O. Calmore, *Critical Race Theory, Archie Shepp, and Fire Music: Securing an Authentic Intellectual Life in a Multicultural World*, 65 S. Cal. L. Rev. 2129, 2145 (1992).
2. Richard J. Herrnstein & Charles Murray, The Bell Curve: Intelligence and Class Structure in American Life (1994).
3. *See id.* at 317–40.
4. *See generally* The Bell Curve Wars: Race, Intelligence, and the Future of America (Steven Fraser ed., 1995).
5. Stephen J. Gould, *Curveball*, New Yorker, Nov. 28, 1994, at 139.
6. *The Bell Curve* devotes several chapters to the discussion of the traditional oppression factors, including poverty and schooling. *See* Herrnstein & Murray, *supra* note 2, at 127–55.
7. *See generally* Anthony M. Platt, The Politics of Riot Commissions, 1917–1970 (1971).
8. *See, e.g.,* Eric Foner, Reconstruction 425–44 (1988). "But the most 'offensive' Blacks of all seemed to be those who achieved a modicum of economic success for, as a White Mississippi farmer commented, the Klan 'do not like to see the negro go ahead.' " *Id.* at 429.
9. *See* Lori Rozsa, *Massacre in a Small Town in 1928*, Atlanta J. & Const., Jan. 17, 1993, at M1.
10. Larry Rohter, *Paying for Racial Attack Divides Florida Leaders*, N.Y. Times, Mar. 14, 1994, at A12. The Florida legislature finally passed, and the governor signed, a claims bill providing $60,000 in scholarships to compensate the Rosewood families and their survivors. *See* C. Jeanne Bassett, *House Bill 591: Florida Compensates Rosewood Victims and Their Families for a Seventy-One-Year-Old Injury*, 22 Fla. St. U. L. Rev. 503, 520 (1995).
11. Ellis Cose, The Rage of a Privileged Class (1993).
12. *Id.* at 1.
13. Derrick A. Bell, And We Are Not Saved: The Elusive Quest for Racial Justice 157–58 (1987).
14. *Id.*
15. David Aldridge, *Companis Admits Error but Maintains Innocence*, Wash. Post, July 3, 1987, at F1.
16. Critical race theory's founding members are usually identified as Derrick Bell, Richard Delgado, Charles Lawrence, Mari Matsuda, and Patricia Williams.
17. For the definitive example of incisive legal analysis utilizing these methods, see Patricia J. Williams, The Alchemy of Race and Rights (1991).
18. Angela P. Harris, *Foreword: The Jurisprudence of Reconstruction*, 82 Cal. L. Rev. 741, 743 (1994).
19. *Id.* Richard Delgado, one of critical race theory's original writers, lists as among the attributes of critical race scholars the following:

> (1) insistence on "naming our own reality"; (2) the belief that knowledge and ideas are powerful; (3) a readiness to question basic premises of moderate/incremental civil rights law; (4) the borrowing of insights from social science on race and racism; (5) critical examination of the myths and stories powerful groups use to justify racial subordination; (6) a more contextualized treatment of doctrine; (7) criticism of liberal legalisms; and (8) an interest in structural determinism—the ways in which legal tools and thought-structures can impede law reform.

Richard Delgado, *When a Story Is Just a Story: Does Voice Really Matter*, 76 Va. L. Rev. 95, 95 n.4 (1990).
20. Stanley E. Fish, There's No Such Thing As Free Speech and It's a Good Thing, Too 21 (1994).
21. Patricia J. Williams, *Alchemical Notes: Reconstructing Ideals from Deconstructed Rights*, 22 Harv. C.R.-C.L. L. Rev. 401, 430 (1987).
22. Veronica Gentilli, Comment, *A Double Challenge for Critical Race Scholars: The Moral Context*, 65 S. Cal. L. Rev. 2361, 2362 (1992).
23. *See* Calmore, *supra* note 1, at 2189.

24. For example, Mari Matsuda is not willing to accede to the prevalent notion that reparations are dead, and has put forth a powerful call that America redress the harms it inflicted on blacks, Native Americans, and Native Hawaiians, as a means of salvaging the national soul. Mari J. Matsuda, *Voices of America: Accent, Antidiscrimination Law, and a Jurisprudence for the Last Reconstruction*, 100 YALE L.J. 1329, 1333 (1991).

25. *See* Calmore, *supra* note 1, at 2146.

26. *Id.* at 2163. A partial listing of these "people of color" can be found in Richard Delgado & Jean Stefancic, *Critical Race Theory: An Annotated Biography*, 79 VA. L. REV. 461 (1993).

27. *See* Gentilli, *supra* note 22, at 2363 (citing Charles R. Lawrence, III, *The Word and the River: Pedagogy as Scholarship as Struggle*, 65 S. CAL. L. REV. 2231, 2282–83 (1992)).

28. *See generally* Charles R. Lawrence, III, *If He Hollers Let Him Go: Regulating Racist Speech on Campus*, 1990 Duke L.J. 431; Mari J. Matsuda, *Public Response to Racist Speech: Considering the Victim's Story*, 87 MICH. L. REV. 2320 (1989).

29. DERRICK A. BELL, FACES AT THE BOTTOM OF THE WELL: THE PERMANENCE OF RACISM 158 (1992).

30. *Id.* at 194.

31. Cheryl I. Harris, *Whiteness as Property*, 106 HARV. L. REV. 1709 (1993).

32. *Id.* at 1710–12.

33. Daniel A. Farber, *The Outmoded Debate over Affirmative Action*, 82 CAL. L. REV. 893, 904 (1994).

34. Edward L. Rubin, *On Beyond Truth: A Theory for Evaluating Legal Scholarship*, 80 CAL. L. REV. 889, 960 (1992) ("Critical Race Theory is only a partial subdiscipline; although it is based on distinctive norms [i.e., distinctive from the liberal positivist tradition], it lacks the distinctive methodology that characterizes [the definite partial subdisciplines of] critical legal studies or law and economics.").

35. Daniel A. Farber & Suzanna Sherry, *Telling Stories out of School: An Essay on Legal Narratives*, 45 STAN. L. REV. 807, 809 (1993).

36. *Id.* at 814.

37. *Id.* at 842, 845.

38. *Id.* at 842.

39. Randall L. Kennedy, *Racial Critiques of Legal Academia*, 102 HARV. L. REV. 1745, 1748 (1989).

40. *Id.* at 1749.

3

Education Policy as an Act of White Supremacy
Whiteness, Critical Race Theory, and Education Reform
David Gillborn

Introduction: Problems and Perspectives

> As I write, I try to remember when the word racism ceased to be the term which best
> expressed for me exploitation of black people and other people of color in this society and
> when I began to understand that the most useful term was white supremacy.
>
> (hooks, 1989, p. 112)

In this paper I consider the role of education policy in the active structuring of racial
inequity. Like bell hooks, my analysis centres on a conceptualization of "white
supremacy" that goes beyond the usual narrow focus on extreme and explicitly racist
organizations. Rather, this analysis focuses on a more extensive, more powerful version
of white supremacy; one that is normalized and taken for granted. Before examining
the evidence for the contemporary manifestation of white supremacist thought, it
may be useful to draw on an historical example that helps to set the scene.

Marcus Wood's book *Blind memory* examines the visual representation of slavery
in England and America during the eighteenth and nineteenth century. He begins
by commenting on the case of Thomas Clarkson's "Abolition map". Produced in
1808, the "map" was an attempt to chart visually the relationships between all the
important people and events involved in bringing about the abolition of slavery. As
Wood states, the map represents:

> . . . a cartographic fantasy which presents abolition as a series of tributary streams and rivers,
> each with the name of a supposed abolitionist attached. The waterways unite to form two
> mighty rivers in England and America, and these in turn unite when they flow into the open
> sea, presumably the sea of emancipation and spiritual renewal.
>
> (Wood, 2000, pp. 1, 4)

Incredibly, not a single slave was mentioned in this "map".

Clarkson's map provides an object-lesson in the reimagining of history to present
a unified tale of the triumph of white civilizing values over the forces of repression.
The erasure of Black people,[1] as an active and ultimately irresistible force for change,
is both obscene and significant. In a similar fashion policy-makers (and many edu-
cationists) tend to imagine education policy as evolving over time, sometimes with
dramatic changes in focus, but always (so policy-makers assure us) with the best of

intentions for all. This sanitized (white-washed) version of history envisions policy as a rational process of change, with each step building incrementally on its predecessor in a more-or-less linear and evolutionary fashion. But such an approach is contrary to the reality of race and politics in England where virtually every major public policy meant to improve race equity has arisen *directly* from resistance and protest by Black and other minoritized communities. Indeed, some of the most significant changes have come about as the result of bloodshed. The most recent example of this is the far-reaching changes made to race equity legislation (affecting all public institutions and every state maintained school) in the wake of *The Stephen Lawrence inquiry* (Macpherson, 1999). This Inquiry was only established after years of campaigning by Doreen and Neville Lawrence in an attempt to bring to justice the white youths who had murdered their 18-year-old son as he waited for a London bus (and was necessary because of the failure of the police force—which treated the Lawrences more like troublemakers than grieving parents). Another notable example in the field of education policy is the establishment, in 1979, of a committee of inquiry into the education of minority ethnic children following growing protests by Black community groups (see Redbridge Community Relations Council, 1978) and activists (see Coard, 1971; Dhondy, 1974, 1978). Similarly, "multicultural" education enjoyed a brief boost to its policy profile following uprisings in Brixton, Bristol and elsewhere in the early 1980s (see Virdee & Cole, 2000; Figueroa, 2004).

There is a pressing need, therefore, to view policy in general, and education policy in particular, through a lens that recognizes the very real struggles and conflicts that lie at the heart of the processes through which policy and practice are shaped. This is a radical challenge that calls into question many of the comforting myths that self-avowedly "democratic" states tell about themselves. But the challenge extends beyond the realms of policy-making and policy-implementation, and reaches into the academy. In particular, such a perspective challenges the kind of "problem-solving" approach that has come to typify a great deal of academic work, especially in the traditions of school effectiveness and management/leadership studies (see Morley & Rassool, 1999). Here, in the words of Thrupp and Wilmott (2003, p. 4) commonsense "ahistorical, individuated and often monocultural views about the purposes and problems of schooling" feed into a kind of uncritical "policy science" (after Grace, 1995) that seeks school-based solutions to school-based problems and totally ignores existing structural and historic relations of domination. Roger Dale (2001) has criticized a similar tendency in English Sociology of Education where, as Rob Moore argued, a weak sociology *for* education (rather than a sociology *of* education) has sometimes focused on "the internal features of the system . . . tending to 'take' its problems rather than 'make' problems through the external criteria of critical social theory" (Moore, 1996, p. 158). As Geoff Whitty (2002) has documented, the election of a New Labour government in 1997 did nothing to challenge the existing aggressively managerialist policy culture and academic research milieu. As several writers have argued, notably Michael Apple (1996), Stephen Ball (2004) and Sara Delamont (2001), there is no such thing as *the* sociology of education. There are competing (and excluding) versions and constructions of the discipline, even within a single time period in a single nation state.

The line of analysis pursued in this paper, therefore, may seem radical (perhaps even insane)[2] but it builds on a growing tradition of critical race scholarship that is especially strong in the US (Crenshaw et al., 1995; Ladson-Billings & Tate, 1995; Ladson-Billings, 1998; Parker, 1998; Delgado & Stefancic, 2000, 2001; Essed & Goldberg, 2002). By applying these perspectives to the English case I hope, first, to illuminate some of the deeper problems and conflicts at the heart of education policy and race inequity, and second, to contribute to the "iterative project of scholarship and social justice" aspired to by critical race theory (Tate, 1997, pp. 234–235).

The main focus of the paper is a reconceptualization of white supremacy and an examination of the empirical evidence in contemporary English education policy. In particular, I examine some fundamental questions about who and what education policy is for. Before looking at the empirical data, however, it is necessary to set out my understanding of whiteness and the construction of white identities.

Troubling Whiteness[3]

> . . . whiteness is not a culture but a social concept.
>
> (Leonardo, 2002, p. 32)

As Rosa Hernandez Sheets (2000, 2003) has argued, focusing on white people (their sense of self, their interests and concerns) has become such a fashionable past-time within parts of the US academy that there is a danger of whiteness studies colonizing and further de-radicalizing multicultural education. However, the field is extremely wide. If the guilt-ridden white introspection that Sheets fears is at one end of the spectrum, at the other pole lie Marxist analyses that firmly identify whiteness as one more "strategy for securing to some an advantage in a competitive society" (Ignatiev, 1997, p. 1). The latter position calls for the "abolition of the white race":

> Various commentators have stated that their aim is to identify and preserve a positive white identity. Abolitionists deny the existence of a positive white identity. We at *Race Traitor*, the journal with which I am associated, have asked some of those who think whiteness contains positive elements to indicate what they are. We are still waiting for an answer. Until we get one, we will take our stand with David Roediger, who has insisted that whiteness is not merely oppressive and false, it is nothing but oppressive and false.
>
> (Ignatiev, 1997, p. 1)[4]

Alastair Bonnett has argued that this position is considerably weakened by its "obsessive focus" on the US and a "persistent romanticization of blackness" that leads the abolitionist position to a form of class reductionism that is unable to deal with the complexities of racism in a more nuanced way that takes account of experiences elsewhere in the world (Bonnett, 2000, p. 141). One attempt to find a critical, but not class reductionist, approach to these issues is to be found in the work of Zeus Leonardo (2002, 2004). Leonardo appropriates concepts from critical pedagogy, globalization studies and whiteness studies, to argue for a "neo-abolitionist" position.

Leonardo begins by addressing a key problematic in this field; the difference between "whiteness" and "white people":

"Whiteness" is a racial discourse, whereas the category "white people" represents a socially constructed identity, usually based on skin color.

(Leonardo, 2002, p. 31)

This is a vital point. Critical scholarship on whiteness is not an assault on white people per se: it is an assault on the socially constructed and constantly reinforced power of white identifications and interests (see Ladson-Billings & Tate, 1995, pp. 58–60). "So-called 'White' people" (Bonnett, 1997, p. 189) do not necessarily reinforce whiteness any more than heterosexual people are *necessary* homophobic, or men are *necessarily* sexist. However, these analogies are useful because they highlight the forces that recreate and extend the kinds of "unthinking" assumptions and actions which mean that very many (probably the majority) of heterosexuals *are* homophobic and most men *are* sexist. It is possible for white people to take a real and active role in deconstructing whiteness but such "race traitors" are relatively uncommon.

Building on a range of work, in particular Ruth Frankenberg (1993) and David Roediger (1992), Leonardo discusses some of the defining characteristics of whiteness (Leonardo, 2000, p. 32). For example:

- "*An unwillingness to name the contours of racism*": inequity (in employment, education, wealth, etc) is explained by reference to any number of alternative factors rather than being attributable to the actions of whites.
- "*The avoidance of identifying with a racial experience or group*": whiteness draws much of its power from "Othering" the very idea of ethnicity. A central characteristic of whiteness is a process of "naturalization" such that white becomes the norm from which other "races" stand apart and in relation to which they are defined. When white-identified groups *do* make a claim for a white ethnic identity alongside other officially recognized ethnic groups (e.g., as has been tried by the Ku Klux Klan in the US and the British National Party in England) it is the very exceptionality of such claims that points to the commonsense naturalization of whiteness at the heart of contemporary political discourse (see Swain & Nieli, 2003; Ratcliffe, 2004, pp. 115–117).
- "*The minimization of racist legacy*": seeking to "draw a line" under past atrocities as if that would negate their continued importance as historic, economic and cultural factors.

This is not to say that whiteness is stable nor unambiguous. Indeed, some of the most striking scholarship in this field has taken as its focus the historically specific, contingent and "slippery" nature of whiteness (Bonnett, 1997). For centuries legislators have struggled to capture the "commonsense" understandings of race in terms that could be legally enforced (see Wright, 1997; Ladson-Billings, 2004). In addition, many groups that at one time or another have been defined as outside whiteness have at other times been redefined and brought within the privileged group. See, for example, Karen Brodkin Sacks (1997) *How did Jews become white folks?* and Noel Ignatiev (1995) *How the Irish became white.*

Whiteness as *Performatively Constituted*

In critical scholarship it is not uncommon to hear whiteness described as a *perform-ance*. Leonardo (2002, p. 31), for example, cites Henry Giroux (1997) in exactly this way. Describing whiteness as a performance can operate as a shorthand means of drawing attention to the importance of actions and constructed identities—rejecting the simplistic assumption that "whiteness" and "white people" are one and the same thing:

> . . . the critical project that largely informs the new scholarship on "whiteness" rests on a singular assumption. Its primary aim is to unveil the rhetorical, political, cultural, and social mechanisms through which "whiteness" is both invented and used to mask its power and privilege.
>
> (Giroux, 1997, p. 102)

However, at risk of seeming pedantic, there is an important distinction to be made here between performance and *performativity*: it is a distinction that directly addresses the power of whiteness and the problems in decentring it.

The idea of likening social "actors" to performers on a stage is far from novel. One of the most insightful analyses remains that connected with the Chicago school of symbolic interaction, especially in the work of Howard Becker and Erving Goffman. The latter, of course, took the analogy as far as describing an entire dramaturgical analysis of social interaction, including "performers", "communication out of char-acter" and "front" and "back" regions, where actors allow different (often contra-dictory) faces to be seen by particular associates (Goffman, 1959). However, one of the problems with such an analysis is the degree to which performers are aware of the performance they are giving. One of the most powerful and dangerous aspects of whiteness is that many (possibly the majority) of white people have no awareness of whiteness as a construction, let alone their own role in sustaining and playing out the inequities at the heart of whiteness. In this sense, the dramaturgical over-tones of the analysis actually *underestimate* the size of the task facing critical antiracists. As Deborah Youdell argues:

> The terms "perform" and "performance" imply a volitional subject, even a self-conscious, choosing performer, behind the "act" which is performed.
>
> (Youdell, 2000, p. 64)

Building on writers like Michel Foucault (1980, 1990, 1991) and Judith Butler (1990, 1993, 1997), Youdell argues for a particular understanding of how power operates on and through the creation of different subject identities. Through a meticulously documented and highly sensitive analysis of teenage identity-work in school, Youdell takes seriously the spaces and possibilities for resistance and subversion. Crucially, however, her analysis also demonstrates the numerous ways in which certain iden-tities are strengthened and legitimized through countless acts of reiteration and reinforcement. These processes are not foolproof but their power is enormous, extending even into the most intimate and apparently idiosyncratic of actions and relationships, including, for example, the particular constellations of heterosexual desire that are deemed possible across race lines in school (Youdell, 2004). Youdell terms this the *performative constitution of identity.*

It is this performative constitution of particular identities and roles that lends whiteness its deep-rooted, almost invisible status. One of the key points about whiteness as a performatively constituted identity is that those who are implicated in whiteness rarely even realize its existence—let alone their own role in its repeated iteration and resignification.

In the next section of this paper I want to take the key conceptual insights discussed above and apply them to the field of education policy and race inequity in England. I view this work as building on two key conceptual pillars: an understanding of critical race theory that includes elements of critical antiracism elaborated outside the US (Gillborn, 1995, 2004a, b; Bonnett, 2000; Dei et al., 2004) and critical white studies, including in particular a notion of whiteness as performatively constituted in numerous discursive arenas including the realms of education policy and classroom practice.

Seeing Supremacy

> Whiteness has developed, over the past two hundred years, into a taken-for-granted experience structured upon a varying set of supremacist assumptions (sometimes cultural, sometimes biological, sometimes moral, sometimes all three). Non-White identities, by contrast, have been denied the privileges of normativity, and are marked within the West as marginal and inferior.
>
> (Bonnett, 1997, p. 188)

Critical race theory promotes a different perspective on white supremacy than the limited and extreme understandings usually denoted by the term in everyday language. "White supremacy" is a term usually reserved for individuals, organizations and/or philosophies that are overtly and self-consciously racist in the most crude and obvious way: organizations that not only claim a distinctiveness for white-identified people, but add a social Darwinist element to argue for intellectual and/or cultural superiority, frequently based on a supposedly fixed genetic inheritance. Even after the genocide of the Nazi era in the previous century, such perspectives continue to be openly preached by some.[5] On both sides of the Atlantic, however, it is interesting that groups whose neo-nazi pedigree is secure (like the British National Party and the Ku Klux Klan) have recently tried to reinvent themselves as slicker, more media astute organizations, calling for a supposed realignment of policy goals and interests to favour the white majority "ethnic" group and denying that their fascistic past has any relevance to their contemporary activities. It should also be remembered that, although mainstream science long ago rejected crude notions of racial genetic separateness and superiority (Selden, 1999), it is *exactly* these beliefs which shaped Herrnstein and Murray's (1994) foray into the *New York Times* bestseller list.[6]

Such extreme and obviously racist positions are highly dangerous but they are by no means the whole story. Indeed, there is a danger that their influence on debate risks obscuring a far more comprehensive and subtle form of race politics—one that actually exerts a more powerful influence. As Paul Gilroy argued, in relation to the British case, more than a decade ago:

> A tension exists between those strands in antiracism which are primarily antifascist and those which work with a more extensive and complex sense of what racism is in contemporary Britain. . . . The price of over-identifying the struggle against racism with the activities of these extremist groups and grouplets is that however much of a problem they may be in a particular area (and I am not denying the need to combat their organizing) they are exceptional. They exist on the fringes. . . . A more productive starting point is provided by focusing on racism in the mainstream and seeing "race" and racism not as fringe questions but as a volatile presence at the very centre of British politics, actively shaping and determining the history not simply of blacks, but of this country as a whole . . .
>
> (Gilroy, 1992, p. 51)

Critical work on race in the US has moved beyond the "commonsense" superficial readings of white supremacy as solely the preserve of obviously extreme racialized politics. Some scholars have penetrated even further the façade of contemporary politics, to argue that mainstream political parties, and the functioning of agencies like the education system itself, are actively implicated in maintaining and extending the grip that white people have on the major sources of power in "Western" capitalist societies.

> [By] "white supremacy" I do not mean to allude only to the self-conscious racism of white supremacist hate groups. I refer instead to a political, economic, and cultural system in which whites overwhelmingly control power and material resources, conscious and unconscious ideas of white superiority and entitlement are widespread, and relations of white dominance and non-white subordination are daily reenacted across a broad array of institutions and social settings.
>
> (Ansley, 1997, p. 592)

Of course, this is not to argue that white people are uniformly powerful, as Noel Ignatiev has argued in relation to poverty among whites; "whiteness does not exempt people from exploitation, it reconciles them to it. It is for those who have nothing else" (Ignatiev, 1997, p. 1). The growing influence of critical race theory has supported this line of analysis but it is a perspective that was present before the advent of CRT in education (see Sleeter, 1993). For example, this paper began with a quotation from bell hooks who, writing in the late 1980s, used the term to explicitly critique a central and extensive form of racism that evades the simplistic definitions of liberal discourse. In particular, hooks identifies white supremacy as a deeply rooted exercise of power that remains untouched by moves to address the more obvious forms of overt discrimination:

> When liberal whites fail to understand how they can and/or do embody white-supremacist values and beliefs even though they may not embrace racism as prejudice or domination (especially domination that involves coercive control), they cannot recognize the ways their actions support and affirm the very structure of racist domination and oppression that they profess to wish to see eradicated.
>
> (hooks, 1989, p. 113)

This perspective echoes precisely the same critique of liberalism that prompted the genesis of critical race theory in legal scholarship.

> CRT begins with a number of basic insights. One is that racism is normal, not aberrant, in American society. Because racism is an ingrained feature of our landscape, it looks ordinary and natural to persons in the culture. Formal equal opportunity—rules and laws that insist on treating blacks and whites (for example) alike—can thus remedy only the more extreme and shocking forms of injustice, the ones that do stand out. It can do little about the business-as-usual forms of racism that people of color confront every day and that account for much misery, alienation, and despair.
>
> (Delgado & Stefancic, 2000, p. xvi)

In the remainder of this paper I work from this critical perspective to explore how contemporary English education policy plays an active role in supporting and affirming exactly these kinds of racist inequities and structures of oppression.[7]

Who and What is Education Policy For?

In previous sections of this paper I have stressed the importance of looking beyond the superficial rhetoric of policies and practices, in order to focus on the material and ideological work that is done to legitimate and extend race inequity. When judging education policy, therefore, it is pertinent to ask some deceptively simple questions. In view of the restrictions of available space, I will structure the discussion in relation to three questions that directly address the material consequences of education policy. These are by no means the only relevant "tests" of equity and policy but they are among the most revealing and fundamental because they go beyond the expressed intent of policy-makers and practitioners to examine how policy works in the real world. First, the question of priorities: who or what is driving education policy? Second, the question of beneficiaries: who wins and who loses as a result of education policy priorities? And finally, the question of outcomes: what are the effects of policy? I will address each question in turn.

Priority

As several studies have shown, over the last half-century issues of racism, "race relations" and "race" equity have featured differently in education policy. From early post-war ignorance and neglect (Lynch, 1986), through periods of overt assimilationist and integrationist policies (Tomlinson, 1977; Mullard, 1982), it has been clear that, although the particular measures meant to address ethnic diversity have changed from time to time, one constant feature has been a place on the margins of education policy. Superficially there have been significant changes. For example, during much of the 1980s and 1990s successive Conservative administrations—reflecting Margaret Thatcher's famous assertion that there is "no such thing as society" (Thatcher, 1993, p. 626)—insisted that the only fair approach was a "colour-blind" perspective that denied any legitimacy to group-based analyses and claims. John Major, who succeeded Thatcher as Prime Minister, asserted:

> Life is lived, people join in, people belong. Darkness, lightness—that's a difference losing

significance with every day crossed off the calendar. . . . Few things would inflame racial tension more than trying to bias systems in favour of one colour—a reverse discrimination that fuels resentment. An artificial bias would damage the harmony we treasure. Equality under the law—yes; equality of opportunity and reward—yes. These promote harmony. Policy must be colour-blind—it must just tackle disadvantage. Faced by British citizens, whatever their background might be.

(Major, 1997, pp. 6–7)

Major's determination to refuse the significance of raced inequality (reducing "race" to "darkness" and "lightness") was highly significant. The sub-text of his attack on "an artificial bias" would seem to have been an acceptance of some form of non-artificial (natural?) bias. In a stark reversal of this language, Tony Blair's incoming New Labour administration of 1997 openly named race inequity as an unacceptable feature of the education system and even cited critical research that had raised questions about teachers' role in producing raced inequities in school (DfEE, 1997). Unfortunately, the tangible outcomes of this approach have mostly concerned granting funding to a handful of minority ethnic schools on the basis of a distinctive religious identity, e.g., creating the first state-funded Muslim schools (see Gillborn, 1998, 2001; Figueroa 2004).

A particularly stark indicator of the place of race equity in contemporary education policy is provided by the Department for Education's "five year strategy" published amid a flurry of publicity in the summer of 2004. Running to more than 100 pages, the document set out Labour's proposals for the next five years of education policy. "Minority ethnic" pupils are granted a single mention in the text; a 25-word paragraph headed *low achieving minority ethnic groups* (DfES, 2004, p. 60). The word "racism" does not appear at all; neither do the more sanitized concepts of "prejudice" and "discrimination". In contrast, "business" and "businesses" appear 36 times, and "standards" appears on 65 separate occasions: the latter equates to an average reiteration of "standards" once every page and a half. Clearly, the five year strategy prioritized an official version of "standards" in education, but one could legitimately ask "standards for whom"?

Regardless of the political persuasion of the incumbent political party, therefore, race equity has constantly to fight for legitimacy as a significant topic for education policy-makers. This is a key part of the way in which education policy is implicated in white supremacy.

Beneficiaries

Since 1988 education policy in England, under both Conservative and Labour governments, has been driven by the assertion that "standards" are too low and must be raised. The dominant measure of standards has been through crude quantitative data, in particular, students' performance in high-stakes tests conducted at the end of their primary and secondary education. These data are published nationally in tabular form and provide a misleading, but easily reproduced, guide to school "standards".[8] These reforms have fundamentally altered how schools operate, placing a premium on those subjects that will count in the school tests[9] and leading to increased selection and separation of students who are thought to be "academic" in secondary schools (more on this below).

A good performance in the official statistics is extremely important for schools: continual "under-performance" can trigger a range of sanctions including, ultimately, school closure. Not surprisingly, therefore, the proportion of 16-year-olds attaining the requisite five "higher grade passes" in their high-stakes examinations has consistently risen since the late 1980s. However, students of minority ethnic backgrounds have not always shared equally in these gains.[10] In fact, of the five principal ethnic categories monitored continuously since the late 1980s, only one group—whites— have enjoyed consistent year-on-year improvement. The proportion of whites attaining the "benchmark" level (at least five higher grade passes) has risen from 30% in 1989 to 55% in 2004 (DfES, 2005, Table A). Each of the other "ethnic" groups counted in official statistics have experienced periods where their rate of success has held constant (as in the case of Indian students between 2000 and 2002) or even where their success rate has fallen back, e.g., Black students in 1992–1994, and between 2000 and 2004; Pakistani students between 1992 and 1996, and between 2002 and 2004; and Bangladeshi students in 1998–2000 (DfES, 2005).

On the whole, therefore, minoritized students have not shared equally in the improved attainments associated with the recent reforms. In particular, "Black" students find themselves even further behind their white counterparts than they were in the 1980s: in 1989, 30% of white students achieved five or more higher grade passes, compared with 18% of Black students (an inequity of 12 percentage points); in 2004, however, the gap was 20 percentage points (with the benchmark being attained by 55% of white students and 35% of their Black peers: DfES, 2005, Table A). Similarly, Pakistani students (who were 11 percentage points behind whites in 1992) have experienced widening inequities of attainment in recent years: in 2004, 37% of Pakistani students reached the required level, i.e., a gap of 18 percentage points behind whites.

A great deal of official attention is often focused on pupils categorized as of "Indian" ethnic heritage: this group was first recognized separately in official statistics in 1992, when 38% attained the benchmark level of success. Since then, Indian students have generally enjoyed *greater* success than the white group: with 72% achieving at least five higher grade passes in the most recent survey. This level of attainment is often highlighted in official press releases and in media coverage: "Minority ethnic pupils make further progress at GCSE" (DfES Press Release, 24 February 2005).

Indeed, the attainment of Indian pupils (along with their other "Asian" peers) is frequently cited as evidence that the system rewards effort and that under achievement can have nothing to do with racism (neither overt nor unintended):

> I'm no educationist, but if you examine the statistics it is certainly difficult to conclude that our schools discriminate against ethnic minorities, even unwittingly. Chinese and some other Asian pupils excel, easily outperforming the whites.
>
> (Liddle, 2005)

Much has been written in the US about how certain groups are held up as "model minorities", a stereotype of hard work and success that harms both the group itself (by obscuring certain other disadvantages, such as higher rates of unemployment) and, by implication, other less successful groups (whose "failure", it is reasoned, must surely be their own fault): see Min (2004) and Takaki (1993). This literature is less well developed in the UK but qualitative research has already established that racism in schools works differently for different ethnic groups (see Youdell, 2000, 2004). A more detailed examination of Indian and Chinese attainments is beyond the scope of the present paper, suffice it to say that their examination success evidences nothing about an absence of racism in their school experiences (see Bhatti, 2004; Archer & Francis, 2005, forthcoming). Furthermore, their relative success should not distract from the much less positive picture that emerges for the other minority groups counted in official data (above).

Outcomes

A major reason for the different patterns of improvement shown by different groups is likely to lie in the ways that schools have responded to the pressure to "raise standards". There is anecdotal evidence, for example, which suggests that some schools have sought to limit the proportion of minority students they admit and to expel disproportionate numbers of Black students. By their very nature, such practices elude official documentation and scrutiny, but it is certainly the case that Black students continue to be significantly more likely to be expelled from school than their white peers (as they have since records began: DfES, 2002) and that Black students are frequently treated more harshly than whites accused of similar offences—a pattern long established in British qualitative research (Wright, 1987, 1992; Mac an Ghaill, 1988; Gillborn, 1990; Figueroa, 1991; Mirza, 1992, 1999; Nehaul, 1996; Connolly, 1998; Gillborn & Youdell, 2000; Wright et al., 2000; Blair, 2001; Sewell, 2004) and now even identified in official school inspection data.[11]

It is also clear that schools are increasingly using "setting by ability" and other forms of internal selection to separate children into hierarchical teaching groups. This kind of development is openly advocated by government. For example, the Labour Party's 1997 election manifesto claimed that setting benefits both high- and low-achieving students (Labour Party, 1997, p. 7), something that is directly contradicted by the international research evidence.[12] In addition, subsequent policies have further extended this principle by first, creating advantaged pathways for those designated as "gifted and talented", and second, by increasing the number of specialist schools, each with increased provision to choose pupils according to "aptitude" and/ or "ability" (see Edwards & Tomlinson, 2002). Wholly predictably, in view of previous research on the racialized nature of selection to "gifted" programmes, evidence is already emerging that certain minority groups, especially Black students, are markedly under-represented in special provision for the so-called "gifted and talented" (Ofsted, 2004, p. 6).

One of the most consistent findings in research on school-based selection processes is that, when asked to judge the potential, attitude and/or motivation of their students, white teachers tend to place disproportionate numbers of Black students in low ranked groups (CRE, 1992; Gillborn & Gipps, 1996; Hallam & Toutounji, 1996; Sukhnandan

& Lee, 1998). These decisions frequently have a cumulative effect whereby the initial decision compounds inequity upon inequity until success can become, literally, impossible. For example, where students are placed in low ranked teaching groups they frequently cover a restricted curriculum; their teachers have systematically lower expectations of them; and, in many high-stakes tests in England, they are entered for low "tiered" examinations where only a limited number of grades are available. In the lowest maths paper, for example, the best available grade is D: that is, *less* than the C grade that is commonly accepted as the minimum necessary for entry into the professions or further dedicated study at advanced level. In a study of these decisions in London secondary schools, it was Black students who were most likely to be placed in this situation: two-thirds of Black students in the schools under study (Gillborn & Youdell, 2000). It is difficult to think of a clearer example of institutional racism than a test, disproportionately taken by Black students, in which the highest possible grade is commonly judged to be a "failure". We have to ask whether such discriminatory processes would be permitted if their victims were white, and especially, middle class whites. Ernest R. House has noted an identical situation in the US in relation to the practice of "retaining students", i.e., holding them back a year:

> Americans will support policies that are harmful to minorities that they would not tolerate if those same policies were applied to majority populations. In education, for example, Americans are strongly in favor of retention—retaining students at the same grade level for another year—even though the research evidence overwhelmingly shows strong negative effects. . . . Retention programs are applied massively to minorities in large cities, but not to majority populations.
>
> (House, 1999, p. 2)

In relation to the three tests I set out earlier, therefore, the English education system appears to be a clear case where the routine assumptions that structure the system encode a deep privileging of white students and, in particular, the legitimization, defence and extension of Black inequity. In terms of policy priorities race equity has been at best a marginal concern, at worst non-existent. In relation to beneficiaries the picture is more complex than usually recognized (some minoritized groups do relatively well), but the most consistent beneficiaries are white students and, in key respects, Black students' position is no better than it was when the whole reform movement began in the late 1980s. Finally, an examination of outcomes clearly shows that central reform strategies (such as the use of selection and hierarchical teaching groups) are known to work against race equity but are nevertheless promoted as "best practice" for all. These reforms are known to discriminate in practice (regardless of intent) and are, therefore, racist in their consequences. These three tests of the system are by no means exhaustive but they are sufficient to establish the education system's active involvement in the defence and extension of the present regime of white supremacy in the contemporary British state.

Conclusions

> . . . white-ness is a state of mind, not a complexion.
>
> (Malcolm X, quoted by Hare, 2002, p. 9)

In this paper I have tried to construct a synthesis of several different arguments in order to arrive at a new understanding of an old problem. Critical race theory and critical work on the nature of whiteness offer a potentially important new way of viewing familiar issues with a fresh eye. Neither approach, however, is without its weaknesses and problems. Quite apart from the internal divisions between scholars working on different specificities of similar approaches, there are problems in the way that both perspectives might yet fall prey to the very mechanisms that they seek to critique. Gloria Ladson-Billings (1998), for example, has pointedly questioned whether education is too "nice" a field (i.e., too majoritarian, too conservative, and too self-satisfied) to ever take forward such a radical challenge. Similarly Rosa Hernandez Sheets warns that whiteness studies threatens to become a "movement" through which white people recolonize the centre of multicultural education, one of the few spaces carved out by people of color in the US academy (Sheets, 2000). These are very real possibilities. But there is also the possibility that, by engaging in work of this kind, critical scholars can raise new questions, challenge so-called "common-sense" and disrupt the assumptions that currently shape education (in policy *and* practice).

This process of radical critique should not be confused with a prophecy of doom. To identify the complex and deep rooted nature of racism is not to assume that it is inevitable nor insurmountable (see Ansley, 1997). Neither is such an analysis an attack on the progress already made in the struggle for greater equity: recognizing how far we must yet travel, is not to deny that we have already moved. This perspective, however, insists on recognizing the scale and difficulty of the task ahead. Critical race theory is frequently accused of pessimism but its recognition of contemporary white supremacy is intended to advance and inform the struggle for greater equity, not to detract from it. As Richard Delgado and Jean Stefancic have asked:

> . . . is [CRT] optimistic, because it believes that race is a social construction? (As such, it should be subject to ready change.) And if CRT does have a dark side [sic], what follows from that? Is medicine pessimistic because it focuses on diseases and traumas?
>
> (Delgado & Stefancic, 2001, p. 13)

Drawing primarily on the work of scholars of color in the US, in this paper I have tried to build on the insights of both CRT and critical white studies. This approach rejects the commonsense (white-sense?) view of education policy and the dominant understanding of the functioning of education in Western societies. This critical perspective is based on the recognition that race inequity and racism are central features of the education system. These are not aberrant nor accidental phenomena that will be ironed out in time, they are fundamental characteristics of the system. *It is in this sense that education policy is an act of white supremacy.* To revisit bell hooks' use of the term white supremacy, the evidence shows that education policy in England clearly acts to "support and affirm the very structure of racist domination and oppression" (after hooks, 1989, p. 113). I have shown how policy assumes and defends white supremacy through the priorities it sets, the beneficiaries that it privileges, and the outcomes that it produces. Far from being the extreme and unhelpful slur that many critics (of both left and right) assume the term to be, white supremacy is actually a wholly apt descriptor of the functioning and structure of contemporary education.

Finally, in view of the particular way in which race critical research uses the term "white supremacy", and its shocking connotations for some readers, it may be useful to add a few words on the question of *intentionality*. Scholarship on race inequity (in numerous disciplines and in many nation states) has long argued that a deliberate intention to discriminate is by no means a necessary requirement in order to recognize that an activity or policy may be racist in its consequences. This point is made powerfully by Kimberlé Crenshaw and her colleagues in relation to legal definitions of racism in the US:

> . . . the dominant legal conception of racism as a discrete and identifiable act of "prejudice based on skin color" placed virtually the entire range of everyday social practices in America—social practices developed and maintained throughout the period of formal American apartheid—beyond the scope of critical examination or legal remediation.
>
> (Crenshaw et al., 1995, p. xv)

The situation in Britain is somewhat different. *The Stephen Lawrence inquiry* defined institutional racism as:

> The collective failure of an organization to provide an appropriate and professional service to people because of their colour, culture, or ethnic origin. It can be seen or detected in processes, attitudes and behaviour which amount to discrimination through unwitting prejudice, ignorance, thoughtlessness and racist stereotyping which disadvantage minority ethnic people.
>
> (Macpherson, 1999, p. 28)

This definition deliberately emphasizes outcome and effect over any question of intent. According to this approach racism may be "unwitting" but what matters is the outcome. This view was enshrined in the amendments to British race equity legislation that followed the Lawrence report. For example, the official definition of a racist incident is "any incident which is perceived to be racist by the victim or any other person" (Home Office, 2000, p. 1).

The amended legislation only became active in 2002 and at the time of writing no education cases have been tested in court. Nevertheless, early indications are far from encouraging: education is among the least active of all public services in relation to the new duties (Schneider-Ross, 2003; Gillborn, 2004c). Notwithstanding the legislation's uncertain impact on practice, the analysis of *The Stephen Lawrence inquiry* and the language of the amended laws remains potentially significant. Finally, for the time being at least, in Britain the law has moved well beyond the perennial claim that it is unfair to talk of racism where no offence was intended. In official terms, in theory at least, racism has finally been de-coupled from questions of intent. But the conscious intent of individual people (whether policy-makers or teachers) is more complex than a simple dichotomy between intended and unintended outcomes.

Work on institutional racism (in the US and UK over more than three decades) has firmly established that even well-intentioned actions can have racist consequences. In a preceding paragraph I stated that the forms of institutional racism in education policy are not accidental: does that mean that they are deliberate? One answer might be that institutional racism and race inequity are deliberate insofar as (at best) there appears to be a judgement that their eradication is simply not important enough to shape the main tenets of education policy: it is possible, of course, that the situation is even worse than this, and that there has been a judgement that race equity is dangerous (electorally, where whites might turn to alternative parties) or socially and economically (where a Marxian/abolitionist analysis would have it that dividing the working class is a good way of protecting ruling class power). Either way, we know enough about education policy and practice to go a long way towards eradicating race injustice in education (funding urban schools to a realistic level; securing testing regimes that do not unfairly discriminate on racial lines; abandoning selective teaching and grouping; broadening the curriculum; diversifying the teaching force; and genuinely acting on the results of ethnic monitoring would all be a good start). In practice, however, high-stakes testing, school performance tables and selection by "ability" are all being used increasingly—despite their *known* detrimental impact on Black students. That racist measures are not only retained, but actually extended, suggests that policy-makers have decided (tacitly, if not explicitly) to place race *equity* at the margins—thereby retaining race *injustice* at the centre.

The evidence suggests that, despite a rhetoric of standards for all, education policy in England is actively involved in the defence, legitimation and extension of white supremacy. The assumptions which feed, and are strengthened by, this regime are not overtly discriminatory but their effects are empirically verifiable and materially real in every meaningful sense. Shaped by long established cultural, economic and historical structures of racial domination, the continued promotion of policies and practices that are known to be racially divisive testifies to a tacit intentionality in the system. The racist outcomes of contemporary policy may not be coldly calculated but they are far from accidental.

Acknowledgements

The ideas in this paper have benefited considerably from discussions with colleagues and friends in numerous contexts, including the annual meetings of the American Educational Research Association (San Diego, 2004), the British Educational Research Association (Edinburgh, 2003), and seminars/meetings in universities and community halls in various parts of the world. In particular, I would like to thank the colleagues who made such events possible through the Stephen Lawrence Charitable Trust, the Birmingham Race Action Partnership and the Universities of Brighton (UK), Melbourne (Australia), Tokyo and Osaka (Japan), Roskilde (Denmark) and Wisconsin-Madison (USA). My thanks to all the participants for their generous, passionate and committed interchange of ideas and experiences. Finally, a special thanks to those who have commented in detail on the text of this paper, Michael W. Apple, Stephen J. Ball, Gregg D. Beratan, Alastair Bonnett, Mike Cole, Paul Connolly, Gloria Ladson-Billings, Zeus Leonardo, Heidi Safia Mirza, Laurence Parker, Peter Ratcliffe, Christine Sleeter and Deborah Youdell: I have tried to learn from their views, all remaining errors are, of course, my responsibility.

Notes

1. In this paper the word "Black" is used to signify those groups of minoritized subjects who would generally identify themselves with the term, and be identified by such a term; most usually people with family heritages that identify with Africa and/or the Caribbean.
2. My first public presentation of the central ideas in this paper was at a major education conference in England in the fall of 2003. A prominent white professor told me later that, although some of my earlier work had been "useful", this talk of "supremacy" meant that I had, in his words, "gone mad".
3. I use "troubling" here in the way that several scholars, in particular those working in post-structuralist and/or queer theory, have applied the term to a destabilizing, decentring of commonly accepted assumptions and definitions: after Butler (1990), Horn (2003), Kumashiro (2001) and Youdell (2000).
4. See also David R. Roediger (1992, 1994).
5. See, for example, the interviews with Matthew Hale and Lisa Turner of the World Church of the Creator, in Swain and Nieli (2003).
6. For more detail on Herrnstein and Murray's claims, and the racist pedigree of their sources (both intellectual and financial) see Lane (1999), Gillborn and Youdell (2000, p. 231) and Apple (2004, pp. 198–199).
7. For an introduction to the basic tenets of CRT see Delgado and Stefancic (2001). For a consideration of the links between CRT in education and British antiracist thought see Gillborn (forthcoming).
8. The annually published data are frequently retabulated by national newspapers and given headlines that proclaim them as a guide to the "top" schools, those with the "highest failure rate" and "bottom of the league" (Gillborn & Youdell, 2000, chapter 2).
9. An official survey, for the Qualifications and Curriculum Authority (QCA), found that in 2001, 10- and 11-year-olds were spending 49% of their classroom time on English and maths: see Mansell and Clark (2003, p. 2).
10. The best guide to students' performance over this time period is the Youth Cohort Study (YCS), a survey of school-leavers' achievements and experiences that has been conducted at least every two years since the late 1980s. The YCS has the advantage of using large, nationally representative samples but it is far from perfect: sub-samples can become quite small, especially when trying to simultaneously examine several elements (such as gender, ethnicity and socioeconomic background). Nevertheless, it does offer a snapshot of how certain minority groups have performed over time.
11. A report by the Office for Standards in Education (Ofsted) noted that "the lengths of fixed-period exclusions varied considerably in some schools between black and white pupils for what were described as the same or similar incidents" (2001, p. 23).
12. See, for example, the reviews offered by Hallam (2002) and Wiliam and Bartholomew (2001).

References

Ansley, F. L. (1997) White supremacy (and what we should do about it), in: R. Delgado & J. Stefancic (Eds) *Critical white studies: looking behind the mirror* (Philadelphia, Temple University Press), 592–595.

Apple, M. W. (1996) Power, meaning and identity: critical sociology of education in the United States, *British Journal of Sociology of Education*, 17(2), 125–144.

Apple, M. W. (2004) *Ideology and curriculum* (New York, RoutledgeFalmer).

Archer, L. & Francis, B. (2005) "They never go off the rails like other ethnic groups": teachers' constructions of British Chinese pupils' gender identities and approaches to learning, *British Journal of Sociology of Education*, 26(2), 165–182.

Archer, L. & Francis, B. (forthcoming) Constructions of racism by British Chinese pupils and parents, *race ethnicity & education*.

Ball, S. J. (2004) The sociology of education: a disputational account, in: S. J. Ball (Ed.) *The RoutledgeFalmer reader in sociology of education* (London, Falmer), 1–12.

Bhatti, G. (2004) Good, bad and normal teachers: the experiences of South Asian children, in: G. Ladson-Billings & D. Gillborn (Eds) *The RoutledgeFalmer reader in multicultural education* (New York, RoutledgeFalmer).

Blair, M. (2001) *Why pick on me? School exclusion and black youth* (Stoke-on-Trent, Trentham).

Bonnett, A. (1997) Constructions of whiteness in European and American anti-racism, in: P. Werbner & T. Modood (Eds) *Debating cultural hybridity: multi-cultural identities and the politics of anti-racism* (London, Zed Books).

Bonnett, A. (2000) *Anti-racism* (London, Routledge).

Butler, J. (1990) *Gender trouble: feminism and the subversion of identity* (London, Routledge).

Butler, J. (1993) *Bodies that matter: on the discursive limits of "sex"* (London, Routledge).

Butler, J. (1997) *Excitable speech: a politics of the performative* (London, Routledge).

Coard, B. (1971) *How the West Indian child is made educationally subnormal in the British school system* (London, New Beacon Books).

Commission for Racial Equality (CRE) (1992) *Set to fail? Setting and banding in secondary schools* (London, Commission for Racial Equality).

Connolly, P. (1998) *Racism, gender identities and young children: social relations in a multi-ethnic, inner-city primary school* (London, Routledge).

Crenshaw, K., Gotanda, N., Peller, G. & Thomas, K. (Eds) (1995) *Critical race theory: the key writings that formed the movement* (New York, The New Press).

Dale, R. (2001) Shaping the sociology of education over half-a-century, in: J. Demaine (Ed.) *Sociology of education today* (New York, Palgrave), 5–29.

Dei, G. J. S., Karumanchery, L. L. & Karumanchery-Luik, N. (2004) *Playing the race card: exposing white power and privilege* (New York, Peter Lang).

Delamont, S. (2001) Reflections on social exclusion, *International Studies in Sociology of Education*, 11(1), 25–40.

Delgado, R. & Stefancic, J. (Eds) (2000) *Critical race theory: the cutting edge* (Philadelphia, Temple University Press).

Delgado, R. & Stefancic, J. (2001) *Critical race theory: an introduction* (New York, New York University Press).

Department for Education and Employment (1997) *Excellence in schools* (London, DfEE).

Department for Education and Skills (2002) *Statistics of education: permanent exclusions from maintained schools in England* (London, DfES).

Department for Education and Skills (2003) *Youth cohort study: the activities and experiences of 16-year-olds: England and Wales* (London, DfES).

Department for Education and Skills (2004) *Five year strategy for children and learners: putting people at the heart of public services* (London, DfES).

Department for Education and Skills (2005) *Youth cohort study: the activities and experiences of 16-year-olds: England and Wales* (London, DfES).

Dhondy, F. (1974) The black explosion in British schools, *Race Today*, February, 44–47.

Dhondy, F. (1978) Teaching young blacks, *Race Today*, May–June, 80–85.

Edwards, T. & Tomlinson, S. (2002) *Selection isn't working: diversity, standards and inequality in secondary education* (London, Central Books).

Essed, P. & Goldberg, D. T. (Eds) (2002) *Race critical theories* (Oxford, Blackwell).

Figueroa, P. (1991) *Education and the social construction of "race"* (London, Routledge).

Figueroa, P. (2004) Multicultural education in the United Kingdom: historical development and current status, in: J. A. Banks & C. A. M. Banks (Eds) *Handbook of research on multicultural education* (San Francisco, Jossey-Bass), 997–1026.

Foucault, M. (1980) *Power/knowledge: selected interviews and other writings* (Hemel Hempstead, Harvester).

Foucault, M. (1990) *Politics philosophy culture: interviews and other writings 1977–1984*, (London, Routledge).

Foucault, M. (1991) *Discipline and punish: the birth of the prison* (London, Penguin).

Frankenberg, R. (1993) *White women, race matters: the social construction of whiteness* (Minneapolis, MN, University of Minnesota Press).

Gillborn, D. (1990) *"Race", ethnicity and education: teaching and learning in multi-ethnic schools* (London, Unwin Hyman).

Gillborn, D. (1995) *Racism and antiracism in real schools. Theory. Policy. Practice* (Buckingham, Open University Press).

Gillborn, D. (1998) Racism, selection, poverty and parents: New Labour, old problems?, *Journal of Education Policy*, 13(6), 717–735.

Gillborn, D. (2001) Racism, policy and the (mis)education of black children, in: R. Majors (Ed.) *Educating our black children: new directions and radical approaches* (London, RoutledgeFalmer), 13–27.

Gillborn, D. (2004a) Anti-racism: from policy to praxis, in: G. Ladson-Billings & D. Gillborn (Eds) *The Routledge-Falmer reader in multicultural education* (New York, RoutledgeFalmer), 35–48.

Gillborn, D. (2004b) Critical race theory: what is it and what use is it to British antiracism?, paper presented at the *British Educational Research Association (BERA) Annual Meeting*, Manchester, September.

Gillborn, D. (2004c) Are your children being set up to fail? *The Stephen Lawrence Charitable Trust 2004–2005* (London, The Stephen Lawrence Charitable Trust), 22–24.

Gillborn, D. (forthcoming) Critical race theory and education: racism and antiracism in educational theory and praxis.

Gillborn, D. & Gipps, C. (1996) *Recent research on the achievements of ethnic minority pupils* (London, HMSO).

Gillborn, D. & Youdell, D. (2000) *Rationing education: policy, practice, reform and equity* (Buckingham, Open University Press).

Gilroy, P. (1992) The end of antiracism, in: J. Donald & A. Rattansi (Eds) *"Race", culture and difference* (London, Sage).

Giroux, H. (1997) *Channel surfing: racism, the media, and the destruction of today's youth* (New York, St Martin's Press).

Goffman, E. (1959) *The presentation of self in everyday life* (London, Penguin).

Grace, G. (1995) *School leadership: beyond education management: an essay in policy scholarship* (London, Falmer).

Hallam, S. & Toutounji, I. (1996) *What do we know about the grouping of pupils by ability? A research review* (London, Institute of Education, University of London).

Hallam, S. (2002) *Ability grouping in schools: a literature review. Perspectives on education policy, number 13* (London, Institute of Education, University of London).

Hare, B. (2002) *2001 race odyssey: African Americans and sociology* (Syracuse, NY, Syracuse University Press).

Hernstein, R. J. & Murray, C. (1994) *The bell curve: intelligence and class structure in American life* (New York, The Free Press).

Home Office (2000) *Code of practice on reporting and recording racist incidents in response to recommendation 15 of the Stephen Lawrence Inquiry report* (London, Home Office).

hooks, b. (1989) *Talking back: thinking feminist. Thinking black* (Boston, MA, South End Press).

Horn, S. (2003) Shifting mosaics, *race ethnicity and education*, 6(1), 95–102.

House, E. R. (1999) Race and policy, *Education Policy Analysis Archives*, 7(16), 1–14. Available online at http:// epaa.asu.edu/epaa/v7n16.html (accessed 9 February 2005).

Ignatiev, N. (1995) *How the Irish became white* (London, Routledge).

Ignatiev, N. (1997) The point is not to interpret whiteness but to abolish it, talk given at the *Making and Unmaking of Whiteness Conference*, University of California, Berkeley, 11–13 April. Available online at: www.postfun.com/ racetraitor (Accessed 11 December 2003).

Kumashiro, K. (2001) *Troubling intersections of race and sexuality: queer students of color and anti-oppressive education* (Oxford, Rowman & Littlefield).

Labour Party (1997) *New Labour: because Britain deserves better* (London, Labour Party).

Ladson-Billings, G. (1998) Just what is critical race theory and what's it doing in a *nice* field like education?, *International Journal of Qualitative Studies in Education*, 11(1), 7–24.

Ladson-Billings, G. (2004) The social funding of race: the role of schooling, paper presented at the *Symposium on Education and Diversity*, University of Melbourne, Australia, September–October.

Ladson-Billings, G. & Tate, W. F. (1995) Toward a critical race theory of education, *Teachers College Record*, 97(1), 47–68.

Lane, C. (1999) The tainted sources of *The bell curve*, in: A. Montagu (Ed.) *Race & IQ: expanded edition* (New York, Oxford University Press), 408–424.

Leonardo, Z. (2002) The souls of white folk: critical pedagogy, whiteness studies, and globalization discourse, *race ethnicity & education*, 5(1), 29–50.

Leonardo, Z. (2004) The color of supremacy: beyond the discourse of "white privilege", *Educational Philosophy and Theory*, 36(2), 137–152.

Liddle, R. (2005) It's not race that keeps black boys back, *Sunday Times*, 13 March. Available online at: www.timesonline.co.uk/article/ø,, 2ø88–152293ø, øø.html (Accessed 20 March 2005).

Lynch, J. (1986) *Multicultural education: principles and practice* (London, Routledge and Kegan Paul).

Mac an Ghaill, M. (1988) *Young, gifted and black: student teacher relations in the schooling of black youth* (Milton Keynes, Open University Press).

Macpherson, W. (1999) *The Stephen Lawrence Inquiry* (London, The Stationery Office).

Major, J. (1997) *Britain—the best place in the world* (London, Conservative Central Office).

Mansell, W. & Clark, E. (2003) Juniors spend half their time on the three Rs, *Times Educational Supplement*, 6 June, p. 2.

Min, P. G. (2004) Social science research on Asian Americans, in: J. A. Banks & C. A. M. Banks (Eds) *Handbook of research on multicultural education* (San Francisco, Jossey-Bass), 332–348.

Mirza, H. S. (1992) *Young, female and black* (London, Routledge).

Mirza, H. S. (1999) Institutional racism and education: myths and realities, paper presentation for *Black History Month Seminar Series; Tackling Institutional Racism*, Middlesex University, October.

Moore, R. (1996) Back to the future: the problem of change and the possibilities of advance in the sociology of education, *British Journal of Sociology of Education*, 17(2), 145–162.

Morley, L. & Rassool, N. (1999) *School effectiveness: fracturing the discourse* (London, Falmer).

Mullard, C. (1982) Multiracial education in Britain: from assimilation to cultural pluralism, in J. Tierney (Ed.) *Race, migration and schooling* (London, Holt, Rinehart & Winston), 120–133.

Nehaul, K. (1996) *The schooling of children of Caribbean heritage* (Stoke-on-Trent, Trentham).

Office for Standards in Education (Ofsted) (2001) *Improving attendance and behaviour in secondary schools* (London, Ofsted).

Office for Standards in Education (Ofsted) (2004) *National academy for gifted and talented youth: summer schools 2003* (London, Ofsted).

Parker, L. (Ed.) (1998) *Race is . . . race isn't: critical race theory and qualitative studies in education* (Boulder, CO, Westview Press).

Ratcliffe, P. (2004) *"Race", ethnicity and difference: imagining the inclusive society* (Maidenhead, Open University Press).

Redbridge Community Relations Council (1978) *Cause for concern—West Indian pupils in Redbridge* (London, Redbridge Community Relations Council).

Roediger, D. R. (1992) *The wages of whiteness: race and the making of the American working class* (New York, Verso).

Roediger, D. R. (1994) *Towards the abolition of whiteness: essays on race, politics, and working class history* (New York, Verso).

Sacks, K. B. (1997) How did Jews become white folks?, in: R. Delgado & J. Stefancic (Eds) *Critical white studies: looking behind the mirror* (Philadelphia, Temple University Press), 395–401.

Schneider-Ross (2003) *Towards racial equality: an evaluation of the public duty to promote race equality and good race relations in England and Wales (2002)* (London, Commission for Racial Equality).

Selden, S. (1999) *Inheriting shame: the story of eugenics and racism in America* (New York, Teachers College Press).

Sewell, T. (2004) Loose canons: exploding the myth of the "black macho" lad, in: G. Ladson-Billings & D. Gillborn (Eds) *The RoutledgeFalmer reader in multicultural education* (New York, RoutledgeFalmer), 103–116.

Sheets, R. H. (2000) Advancing the field or taking center stage: the white movement in multicultural education, *Educational Researcher*, 29(9), 15–21

Sheets, R. H. (2003) Competency vs. good intentions: diversity ideologies and teacher potential, *International Journal of Qualitative Studies in Education*, 16(1), 111–120.

Sleeter, C. E. (1993) How white teachers construct race, in: G. Ladson-Billings & D. Gillborn (Eds) *The Routledge-Falmer reader in multicultural education* (New York, RoutledgeFalmer), 163–178.

Sukhnandan, L. & Lee, B. (1998) *Streaming, setting and grouping by ability* (Slough, National Foundation for Educational Research).

Swain, C. M. & Nieli, R. (Eds) (2003) *Contemporary voices of white nationalism in America* (Cambridge, Cambridge University Press).

Takaki, R. (1993) *A different mirror: a history of multicultural America* (New York, Little, Brown).

Tate, W. F. (1997) Critical race theory and education: history, theory, and implications, in: M. W. Apple (Ed.) *Review of research in education* (Washington, DC, American Educational Research Association), 234–235.

Thatcher, M. (1993) *The Downing Street years* (New York, HarperCollins).

Thrupp, M. & Wilmott, R. (2003) *Educational management in managerialist times: beyond the textual apologists* (Maidenhead, Open University Press).

Tomlinson, S. (1977) Race and education in Britain 1960–1977: an overview of the literature, *Sage Race Relations Abstracts*, 2(4), 3–33.

Virdee, S. & Cole, M. (2000) "Race", racism and resistance, in: M. Cole (Ed.) *Education, equality and human rights: issues of gender, "race", sexuality, special needs and social class* (London, RoutledgeFalmer).

Whitty, G. (2002) *Making sense of education policy* (London, Paul Chapman Publishing).

Wiliam, D. & Bartholomew, H. (2001) The influence of ability-grouping practices on student achievement in mathematics, paper presented at the *Conference of the British Educational Research Association*, University of Leeds, September 2001.

Wood, M. (2000) *Blind memory: visual representations of slavery in England and America 1780–1865* (Manchester, Manchester University Press).

Wright, C. (1987) Black students–white teachers, in: B. Troyna (Ed.) *Racial inequality in education* (London, Tavistock).

Wright, C. (1992) *Race relations in the primary school* (London, David Fulton).

Wright, C., Weekes, D. & McGlaughlin, A. (2000) *"Race", class and gender in exclusion from school* (London, Falmer).

Wright, L. (1997) Who's black, who's white, and who cares, in: R. Delgado & J. Stefancic (Eds) *Critical white studies: looking behind the mirror* (Philadelphia, Temple University Press), 164–169.

Youdell, D. (2000) *Schooling Identities: an ethnography of the constitution of pupil identities.* Unpublished Ph.D. thesis, Institute of Education, University of London.

Youdell, D. (2004) Identity traps or how black students fail: the interactions between biographical, sub-cultural, and learner identities, in: G. Ladson-Billings & D. Gillborn (Eds) *The RoutledgeFalmer reader in multicultural education* (New York, RoutledgeFalmer), 84–102.

Part Two

History and Evolution

4

Brown v. Board of Education and the Interest Convergence Dilemma

Derrick A. Bell, Jr.

In 1954, the Supreme Court handed down the landmark decision *Brown v. Board of Education*[1] in which the court ordered the end of state-mandated racial segregation of public schools. Now, more than twenty-five years after that dramatic decision, it is clear that *Brown* will not be forgotten. It has triggered a revolution in civil rights law and in the political leverage available to blacks in and out of court. As Judge Robert L. Carter put it, *Brown* transformed blacks from beggars pleading for decent treatment to citizens demanding equal treatment under the law as their constitutionally recognized right.[2]

Yet today most black children attend public schools that are both racially isolated and inferior.[3] Demographic patterns, white flight, and the inability of the courts to effect the necessary degree of social reform render further progress in implementing *Brown* almost impossible. The late Alexander Bickel warned that *Brown* would not be overturned but, for a whole array of reasons, "may be headed for—dread word—irrelevance."[4] Bickel's prediction is premature in law where the *Brown* decision remains viable, but it may be an accurate assessment of its current practical value to millions of black children who have not experienced the decision's promise of equal educational opportunity.

Shortly after *Brown*, Herbert Wechsler rendered a sharp and nagging criticism of the decision.[5] Though he welcomed its result, he criticized its lack of a principled basis. Wechsler's views have since been persuasively refuted,[6] yet within them lie ideas that may help to explain both the disappointment of *Brown* and also what can be done to renew its promise.

In this comment, I plan to take a new look at Wechsler within the context of the subsequent desegregation campaign. By doing so, I hope to offer an explanation of why school desegregation has in large part failed and what can be done to bring about change.

I. Professor Wechsler's Search for Neutral Principles in Brown

The year was 1959, five years after the Supreme Court's decision in *Brown*. If there was anything the hard-pressed partisans of the case did not need, it was more criticism of a decision ignored by the President, condemned by much of Congress, and resisted wherever it was sought to be enforced.[7] Certainly, civil rights adherents did not welcome adding to the growing list of critics the name of Professor Herbert Wechsler, an outstanding lawyer, a frequent advocate for civil rights causes, and a scholar of prestige and influence.[8] Nevertheless, Wechsler chose that time and an invitation to deliver Harvard Law School's Oliver Wendell Holmes Lecture as the occasion to raise new questions about the legal appropriateness and principled shortcomings of *Brown* and several other major civil rights decisions.[9]

Here was an attack that could not be dismissed as after-the-fact faultfinding by a conservative academician using his intellect to further a preference for keeping blacks in their "separate but equal" place. Wechsler began by saying that he had welcomed the result in *Brown*; he noted that he had joined with the NAACP's Charles Houston in litigating civil rights cases in the Supreme Court.[10] He added that he was not offended because the court failed to uphold earlier decisions approving segregated schools; nor was he persuaded by the argument that the issue should have been left to Congress because the court's judgment might not be honored.[11]

Wechsler did not align himself with the "realists," who "perceive in law only the element of fiat, in whose conception of the legal cosmos reason has no meaning or no place,"[12] nor with the "formalists," who "frankly or covertly make the test of virtue in interpretation whether its result in the immediate decision seems to hinder or advance the interests or the values they support."[13] Wechsler instead saw the need for criteria of decision that could be framed and tested as an exercise of reason and not merely adopted as an act of willfulness or will. He believed, in short, that courts could engage in a "principal appraisal" of legislative actions that exceeded a fixed "historical meaning" of constitutional provisions without, as Judge Learned Hand feared, becoming "a third legislative chamber."[14] Courts, Wechsler argued, "must be genuinely principled, resting with respect to every step that is involved in reaching judgment on analysis and reasons quite transcending the immediate result that is achieved."[15] Applying these standards, which included constitutional and statutory interpretation, the subtle guidance provided by history, and appropriate but not slavish fidelity to precedent, Wechsler found difficulty with Supreme Court decisions where principled reasoning was, in his view, either deficient or, in some instances, nonexistent.[16] He included the *Brown* opinion in the latter category.

Wechsler reviewed and rejected the possibility that *Brown* was based on a declaration that the Fourteenth Amendment barred all racial lines in legislation.[17] He also doubted that the opinion relied upon a factual determination that segregation caused injury to black children, since evidence as to such harm was both inadequate and conflicting.[18] Rather, Wechsler concluded, the court in *Brown* must have rested its holding on the view that "racial segregation is, *in principle*, a denial of equality to the minority against whom it is directed; that is, the group that is not dominant politically and, therefore, does not make the choice involved."[19] Yet Wechsler found this argument untenable as well, because, among other difficulties, it seemed to require an inquiry into the motives of the legislature, a practice generally foreclosed to the courts.[20]

After dismissing these arguments, Wechsler then asserted that the legal issue in state-imposed segregation cases was not one of discrimination at all but, rather, of associational rights: "the denial by the state of freedom to associate, a denial that impinges in the same way on any groups or races that may be involved."[21] Wechsler reasoned that "if the freedom of association is denied by segregation, integration forces an association upon those for whom it is unpleasant or repugnant."[22] Concluding with a question that has challenged legal scholars, Wechsler asked, "Given a situation where the state must practically choose between denying the association to those individuals who wish it or imposing it on those who would avoid it, is there a basis in neutral principles for holding that the Constitution demands that the claims for association should prevail?"[23]

In suggesting that there was a basis in neutral principles for holding that the Constitution supports a claim by blacks for an associational right, Wechsler confessed that he had not yet written an opinion supporting such a holding. "To write it is for me the challenge of the school-segregation cases."[24]

II. The Search for a Neutral Principle: Racial Equality and Interest Convergence

Scholars who accepted Wechsler's challenge had little difficulty finding a neutral principle on which the *Brown* decision could be based. Indeed, from the hindsight of a quarter century of the greatest racial consciousness-raising the country has ever known, much of Wechsler's concern seems hard to imagine. To doubt that racial segregation is harmful to blacks, and to suggest that what blacks really sought was the right to associate with whites, is to believe in a world that does not exist now and could not possibly have existed then. Charles Black, therefore, correctly viewed racial equality as the neutral principle that underlay the *Brown* opinion.[25] In Black's view, Wechsler's question "is awkwardly simple,"[26] and he states his response in the form of a syllogism. Black's major premise is that "the equal protection clause of the fourteenth amendment should be read as saying that the Negro race, as such, is not to be significantly disadvantaged by the laws of the states."[27] His minor premise is that "segregation is a massive intentional disadvantaging of the Negro race, as such, by state law."[28] The conclusion, then, is that the equal protection clause clearly bars racial segregation because segregation harms blacks and benefits whites in ways too numerous and obvious to require citation.[29]

Logically, the argument is persuasive, and Black has no trouble urging that "[w]hen the directive of equality cannot be followed without displeasing the white[s], then something that can be called a 'freedom' of the white[s] must be impaired."[30] It is precisely here, though, that many whites part company with Professor Black. Whites may agree in the abstract that blacks are citizens and are entitled to constitutional protection against racial discrimination, but few are willing to recognize that racial segregation is much more than a series of quaint customs that can be remedied effectively without altering the status of whites. The extent of this unwillingness is illustrated by the controversy over affirmative action programs, particularly those where identifiable whites must step aside for blacks they deem less qualified or less deserving. Whites simply cannot envision the personal responsibility and the potential sacrifice inherent in Black's conclusion that true equality for blacks will require the surrender of racism-granted privileges for whites.

This sober assessment of reality raises concern about the ultimate import of

Black's theory. On a normative level, as a description of how the world *ought* to be, the notion of racial equality appears to be the proper basis on which *Brown* rests, and Wechsler's framing of the problem in terms of associational rights thus seems misplaced. Yet on a positivistic level—how the world *is*—it is clear that racial equality is not deemed legitimate by large segments of the American people, at least to the extent it threatens to impair the societal status of whites. Hence, Wechsler's search for a guiding principle in the context of associational rights retains merit in the positivistic sphere, because it suggests a deeper truth about the subordination of law to interest group politics with a racial configuration.

Although no such subordination is apparent in *Brown*, it is possible to discern in more recent school decisions the outline of a principle, applied without direct acknowledgment, that could serve as the positivistic expression of the neutral statement of general applicability sought by Wechsler. Its elements rely as much on political history as legal precedent and emphasize the world as it is rather than how we might want it to be. Translated from judicial activity in racial cases both before and after *Brown*, this principle of "interest convergence" provides: The interest of blacks in achieving racial equality will be accommodated only when it converges with the interests of whites. However, the Fourteenth Amendment, standing alone, will not authorize a judicial remedy providing effective racial equality for blacks where the remedy sought threatens the superior societal status of middle- and upper-class whites.

It follows that the availability of Fourteenth Amendment protection in racial cases may not actually be determined by the character of harm suffered by blacks or the quantum of liability proved against whites. Racial remedies may instead be the outward manifestations of unspoken and perhaps subconscious judicial conclusions that the remedies, if granted, will secure, advance, or at least not harm societal interests deemed important by middle- and upper-class whites. Racial justice—or its appearance—may, from time to time, be counted among the interests deemed important by the courts and by society's policymakers.

In assessing how this principle can accommodate both the *Brown* decision and the subsequent development of school desegregation law, it is necessary to remember that the issue of school segregation and the harm it inflicted on black children did not first come to the court's attention in the *Brown* litigation: blacks had been attacking the validity of these policies for one hundred years.[31] Yet, prior to *Brown*, black claims that segregated public schools were inferior had been met by orders requiring merely that facilities be made equal.[32] What accounted, then, for the sudden shift in 1954 away from the separate but equal doctrine and toward a commitment to desegregation?

I contend that the decision in *Brown* to break with the court's long-held position on these issues cannot be understood without some consideration of the decision's value to whites, not simply those concerned about the immorality of racial inequality, but also those whites in policymaking positions able to see the economic and political advances at home and abroad that would follow abandonment of segregation. First, the decision helped to provide immediate credibility to America's struggle with communist countries to win the hearts and minds of emerging third world people. At least this argument was advanced by lawyers for both the NAACP and the federal government.[33] The point was not lost on the news media. *Time* magazine, for example, predicted that the international impact of *Brown* would be scarcely less important than its effect on the education of black children: "In many countries, where U.S. prestige and leadership have been damaged by the fact of U.S. segregation, it will come as a timely reassertion of the basic American principle that 'all men are created equal.' "[34]

Second, *Brown* offered much needed reassurance to American blacks that the precepts of equality and freedom so heralded during World War II might yet be given meaning at home. Returning black veterans faced not only continuing discrimination but also violent attacks in the South which rivaled those that took place at the conclusion of World War I.[35] Their disillusionment and anger were poignantly expressed by the black actor, Paul Robeson, who in 1949 declared, "It is unthinkable . . . that American Negroes would go to war on behalf of those who have oppressed us for generations . . . against a country [the Soviet Union] which in one generation has raised our people to the full human dignity of mankind."[36] It is not impossible to imagine that fear of the spread of such sentiment influenced subsequent racial decisions made by the courts.

Finally, there were whites who realized that the South could make the transition from a rural plantation society to the sunbelt with all its potential and profit only when it ended its struggle to remain divided by state-sponsored segregation.[37] Thus, segregation was viewed as a barrier to further industrialization in the South.

These points may seem insufficient proof of self-interest leverage to produce a decision as important as *Brown*. They are cited, however, to help assess—and not to diminish—the Supreme Court's most important statement on the principle of racial equality. Here, as in the abolition of slavery, there were whites for whom recognition of the racial equality principle was sufficient motivation. As with abolition, though, the number who would act on morality alone was insufficient to bring about the desired racial reform.[38]

Thus, for those whites who sought an end to desegregation on moral grounds or for the pragmatic reasons outlined above, *Brown* appeared to be a welcome break with the past. When segregation was finally condemned by the Supreme Court, however, the outcry was nevertheless great, especially among poorer whites who feared loss of control over their public schools and other facilities. Their fear of loss was intensified by the sense that they had been betrayed. They relied, as had generations before them, on the expectation that white elites would maintain lower-class whites in a societal status superior to that designated for blacks.[39] In fact, there is evidence that segregated schools and facilities were initially established by legislatures at the insistence of the white working class.[40] Today, little has changed: many poorer whites oppose social reform as "welfare programs for blacks" although, ironically, they have employment, education, and social service needs that differ from those of poor blacks by a margin that, without a racial scorecard, is difficult to measure.[41]

Unfortunately, poorer whites are now not alone in their opposition to school desegregation as well as to other attempts to improve the societal status of blacks: recent decisions, most notably by the Supreme Court, indicate that the convergence of black and white interests that led to *Brown* in 1954 and influenced the character of its enforcement has begun to fade. In *Swann v. Charlotte-Mecklenburg Board of*

Education,[42] Chief Justice Warren Burger spoke of the "reconciliation of competing values" in desegregation cases.[43] If there was any doubt that "competing values" referred to the conflicting interests of blacks seeking desegregation and whites who prefer to retain existing school policies, then the uncertainty was dispelled by *Milliken v. Bradley,*[44] and *Dayton Board of Education v. Brinkman (Dayton I).*[45] In both cases, the court elevated the concept of "local autonomy" to a "vital national tradition."[46] "No single tradition in public education is more deeply rooted than local control over the operation of schools; local autonomy has long been thought essential both to the maintenance of community concern and support for public schools and to quality of the educational process."[47] Local control, however, may result in the maintenance of a status quo that will preserve superior educational opportunities and facilities for whites at the expense of blacks. As one commentator has suggested, "It is implausible to assume that school boards guilty of substantial violations in the past will take the interests of black school children to heart."[48]

As a result of its change in attitudes, the court has increasingly erected barriers to achieving the forms of racial balance relief it earlier had approved.[49] Plaintiffs must now prove that the complained-of segregation was the result of discriminatory actions intentionally and individuously conducted or authorized by school officials.[50] It is not enough that segregation was the "natural and foreseeable" consequence of their policies.[51] Even when this difficult standard of proof is met, moreover, courts must carefully limit the relief granted to the harm actually proved.[52] Judicial second thoughts about racial balance plans with broad-range busing components, the very plans that civil rights lawyers have come to rely on, is clearly evident in these new proof standards.

There is, however, continuing if unpredictable concern in the Supreme Court about school boards whose policies reveal long-term adherence to overt racial discrimination. In many cases, trial courts exposed to exhaustive testimony regarding the failure of school officials to desegregate or to provide substantial equality of schooling for minority children become convinced that school boards are violating *Brown.* Thus far, unstable Supreme Court majorities have upheld broad desegregation plans ordered by these judges,[53] but the reservations expressed by concurring justices[54] and the vigor of those justices who dissent[55] caution against optimism in this still controversial area of civil rights law.[56]

At the very least, these decisions reflect a substantial and growing divergence in the interests of whites and blacks. The result could prove to be the realization of Wechsler's legitimate fear that, if there is not a change of course, the purported entitlement of whites not to associate with blacks in public schools may yet eclipse the hope and the promise of *Brown.*

III. Interest Convergence Remedies Under Brown

Further progress to fulfill the mandate of *Brown* is possible to the extent that the divergence of racial interests can be avoided or minimized. Whites in policymaking positions, including those who sit on federal courts, can take no comfort in the conditions of dozens of inner-city school systems where the great majority of nonwhite children attend classes that are as segregated and ineffective as those so roundly condemned by Chief Justice Warren in the *Brown* opinion. Nor do poorer whites gain from their opposition to the improvement of educational opportunities for blacks: as noted earlier, the needs of the two groups differ little.[57] Hence, over time, all will reap the benefits from a concerted effort toward achieving racial equality.

The question still remains as to the surest way to reach the goal of educational effectiveness for both blacks and whites. I believe that the most widely used programs mandated by the courts—"antidefiance, racial balance" plans—may in some cases be inferior to plans focusing on "educational components," including the creation and development of "model" all-black schools. A short history of the use of the anti-defiance strategy would be helpful at this point.

By the end of the fifties, it was apparent that compliance with the *Brown* mandate to desegregate the public schools would not come easily or soon. In the seventeen border states and the District of Columbia, fewer than two hundred thousand blacks were actually attending classes with white children.[58] The states in the deep South had not begun even token desegregation,[59] and it would take Supreme Court action to reverse the years-long effort of the Prince Edward County School Board in Virginia to abolish rather than desegregate its public schools.[60] Supreme Court orders[61] and presidential action had already been required to enable a handful of black students to attend Central High School in Little Rock, Arkansas.[62] Opposition to *Brown* was clearly increasing; its supporters were clearly on the defensive, as was the Supreme Court itself.

For blacks, the goal in school desegregation suits remained the effective use of the *Brown* mandate to eliminate state-sanctioned segregation. These efforts received unexpected help from the excesses of the massive resistance movement that led courts to justify relief under *Brown* as a reaffirmation of the supremacy of the judiciary on issues of constitutional interpetation. Brown, in the view of many, might not have been a wise or proper decision, but violent and prolonged opposition to its implementation posed an even greater danger to the federal system.

The Supreme Court quickly recognized this additional basis on which to ground school desegregation orders. "As this case reaches us," the court began its dramatic opinion in *Cooper v. Aaron*,[63] "it raises questions of the highest importance to the maintenance of our federal system of government."[64] Reaching back to *Marbury v. Madison*,[65] the court reaffirmed Chief Justice John Marshall's statement that "[i]t is emphatically the province and duty of the judicial department to say what the law is."[66] There were few opponents to this stand, and Professor Wechsler was emphatic-ally not one of them. His criticism of *Brown* concluded with a denial that he intended to offer "comfort to anyone who claims legitimacy in defiance of the courts."[67] Those who accept the benefits of our constitutional system, Wechsler felt, cannot deny its allegiance when a special burden is imposed. Defiance of court orders, he asserted, constituted the "ultimate negation of all neutral principles."[68]

For some time, then, the danger to federalism posed by the secessionist-oriented resistance of southern state and local officials provided courts with an independent basis for supporting school desegregation efforts.[69] In the lower federal courts, the perceived threat to judicial status was often quite personal. Surely, I was not the only civil rights attorney who received a favorable decision in a school desegregation case less by legal precedent than because a federal judge, initially hostile to those precedents, my clients, and their lawyer, became incensed with school board litigation tactics that exhibited as little respect for the court as they did for the constitutional rights of black children.

There was a problem with school desegregation decisions framed in this antidefiance form which was less discernible then than now. While a prerequisite to the provision of equal educational opportunity, condemnation of school board evasion was far from synonymous with that long-promised goal. Certainly, it was cause for celebration when the court recognized that some pupil assignment schemes,[70] "freedom-of-choice" plans,[71] and similar "desegregation plans" were in fact designed to retain constitutionally condemned dual school systems. When the court, in obvious frustration with the slow pace of school desegregation, announced in 1968 what Justice Lewis Powell later termed "the *Green/Swann* doctrine of 'affirmative duty,' "[72] which placed on school boards the duty to disestablish their dual school systems, the decisions were welcomed as substantial victories by civil rights lawyers. Yet the remedies set forth in the major school cases following *Brown*—balancing the student and teacher populations by race in each school, eliminating single-race schools, redrawing school attendance lines, and transporting students to achieve racial balance[73]— have not in themselves guaranteed black children better schooling than they received in the pre-*Brown* era. Such racial balance measures have often altered the racial appearance of dual school systems without eliminating racial discrimination. Plans relying on racial balance to foreclose evasion have not eliminated the need for further orders protecting black children against discriminatory policies, including resegregation within desegregated schools,[74] the loss of black faculty and administrators,[75] suspensions and expulsions at much higher rates than white students,[76] and varying forms of racial harassment ranging from exclusion from extracurricular activities[77] to physical violence.[78] Antidefiance remedies, then, while effective in forcing alterations in school system structure, often encourage and seldom shield black children from discriminatory retaliation.

The educational benefits that have resulted from the mandatory assignment of black and white children to the same schools are also debatable.[79] If benefits did exist, they have begun to dissipate as whites flee in alarming numbers from school districts ordered to implement mandatory reassignment plans.[80] In response, civil rights lawyers sought to include entire metropolitan areas within mandatory reassignment plans in order to encompass mainly white suburban school districts, where so many white parents sought sanctuary for their children.[81]

Thus, the antidefiance strategy was brought full circle from a mechanism for preventing evasion by school officials of *Brown*'s antisegregation mandate to one aimed at creating a discrimination-free environment. This approach to the implementation of *Brown*, however, has become increasingly ineffective; indeed, it has in some cases been educationally destructive. A preferable method is to focus on obtaining real educational effectiveness, which may entail the improvement of presently desegregated schools as well as the creation or preservation of model black schools.

Civil rights lawyers do not oppose such relief, but they clearly consider it secondary to the racial balance remedies authorized in the *Swann*[82] and *Keyes*[83] cases. Those who espouse alternative remedies are deemed to act out of suspect motives. *Brown* is law, and racial balance plans are the only means of complying with the decision. The position reflects courage, but it ignores the frequent and often complete failure of programs that concentrate solely on achieving a racial balance.

Desegregation remedies that do not integrate may seem a step backward toward the *Plessy* "separate but equal" era. Some black educators, however, see major educational benefits in schools where black children, parents, and teachers can utilize the real cultural strengths of the black community to overcome the many barriers to educational achievement.[84] As Laurence Tribe has argued, "[J]udicial rejection of the 'separate but equal' talisman seems to have been accompanied by a potentially troublesome lack of sympathy for racial separateness as a possible expression of group solidarity."[85]

This is not to suggest that educationally oriented remedies can be developed and adopted without resistance. Policies necessary to obtain effective schools threaten the self-interest of teacher unions and others with vested interests in the status quo. However, successful magnet schools may provide a lesson that effective schools for blacks must be a primary goal rather than a secondary result of integration. Many white parents recognize a value in integrated schooling for their children, but they quite properly view integration as merely one component of an effective education. To the extent that civil rights advocates also accept this reasonable sense of priority, some greater racial interest conformity should be possible.

Is this what the *Brown* opinion meant by "equal educational opportunity?" Chief Justice Warren said the court could not "turn the clock back to 1868 when the [Fourteenth] Amendment was adopted, or even to 1896 when *Plessy v. Ferguson* was written."[86] The change in racial circumstances since 1954 rivals or surpasses all that occurred during the period that preceded it. If the decision that was at least a catalyst for that change is to remain viable, those who rely on it must exhibit the dynamic awareness of all the legal and political considerations that influenced those who wrote it.

Professor Wechsler warned us early on that there was more to *Brown* than met the eye. At one point, he observed that the opinion is "often read with less fidelity by those who praise it than by those by whom it is condemned."[87] Most of us ignored that observation openly and quietly raised a question about the sincerity of the observer. Criticism, as we in the movement for minority rights have every reason to learn, is a synonym for neither cowardice nor capitulation. It may instead bring awareness, always the first step toward overcoming still another barrier in the struggle for racial equality.

Notes

1. 347 U.S. 483 (1954).
2. Carter, "The Warren Court and Desegregation," in D. Bell, ed., *Race, Racism and American Law*, 456–61 (1973).
3. See Bell, Book Review, 92 *Harv. L. Rev.* 1826, 1826 n. 6 (1979). See also C. Jencks, *Inequality*, 25–28 (1972).
4. A. Bickel, *The Supreme Court and the Idea of Progress* 151 (1970).
5. Wechsler, "Toward Neutral Principles of Constitutional Law," 73 *Har. L. Rev.*, 1 (1959); the lecture was later published in a collection of selected essays. H. Wechsler, *Principles, Politics, and Fundamental Law*, 3 (1961).

6. See e.g., Black, "The Lawfulness of the Segregation Decisions," 69 *Yale L. J.*, 421 (1960); Heyman, "The Chief Justice, Racial Segregation, and the Friendly Critics," 49 *Calif. L. Rev.*, 104 (1961); Pollack, "Racial Discrimination and Judicial Integrity: A Reply to Professor Wechsler," 108 *U. Pa. L. Rev.*, 1 (1959).

7. The legal campaign that culminated in the *Brown* decision is discussed in great depth in R. Kluger, *Simple Justice* (1976). The subsequent fifteen years are reviewed in S. Wasby, A. D'Amato, and R. Metrailer, *Desegregation from* Brown *to* Alexander (1977).

8. Wechsler is the Harlan Fiske Stone Professor of Constitutional Law Emeritus at the Columbia University Law School. His work is reviewed in 78 *Colum. L. Rev.*, 969 (1978) (issue dedicated in Professor Wechsler's honor upon his retirement).

9. See Wechsler, *supra* note 5, at 31–35.

10. Wechsler recalled that Houston, who was black, "did not suffer more than I in knowing that we had to go to Union Station to lunch together during the recess"; *id.* at 34.

11. *Id.* at 31–32.

12. *Id.* at 11.

13. *Id.*

14. *Id.* at 16.

15. *Id.* at 15.

16. *Id.* at 19.

17. *Id.* at 32.

18. *Id.* at 32–33.

19. *Id.* at 33 (emphasis added).

20. *Id.* at 33–34.

21. *Id.* at 34.

22. *Id.*

23. *Id.*

24. *Id.*

25. See Black, *supra* note 6, at 428–29.

26. *Id.* at 423.

27. *Id.*

28. *Id.*

29. *Id.* at 425–26.

30. *Id.* at 429.

31. See, e.g. *Roberts v. City of Boston*, 59 Mass. (5 Cush.) 198 (1850).

32. The cases are collected in Larson, "The New Law of Race Relations," 1969. *Wis. L. Rev.*, 470, 482, 483 n. 27; Leflar and Davis, "Segregation in the Public Schools—1953," 67 *Harv. L. Rev.*, 377, 430–35 (1954).

33. See Bell, "Racial Remediation: An Historical Perspective on Current Conditions," 52 *Notre Dame Law.*, 5, 12 (1976).

34. *Id.* at 12 n. 31.

35. C. Vann Woodward, *The Strange Career of Jim Crow*, 114 (3d rev. ed. 1974): I. Franklin, *From Slavery to Freedom*, 428–86 (2d ed. 1967).

36. D. Butler, "Paul Robeson," 137 (1976) (unwritten speech before the Partisans of Peace, World Peace Congress in Paris).

37. Professor Robert Higgs argued that the "region's economic development increasingly undermined the foundations of its traditional racial relations"; Higgs, "Race and Economy in the South, 1890–1950," in R. Haws, ed. *The Age of Segregation*, 89–90 (1978). Sociologists Frances Fox Piven and Richard Cloward have also drawn a connection between this economic growth and the support for the civil rights movement in the forties and fifties, when various white elites in business, philanthropy, and government began to speak out against racial discrimination. F. Piven and R. Cloward, *Regulating The Poor*, 229–30 (1971); see also F. Piven and R. Cloward, *Poor People's Movements*, 189–94 (1977).

38. President Abraham Lincoln, for example, acknowledged the moral evil in slavery. In his famous letter to publisher Horace Greeley, however, he promised to free all, some, or none of the slaves, depending on which policy would most help save the Union: M. Roe, ed., *Speeches and Letters of Abraham Lincoln, 1832–65*, at 194–95.

39. See Piven and Cloward, *Poor People's Movements*, 187 (1977), and, generally, Bell, *supra* note 33.

40. See Woodward, *supra* note 35, at 6.

41. Robert Heilbronner suggests that this country's failure to address social issues including poverty, public health, housing, and prison reform as effectively as many European countries is due to the tendency of whites to view reform efforts as "programs to 'subsidize' Negroes. . . . In such cases the fear and resentment of the Negro takes precedence over the social problem itself. The result, unfortunately, is that the entire society suffers from the

results of a failure to correct social evils whose ill effects refuse to obey the rules of segregation"; Heilbronner, "The Roots of Social Neglect in the United States," in E. Rostow, ed., *Is Law Dead?*, 288, 296 (1971).

42. 402 U.S. 1 (1971).

43. *Id.* at 31.

44. 418 U.S. 717 (1974) (limits power of federal courts to treat a primarily black urban school district and largely white suburban districts as a single unit in mandating desegregation).

45. 433 U.S. 406 (1977) (desegregation orders affecting pupil assignments should seek only the racial mix that would have existed absent the constitutional violation).

46. *Id.* at 410, 418 U.S. at 741–742.

47. 418 U.S. at 741.

48. The Supreme Court, 1978 Term, 93 *Harv. L. Rev.*, 60, 130 (1979).

49. See generally Fiss, "School Desegregation: The Uncertain Path of the Law," 4 *Philosophy and Pub. Aff.* 3 (1974); Kanner, "From Denver to Dayton: The Development of a Theory of Equal Protection Remedies," 72 *NW. U. L. Rev.*, 382 (1977).

50. *Dayton Bd. of Educ. v. Brinkman (Dayton I)*, 433 U.S. 406 (1977).

51. *Columbus Bd. of Educ. v. Penick*, 99 S. Ct. 2941, 2950 (1979).

52. *Austin Independent School Dist. v. United States*, 429 U.S. 990, 991 (1976) (Powell, J., concurring).

53. *Dayton Bd. of Educ. v. Brinkman (Dayton II)*, 99 S. Ct. 2917 (1979); *Columbus Bd. of Educ. v. Penick*, 99 S. Ct. 2941 (1979).

54. See *Columbus Bd. of Educ. v. Penick*, 99 S. Ct. 2941, 2952 (1979) (Burger, C. J., concurring); *id.* at 2983 (Stewart J., concurring).

55. See *id.* at 2952 (Rehnquist, J., dissenting); *id.* at 2988 (Powell, J., dissenting). See also *Dayton Bd. of Educ. v. Brinkman (Dayton II)*, 99 S. Ct. 2971, 2983 (1979) (Stewart, J., dissenting).

56. The court faces another difficult challenge in the 1979 term when it reviews whether the racial balance plan in Dallas, Texas, goes far enough in eliminating one-race schools in a large district that is now 65 percent black and Hispanic. *Tasby v. Estes*, 572 F. 2d 1010 (5th Cir. 1978), *cert. granted sub nom. Estes v. Metropolitan Branches of Dallas* NAACP, 440 U.S. 906 (1979).

57. See p. 21 *supra*.

58. P. Bergman, *The Chronological History of the Negro in America*, 561 (1969).

59. *Id.* at 561–62.

60. *Griffin v. County School Bd.*, 372 U.S. 218 (1964).

61. *Cooper v. Aaron*, 358 U.S. 1 (1958).

62. P. Bergman, *supra* note 58, at 555–56, 561–62.

63. 358 U.S. 1 (1958).

64. *Id.* at 4.

65. 5 U.S. (1 Cranch) 137, 177 (1803).

66. 358 U.S. at 18.

67. Wechsler, *supra* note 5, at 35.

68. *Id.*

69. See, e.g., *Goss v. Board of Educ.*, 373 U.S. 683 (1963) (struck down "minority to majority" transfer plans enabling resegregation of schools); *Bush v. New Orleans Parish School Bd.*, 188 F. Supp. 916 (E. D. La.), *aff'd*, 365 U.S. 569 (1961) (invalidation of state "interposition acts"); *Pointdexter v. Louisiana Financial Comm'n.*, 275 F. Supp. 833 (E. D. La. 1967), *aff'd per curiam*, 389 U.S. 215 (1968) ("tuition grants" for children attending private schools voided).

70. These plans, requiring black children to run a gauntlet of administrative proceedings to obtain assignment to a white school, were at first judicially approved. See *Covington v. Edwards*, 264 F. 2d 780 (4th Cir.), *cert. denied*, 361 U.S. 840 (1959); *Shuttlesworth v. Birmingham Bd. of Educ.*, 162 F. Supp. 372 (N. D. Ala.), *aff'd*, 358 U.S. 101 (1958).

71. *Green v. County School Bd.*, 391 U.S. 430 (1968) (practice of "free choice"—enabling each student to choose whether to attend a black or white school—struck down).

72. *Keyes v. School Dist. No. 1*, 413 U.S. 189, 224 (1973) (Powell, J., concurring in part and dissenting in part).

73. See, e.g., *Swann v. Charlotte-Mecklenburg Bd. of Educ.*, 402 U.S. 1 (1976); *Green v. County School Bd.*, 391 U.S. 430 (1968).

74. See, e.g., *Jackson v. Marvell School Dist. No. 22*, 425 F. 2d 211 (8th Circ. 1970). There were also efforts to segregate students within desegregated schools by the use of standardized tests and achievement scores. See *Singleton v. Jackson Mun. Separate School Dist.*, 419 F. 2d 1211 (5th Cir.), *rev'd per curiam*, 396 U.S. 290 (1970); *Hobson v. Hansen*, 269 F. Supp. 401 (D. D. Cir. 1967), *aff'd sub nom. Smuck v. Hobson*, 408 F 2d 175 (D. C. Cir. 1969).

75. See, e.g., *Chambers v. Hendersonville City Bd. of Educ.*, 364 F. 2d 189 (4th Cir. 1966). For a discussion of the wholesale dismissal and demotion of black teachers in the wake of school desegregation orders, see materials

compiled in 2 N. Dorsen, P. Bender, B. Neuborne, and S. Law, *Enerson, Haber, and Dorsen's Political and Civil Rights in the United States*, 679–80 (4th ed. 1979).

76. *Hawkins v. Coleman*, 376 F. Supp. 1330 (N. D. Tex. 1974); *Dunn v. Tyler Independent School Dist.*, 327 F. Supp. 528 (E. D. Tex. 1971), *aff'd in part and rev'd in part*, 460 F. 2d 137 (5th Cir. 1972).

77. *Floyd v. Trice*, 490 F. 2d 1154 (8th Cir. 1974); *Augustus v. School Bd.*, 361 F. Supp. 383 (N. D. Fla. 1973), *modified*, 307 F. 2d 152 (5th Cir. 1975).

78. For a recent example, see the account of racial violence resulting from desegregation in Boston, in Husoch, "Boston: The Problem That Won't Go Away," *New York Times*, Nov. 25, 1979, SS 6 (Magazine), at 32.

79. See N. St. John, *School Desegregation*, 16–41 (1975).

80. See D. Armor, "White Flight, Demographic Transition, and the Future of School Desegregation" (1978) (Rand Paper Series, the Rand Corp.); J. Colemen, S. Kelly, and J. Moore, "Trends in School Segregation, 1968–1973" (1975) (Urban Institute Paper). But see Pettrigrew and Green, "School Desegregation in Large Cities: A Critique of the Coleman 'White Flight' Thesis," 46 *Harv. Educ. Rev.*, 1 (1976); Rossell, "School Desegregation and White Flight," 90 *Pol. Sci. Q.* 675 (1975), R. Farley, "School Integration and White Flight" (1975) (Population Studies Center, U. Mich.).

81. See, e.g., *Milliken v. Bradley*, 418 U.S. 717 (1974). In Los Angeles, where the court ordered reassignment of sixty-five thousand students in grades four through eight, 30–50 percent of the twenty-two thousand white students scheduled for mandatory busing boycotted the public schools or enrolled elsewhere: U.S. Commission on Civil Rights, *Desegregation of the Nation's Public Schools: A Status Report*, 51 (1979).

82. *Swann v. Charlotte-Mecklenburg Bd. of Educ.*, 402 U.S. 1 (1971).

83. *Keyes v. School Dist. No. 1*, 413 U. S. 189 (1973).

84. S. Lightfoot, *Worlds Apart*, 172 (1978). For a discussion of the Lightfoot theory, see Bell, *supra* note 3, at 1838.

85. L. Tribe, *American Constitutional Law*, §16–15, at 1022 (1978) (footnote omitted).

86. *Brown v. Board of Educ.*, 347 U.S. 483, 492 (1954).

87. Wechsler, *supra* note 5, at 32.

5

Desegregation as a Cold War Imperative

Mary L. Dudziak

At the height of the McCarthy era, when Congressional committees were exposing "communist infiltration" in many areas of American life, the Supreme Court was upholding loyalty oath requirements, and the executive branch was ferreting out alleged communists in government, the U.S. Attorney General filed a pro-civil rights brief in what would become one of the most celebrated civil rights cases in American history: *Brown v. Board of Education*. Although seemingly at odds with the restrictive approach to individual rights in other contexts, the U.S. government's participation in the desegregation cases during the McCarthy era was no anomaly.

In the years following World War II, racial discrimination in the United States received increasing attention from other countries. Newspapers throughout the world carried stories about discrimination against non-white visiting foreign dignitaries, as well as against American blacks. At a time when the U.S. hoped to reshape the postwar world in its own image, the international attention given to racial segregation was troublesome and embarrassing. The focus of American foreign policy at this point was to promote democracy and to "contain" communism. However, the international focus on U.S. racial problems meant that the image of American democracy was tarnished. The apparent contradictions between American political ideology and practice led to particular foreign policy difficulties with countries in Asia, Africa, and Latin America. U.S. government officials realized that their ability to sell democracy to the Third World was seriously hampered by continuing racial injustice at home. Accordingly, efforts to promote civil rights within the United States were consistent with, and important to, the more central U.S. mission of fighting world communism.

The literature on desegregation during the 1940s and 1950s has failed to consider the subject within the context of other important aspects of American cultural history during the postwar era. Most scholars seem to assume that little outside the subject of race relations is relevant to the topic.[1] As a result, historians of *Brown* seem to write about a different world than do those who consider other aspects of postwar American culture. The failure to contextualize *Brown* reinforces the sense that the movement against segregation somehow happened in spite of everything else that was going on. During a period when civil liberties and social change were repressed in other contexts, somehow, some way, *Brown* managed to happen.

This chapter represents an effort to begin to examine the desegregation cases within the context of the cultural and political period in which they occurred. The wealth of primary historical documents on civil rights during the Cold War that explicitly draw connections between civil rights and anticommunism suggests that an effort to examine desegregation within the context of Cold War American culture may be more than an interesting addition to a basically well told tale. It may ultimately cause us to recast our interpretations of the factors motivating the critical legal and cultural transformation that *Brown* has come to represent.

In one important deviation from the dominant trend in scholarship on desegregation, Derrick Bell has suggested that the consensus against school segregation in the 1950s was the result of a convergence of interests on the part of whites and blacks, and that white interests in abandoning segregation were in part a response to foreign policy concerns and an effort to suppress the potential of black radicalism at home. According to Bell, without a convergence of white and black interests in this manner, *Brown* would never have occurred.[2] While Bell's work is important and suggestive, neither Bell nor other scholars have developed this approach historically.

One need not look far to find vintage '50s Cold War ideology in primary historical documents relating to *Brown*. For example, the amicus brief filed in *Brown* by the U.S. Justice Department argued that desegregation was in the national interest in part due to foreign policy concerns. According to the Department, the case was important because "[t]he United States is trying to prove to the people of the world, of every nationality, race and color, that a free democracy is the most civilized and most secure form of government yet devised by man."[3] Following the decision, newspapers in the United States and throughout the world celebrated *Brown* as a "blow to communism" and as a vindication of American democratic principles. As was true in so many other contexts during the Cold War era, anticommunist ideology was so pervasive that it set the terms of the debate on all sides of the civil rights issue.

In addition to its important consequences for U.S. race relations, *Brown* served U.S. foreign policy interests. The value of a clear Supreme Court statement that segregation was unconstitutional was recognized by the State Department. Federal government policy on civil rights issues during the Truman Administration was framed with the international implications of U.S. racial problems in mind. And through a series of amicus briefs detailing the effect of racial segregation on U.S. foreign policy interests, the Administration impressed upon the Supreme Court the necessity for world peace and national security of upholding black civil rights at home.

As has been thoroughly documented by other historians, the federal government's efforts in the late 1940s and early 1950s to achieve some level of racial equality had much to do with the personal commitment on the part of some in government to racial justice, and with the consequences of civil rights policies for domestic electoral politics. In addition to these motivating factors, the effect of U.S. race discrimination on international relations during the postwar years was a critical motivating factor in the development of federal government policy. Without attention to the degree to which desegregation served important foreign policy interests, the federal government's posture on civil rights issues in the postwar years cannot be fully understood.

American Racism in the Eyes of the World

Apart from pressure from civil rights activists and electoral politics at home, the Truman Administration had another reason to address domestic racism: other countries were paying attention to it. Newspapers in many corners of the world covered stories of racial discrimination against visiting non-white foreign dignitaries and Americans. And as tension between the United States and the Soviet Union increased in the years after the war, the Soviets made effective use of U.S. failings in this area in anti-American propaganda. Concern about the effect of U.S. race discrimination on Cold War American foreign policy led the Truman Administration to consider a pro-civil rights posture as part of its international agenda to promote democracy and contain communism.

In one example of foreign press coverage, in December 1946 the *Fiji Times & Herald* published an article entitled "Persecution of Negroes Still Strong in America." According to the Fiji paper, "the United States has within its own borders, one of the most oppressed and persecuted minorities in the world today." In the Southern states, "hundreds of thousands of negroes exist today in an economic condition worse than the out-and-out slavery of a century ago." Treatment of blacks was not merely a question of race discrimination; "it is frequently a question of the most terrible forms of racial persecution."

The article described the 1946 lynching of four blacks in Georgia. "This outrage," the article continued, followed Supreme Court action invalidating Georgia voting restrictions. "The decision gave the negro the legal right to vote but [Georgia Governor] Talmadge challenged him to exercise it. He also flung a defiance to the Court itself and asked the voters of his State to back him up, which they did." According to the paper, "[v]ery few negroes dared to vote, even though the country's highest tribunal had found them entitled to. Most of those who did, or tried to, were badly mauled by white ruffians." The article noted that federal anti-lynching legislation had been proposed in the past, and "further attempts are certain in the next Congress."

The *Fiji Times & Herald* was not entirely critical. Reporting that a recent dinner honoring black journalists had brought together blacks and white Southerners, the paper concluded that "[t]he point is that the best culture of the south, in America, is opposed to the Bilbo-Talmadge anti-negro oppression and seems today more than ever inclined to join with the north in fighting it." Efforts against racial intolerance had particular consequences in the U.S., for "there cannot be, on the basic tenants [sic] of Americanism, such a thing as second class citizenship." The issue also had broader implications, however. "The recognition and acceptance of the concept of a common humanity should, and must, shatter the longstanding bulwarks of intolerance, racial or otherwise, before anything entitled to call itself true civilisation can be established in America or any other country."

The American Consul in Fiji was unhappy with the *Times & Herald* article, which it saw as "an indication of certain of the anti-American and/or misinformation or propaganda now carried" in the paper. A response to the article seemed appropriate and necessary. "If and when a favorable opportunity occurs, the matter of the reasonableness or justification in the publication of such biased and unfounded material, obviously prejudicial to American prestige throughout this area, will be tactfully broached to the Editor and appropriate government officials."

In Ceylon, American Embassy officials were concerned about what they considered to be "Asian preoccupation with racial discrimination in the United States." Ceylon newspapers ran stories on U.S. racial problems picked up from Reuters wire service. In addition, a Ceylon *Observer* columnist focused on the issue, particularly the seeming contradiction of segregation in the capital of American democracy. In his article, Lakshman Seneviratne quoted *Time* magazine as saying, "[i]n Washington, the seated figure of Abraham Lincoln broods over the capital of the U.S. where Jim Crow is the rule." According to Seneviratne, in Washington "the colour bar is the greatest propaganda gift any country could give the Kremlin in its persistent bid for the affections of the coloured races of the world, who, if industrialized, and technically mobilized, can well dominate, if domination is the obsession, the human race."

The effect of U.S. race discrimination on the country's leadership in postwar world politics was discussed in the Chinese press. The Shanghai *Ta Kung Pao* covered the May 2, 1948, arrest of U.S. Senator Glen Taylor for violating Alabama segregation laws. Criticizing Taylor's arrest, the paper noted that "[t]he Negro problem is a problem of U.S. internal politics, and naturally, it is unnecessary for anybody else to meddle with it." However, the issue had international ramifications.

> [W]e cannot help having some impressions of the United States which actually already leads half of the world and which would like to continue to lead it. If the United States merely wants to "dominate" the world, the atomic bomb and the U.S. dollar will be sufficient to achieve this purpose. However, the world cannot be "dominated" for a long period of time. If the United States wants to "lead" the world, it must have a kind of moral superiority in addition to military superiority.

According to the paper, "the United States prides itself on its 'liberal traditions,' and it is in the United States itself that these traditions can best be demonstrated."

The American Consul General in Shanghai believed that the *Ta Kung Pao* editorial "discusses the Negro problem in the U.S. in a manner quite close to the Communist Party line." The Consul General preferred an editorial in the *China Daily Tribune* which cast American race discrimination as a problem generated by a small minority who were acting against the grain. According to that paper, "Prejudice against people of color seems to die hard in some parts of the United States despite all that President Truman and the more enlightened leaders of the nation are doing to ensure that race equality shall become an established fact."

Indian newspapers were particularly attuned to the issue of race discrimination in the U.S. According to the American Consul General in Bombay, "[t]he color question is of intense interest in India." Numerous articles with titles like "Negro Baiting in America," "Treatment of Negroes a Blot on U.S.," and "Untouchability Banished in India: Worshipped in America" appeared in the Indian press. Regarding the latter article, the American Consul General commented that it was "somewhat typical of the irresponsible and malicious type of story on the American Negro which appears not too infrequently in segments of the Indian press. . . ." The article was written by Canadian George T. Prud'homme, who the Consul General described as a "communist writer." It concerned a trip through the South, and included a photo-graph of a chain gang. According to Prud'homme, "[t]he farther South one travels, the less human the Negro status becomes, until in Georgia and Florida it degenerates to the level of the beast in the field."

Prud'homme described an incident following his attempt to speak to blacks seated behind him on a segregated bus. He was later warned "not to talk to 'those damned niggers.' "

> "We don't even talk to niggers down here," said [a] blond young man.
> "You better not either . . . unless you want to get beaten up."

> I replied I didn't think the Negroes would attempt to beat me up with the bus half-filled with whites.

> *"It isn't the niggers that will beat you up, it's the whites you have to look out for,"* confided the driver. *"This ain't the North. Everything is different down here."*

The article discussed segregation, the history of the Ku Klux Klan, and the denial of voting rights through poll taxes and discriminatory voter registration tests. The writer believed that American treatment of blacks "strangely resembles the story of India under British domination." The "only bright spot in this picture" was provided by individuals such as a white Baptist pastor who was committed to racial equality. But the minister told Prud'homme, "If one of us fights for true democracy and progress, he is labelled a Communist. . . . That is an effective way of shutting him up."

Of particular concern to the State Department was coverage of U.S. racism by the Soviet media. The U.S. Embassy in Moscow believed that a number of articles in 1946 "may portend stronger emphasis on this theme as [a] Soviet propaganda weapon." In August 1946, the U.S. Embassy in Moscow sent the State Department a translation of an editorial from the periodical *Trud* which was "representative of the frequent Soviet press comment on the question of Negro discrimination in the United States." The *Trud* article was based on information the Soviets had gathered from the "progressive American press," and it concerned lynching and black labor in the South.

According to *Trud*, American periodicals had reported "the increasing frequency of terroristic acts against negroes," including "the bestial mobbing of four negroes by a band of 20 to 25 whites" in July 1946 in Monroe, Georgia. In another incident near Linden, Louisiana, "a crowd of white men tortured a negro war veteran, John Jones, tore his arms out and set fire to his body. The papers stress the fact that the murder-ers, even though they are identified, remain unpunished." U.S. census figures indi-cated that three quarters of American blacks lived in the South. In the Southern "Black Belt," "the negroes are overwhelmingly engaged in agriculture, as small tenant-farmers, share-croppers and hired hands. Semi-slave forms of oppression and exploitation are the rule. . . ." Blacks were denied economic rights due to the way the legal system protected the interests of the landowners upon whose property share-croppers and tenant farmers labored. In addition, "[t]he absence of economic rights is accompanied by the absence of social rights. The poll tax, in effect in the Southern

States, deprives the overwhelming majority of negroes of the right to vote." *Trud* observed that "[t]he movement for full economic, political and social equality is spreading among the negro population," but that "[t]his movement has evoked exceptional fury and resistance." According to the paper, "[t]he progressive public opinion of the USA is indignant at the baiting of negroes, and rightly sees in this one of the means by which reaction is taking the offensive against the working people."

By 1949, according to the U.S. Embassy in Moscow, "the 'Negro question' [was] [o]ne of the principal Soviet propaganda themes regarding the United States." "[T]he Soviet press hammers away unceasingly on such things as 'lynch law,' segregation, racial discrimination, deprivation of political rights, etc., seeking to build up a picture of an America in which the Negroes are brutally down-trodden with no hope of improving their status under the existing form of government." An Embassy official believed that "this attention to the Negro problem serves political ends desired by the Soviet Union and has nothing whatsoever to do with any desire to better the Negro's position. . . ." The "Soviet press seizes upon anything showing the position of the US Negro in a derogatory light while ignoring entirely the genuine progress being made in America in improving the situation."

A powerful critique of U.S. racism, presented before the United Nations, came from American blacks. On October 23, 1947, the NAACP filed a petition in the United Nations protesting the treatment of blacks in the U.S. called *An Appeal to the World*. The petition denounced U.S. race discrimination as "not only indefensible but barbaric." It claimed that racism harmed the nation as a whole. "It is not Russia that threatens the United States so much as Mississippi; not Stalin and Molotov but Bilbo and Rankin; internal injustice done to one's brothers is far more dangerous than the aggression of strangers from abroad." The consequences of American failings were potentially global. "[T]he disfranchisement of the American Negro makes the functioning of all democracy in the nation difficult; and as democracy fails to function in the leading democracy in the world, it fails the world." According to W.E.B. Du Bois, the principal author of the petition, the purpose behind the appeal was to enable the UN "to prepare this nation to be just to its own people."

The NAACP petition "created an international sensation." It received extensive coverage in the American and foreign media. Meanwhile, U.S. Attorney General Tom Clark remarked, "I was humiliated . . . to realize that in our America there could be the slightest foundation for such a petition." Although she was a member of the Board of Directors of the NAACP, Eleanor Roosevelt, who was also a member of the American UN delegation, refused to introduce the NAACP petition in the United Nations out of concern that it would harm the international reputation of the United States. The Soviet Union, however, proposed that the NAACP's charges be investigated. On December 4, 1947, the UN Commission on Human Rights rejected that proposal, and the UN took no action on the petition. Nevertheless, the *Des Moines Register* remarked that the petition had "accomplished its purpose of arousing interest in discrimination." Although the domestic press reaction was generally favorable, the West Virginia *Morgantown Post* criticized the NAACP for "furnishing Soviet Russia with new ammunition to use against us."

The Truman Justice Department first participated as amicus curiae in civil rights cases involving restrictive covenants.[4] In previous civil rights cases, the Solicitor

General participated when the litigation involved a federal agency,[5] and when the question in the case concerned the supremacy of federal law.[6] A different sort of federal interest was involved in the restrictive covenant cases. According to Solicitor General Phillip Perlman, racially restrictive covenants hampered the federal government "in doing its duty in the fields of public health, housing, home finance, and in the conduct of foreign affairs."[7] The Brief for the United States in *Shelley v. Kraemer*[8] relied on the State Department's view that "the United States has been embarrassed in the conduct of foreign relations by acts of discrimination taking place in this country."[9] To support this argument, the brief quoted at length from the letter Acting Secretary of State Acheson had written to the FEPC in 1946.

Although not addressing the international implications of the case, the Supreme Court agreed with the result sought by the Justice Department. The Court ruled that enforcement of racially restrictive covenants in state courts constituted state action which violated the rights of blacks to equal protection of the laws.[10]

The Solicitor General's office continued its efforts in civil rights cases in 1949. In *Henderson v. United States*,[11] the Department of Justice took a position contrary to the Interstate Commerce Commission on the question of the validity of railroad dining car segregation under the Interstate Commerce Act.[12] As in *Shelley*, an important motivation behind the government's anti-segregation position was the international implications of segregation.[13] The *Henderson* brief elaborated more fully on the problem. One area in which international criticism of the U.S. manifested itself was the United Nations. The brief quoted from recent statements made by representatives of other governments in a UN subcommittee meeting which "typify the manner in which racial discrimination in this country is turned against us in the international field."[14] For example, a representative of the Soviet Union had commented: "Guided by the principles of the United Nations Charter, the General Assembly must condemn the policy and practice of racial discrimination in the United States and any other countries of the American continent where such a policy was being exercised."[15] Similarly, the representative from Poland "did not . . . believe that the United States Government had the least intention to conform to the recommendations which would be made by the United Nations with regard to the improvement of living conditions of the coloured population of that country."[16]

As it had in *Shelley*, the Justice Department made reference to foreign press coverage of U.S. race discrimination, noting that "[t]he references to this subject in the unfriendly foreign press are frequent and caustic."[17] This time the brief bolstered this claim with examples from Soviet publications. *The Bolshevik*, for example, carried an article which claimed that

> [t]he theory and practice of racial discrimination against the negroes in America is known to the whole world. The poison of racial hatred has become so strong in post-war America that matters go to unbelievable lengths; for example a Negress injured in a road accident could not be taken to a neighbouring hospital since this hospital was only for "whites."[18]

Through its reliance on UN statements and the Soviet press, the *Henderson* brief powerfully made the point that racial segregation hampered the U.S. government's fight against world communism.

The Impact of *Brown* on American Foreign Policy Interests

When *Brown v. Board of Education* was decided, the opinion gave the State Department the counter to Soviet propaganda it had been looking for, and the State Department wasted no time in making use of it. Within an hour after the decision was handed down, the Voice of America broadcast the news to Eastern Europe.[19] An analysis accompanying the "straight news broadcasts" emphasized that "the issue was settled by law under democratic processes rather than by mob rule or dictatorial fiat."[20] The *Brown* broadcast received "top priority on the Voice's programs," and was to be "beamed possibly for several days, particularly to Russian satellites and Communist China." The *New York Times* quoted a Voice of America official as commenting that "[i]n these countries . . . the people would know nothing about the decision except what would be told them by the Communist press and radio, which you may be sure would be twisted and perverted. They have been told that the Negro in the United States is still practically a slave and a declassed citizen."[21]

The *Brown* decision had the kind of effect on international opinion that the U.S. government had hoped for. Favorable reaction to the opinion spanned the globe. On May 21, 1954, for example, the President of the Municipal Council of Santos, São Paulo, Brazil, sent a letter to the U.S. Embassy in Rio de Janeiro celebrating the *Brown* decision. The Municipal Council had passed a motion recording "a vote of satisfaction" with the ruling. They viewed *Brown* as "establishing the just equality of the races, essential to universal harmony and peace." The Council desired that "the Consul of that great and friendly nation be officially notified of our desire to partake in the rejoicing with which the said decision was received in all corners of the civilized world."

Newspapers in Africa gave extensive coverage to the decision. According to a dispatch from the American Consul in Dakar, *Brown* was "greeted with enthusiasm in French West Africa although the press has expressed some slight skepticism over its implementation." *Afrique Nouvelle*, a weekly paper that was a "highly vocal opponent of all racial discrimination," carried an article under the headline "At last! Whites and Blacks in the United States on the same school benches." The dispatch noted that the writer was concerned that there would be

> "desperate struggles" in some states against the decision but expresses the hope that the representatives of the negroes and the "spiritual forces" of the United States will apply themselves to giving it force and life. The article concludes by saying that "all the peoples of the world can salute with joy this measure of progress."

The American Consul concluded the dispatch by observing that

> [w]hile it is, of course, too soon to speculate on the long range effects of the decision in this area, it is well to remember that school segregation more than any other single factor has lowered the prestige of the United States among Africans here and the over-all results, therefore, can hardly fail to be beneficial.

Although the initial decision to participate in *Brown* had been made by the Truman Administration, the Republican National Committee (RNC) was happy to take credit for it. On May 21, 1954, the RNC issued a statement which claimed that the decision "falls appropriately within the Eisenhower Administration's many-frontal attack on global Communism. Human equality at home is a weapon of freedom. . . . [I]t helps guarantee the Free World's cause."[22]

Conclusion

The desegregation cases came before the Court at a time when the sanctity of American democracy had tremendous implications for U.S. foreign policy interests. The U.S. hoped to save the world for democracy, and promoted its ideology and form of government as providing for greater personal freedom. In the U.S., the Voice of America proclaimed, the Bill of Rights and the Constitution protected American citizens from state tyranny. Yet as news story after news story of voting rights abuses, state-enforced segregation, and lynchings appeared in the world media, many questioned whether American constitutional rights and democratic principles had any meaning. In many African and Asian countries, where issues of race, nationalism, and anti-colonialism were of much greater import than Cold War tensions between the superpowers, the reality of U.S. racism was particularly problematic. America could not save the Third World for democracy if democracy meant white supremacy. The Soviet Union's efforts to take advantage of this American dilemma reinforced its Cold War implications.

In responding to foreign critics, State Department officials attempted to characterize American racism as a regional, rather than a national, problem, and as something that was on its way out. They argued that democracy was working, and that it would eventually overcome the anachronistic practices of a marginal few. The desegregation cases posed a threat to this characterization. If the Supreme Court had ruled in favor of the defendants in *Shelley, Henderson, Sweatt, McLaurin,* and *Brown,* the Court would have reaffirmed the idea that the American Constitution accommodated the racist practices challenged in those cases. American Embassy officials in Nigeria would have found it difficult to counter arguments that the Communist Party was more committed to the interests of people of color, if the Court had interpreted the document embodying the principles of democracy and individual rights to be consistent with racial segregation.

Notes

1. As Gerald Horne has noted, "the fact that the *Brown* ruling came in the midst of a concerted governmental campaign against international and domestic communism is one of the most overlooked aspects of the decision." G. HORNE, BLACK AND RED: W.E.B. DU BOIS AND THE AFRO-AMERICAN RESPONSE TO THE COLD WAR, 1944–1963, at 227 (1986).
2. D. Bell, *Brown v. Board of Education and the Interest-Convergence Dilemma,* 93 HARV. L. REV. 518 (1980), reprinted in D. BELL, SHADES OF BROWN: NEW PERSPECTIVES ON SCHOOL DESEGREGATION (1980) [hereinafter Bell, *Convergence Dilemma*]; *see also* D. Bell, *Racial Remediation: An Historical Perspective on Current Conditions,* 52 NOTRE DAME L. REV. 5, 12 (1976).
3. Brief for the United States as Amicus Curiae at 6, Brown v. Board of Education, 347 U.S. 483 (1954).
4. *See* Shelley v. Kraemer, 334 U.S. 1 (1948); Hurd v. Hodge, 334 U.S. 24 (1948). According to Solicitor General

Perlman, the brief filed in the restrictive covenant cases was "the first instance in which the Government had intervened in a case to which it was not a party and in which its sole purpose was the vindication of rights guaranteed by the Fifth and Fourteenth Amendments." J. ELLIFF, THE UNITED STATES DEPARTMENT OF JUSTICE AND INDIVIDUAL RIGHTS 1937–1962, 258 (1987) (quoting Address by Perlman to the National Civil Liberties Clearing House (Feb. 23, 1950)).

Because my purpose is to examine the Truman Administration's participation in these cases, this article does not dwell on the crucial role in the cases played by the NAACP. For excellent treatments of the NAACP's litigation efforts, see M. TUSHNET, THE NAACP's LEGAL STRATEGY AGAINST SEGREGATED EDUCATION, 1925–1950 (1987); R. KLUGER, SIMPLE JUSTICE (1975).

5. *See* Mitchell v. United States, 313 U.S. 80 (1941).

6. *See* Taylor v. Georgia, 315 U.S. 25 (1942).

7. Oral argument of Solicitor General Perlman, 16 U.S.L.W. 3219 (Jan. 20, 1948) (paraphrased account of argument); see also C. VOSE, CAUCASIANS ONLY: THE SUPREME COURT, THE NAACP, AND THE RESTRICTIVE COVENANT CASES 200 (1959).

8. 334 U.S. 1 (1948). In *Shelley*, whites sold residential property to blacks in violation of a covenant among landowners prohibiting sales to nonwhites. State Supreme Courts in Missouri and Michigan had ruled that the covenants were enforceable. *Id.* at 6–7. The question in *Shelley* was whether judicial enforcement of the covenants constituted state action violating the fourteenth amendment rights of the blacks who purchased the property. The Supreme Court ruled that it did. *Id.* at 20.

9. Brief for the United States as Amicus Curiae at 19, Shelley v. Kraemer, 334 U.S. 1 (1948) (quoting letter from Ernest A. Gross, Legal Adviser to the Secretary of State, to the Attorney General (Nov. 4, 1947)).

10. 334 U.S. at 20.

11. 339 U.S. 816 (1950).

12. The Interstate Commerce Act provided that "[i]t shall be unlawful for any common carrier . . . to make, give, or cause any undue or unreasonable preference or advantage to any particular person . . . in any respect whatsoever; or to subject any particular person . . . to any undue or unreasonable prejudice or disadvantage in any respect whatsoever. . . ." Interstate Commerce Act, ch. 722, § 5(a), 54 Stat. 898, 902, 49 U.S.C. § 3(1) (1946) (codified as amended at 49 U.S.C. § 1074(b) (1982)). The Interstate Commerce Commission ruled that the Southern Railway Company's practice of providing separate seating behind a curtain in dining cars for black passengers did not violate the Act. *See* Henderson v. United States, 339 U.S. 816, 820–22 (1950). On appeal, the ICC defended its interpretation of the Act, and the Justice Department filed a brief on behalf of the United States arguing that (1) dining car segregation violated the Act, and (2) segregation violated the equal protection clause. *See* Brief for the United States at 9–11, Henderson v. United States, 339 U.S. 816 (1950).

13. The brief quoted from the same letter from Dean Acheson that the Department had relied on in *Shelley*. *See* Brief for the United States at 60–61, Henderson v. United States, 339 U.S. 816 (1950).

14. *Id.* at 61.

15. *Id.* (quoting United Nations, General Assembly, *Ad Hoc* Political Committee, Third Session, Part II, Summary Record of the Fifty-Third Meeting (May 11, 1949), at 12).

16. *Id.* (quoting United Nations, General Assembly, *Ad Hoc* Political Committee, Third Session, Part II, Summary Record of Fifty-Fourth Meeting (May 13, 1949), at 6).

17. *Id.*

18. *Id.* at 61 n.73 (quoting Frantsov, *Nationalism—The Tool of Imperialist Reaction*, THE BOLSHEVIK (U.S.S.R.), No. 15 (1948)).

In another example, a story in the Soviet *Literary Gazette* titled "The Tragedy of Coloured America" stated:

> It is a country within a country. Coloured America is not allowed to mix with the other white America, it exists within it like the yolk in the white of an egg. Or, to be more exact, like a gigantic ghetto. The walls of this ghetto are invisible but they are nonetheless indestructible. They are placed within cities where the Negroes live in special quarters, in buses where the Negroes are assigned only the back seats, in hairdressers where they have special chairs.

Id. (quoting Berezko, *The Tragedy of Coloured America*, The LITERARY GAZETTE (U.S.S.R.), No. 51 (1948)).

19. N.Y. TIMES, May 18, 1954, at 1, col. 7. The Voice of America's ability to effectively use the decision was enhanced by the fact that the opinion was short and easily understandable by lay persons. Chief Justice Earl Warren intended to write "a short opinion so that any layman interested in the problem could read the entire opinion [instead of getting just] a little piece here and a little piece there. . . . I think most of the newspapers printed the entire decision." *See* J. WILKINSON, FROM BROWN TO BAKKE: THE SUPREME COURT AND SCHOOL INTEGRATION, 1954–1978 30 (1979) (quoting H. ABRAHAM, FREEDOM AND THE COURT 372 n. 90 (3d ed. 1977)).

20. N.Y. TIMES, May 18, 1954, at 1, col. 7.

21. *Id.*

22. Republican National Committee, News Release, May 21, 1954, at 3, White House Files—Civil Rights—Republican National Committee 1954, Box 37, Philleo Nash Papers, Harry S. Truman Library.

President Eisenhower himself was less enthusiastic. He repeatedly refused to publicly endorse *Brown. See* R. BURK, THE EISENHOWER ADMINISTRATION AND BLACK CIVIL RIGHTS 144, 162, 165–66 (1984). *See generally* Mayer, *With Much Deliberation and Some Speed: Eisenhower and the Brown Decision,* 52 J. SOUTHERN HIST. 43 (1986). Eisenhower criticized "foolish extremists on both sides" of the school desegregation controversy, R. BURK, *supra* at 163, and, in an effort to distance his administration from the Supreme Court's ruling, he "rebuked Vice President Nixon for referring to Earl Warren as the 'Republican Chief Justice'. . . ." *Id.* at 162. Chief Justice Warren was angered by Eisenhower's stance. He believed that if Eisenhower had fully supported *Brown,* "we would have been relieved . . . of many of the racial problems that have continued to plague us." E. WARREN, THE MEMOIRS OF EARL WARREN 291 (1977); *see* J. WILKINSON, *supra* note 19, at 24.

Part Three

Affirmative Action

6

The "We've Done Enough" Theory of School Desegregation

Mark V. Tushnet

After its periodic outbursts of support for African–American interests—provoked by a combination of idealism and self-interest—white America ordinarily decides that it has done enough, and withdraws.[1] The Supreme Court articulated this "we've done enough" theory in the Civil Rights Cases of 1883,[2] less than a decade after Reconstruction's end. According to Justice Bradley, "When a man has emerged from slavery, and by the aid of beneficent legislation has shaken off the inseparable concomitants of that state, there must be some stage in the progress of his elevation when he takes the rank of a mere citizen, and ceases to be the special favorite of the law."[3] White America had done enough before 1875, so, in the Court's eyes, the Civil Rights Act of 1875 unconstitutionally sought to maintain African Americans as "special favorites of the law."[4]

The "we've done enough" theory resurfaced in 1995 when the Court held in Missouri v. Jenkins[5] that federal courts lacked power to order that a state provide financial resources to an urban school district that would attract white students back to the city's schools.[6] Jenkins involved the Kansas City, Missouri, school district, which had been operated under Missouri's segregated school system before the Supreme Court's decision in Brown v. Board of Education.[7] In 1984 a federal district judge found that the city and the state had continued to maintain a segregated system by giving white parents a wide choice of schools to educate their children.[8] After further proceedings the judge ordered the city and the state to create a number of well-funded "magnet schools" designed to attract white children to the city's schools.[9]

As the Court's majority saw the case, in making such an order, the district court had attempted an end-run around the Court's earlier proscription of desegregation remedies reaching across district boundaries.[10] In the majority's view, the district court attempted to remedy "white flight," the withdrawal of white students from the city's public schools as the schools implemented prior desegregation orders.[11] According to the Court, however, the schools were not responsible for white flight; therefore, federal courts could not "remedy" something resulting from uncoerced choices by white parents rather than from decisions by some public agencies.[12] As Chief Justice Rehnquist stated, the district court's purpose was "to attract nonminority students from outside" the city, an "interdistrict goal [that] is beyond the scope of the intradistrict violation."[13]

We can understand Jenkins best by seeing it against the background of desegregation politics and the Court's decisions. Between 1954 and 1995 political support for
desegregation eroded under the pressure of white opposition to forced busing.[14]
According to Brown, "separate educational facilities are inherently unequal."[15] Read
against Brown's doctrinal background, this had two meanings. First, as the Court
expressly said, African–American children in segregated schools suffer a stigma—"a
feeling of inferiority as to their status in the community that may affect their hearts
and minds in a way unlikely ever to be undone"[16]—communicated to them by the
white majority's insistence that the law endorse the majority's refusal to associate
with African Americans.

Second, separate education facilities were inherently unequal because they could
not provide access to educational opportunities equal to those available to whites.
The Court knew, of course, that separate schools were unlikely ever to be equal in
material endowments.[17] Only four years earlier it had confronted and rejected the
ridiculous claim that a makeshift law school for African Americans was equal to the
well-endowed University of Texas Law School.[18] The record there showed gross
material inequalities, but the Court perhaps unfortunately paid attention to non-
material features of legal education as well, emphasizing that the new school could
not compete with the University of Texas's role as the place where the state's future
lawyers got to know each other.[19] These non-material factors provided the essential
background for Brown. The lower courts in Kansas, South Carolina, and Virginia
found as a matter of fact that the schools provided for African Americans were
equal in material features to those available to whites.[20] No one familiar with
the South could have accepted those "findings" with a straight face.[21] But, concerned not to insult people the justices thought of as responsible white Southerners,
the Court chose to rely on the findings and emphasized, as in the Texas law
school case, other inequalities "inherent" in a segregated system.[22] This emphasis on
other inequalities had the unfortunate effect of diverting attention from material
inequalities.[23]

Over the next decade the Court focused on stigmatic injury. In Brown's immediate aftermath the justices may have thought that eliminating legally sanctioned
segregation would eliminate the stigma: the theory would have been that stigma
arose from white insistence that law endorse their prejudices, not from the prejudices
themselves. White resistance led the justices to a different view. By the time the Court
heard Green,[24] they began to lean toward the belief that stigma arose from white
refusal to associate with African Americans, whether or not endorsed by law.[25] That
belief rather naturally led to Swann:[26] the only way to eliminate the stigma was to
insist that whites attend schools with African Americans.[27]

By the time Swann was decided, however, the political context had changed.
Following Barry Goldwater's lead, Richard Nixon saw political advantages for the
Republican party in breaking the Democratic hold on the South by taking a stand
against further efforts to desegregate Southern schools.[28] Nixon's Department of
Justice argued against busing remedies in the Supreme Court,[29] and Nixon's Southern
strategy led him to appoint busing opponents to the Court.[30] At the same time,
Nixon's Department of Health, Education, and Welfare kept the issue alive by
forcefully insisting that Southern schools desegregate.[31]

When desegregation and busing were issues in the South alone, white Americans
—at least those in the North—could say, "We—the people of the United States as a
whole [meaning those other whites in the South]—have not yet done enough." As
the issues moved North, however, white Americans all over the country began to
think, "We've done enough." One might imagine a truly Machiavellian strategy at
work: Republicans benefited by keeping the issues alive rather than by resolving
them, because that allowed them to continue to weaken Democratic strength among
white Southerners and the white working-class in the North; and Democrats stepped
into the trap by continuing to be committed to busing as a remedy for segregation.

On one level, however, the real story is messier. Nixon appointed four justices
to the Supreme Court.[32] The Court's liberals could occasionally cobble together a
majority to support a lower court's decision to remedy segregation by busing, but
they lacked the resources to rethink desegregation policy in light of changing circumstances. By endorsing busing in Swann, the Court made it much more difficult for
lower courts to develop more imaginative remedies to ensure that substantial numbers of white students attended city schools. As a result, the few cases that reached the
Supreme Court all involved busing.[33] The Court's liberals did not have the votes to
support rulings that would have required lower courts to be more imaginative. The
best they could do was occasionally affirm a busing order. The liberals were fighting a
rear-guard action and thought they had done well when they persuaded five justices
not to retreat from Swann.[34]

Desegregation politics and doctrine interacted with desegregation seen as education policy. Most who support desegregation believe it has various educational benefits. One can imagine several educational theories in which learning suffers in
one-race environments. For example, members of both races may learn less about
each other. Optimists believe that "increased racial contact can lead to "more
favorable attitudes and friendlier relations between the races' rather than increased
hostility or reinforcement of stereotypes,"[35] while pessimists rely on social scientific
surveys that show few consistent positive improvements in race relations from
desegregation.[36] Those conclusions deal with non-cognitive effects of interracial
contact; that students learn something from such contact seems undeniable.

More important for Jenkins, one might focus on the politics of school financing.
White Americans are primarily responsible for setting tax rates and expenditure
levels for public schools simply because whites are a majority in every state, and
statewide tax and expenditure policies substantially determine education expenditures. One might reasonably believe that white Americans will not provide stably
adequate funding for schools unless the schools contain substantial numbers of white
students,[37] and that stably adequate funding is necessary for positive educational
outcomes.[38]

If a decent education system requires stably adequate funding, and if stably
adequate funding requires that there be a substantial number of white students in the
system, how can that be accomplished?[39] For a decade after Brown v. Board of
Education,[40] the courts seemed to hope that removing legal barriers to maintaining
schools with multiracial enrollments would lead to such enrollments. White resistance to desegregation made the Supreme Court impatient, and in Green v. New Kent
County Board of Education[41] the Court set out on a new course. Under Green, results

mattered. Courts would check to see what the enrollments were and would take steps to ensure that, as Justice Brennan put it, each district was "a system without a "white' school and a "Negro' school, but just schools."[42]

Swann v. Charlotte-Mecklenburg Board of Education[43] took the next step. District courts, the Supreme Court held, had discretion to require substantial amounts of transportation within a school district to achieve a degree of biracial enrollment in each school roughly equivalent to that in the district as a whole.[44] To accomplish that, district courts could develop busing plans.

Even in 1971 when Swann was decided, the Court knew that busing might not produce city schools with a substantial number of white students, because, as Chief Justice Burger put it in Swann, "in a growing, mobile society," few districts would "remain demographically stable."[45] How, then, could stably adequate funding for city schools be assured?

The Court rejected two obvious answers. Shortly after Swann, the Court rejected constitutional challenges to school financing systems based on local property taxes.[46] Justice Powell's opinion for the Court correctly observed that eliminating property-tax financing would not necessarily guarantee that city schools would receive stably higher levels of funds.[47] Had the constitutional challenge succeeded, however, it would have opened the way for a more reflective consideration of the range of issues raised by educational funding, and might have been the occasion for redesigning financing systems to assure stably adequate funding for city schools. Still, even redesigning school financing systems would not ensure that city schools would enroll substantial numbers of white students, which, as I have suggested, may be essential to having stably adequate financing.

Another solution was equally obvious: define the "city's" boundaries to include substantial numbers of white students. As the cases were litigated, they unfortunately combined two issues that could have been kept distinct—expansion of boundaries and elimination of all but a few one-race schools within the expanded district, by means of busing. Milliken v. Bradley rejected that solution.[48] As in Jenkins, the Court insisted that remedies for segregation had to be confined to the districts whose governing authorities had violated the Constitution.

A third solution was possible: provide incentives to white parents to keep their children in the city's schools. This solution expands the city's boundaries meta-phorically, by including within the city all parents who might choose to send their children to the city's schools. It retains the compulsion associated with the tax system, as people—parents and others—are taxed to pay for the incentives, but it eliminates the compulsion associated with student-assignment policies and busing. Notice that this approach does not place much direct value on the fact that whites attend schools with African Americans, and so does not "assume that anything that is predominantly black must be inferior"[49] with respect to anything other than financing (controlled at bottom by whites). Rather, it assumes only that white parents and taxpayers will not adequately fund schools that their children do not attend.

Adopting this solution has a number of attractive features. Swann turned out to be quite problematic, both politically and educationally. "Forced busing" was politically unpopular.[50] Frequently liberals defended busing on educational grounds: they asserted that children, particularly African-American children, learned cognitive skills more effectively in biracial schools.[51] That claim turned out to be hard to defend. Evidence accumulated showing relatively few of these educational benefits from student-assignment policies involving substantial amounts of busing.[52]

At the same time, the evidence did suggest that the compulsion involved in student-assignment policies reduced the desegregation's educational benefits.[53] White parents did not want to be told that their children had to attend schools with African Americans. When they chose to send their children to schools with African Americans, however, the educational benefits occurred. Incentives, in short, might work, as Green required.[54]

The most effective voluntary desegregation plans involved creating magnet schools, where students were offered specialized programs, usually at a per-student outlay well above the average in non-magnet schools.[55] White parents' misgivings about sending their children to school with African Americans were overcome by the attraction of the higher expenditures or the magnet schools' programs.[56] Where voluntary desegregation plans were implemented, white flight decreased significantly.[57] Summarizing one important study, David Armor writes, "Mandatory plans produced greater interracial exposure . . . than voluntary magnet plans during the first several years of implementation, but the voluntary magnet plans produced greater exposure over the long run," and "mandatory plans produced greater racial balance for longer periods . . ., but voluntary magnet plans eventually caught up . . . and produced about the same level of racial balance."[58] As one scholar puts it, "plans that provide incentives for desegregation . . . make citizens happier than mandatory assignment plans and usually produce more interracial exposure."[59] White parents "show strong . . . support for various voluntary desegregation techniques such as magnet schools," as do African-American parents.[60] Uncomfortable or dissatisfied with "forced busing," these scholars agree that "both mandatory and voluntary plans appear to contribute to the loss of white enrollment"[61] but believe that voluntary plans have greater promise. As Armor states, "Other than mandatory assignment, the only effective way to attract sizable numbers of white students to predominantly minority schools is to install magnet programs."[62]

The district court in Jenkins somewhat unartfully understood the educational lessons of the decades since Swann. District Judge Russell Clark believed that substantial white enrollment in the city's schools was necessary, both for the direct educational reasons liberals had pinned their hopes on, and for the indirect educational reason of ensuring stably adequate funding. He ordered the state to provide substantial funding for schools that would attract white students, both because they provided programs more attractive than those available elsewhere and because they had "state of the art" physical facilities.[63]

In the terms used by scholars of the desegregation process, the district judge's plan was voluntary, not mandatory. Of course it was financed by taxes that white parents had no choice about paying, but no white parent was told which school to send her or his children to. Increased investments in the city's schools provided incentives for white parents to select the city's schools over the suburbs'.[64]

From all the evidence, the district court had picked a program that would work. The city's schools were likely to attract more white students than any mandatory plan would, thereby making stably adequate funding more likely, even after the district court withdrew from supervision, and increasing the likelihood of the educational benefits thought to flow from interracial enrollments.

But, the Supreme Court said, the district judge went too far.[65] Why did the Court reject a program lacking the compulsion that had made "forced busing" so unpopular among whites, a program that seemed likely to guarantee biracial enrollments in the city's schools as Green contemplated?[66]

Legal doctrine alone could not have determined the outcome. Justice Souter's dissent made the legal realist response to the Court's holding that the district court improperly used a violation occurring within the city to order a remedy reaching outside its boundaries.[67] The issue, according to the Court's doctrine, was causation: a federal court could issue a remedy for harms caused by legal segregation.[68] The majority concluded that "white flight" was caused by desegregation, not by segregation.[69] Justice Souter made two points. First, he offered a narrow interpretation of causation.[70] Consider, he said, a parent with a child in the city's public schools just before the district court found them to be unconstitutionally segregated. The schools were in terrible condition, and "the cost of turning this shambles into habitable schools was enormous."[71] A parent concerned about the tax burden of rehabilitating the schools' physical condition "could well have decided that the inevitable cost of clean-up would produce an intolerable tax rate."[72] Was that parent's decision to move to the suburbs caused by segregation or by desegregation? "The distinction," Justice Souter wrote, "has no significance."[73]

Justice Souter acknowledged that this scenario might not accurately describe the process by which white parents decided to withdraw their children from the public schools.[74] He provided another, broader way of looking at the problem: "There is in fact no break in the chain of causation linking the effects of desegregation with those of segregation. There would be no desegregation orders and no remedial plans without prior unconstitutional segregation ... An adverse reaction to a desegregation order is traceable in fact to the segregation that is subject to the remedy."[75] This is standard legal-realist reasoning familiar to every first-year law student. Causation, we learn, is not a "fact" about the universe. It is instead a choice we make for policy or other reasons. When we select one point in the infinite causal chain linking the world together and say, "Before this point, no causation that the legal system needs to—or may—address, but after it, sufficient causation," we are making a choice that must be defended on policy or other grounds.

Perhaps there are such grounds available in Jenkins, but neither Chief Justice Rehnquist's majority opinion nor Justice Thomas's concurrence provides them. In particular, Justice Thomas's widely noted opinion, castigating the district court and by inference white liberals for their "willingness to assume that anything that is predominantly black must be inferior,"[76] focused on the district court's findings regarding the inadequate education provided in the city's schools. Those findings, according to Justice Thomas, relied on "the theory that black students suffer an unspecified psychological harm from segregation that retards their mental and educational development," a theory that "rests on an assumption of black inferiority."[77] I am inclined to think that Justice Thomas is right about that proposition, at least when stated in its broadest form. African-American students surely can learn as much, in a cognitive sense at least, without white students as with them.

Justice Souter's dissent showed that the result in Jenkins was not compelled by existing doctrine, and the majority did not provide adequate policy reasons for the choice it made among available definitions of causation.[78] For the Court's majority Jenkins was a school desegregation case in which an overly aggressive federal judge pushed beyond the limits of his authority. It did not matter that the case did not involve forced busing, the issue that had propelled opposition to desegregation orders for twenty years. It did not matter that the case did involve a program that used incentives rather than coercion to produce schools likely to have substantial numbers of white and African-American students. It did not matter, in short, that Jenkins involved a desegregation plan that might actually work.

What, then, accounts for the outcome? I can imagine ingenious defenses of the majority decision. In the end, however, the answer historians will give seems likely to be, "The Court agreed with a majority of white Americans: "We've done enough,' the justices said."[79]

Notes

1. The "we've done enough" theory is no more than a particular version of the argument pioneered by Derrick Bell, Brown v. Board of Education and the Interest-Convergence Dilemma, 93 Harv. L. Rev. 518 (1980). I should add that in writing this essay I have often inadvertently thought of the theory as the "we've had enough" theory, and I do not disclaim the accuracy of such a recharacterization.
2. The Civil Rights Cases, 109 U.S. 3 (1883).
3. Id. at 25.
4. Id.
5. Missouri v. Jenkins, 115 S. Ct. 2038 (1995).
6. Id. at 2051.
7. Brown v. Board of Educ., 347 U.S. 483 (1954).
8. Jenkins v. Missouri, 593 F. Supp. 1485 (W.D. Mo. 1984).
9. The district court's order is unreported, but is quoted in Jenkins, 115 S. Ct. at 2043–44. The Supreme Court has defined "magnet schools" as "public schools of voluntary enrollment designed to promote integration by drawing students away from their neighborhoods and private schools through distinctive curricula and high quality." Missouri v. Jenkins, 495 U.S. 33, 40 n.6 (1990).
10. Milliken v. Bradley, 418 U.S. 717 (1974). For the Court's criticism of the district court's order, see Jenkins, 115 S. Ct. at 2052.
11. Jenkins, 115 S. Ct. at 2052.
12. Id. at 2052–53.
13. Id. at 2051.
14. For an overview of the social and political history of school desegregation as of 1984, see Jennifer L. Hochschild, The New American Dilemma: Liberal Democracy and School Desegregation (1984).
15. Brown v. Board of Educ., 347 U.S. 483, 495 (1954).
16. Id. at 494.
17. At the oral argument in Brown, for example, Thurgood Marshall argued that segregation "produced . . . inevitable inequalities in physical facilities." Mark V. Tushnet, Making Civil Rights Law: Thurgood Marshall and the Supreme Court, 1936–1961, at 175 (1994).
18. Sweatt v. Painter, 339 U.S. 629 (1950). The Supreme Court directed the desegregation of the University of Texas's Law School, finding that the state's creation of a new, small school for African-Americans did not satisfy the equality component of the "separate but equal" doctrine.
19. Id. at 634.
20. The lower court findings are summarized in Brown, 354 U.S. at 486 n.1; see also Sweatt, 339 U.S. at 492 n.9.
21. An ingenious demonstration of the point is made by Wenona Y. Whitfield, Brown v. Board of Education: A Substitute Opinion, 20 South. Ill. U. L.J. 15 (1995), proposing a form of relief to the plaintiffs in Brown that would not have required rejection of the "separate but equal" doctrine: assignment of all African-American children to previously white schools, and white children to previously African-American schools. No one in

1954 seriously proposed this remedy because no one took seriously the claim that the separate schools were in fact equal.

22. Brown, 347 U.S. at 493–94.

23. For speculation that the white South would have accepted a decision requiring substantially increased investment in African-American schools with less resistance than it threw up against Brown, see L. Michael Seidman, Brown and Miranda, 80 Cal. L. Rev. 673 (1992).

24. Green v. County Sch. Bd. of New Kent County, 391 U.S. 430 (1968).

25. Green was the Court's first extended confrontation with Southern resistance to desegregation, resistance that had produced a situation in which the degree of desegregation in the deep South was minuscule, and in the upper South was little more than "token." For a description of the limited impact of Brown, see Gerald N. Rosenberg, The Hollow Hope: Can Courts Bring About Social Change 42–54 (1991) (providing a statistical analysis of Southern integration rates for the two decades after Brown).

26. Swann v. Charlotte-Mecklenburg Bd. of Educ., 402 U.S. 1 (1971).

27. Id. at 26 (discussing exacting scrutiny courts should use when proposed integration plan results in one-race schools).

28. See Theodore H. White, The Making of a President: 1968, at 137–38 (1969).

29. See Alexander v. Holmes County Bd. of Educ., 396 U.S. 19 (1969).

30. See Joan Hoff, Richard M. Nixon, in 3 Encyclopedia of the Am. Presidency 1081, 1084 (Leonard W. Levy & Louis Fisher eds., 1994).

31. For an overview of civil rights policy through the Nixon administration, see Hugh D. Graham, The Civil Rights Era: Origins and Development of National Policy, 1960–1972 (1990) (discussing national civil rights policy through three Presidents' administrations).

32. The four were Chief Justice Warren Burger and Justices Harry A. Blackmun, Lewis F. Powell, and William H. Rehnquist.

33. In addition to Swann, the most important cases were Dayton Bd. of Educ. v. Brinkman, 433 U.S. 406 (1977), after remand, 443 U.S. 526 (1979), and Columbus Bd. of Educ. v. Penick, 443 U.S. 449 (1979).

34. The Court's most consistent adherents to Swann were Justices William F. Brennan and Thurgood Marshall. They could ordinarily count on Justice Byron R. White to agree with them, and sometimes Justice Potter Stewart would agree as well. Justice John Paul Stevens typically provided the fifth vote. See, e.g., Dayton Bd. of Educ. v. Brinkman, 443 U.S. 526 (1979); Keyes v. School Dist. No. 1, Denver, Colo., 413 U.S. 189 (1973).

35. David Armor, Forced Justice: School Desegregation and the Law 102 (1995) (describing one version of the argument). Armor also describes, and criticizes, other versions, but I believe the one quoted in the text is the most plausible.

36. Id. at 103–06.

37. The term stably is important to this formulation. As a matter of abstract theory, courts could presumably permanently oversee educational taxation and expenditures. As a practical matter, however, they will not do so. When they withdraw from supervision, stably adequate funding must continue. When schools have substantial numbers of white students, they will receive adequate funding. And when they are attractive enough to continue to enroll substantial numbers of white students, their funding will be stable. The idea here is that the district court's requirement of substantial additional funding would produce an "equilibrium" resulting in permanently adequate funding as the schools attracted more white students, thereby allowing the court to lift its orders directing additional funding.

38. One sometimes runs across skepticism that funding has much relation to education, but I doubt that even the skeptics vote with their pocketbooks in a manner consistent with their skepticism: Consider two private schools charging the same tuition and using the same educational philosophy, one with a large endowment and one with none at all. As a result, per-student expenditures at the first school are much higher than those at the second. Suppose it takes an extra hour each day to get to the better-endowed school. How many of those who deride throwing money at schools would send their children to the school without an endowment, on the ground that the educational benefits from the extra expenditures did not offset the inconvenience of the additional travel? The Court somewhat grudgingly conceded that it was "certainly theoretically possible that the greater the expenditure per pupil . . ., the more likely it is that some unknowable number of nonminority students not presently attending schools in the [city] will choose to enroll in those schools." Missouri v. Jenkins, 115 S. Ct. 2038, 2054 (1995); see also Armor, supra note 35, at 207. Armor concludes that white parents use "a personal cost-benefit model of community support for school desegregation techniques," which explains the effectiveness of magnet programs.

39. Perhaps there are better ways to use the money the district court ordered invested in schools to improve the condition of African Americans. There is essentially no reason to believe, however, that anyone was going to do so. The money used for the schools might have been left in taxpayers' hands, or it might have been used for other

programs, but it seems massively unlikely that it would have been used to improve public assistance programs in Missouri's cities, for example.

40. Brown v. Board of Educ., 347 U.S. 483 (1954).
41. Green v. County Sch. Bd. of New Kent County, 391 U.S. 430 (1968).
42. Id. at 442.
43. Swann v. Charlotte-Mecklenburg Bd. of Educ., 402 U.S. 1 (1971).
44. Id. at 25.
45. Id. at 31.
46. San Antonio Indep. Sch. Dist. v. Rodriguez, 411 U.S. 1 (1973).
47. Id. at 56–58.
48. Milliken v. Bradley, 418 U.S. 717 (1974). Justice Thurgood Marshall's dissent foretold the difficulties the decision would create:

> Desegregation is not and was never expected to be an easy task. Racial attitudes ingrained in our Nation's childhood and adolescence are not quickly thrown aside in its middle years. But just as the inconvenience of some cannot be allowed to stand in the way of the rights of others, so public opposition, no matter how strident, cannot be permitted to divert this Court from the enforcement of the constitutional principles at issue in this case. Today's holding, I fear, is more a reflection of a perceived public mood that we have gone far enough in enforcing the Constitution's guarantee of equal justice than it is the product of neutral principles of law. In the short run, it may seem to be the easier course to allow our great metropolitan areas to be divided up each into two cities—one white, the other black—but it is a course, I predict, our people will ultimately regret.

Id. at 814–15 (Marshall, J., dissenting).
49. Missouri v. Jenkins, 115 S. Ct. at 2061 (Thomas, J., concurring).
50. For a description of one of the most highly publicized controversies, see Robert A. Dentler & Marvin B. Scott, Schools on Trial: An Inside Account of the Boston Desegregation Case (1981) (describing controversy over busing in Boston, Massachusetts).
51. See Armor, supra note 35, at 67 (quoting U.S. Commission on Civil Rights Report stating, "Negro children who attend predominantly Negro schools do not achieve as well as other children, Negro and white.").
52. See id. at 69–71 (summarizing studies and concluding that there is "a lack of consistent research findings").
53. See id. at 114 (concluding summary of studies with statement, "To the extent that desegregation can improve educational achievement and race relations, most desegregation experts might agree that benefits are optimized if desegregation is voluntary . . .").
54. Green v. County Sch. Bd. of New Kent County, 391 U.S. 430, 439–41 (1968) (holding that a desegregation plan may take any form so long as the plan effectively eliminates segregated schools).
55. See Armor, supra note 35, at 182 (summarizing study concluding that voluntary magnet plans produced more interracial exposure, and equivalent racial balance, over the long run compared to mandatory plans).
56. Put another way, the significance of race would be reduced in the eyes of white parents by the availability of high quality education in desegregated schools.
57. See Armor, supra note 35, at 176–78 (summarizing studies and concluding that "the white flight rate is lower in voluntary plans than in mandatory plans").
58. Id. at 182.
59. Christine H. Rossell, The Carrot or the Stick For School Desegregation Policy: Magnet Schools or Forced Busing 182 (1990).
60. Armor, supra note 35, at 203–04.
61. Id. at 193.
62. Id. at 223. Somewhat inconsistently, Armor expresses concern that court orders like that in Jenkins somehow make it less likely that states will spend the money required to make magnet school programs work. "With many states facing significant budget shortages and deficits," Armor writes, "education funding is in fierce competition with other state priorities . . . In this climate, obtaining or maintaining funds for a desegregation program without clear and concrete educational advantages can be very difficult." Id. at 225. Nowhere in Armor's book does he expressly state that magnet programs do not provide clear and concrete educational advantages. His expressed concern about the Jenkins order is that it might lead states to be "justifiably worried that, if they volunteer to fund some type of desegregation program, a court may later force them to spend much more than they had planned." Id. The Jenkins order, however, rested on an uncontested finding that the state had violated its obligation to desegregate after Brown, not that it had inadequately funded a desegregation effort. Armor—a social scientist who has testified on behalf of school systems seeking relief from court-ordered desegregation plans—does not explain how the concerns he describes would be legally justifiable.
63. See Missouri v. Jenkins, 115 S. Ct. 2038, 2044–45 (1995) (describing district court orders).

64. See id. at 2050–51 (describing district court's theory of "desegregative attractiveness").

65. Id. at 2051.

66. See supra text accompanying notes 41–42.

67. Jenkins, 115 S. Ct. at 2073, 2083–91 (Souter, J., dissenting).

68. See, e.g., id. at 2052 ("What we meant . . . by an interdistrict violation was a violation that caused segregation between adjoining districts.").

69. Id. at 2052.

70. Id. at 2086 (Souter, J., dissenting).

71. Id.

72. Id.

73. Id.

74. He offered a second, parallel scenario involving parents anticipating desegregation who created private schools for their children because they concluded that taxpayers would not continue to fund the city's schools at acceptable levels, and similarly acknowledged the uncertainties associated with that scenario. Id.

75. Id. at 2085.

76. Id. at 2061 (Thomas, J., concurring).

77. Id. at 2062.

78. The dissent also criticized the majority for reaching out to discuss the underlying remedial orders when the Court had granted review on only two aspects of the case, and had earlier denied review when the state sought to challenge the underlying orders. Id. at 2075–78 (Souter, J., dissenting).

79. This conclusion, in the words of my colleague, J. Clay Smith, Jr., "may challenge the premises of Charles Hamilton Houston and Thurgood Marshall's advocacy, that African-Americans should have and maintain faith in the courts as racism continues to grow in the country. Ultimately, it will be determined whether "enough' is too little." (personal communication made to the author).

7

Affirmative Action as a Majoritarian Device
Or, Do You Really Want to be a Role Model?

Richard Delgado

Have you ever noticed how affirmative action occupies a place in our system of law and politics far out of proportion to its effects in the real world? Liberals love talking about and sitting on committees that define, oversee, defend, and give shape to it.[1] Conservatives are attached to the concept for different reasons: they can rail against it, declare it lacking in virtue and principle, and use it to rally the troops.[2] Affirmative action is something they love to hate. The program also generates a great deal of paper, conversation, and jobs—probably more of the latter for persons of the majority persuasion than it has for its intended beneficiaries. Yet, despite its rather meager accomplishments and dubious lineage, a number of us have jumped on the bandwagon,[3] maybe because it seemed one of the few that would let us on.

But should we? Lately, I have been having doubts, as have other writers of color.[4] In this essay I examine several of the reasons why. First, I address some doubts about affirmative action generally. Then I focus on the role model argument, a component of affirmative action that until recently has received less scrutiny than it deserves.[5] I explain the majority group's attraction to the role model argument, but urge professionals of color to reject that approach in favor of other, more liberating relations between themselves and their communities.

I. The Affirmative Action Mystique: Let the Bandwagon Roll Right on

Scholars of color have grown increasingly skeptical about both the way in which affirmative action frames the issue of minority representation and the effects that it produces in the world. Affirmative action, I have noticed, generally frames the question of minority representation in an interesting way: Should we as a society admit, hire, appoint, or promote some designated number of people of color in order to promote certain policy goals, such as social stability, an expanded labor force, and an integrated society?[6] These goals are always forward-looking; affirmative action is viewed as an instrumental device for moving society from state *A* to state *B*.[7] The concept is neither backward-looking nor rooted in history; it is teleological rather than deontological.[8] Minorities are hired or promoted not because we have been unfairly treated, denied jobs, deprived of our lands, or beaten and brought here in chains.[9] Affirmative action neatly diverts our attention from all those disagreeable details and calls for a fresh start.[10] Well, where are we now? So many Chicano bankers and chief executive officers, so many black lawyers, so many Native American engineers, and so many women physicians. What can we do to increase these numbers over the next ten or twenty years? The system thus bases inclusion of people of color on principles of social utility, not reparations or *rights*. When those in power decide the goal has been accomplished, or is incapable of being reached, what logically happens? Naturally, the program stops.[11] At best, then, affirmative action serves as a homeostatic device, assuring that only a small number of women and people of color are hired or promoted.[12] Not too many, for that would be terrifying, nor too few, for that would be destabilizing. Just the right small number, generally those of us who need it least, are moved ahead.[13]

Affirmative action also neatly frames the issue so that even these small accomplishments seem troublesome, requiring great agonizing and gnashing of teeth. Liberals and moderates lie awake at night, asking how far they can take this affirmative action thing without sacrificing innocent white males.[14] Have you ever wondered what that makes *us*—if not innocent, then . . .? Affirmative action enables members of the dominant group to ask, "Is it fair to hire a less-qualified Chicano or black over a more-qualified white?"[15] This is a curious way of framing the question, as I will argue in a moment, in part because those who ask it are themselves the beneficiaries of history's largest affirmative action program. This fact is rarely noticed, however, while the question goes on causing the few of us who are magically raised by affirmative action's unseen hand to feel guilty, undeserving, and *stigmatized*.[16]

Affirmative action, as currently understood and promoted, is also ahistorical. For more than 200 years, white males benefited from their own program of affirmative action, through unjustified preferences in jobs and education resulting from old-boy networks and official laws that lessened the competition.[17] Today's affirmative action critics never characterize that scheme as affirmative action, which of course it was. By labeling problematic, troublesome, and ethically agonizing a paltry system that helps a few of us get ahead, critics neatly take our eyes off the system of arrangements that brought and maintained them in power, and enabled them to develop the rules and standards of quality and merit that now exclude us, make us appear unworthy, dependent (naturally) on affirmative action.

Well, if you were a member of the majority group and invented something that cut down the competition, made you feel good and virtuous, made minorities grateful and humble, and framed the "minority problem" in this wondrous way, I think you would be pretty pleased with yourself. Moreover, if you placed the operation of this program in the hands of the very people who brought about the situation that made it necessary in the first place, society would probably reward you with prizes and honors.

Please do not mistake what I am saying. As marginalized people we should strive to increase our power, cohesiveness, and representation in all significant areas of society.[18] We should do this, though, because we are entitled to these things and because fundamental fairness requires this reallocation of power. We should reformulate the issue. Our acquiescence in treating it as "a question of standards" is absurd and self-defeating when you consider that we took no part in creating those standards and their fairness is one of the very things we want to call into question.[19]

Affirmative action, then, is something no self-respecting attorney of color ought to support. We could, of course, take our own program, with our own goals, our own theoretical grounding, and our own managers and call it "Affirmative Action." But we would, of course, be talking about something quite different. My first point, then, is that we should demystify, interrogate, and destabilize affirmative action. The program was designed by others to promote their purposes, not ours.[20]

II. The Role Model Argument

In this section, I address an aspect of affirmative action mythology, the role model argument, that in my opinion has received less criticism than it deserves.[21] This argument is a special favorite of moderate liberals, who regard it as virtually unassailable.[22] Although the argument's inventor is unknown, its creator must have been a member of the majority group and must have received a prize almost as large as the one awarded the person who created affirmative action itself. Like the larger program of which it is a part, the role model argument is instrumental and forward-looking. It makes us a means to another's end.[23] A white-dominated institution hires you not because you are entitled to or deserve the job. Nor is the institution seeking to set things straight because your ancestors and others of your heritage were systematically excluded from such jobs. Not at all. You're hired (if you speak politely, have a neat haircut, and, above all, can be trusted) not because of your accomplishments, but because of what others think you will do for them. If they hire you now and you are a good role model, things will be better in the next generation.[24]

Suppose you saw a large sign saying, "ROLE MODEL WANTED. GOOD PAY. INQUIRE WITHIN." Would you apply? Let me give you five reasons you should not.

Reason Number One. Being a role model is a tough job, with long hours and much heavy lifting.[25] You are expected to uplift your entire people. Talk about hard, sweaty work![26]

Reason Number Two. The job treats you as a means to an end. Even your own constituency may begin to see you this way. "Of course Tanya will agree to serve as our faculty advisor, give this speech, serve on that panel, or agree to do us X, Y, or Z favor, probably unpaid and on short notice. What is her purpose if not to serve us?"[27]

Reason Number Three. The role model's job description is monumentally unclear. If highway workers or tax assessors had such unclear job descriptions, they would strike. If you are a role model, are you expected to do the same things your white counterpart does, in addition to counseling and helping out the community of color whenever something comes up?[28] Just the latter? Half and half? Both? On your own time, or on company time?[29] No supporter of the role model argument has ever offered satisfactory answers to these questions.

Reason Number Four. To be a good role model, you must be an assimilationist,[30] never a cultural or economic nationalist, separatist, radical reformer, or anything remotely resembling any of these. As with actual models (who walk down runways wearing the latest fashions), you are expected to conform to prevailing ideas of beauty, politeness, grooming, and above all responsibility. If you develop a quirk, wrinkle, aberration, or, heaven forbid, a vice, look out![31] I have heard more than once that a law school would not hire X for a teaching position because, although X might be a decent scholar and good classroom teacher, he was a little exuberant or rough around the edges and thus not good role model material. Not long ago, Margaret Court, the ex-tennis star and grand dame of English tennis officialdom, criticized Martina Navratilova as a poor role model for young tennis players.[32] Martina failed Court's assessment not because she served poorly, wore a wrinkled tennis uniform, displayed bad sportsmanship, or argued with the referees. Rather, in Court's opinion, Martina was not "straight," not "feminine" enough, and so could not serve as a proper role model.[33] Our white friends always want us to model behavior that will encourage our students and proteges to adopt majoritarian social mores; you never hear of them hiring one of their number because he or she is bilingual, wears dashikis, or is in other ways like us.

Reason Number Five (the most important one). The job of role model requires that you *lie*—that you tell not little, but big, whopping lies, and that is bad for your soul. Suppose I am sent to an inner city school to talk to the kids and serve as role model of the month. I am *expected* to tell the kids that if they study hard and stay out of trouble, they can become a law professor like me.[34] That, however, is a very big lie: a whopper. When I started teaching law sixteen years ago, there were about thirty-five Hispanic law professors, approximately twenty-five of which were Chicano. Today, the numbers are only slightly improved.[35] In the interim, however, a nearly complete turnover has occurred. The faces are new, but the numbers have remained the same from year to year.[36] Gonzalez leaves teaching; Velasquez is hired somewhere else. Despite this, I am expected to tell forty kids in a crowded, inner city classroom that if they work hard, they can each be among the chosen twenty-five.[37] Fortunately, most kids are smart enough to figure out that the system does not work this way. If I were honest, I would advise them to become major league baseball players, or to practice their hook shots. As Michael Olivas points out, the odds, pay, and working conditions are much better in these other lines of work.[38]

Recently, the California Postsecondary Commission, concerned about the fate of minorities in the state's colleges and universities,[39] had its statisticians compile a projection for all young blacks starting public school in California that year. That number was about 35,000. Of these, the statisticians estimated that about one half would graduate from high school, the rest having dropped out. Of those completing high school, approximately one out of nine would attend a four-year college. Of that number, about 300 would earn a bachelor's degree. You can form your own estimate of how many of this group, which began as 35,000, will continue on to earn a law degree. Thirty? Fifty? And of these, how many will become law professors? My guess is one, at most. But I may be an optimist.[40]

Suppose I told the ghetto kids these things, that is, the truth. And, while I am at it, told them about diminishing federal and state scholarship funds that formerly enabled poor kids to go to college,[41] about the special threat to assistance for minority college students,[42] and about a climate of increasing hostility, slurs, and harassment on the nation's campuses.[43] Suppose I told them, in short, what the system is really like, how the deck is stacked against them. What would happen? I would quickly be labeled a poor role model and someone else sent to give the inspiring speech next month.

III. Why Things are the Way They are and What can be Done

The role model theory is a remarkable invention. It requires that some of us lie and that others of us be exploited and overworked. The theory is, however, highly functional for its inventors. It encourages us to cultivate nonthreatening behavior in our own people. In addition, it provides a handy justification for affirmative action, which, as I have pointed out, is at best a mixed blessing for communities of color.

As with any successful and popular program, I think we need only examine the functions served by the role model argument to see why our white friends so readily embrace it. Demographers tell us that in about ten years, Caucasians will cease to be the largest segment of California's population.[44] In approximately sixty years, around the year 2050, the same will happen nationally.[45] While this radical demographic shift is occurring, the population also will be aging.[46] The baby boomers, mostly white, will be retired and dependent on social security for support.[47] These retirees will rely on the continuing labor of a progressively smaller pyramid of active workers, an increasing proportion of them of color. You see, then, why it is essential that we imbue our next generation of children with the requisite respect for hard work. They must be taught to ask few questions, pay their taxes, and accept social obligations, even if imposed by persons who look different from them and who committed documented injustices on their ancestors.[48]

If you want the job of passing on *that* set of attitudes to young people of color, go ahead. You will be warmly received and amply rewarded. But you do not have to be a role model. You can do other more honorable, authentic things. You can be a mentor.[49] You can be an "organic intellectual,"[50] offering analysis and action programs for our people. You can be a matriarch, a patriarch, a legend, or a provocateur.[51] You can be a socially committed professional who marches to your own drummer. You can even be yourself. But to the ad, ROLE MODEL WANTED, the correct answer, in my view, is: NOT ME!

Notes

1. Almost every major law review has devoted space to the treatment, usually sympathetic and from a liberal standpoint, of affirmative action. *See, e.g.,* sources noted in Delgado, *The Imperial Scholar: Reflections on a Review of Civil Rights Literature,* 132 U. PA. L. Rev. 561, 562 n.3 (1984); *see also* L. Tribe, American Constitutional Law 1521–44, 1565–71 (2d ed. 1988) (discussion of affirmative action, or "benign" classification, in areas of race and sex).

2. *See e.g.,* Abram, *Affirmative Action: Fair Shakers and Social Engineers,* 99 Harv. L. Rev. 1312 (1986); Graglia, *Special Admission of the "Culturally Deprived" to Law School,* 119 U. PA. L. Rev. 351 (1970); *see also* Carter, *The Best Black and Other Tales,* Reconstruction, Winter 1990, at 6 (middle-of-the-road criticism of affirmative action as psychologically deleterious to its purported beneficiaries).

3. Some writers of color who have supported affirmative action are cited in Delgado, *supra* note 1, at 576 n.76; *see also* Leonard, *A Step Toward Equality: Affirmative Action and Equal Employment Opportunity,* 4 Black L.J. 214 (1974).

4. *E.g.,* D. Bell, And We Are Not Saved: The Elusive Quest for Racial Justice 140–61 (1987); Carter, *supra* note 2; Delgado, Book Review, *Derrick Bell and the Ideology of Racial Reform: Will We Ever Be Saved?,* 97 Yale L.J. 923, 923–24, 933 (1988).

5. The role model argument, in simplest form, holds that affirmative action is justified in order to provide communities of color with exemplars of success, without which they might conclude that certain social roles and professional opportunities are closed to them. Role models are expected to communicate to their communities

that opportunities are indeed available and that hard work and perseverance will be rewarded. *See* Kennedy, *Persuasion and Distrust: A Comment on the Affirmative Action Debate*, 99 Harv. L. Rev. 1327, 1329 (citing as benefits of affirmative action "the expansion of a professional class able to pass . . . elevated aspirations to subsequent generations" and "teaching whites that blacks, too, are capable of handling responsibility."). *But see* Wygant v. Jackson Bd. of Educ., 416 U.S. 267, 274–76 (1986) (plurality opinion) (rejecting role modeling as justification for racial classifications protecting minority teachers against disproportionate layoffs).

Recently, the issue of role modeling was brought to the fore when Derrick Bell, a prominent African-American law professor, took unpaid leave from his position at Harvard because of the school's refusal to hire a black woman professor. *See* Markoff, *Action of Harvard's Prof. Bell Focuses Attention on Diversity*, Natl. L.J., May 7, 1990, at 4. Bell, the country's most noted black law professor, left his position in part because of his growing realization that he could not serve as an adequate role model for black women law students.

6. I discuss this cheerful, forward-looking perspective in Delgado, *supra* note 1, at 569–71. Lyndon Johnson created affirmative action when he issued Executive Order 11,246 on September 24, 1965, during a period of intense racial turmoil. Exec. Order No. 11,246, 30 Fed. Reg. 12,319 (1965). For cases and materials relating to its early implementation, see J. Jones, W. Murphy & R. Belton, Discrimination in Employment 587–683, 989–1012 (5th ed. 1987). For interpretive discussion of affirmative action's role in maintaining white ascendancy, see *infra* text accompanying notes 10–17 and sources cited therein.

7. Delgado, *supra* note 1, at 570 ("The past becomes irrelevant; one just asks where things are now and where we ought to go from here, a straightforward social-engineering inquiry of the sort that law professors are familiar with and good at.").

8. *Id.* (forward-looking perspective avoids need to dwell on "unpleasant matters like lynch mobs, segregated bathrooms, Bracero programs, or professional schools that, until recently, were lily white").

9. See Delgado, *supra* note 4, at 934–41 for a brief description. For a longer treatment, see L. Higginbotham, In the Matter of Color (1978).

10. Delgado, *supra* note 1, at 569–70. For the view that this future-oriented approach is, in fact, desirable, see Sullivan, *The Supreme Court, 1985 Term—Comment: Sins of Discrimination: Last Term's Affirmative Action Cases*, 100 Harv. L. Rev. 78 (1986). For the contrary view that affirmative action *is* based on making amends for past injustices or providing a "level playing field," see Sher, *Justifying Reverse Discrimination*, in Equality and Preferential Treatment 49 (1977).

11. Delgado, *supra* note 1, at 570 ("Moreover, what if the utility calculus changes in the future, so that the programs no longer appear 'useful' to the majority? Can society then ignore those who still suffer the effects of past discrimination?").

12. Delgado, *supra* note 4, at 923–24 (attributing this general view to Derrick Bell, whose "interest-convergence" approach to racial jurisprudence has revolutionized critical thought on matters of race). For discussion of "interest convergence" see Bell, Brown v. Board of Education *and the Interest-Convergence Dilemma*, 93 Harv. L. Rev. 518 (1980).

13. *See* D. Bell, *supra* note 4, at 140–61.

14. *See* Sullivan, *supra* note 10, at 91–96 (arguing that sin-based approach to affirmative action causes this problem).

15. For a poignant recounting of a talented black's encounter with this attitude, see Carter, *supra* note 2.

16. *See id.*; Kennedy, *Racial Critiques of Legal Academia*, 102 Harv. L. Rev. 1745, 1795–96, 1801–07, 1817–18 (1989).

17. Delgado, *Approach-Avoidance in Law School Hiring: Is the Law a WASP?*, 34 St. Louis U. L.J. 631, 639 (1990).

18. For a discussion of whether the dominant group will ever peaceably allow this to happen to any significant extent, see Delgado, *supra* note 4, at 942–45.

19. On the absurdity of using current standards to judge challenges to those very standards, see Delgado, *When A Story Is Just a Story: Does Voice Really Matter?*, 76 Va. L. Rev. 95, 100–02 (1990); Delgado, *Brewer's Plea: Critical Thoughts On Common Cause*, 44 Vand. L. Rev. 1, 8–10 (1991) [hereinafter *Brewer's Plea*].

20. *See supra* text accompanying notes 6–18 (Affirmative action is soothing, limiting, and therapeutic for whites but psychologically and materially injurious to populations of color.).

21. The term is defined *supra* note 5.

22. The argument is unanswerable only in a factual sense: common-sense understandings of human nature hold that persons tend to emulate successful individuals who are like themselves.

23. *See infra* notes 44–48 and accompanying text (speculating that role modeling, as currently understood, is aimed at perpetuating current social relations in the years ahead, when the demography of the United States will have radically changed).

24. In other words, the next generation of people of color will be like the industrious, well-mannered role model. *See infra* notes 44–48 and accompanying text.

25. For a dreary picture of such a life, see Delgado, *Minority Law Professors' Lives: The Bell-Delgado Survey*, 24 Harv. C.R.-C.L. L. Rev. 349, 369 (1989) (reporting survey results and concluding: "It is impossible to read the . . . returns without being acutely conscious of the pain and stress they reflect. Large numbers of minority law

professors are overworked, excluded from informal information networks and describe their work environment as hostile, unsupportive, or openly or subtly racist."); Pierce, *Unity in Diversity: Thirty-Three Years of Stress, Solomon Carter Fuller Lecture*, Am. Psychiatric Assn. Meeting, Wash., D.C. (May 12, 1986) (on file with author) (same).

26. Pierce, *supra* note 25, *see also* Brooks, *Life After Tenure: Can Minority Law Professors Avoid the Clyde Ferguson Syndrome?*, 20 U.S.F.L. Rev. 419 (1986) (overwork and overcommitment produce serious risk of early death for professionals of color in high-visibility positions).

27. *See* Delgado, *supra* note 25, at 360, 367–68.

28. *Id.* Most professors of color of my acquaintance do an inordinate amount of counseling, recruiting, and speaking on behalf of minority causes. *See also* Brooks, *supra* note 26.

29. On the time pressures minority professors of color labor under, see generally Delgado, *supra* note 25, at 355–56.

30. On assimilationism, see *Brewer's Plea, supra* note 19. On black nationalism and separatism, see D. Bell, *supra* note 4, at 215–35 and D. Bell, Race, Racism and American LAW 47–51 (2d ed. 1980).

31. On the intense scrutiny that role models encounter, see Brooks, *supra* note 26 and Delgado, *supra* note 25.

32. Downey, *She Succeeds As A Person, As An Athlete*, L.A. Times, July 16, 1990, at C1, col. 2.

33. *Id.* (hinting that Navratilova's alleged bisexuality disabled her from serving as a role model for aspiring female tennis players).

34. Most minority law professors of color (if we are honest) know we got our positions either by luck—by being in the right place at the right time—or as a result of student pressure and activism. This, of course, is *not* what our majority-race friends and supervisors want us to say to our proteges and communities.

35. Telephone interview with Michael Olivas, Professor of Law, University of Houston, Director, Institute of Higher Education Law and Governance (Sept. 1990). Professor Olivas is a member of various Association of American Law Schools and other professional committees that track the numbers of professors of color in law teaching. For current figures, see Lempinen, *A Student Challenge to the Old Guard*, Student Law., Sept. 1990, at 12, 15 (citing 1990 figure from Olivas of 51 Latino faculty members).

36. *See* Delgado, *supra* note 25, at 350–51 n. 7 (noting the high attrition and turnover rates of law professors of color).

37. This is, of course, mathematically impossible. Perhaps we are only expected to announce that *any given one* of the students could aspire to be in the circle of 25, or more modestly, could become *any* type of professor, or lawyer, or professional, or white-collar worker, or cler, or paralegal, or legal secretary, or. . . . But this would rob the role-model argument of any significance. It would also leave unexplained why sending a Chicano legal assistant (not a law professor) would not do.

38. Interview with Michael Olivas, *supra* note 35. Olivas has recounted this story to several professional groups and committees, where it has always been greeted with dismay. The message is clear. Even if true, one should not say such things!

39. Address by Manning Marable, University of Colorado (Sept. 1990), reporting apparently unpublished results of the Commission's survey. *See Why All the Dropouts?* (editorial), L.A. Times, Dec. 27, 1985, Part II, at 4, col. 1.

40. The future looks grim especially given that these dismal statistics came from California, our most populous, most ethnically diverse, and possibly most progressive state.

41. *See Making College More Costly: Tighter Loan Rules Will Squeeze Schools, Parents and Students*, Time, Mar. 23, 1981, at 89 (working- and middle-class families hard hit by decreases in federal scholarship and loan aid).

42. On the cutback of tutoring and other support services for disadvantaged students that is occurring nationwide see Marriott, *Scholarships Aimed at Minorities Banned*, Denver Post, Dec. 12, 1990, at 1, col. 4.

43. For a survey of some of the more notorious incidents, see Delgado, *Campus Antiracism Rules: Constitutional Narratives in Collision*, 85 NW. U. L. Rev. 343 (1991).

44. Several national magazines have covered the increasing influence of nonwhite cultures on American society, *e.g., A Surging New Spirit*, Time, July 11, 1988, at 46 (growing Hispanic population and changes it is producing in national culture).

45. Marable, *supra* note 39; *cf.* Barringer, *census shows Profound Changes in Racial Makeup of the Nation*, N.Y. Times, Mar. 11, 1991, at A1, col. 1 (regional and ethnic group analysis of changes in U.S. population based on latest census).

46. *See* DeMott, *New Look at the Elderly*, Time, Feb. 18, 1985, at 81; Hornblower, *Gray Power!*, Time, Jan. 4, 1988, at 36.

47. *See* sources cited *supra* note 46.

48. *See* Delgado, *supra* note 4, at 935–41. For an arresting account of Native Americans' fate at the hands of the early U.S. political-legal system, see R. Williams, the American Indian in Western Legal thought: The Discourses of Conquest 227–323 (1990).

49. *I.e.* one who tells aspiring young persons of color *truthfully* what it is like to practice your profession in a society dominated by race.

50. Attributed to Italian Criticalist Antonio Gramsci, the term refers to a people's intellectual who operates in a nonhierarchical fashion and places his or her talents at the service of social reform.
51. In recent times, the most inspired (and maligned) example of most of these things is Derrick Bell, whose imaginative chronicles and acts of nonviolent resistance at Harvard (including a sit-in in his own office and, later, teaching his own classes while on unpaid leave) have galvanized us all.

8

Critical Race Theory and Interest Convergence in the Backlash Against Affirmative Action
Washington State and Initiative 200

Edward Taylor

Washington state became yet another lost battleground in the national debate on affirmative action with its passage of Initiative 200 (November 1998), which promises to "end discrimination" by eliminating most forms of affirmative action. Washington thus follows in the footsteps of California and Texas, where the passage of Initiative 209 and the Hopwood decision, respectively, have resulted in much lower numbers of African American and Hispanic students in undergraduate and graduate programs and have reversed decades of affirmative action policy in state hiring.

How did Washington come to share national billing with such populous and ethnically diverse states as California and Texas as the next test case for the elimination of affirmative action? How is it that the spotlight should now be focused on this fairly small, relatively homogeneous state? Asking of this question leads to an even more central one: How is it that affirmative action, once the bulwark of liberalism and racial progress, is looking so frail?

This article is the result of my quest to understand not only the story of Initiative 200 (I-200), but to look at it as a useful metaphor for the failure of liberalism's promises. Critical examination of I-200 challenges both traditional liberalism and conservative calls for color blindness. It is also an opportunity to look at the backlash against affirmative action through the lens of a newer form of oppositional scholarship, called critical race theory. Critical race theory (CRT) uses a paradigm of racial realism to critique the incrementalism of liberalism and traditional civil rights programs. My purpose is to introduce some of the tenets of CRT into the national debate about affirmative action, in search of a cogent explanation for current trends and a road map toward resistance and hope, away from the impending reality of fatalism and despair. [. . .]

Washington State

Washington, unlike California or Texas, is neither particularly populous nor diverse. Of its 5.5 million residents, 82.2% are white (Washington State Higher Education Coordinating Board [HECB], 1997). Although there have been changes in demographic trends, none amount to seismic shifts. For the last decade, the American Indian population has been steady at 2% and the African American population at just over 3%. Asian/Pacific Islander and Hispanic groups have grown, from 4% or so to just over 6% each. In a parallel way, Washington's colleges and universities are fairly homogenous. At four-year institutions, whites make up 82% of students. The more rural state universities (such as Washington State University and Western Washington University) are 87% white (HECB, 1996). Undergraduate enrollments at community colleges are 19.3% ethnic minority, 80.7% white.

Washington has a racial history that, while far from ideal, is less virulent than many other states'. The first African Americans came to Seattle around the time of the Civil War (Taylor, 1994). Because they were excluded from the main industries of logging and shipbuilding by the labor unions, most job opportunities open to African Americans were menial in nature. But, ironically, there was far more racial antipathy directed toward Asian immigrants and American Indians than toward African Americans, in part because of the latter's low numbers. African Americans thus escaped the savage, organized violence prevalent in other parts of the United States and built a small but vigorous community. However, the progression of the twentieth century saw increasing residential and educational segregation and continued, severe economic hardships due to exclusionary employment practices. Washington, nonetheless, was relatively more racially tolerant than other places; for example, it was one of a handful of states that did not have antimiscegenation laws (Taylor, 1994).

The civil rights movement mobilized Washington's African American population, especially in Seattle, to seek equitable economic and educational opportunities by the use of marches, sit-ins, and boycotts. Outcomes of this activism included the reduction of racial barriers in labor unions, fairer employment practices, and a busing program that took African American students from the Central District to white, suburban schools (Taylor, 1994). Although busing programs have ended, in part because of contemporary objections by African American parents, a variety of affirmative action programs continue to operate.

Affirmative action programs in Washington include outreach programs in middle and high schools to encourage girls and ethnic minorities to participate in math and science, college mentorship programs targeting high schools with majority African American, Hispanic, and Asian enrollment, and training programs for those traditionally excluded from skilled trades. Affirmative action programs also help shape state hiring goals and provide opportunities for women and minority-owned businesses to receive city, county, and state contracts. For example, of the state's near 16,000 hirings over the past five years, 7% have been under affirmative action (Brune, 1998). Notably, nearly half of those were whites. In 1997, the state's "Plus Three" program, which adds three persons who qualify for affirmative action to the traditional list of seven applicants for state job openings, hired more white men than any minority group. Vietnam-era veterans, veterans with disabilities, and disabled persons all qualify for affirmative action programs, and in Washington, most of these people are white men. Thus under the "Plus Three" program, 48 white men, 45 white women, 40 African Americans, and 36 Asian Americans were hired (Brune, 1998).

Responsibility for issues regarding diversity in higher education rests with the Higher Education Coordinating Board (HECB). Beginning in 1987, the Board included in its master plan for higher education the goal of "establishing and implementing policies and practices that ensure the full participation of minorities in higher education programs as students, faculty, staff, and administrators" (1987, p. 36). As part of this plan, alternative standards for admissions were put into place. These standards allow access for students whose combined indices of grades and standardized test scores do not meet regular admissions criteria, and take into account issues of race, income, educational attainment of family members, and college preparation.

According to the Washington State Commission on African American Affairs (1995), white students are by far the greatest beneficiaries. In 1994, for example, 978 first-time freshmen (or 1.4% of a total of 70,883 undergraduates) were admitted under the alternative standards. Eighty percent were white.

Nor have policies aimed at increasing the diversity of college staff and faculty marked much change. People of color comprise 14.7% of staff at community colleges (1996) and 9.8% at four-year institutions, numbers that have not changed significantly since 1990. Whites comprise 90.8% at four-year institutions and 88.9% of faculty at community colleges, also consistent over this decade. Against this backdrop of modest policies and practices comes the "Washington State Civil Rights Initiative."

Initiative 200

Initiative 200 originated from the Center for Equal Opportunity, a conservative Washington, D.C.-based think tank. Modeled closely after California's Proposition 209, I-200 uses the language of civil rights. In full, the text reads:

> The state shall not discriminate against or grant preferential treatment to any individual or group on the basis of race, sex, color, ethnicity, or national origin in the operation of public employment, public education, or public contracting.[1]

With the financial support of Steve Forbes, former Republican presidential candidate, and buoyed by appearances by William Bennett, drug czar under President Bush, I-200 began collecting signatures to qualify for the ballot in 1997. The state Republican party contributed statewide mailings. Mr. Forbes gave $35,000 to the campaign, much of it in the three weeks before the January 2, 1998, deadline for signatures, and over $10,000 for radio ads primarily heard on KVI-AM. I-200 came to public consciousness by the efforts of John Carlson, a conservative talk show host at KVI-AM and chair of the I-200 campaign. Affirmative action became the daily subject for his radio call-in show. Management concerns about this "one-beat" programming (as well as low ratings) led to his ouster at KVI in February 1998 (Serrano, 1998).

I-200 came to national awareness with a *New York Times* story in December 1997 that chronicled the unusual experience of signature gatherers recruited by a firm hired by the I-200 campaign. African Americans from California and the Midwest had been offered bus fare, meals, motel expenses, and $600 a week to work on a "civil rights drive." Pro Mayes, from Rancho Tehama, California, said the recruiter came to his house and "brought my family a turkey for Thanksgiving" (Egan, 1997, p. A12). For many, it seemed like a good opportunity to earn Christmas money. Five African Americans, including one disabled woman and a homeless man, were bused to Seattle.

Problems arose as soon as they began work. "I was getting cursed at by people and having a lot of trouble getting signatures," said Arthur Tillis, of Chicago. "Then I finally read the thing real carefully and I said: Wait a minute. This is against affirmative action. It's not a civil rights thing like it says." Beverly Mosely of Milwaukee had a similar experience. "I got all the way to Seattle and they still wouldn't tell me what the initiative was all about. I'm out there with a clipboard and a couple of people came up to me and said, 'Do you know what you're doing?' I said yes. Getting signatures to keep affirmative action from being abolished. After reading it real carefully, then, let me tell you: I decided I would never sign something like this myself" (p. A12).

All left the state, broke and discouraged. "They wanted some black faces," said Tyrone Wells of Toledo, Ohio. "We were used." Mayes summed up his feelings: "You want to know what this whole thing really cost me? My pride. I was duped. And now I got nothing to bring home to my two kids."

According to the Sherry Bockwinkel, owner of the recruiting firm: "The only way they could be misled is if they can't read. Petitioners are motivated by money. They tend to be lazy. If they say they were misled, they are lying" (Egan, p. A12). Dee Jones, who hired the workers, said they were fired for failing to meet their quotas: "They wanted to do was sleep and treat this like a vacation" (Brune & Serrano, 1998, p. A1).

John Carlson, campaign manager and talk-show host, defended the use of African Americans. He said, "You want people who are known as 'horses,' people who can get the signatures, and get them fast. You don't want people with little or no experience of any race." He denied race was a factor in the petition drive and said that, although the ballot measure "deliberately borrows" language from the 1964 Civil Rights Act, it is not misleading. From his view, "This initiative will restore the moral principle of protecting all Americans from discrimination" (Egan, p. A12).

This "borrowed language" has been controversial. When Proposition 209 passed in California, exit polling showed that 28% of those who had voted in favor did not realize that 209 banned affirmative action (Foster, 1997). The American Civil Liberties Union went to the Thurston County Superior Court in Washington to have the words "affirmative action" added to the language of Initiative 200. The judge ruled against changing the language. The state attorney general's office, who wrote the title and text of the initiative, had decided to basically reflect the language that was in the ballot itself, "trusting that voters would make an informed choice if and when the time comes" and deliberately avoiding "loaded" terms, said James Pharris, senior assistant state attorney general (King, 1997, on-line).

A similar measure banning affirmative action in the city of Houston failed after Mayor Bob Lanier insisted that Proposition A be described as ending affirmative action. This choice of wording was believed to be a key factor in voters' rejection of Proposition A.

I-200, after obtaining the required 180,000 signatures, went to the Washington State Legislature. Without enough support (35 of 98 House members and 17 of 49 senators) to pass the initiative, it was referred to the November ballot as a referendum election ("Initiative Process," 1997) and approved by 58% of the voters. Buoyed by this success, national opponents of affirmative action plan to pursue similar ballot measures in Florida, Nebraska, and Michigan (Holmes, 1998).

Public Opinion

Like voters in California and Houston, Washington residents' opinion appeared to be language dependent. Early polls (conducted by *The Seattle Times*) found 64% of respondents in favor of I-200. Knowing that I-200 would eliminate affirmative action in state employment, contracting, and education, support dropped to 49% (Postman & Brune, 1998). Although 93% believed that racial discrimination still exists and 80% felt that bias against women was still a problem, 48% thought that affirmative action programs, while good in principle, needed to be reformed. There was a significant racial gap—55% of whites and 37% of minorities—initially in favor of the initiative.

When specific affirmative action programs were polled, the response ranged widely. Eighty-five percent supported programs encouraging girls and minorities in math and science, 62% favored the alternative admissions standards in higher education admissions, and 56% wanted to continue apprenticeship programs for those previously excluded from skilled trades. Only 44% defended set-asides for women and minorities in government contracting and 36% endorsed specific hiring goals for women and minorities (Postman & Brune, 1998). In sum, outreach (especially for white women) met with general approval; numeric goals were disliked.

How did the loss of affirmative action affect minority enrollment in colleges? At the University of Washington, for example, the number of minorities is already quite low, at 7.5% of entering freshmen. Passage of I-200 has resulted in about 40% fewer African Americans, 30% fewer Hispanics, and 20% fewer American Indians (Verhovek, 1999).

I-200 Through the Lens of CRT

To examine whether or not the case of I-200 provides supportive evidence for the central tenets of CRT, several issues must be addressed.

Racism as Normal

Charging racism is a volatile exercise, but much depends on how it is defined. The insistence "I'm not a racist" has become the defense de jour of even the most blatant of hate criminals. When racism is defined as specific, individual acts against persons of color, most whites can rightly deny this charge. They see themselves as good and fair people, not as members of a group that enjoys special, undeserved privileges. Such a perspective is distressing, and many whites react with defensiveness and withdrawal if confronted.

If, on the other hand, racism is defined as a political and social force that has benefited a certain group, through no single action on the part of individuals, the terms change. If those benefits include nonsegregated housing, employment opportunities reserved for persons of European ancestry, access to better schools, absence of organized racial violence, and protection from negative racial stereotyping, the net casts wide. Almost no white can reasonably claim to have avoided some of the privileges that are part and parcel of whiteness. Then the equation inverts. As Sleeter (1996) asserts, "I am a racist . . . because I benefit from racism" (p. 30).

Here, what is more important than attempting to prove widespread acts of racial discrimination against ethnic minorities in Washington state is examining the centrality, and invisibility, of white privilege. The problem in Washington is the multitude of benefits extended to the majority population by virtue of group membership—benefits enjoyed at the expense, and exclusion, of others. Yet few look at it that way.

Affirmative action programs attempt to widen some of this privilege base with women and people of color. But many perceive it as victimizing legitimate and honest people who are not personally guilty of racist acts. Ultimately, and as I-200 sees it, the protection of "innocent" whites from displacement is more important than the protection of ethnic minorities from long-standing, "normal," race-based exclusion. Although nearly all agree that racial and gender discrimination still exists, the imperative of protecting even a few blameless whites outweighs the importance of achieving access to groups previously (and presently) denied. Their innocence, both individual and collective, does not appear to factor in the decision making process for most whites.

As Crenshaw describes this dilemma (1988):

> . . . even when injustice is found, efforts to redress it must be balanced against, and limited by, competing interests of white workers—even when those interests were actually created by the subordination of Blacks. The innocence of whites weighs more heavily than do the past wrongs committed upon Blacks and the benefits that whites derived from these wrongs. (p. 1342)

Role of Social/Historic Context

Perhaps because of its relatively benign history, at least as compared to the South, Washington voters may be relying on a "things haven't been that bad here" theory. Thus the groundwork is laid for assumptions about equality in opportunities for jobs, contracts, and college preparation. The systemic ways in which the majority has favored its own in housing, employment, schooling, and contracting, to name a few, are not seen as aberrant or unjust.

The reasoning goes something like this: Although there is a history of racial and gender discrimination in Washington (that still exists), it is now time to end programs designed to reverse its effects. Affirmative action has been a useful tool to give women and minorities equal opportunity but is no longer needed. Such policies force employers to hire unqualified women and minorities over qualified white men (Postman & Brune, 1998).

I-200 guides the state into what Tushnet (1996) calls the "We've done enough" phase. He says that a common pattern in antidiscrimination law is that, after whites have one of their periodic outbursts of support for minorities, particularly African Americans, they eventually and inevitably decide to reverse themselves.

The "We've done enough" principle, although recently advanced by Initiative 200, is deeply rooted in our federal judiciary. During the Reconstruction period, in which African Americans lived in a fear-haunted limbo between slavery and freedom, Supreme Court Justice Bradley made the argument to end what he saw as the new favoritism enjoyed by African Americans:

> When a man has emerged from slavery, and by the aid of benefent legislation has shaken off the inseparable concomitants of that state, there must be some stage in the progress of this elevation when he takes the rank of a mere citizen, and ceases to be the favorite of the law.
>
> (1883, p. 25)

Narrative

The role narrative plays in Initiative 200 is dual. Notable is the absence of the voices of minorities or women and their experiences seeking college admissions, public employment, promotions, or public contracting. Second is the curious story of the African Americans recruited to gather signatures.

Stories wield influence—perhaps more than they should. Think scientifically, as the saying goes, act anecdotally. In the case against affirmative action, there is a story told of almost mythic proportions, of the son or daughter of a neighbor who did not get accepted into his or her college of choice because of minority set-asides. There is the report of the friend not hired by the school district because of "diversity needs," or the long-deserved promotion lost to someone less qualified. I-200 taps into such stories. Data-based evidence that affirmative action has largely benefited whites seems to hold little sway.

What I-200 avoids are the stories of those who have lived lives continuously shaped, and limited, by racism and sexism in schooling and employment. It is unclear if there exists a collective consciousness of these stories among whites—the grandmothers who spent lives scrubbing floors, the fathers denied all but the most menial of jobs, the school counselors who insisted on shop classes or home ec rather than algebra. These experiences have forged a collective consciousness for African Americans and feminists that have informed a political agenda. I-200 ignores, by necessity, this collective identity. The terms of the debate are defined by a rhetoric that does not permit the telling of these stories, much less access a reservoir of public support.

The unusual story of the I-200 signature gatherers is illustrative of this point. The decision of I-200 to recruit African Americans was disingenuous at best, cynical at worst. Some whites, who felt they were misled, asked to have their names removed from the ballot. As one sociology professor said, "I guess I thought that African Americans, being a minority, would not engage in any activity that would make their life chances less." The paradox of using race-neutral language to advance a race-based cause is difficult to explain. John Carlson's confusing explanation underscored this quandary: Race was not a factor in the petition drive, he insisted, yet, "You don't want people with little or no experience of any race" (Egan, 1997, p. A12).

The explanation offered by Sherry Bockwinkel was more direct, charging that the African Americans couldn't read, were lazy, and lying. These accusations resonate deeply with commonly held stereotypes about African Americans. Claims of race-neutrality, however, make defense difficult.

Interest Convergence

Assessing the degree of interest convergence in affirmative action programs requires some tally of advantages. Measurement of such interests is difficult. In a state with a relatively small minority population, race specific policies and goals have a correspondingly small impact. And, when over 70% of the state workforce qualifies for consideration under affirmative action (women plus minorities), it is difficult to distinguish interest divergence or convergence. Although the case can be made that whites, especially white women, have benefited considerably, it does not change public perception that affirmative action is about favoritism for unqualified blacks (Sniderman & Carmines, 1997).

Does the popularity of I-200 then contradict the principle of interest convergence? Would not programs that benefit whites enjoy the support of other whites? That turns out to be true for those programs that are targeted toward whites, such as those promoting math and science to girls or assisting displaced homemakers. Those that specify race, for hiring goals or contract set-asides, are distinctly unpopular. What appears to be objectionable about affirmative action in Washington state is not its whiteness, but its blackness.

Sniderman and Carmines (1997) have conducted extensive national public opinion polls about affirmative action using computer assisted interviewing. They found white opposition to affirmative action is "intense, unvarying, and pervasive" (p. 30) and that its primary beneficiaries are believed to be black. In fact, the mere mention of affirmative action causes whites to significantly increase their expressed dislike for blacks and makes them more likely to describe blacks as lazy, irresponsible, and arrogant (p. 39). This is true for men and women of all classes, and true for self-described liberals (57%), Democrats (65%), and Republicans (64%). Whites also overwhelmingly believe that most blacks are poor and violent.

Although national studies of public opinion have shown an overall reduction in overt racial prejudice, Sniderman and Carmines found no shortage of whites who are willing to admit their racist stereotypes: 52% describe blacks as violent; 45% as boastful; 42% as complaining; and 34% as lazy. The authors comment:

> Given that it is virtually cost-free to say something nice about black Americans in the course of a public opinion interview, what is striking is how few white Americans actually do. Apart from a general willingness of 3 out of 4 whites to describe blacks as "friendly"—surely as innocuous a positive quality as one can imagine—only a modest majority of whites are willing to attribute specific positive characteristics to most blacks. (p. 61)

Because of these widespread antiblack sentiments, Sniderman and Carmines recommend that future attempts to garner support for affirmative action policies refrain from any mention of race. They also note that arguments based on underrepresentation or a history of discrimination are fairly ineffective. Even if a company has a proven policy of racist hiring policies, support for affirmative action within that same company goes only from 21% to 42%. Rather, Sniderman and Carmines suggest changing the terms of the argument to the grounds of moral principles centered on broader views of social justice. This "color blind" strategy, they believe, can increase the support of both prejudiced and self-interested whites.

Affirmative action policies aimed at helping the poor or disabled, if they specifically avoid any mention of race, can garner up to two-thirds of white support (p. 25). Such a strategy, they maintain, is not based on interest convergence, but on common, shared principles of fairness and justice.

This is a distinction without much difference. Others have argued that replacing race- and gender-based affirmative action with a need-based approach is not an adequate substitute but will, because of absolute numbers, redirect resources back to white males (Feinberg, 1996). Nonetheless, theirs is a point not lost on the No-200 campaign. Their ineffective strategy was to avoid mention of race and to direct appeals to white men who may worry that their daughters or wives could be denied equal pay or benefits or lose funding to participate in sports. Appeals to economic prosperity (again, avoiding any mention of race) were the thrust of a series of full-page ads in the *Seattle Times* endorsed by Microsoft, Boeing, and others that urge votes against I-200 "because it's bad for business" (1998, September 6).

Summary

The case of I-200 not only illustrates and confirms some of the tenets of CRT, but suggests CRT as a model with explanatory power. The counter-argument, however, is this: from the point of view of the I-200 supporters, they are endorsing fundamental principles of fairness. It is unfair to discriminate by race or gender in public hiring, contracting, or college admissions. Affirmative action discriminates against people who, by no fault of their own, lose out to women and minorities. And despite their commitment to ideals of justice, they are being criticized as racist.

What has gone wrong? CRT believes that the problem lies in the methods and process of our legal system, where insistence on race neutral language has negated social/historical context. Worse still, the benefits of racial exclusion and white privilege go unrecognized and unchallenged.

Brown (1992) in her analysis of the legal principles of race-neutrality, points out the fallacious assumption that blacks and whites occupy equal positions in society. By disengaging cases from their historical context, in a process known as "disaggregation," the legal process removes the voices of people negatively affected by racism and refuses to acknowledge the deeply held beliefs of black inferiority and white superiority.

In the case of I-200, although white women, veterans, and persons with disabilities have also had their choices widened to include opportunities provided by affirmative action, the greater concern is the protection of those whites displaced by such policies. In short, the protection of whites trumps that of blacks. [. . .]

Conclusion

For advocates of affirmative action, the options come down to this: trust in traditional liberalism versus racial realism. The distinction is more than an academic exercise. The choice between the two makes all the difference, not only in how we conceptualize and formulate public policy, but in how we vote. Liberalism, to its discredit, has underestimated the depth of resentment among whites for race-based policies and has avoided facing the dilemma that exists between its stated goal of racial equality and its reluctance to confront white privilege. Liberalism may be too weakened to mount a serious defense of affirmative action.

Not all critical race theorists agree with this dismissal of liberalism. Crenshaw (1988) has argued that liberal ideology, although far from being perfect, has visionary ideals that should be developed. She also notes that, given the limited range of options for blacks to challenge racism, liberalism should not be too quickly discarded.

Racial realism, on the other hand, directly confronts racism and white privilege. This approach offends many, who accuse it of excessive cynicism and nihilism. Yet West (1995) says that CRT "compels us to confront critically the most explosive issue in American civilization: the historical centrality and complicity of law in upholding white supremacy" (p. xi). For those attempting to make sense of the legal and political trends toward ending affirmative action, CRT poses challenges on several fronts. First is the importance of keeping race and racism at the center of the argument. Second is acknowledging the debate in its historic and social context. Last is the call to pay attention to the real life experiences of African Americans. CRT's usefulness in formulating political and policy strategy remains to be seen but the utility of some of its principles can be recognized in two recent works, the study done by William Bowen and Derek Bok, and President Clinton's review of federal affirmative action practices.

In one of the largest studies of African Americans affected by affirmative action, Bowen and Bok (1998) tracked the lives of over 45,000 students admitted to highly selective colleges under racial preferences policies. Their data underscore the success of affirmative action in creating a generation of African American intellectual, professional, and community leadership. By focusing attention on the experiences of these students, and their lives after college, Bowen and Bok help publicize the accomplishments of race-factored admissions policies and reveal us as a nation that has not only rejected, but is actively reversing, its racist past.

President Clinton's order for a review of the federal government's affirmative action policy also utilized several methods of CRT. By tracing the long history of U.S. racial and gender discrimination, and presenting numeric data and detailed stories of the experiences of random testers documenting widespread racist disparities in hiring practices, the Administration was able to support its "mend it, don't end it" policy. In this way, the debate was placed in its historic/social context, systemic racist practices were revealed, and yet, valid concerns about fairness and effectiveness were addressed (White House, 1996).

What can CRT offer multiculturalism? Both are descendants of that proud forebear, the civil rights movement, and are inspired by centuries of African American resistance. Both must respond to the backlash against affirmative action, even if such efforts, as in the case of I-200, seem in vain.

CRT can inform the debate on affirmative action as well as help articulate and reinvigorate multiculturalism's political roots. It may take a dose of racial realism to discover a new vision and the will to struggle toward that vision, whether it be the dream of a workforce and classroom that genuinely reflect our nation's diversity or the hope of a multicultural curriculum so authentic and powerful as to eradicate racism and sexism in our society. The likelihood of this happening may seem as remote a hope as freedom must have seemed for our chained forebears. Their heroism and ultimate victory lay not in armed revolt or illustrious gestures, but in the cumulative effect of countless, small acts of resistance. In the same way, we prevail by the act of resistance itself. For it is at the point when we begin to question our own assumptions and privileges, resist stereotyping, classism, and patriarchy, and critically examine the contextualized, racial meanings of our lives—it is at that point—that we are triumphant.

Note

1. State affirmative action hiring programs for Vietnam-era veterans, veterans with disabilities, and disabled persons are exempt from this ban. Collegiate athletic programs would also be immune. Whether or not recruiting efforts would also be prohibited remains unclear.

References

Because it's bad for business. (1998, September 6). *The Seattle Times*, pp. A22.

Bowen, W. G., & Bok, D. (1998). *The shape of the river: Long-term consequences of considering race in college and university admissions*. Princeton, NJ: Princeton University Press.

Bronner, E. (1998, September 9). Study strongly supports affirmative action in admissions to elite colleges. *The New York Times*, A24.

Brooks, R. L., & Newborn, M. J. (1994). Critical race theory and classical liberal civil rights scholarship: A distinction without a difference. *California Law Review, 82*(4), 787–845.

Brown, W. R. (1992). The convergence of neutrality and choice: The limits of the state's affirmative duty to provide equal educational opportunity. *Tennessee Law Review, 60*, 63–133.

Brune, T. (1998, February 9). Nearly half of all affirmative action hires are white. *The Seattle Times* [On-line], www.seattletimes.com.

Brune, T. (1998, July 3). I-200 backers faulted over gifts. *The Seattle Times*, pp. B1, B2.

Brune, T., & Serrano, B. A. (1998, December 12). Signature gatherers, their race become issues Initiative 200 effort. *The Seattle Times*, A1, A22.

Civil Rights Cases, 109 U.S. 3 (1883).

Crenshaw, K. W. (1988). Race, reform, and retrenchment: Transformation and legitimation in antidiscrimination law. *Harvard Law Review, 101*(7), 1331–1387.

Egan, T. (1997, December 17). Blacks recruited by "rights" drive to end preferences. *The New York Times*, A12.

Farber, D. A., & Sherry, S. (1997). *Beyond all reason: The radical assault on truth in American Law*. New York: Oxford University Press.

Feinberg, W. (1997). Affirmative action and beyond: A case for a backward-looking gender-and race-based policy. *Teachers College Record, 97*(3), 362–381.

Foster, H. (1997, December 31). I-200 nets signatures—and a controversy. *Seattle Post-Intelligencer*, A1, A4.

Foster, H. (1998, September 14). Most in poll support I-200. *Seattle Post-Intelligencer*, A1, A4.

Holmes, S. (1998, November 10). Victorious preference foes look for new battlefields. *The New York Times*, A23.

King, M. (1997, November 13). Debate over affirmative action moves to this state. *The Seattle Times* [On-line], www.seattletimes.com.

Ladson-Billings, G. (1994, April). *Your blues ain't like mine: Keeping issues of race on the multicultural agenda*. Paper presented at the annual meeting of the American Educational Research Association, New Orleans, LA.

Postman, D., & Brune, T. (1998, July 12). Across state, thirst is strong for reforming affirmative action. *The Seattle Times*, A1, A8–9.

Postman, D., & Mapes, L. V. (1998, February 10). I-200 lacks lawmakers' votes; it's likely headed for ballot. *The Seattle Times*, A1, A7.

Serrano, B. A. (1998, February 4). Carlson out at KVI over I-200 focus. *The Seattle Times*, A1, A10.

Sniderman, P. M., & Carmines, E. G. (1997). *Reaching beyond race.* Cambridge, MA: Harvard University Press.

Tate, W. (1997). Critical race theory in education: History, theory, and implications. In M. W. Apple (Ed.), *Review of research in education* (pp. 195–247). Washington DC: American Educational Research Association.

Taylor, Q. (1994). *The forging of a black community: Seattle's central district from 1870 through the civil rights era.* Seattle, WA: University of Washington Press.

Tushnet, M. V. (1996). The "We've done enough" theory of school desegregation. *Howard Law Journal, 39*(3), 767–779.

Verhovek, S. H. (1999, September 17). Gates, "spreading the wealth," makes scholarship gift official. *The New York Times,* A19.

Washington State Commission on African American Affairs. (1995, November). *Affirmative action: Who's really benefiting? Part II on public higher education.*

Washington State Higher Education Coordinating Board. (1987). *The Washington state master plan for higher education.* Olympia, WA: Higher Education Coordinating Board.

Washington State Higher Education Coordinating Board. (1996, April). *Briefing paper on affirmative action and diversity.* Olympia, WA: Higher Education Coordinating Board.

Washington State Higher Education Coordinating Board. (1997, December). *1997 statewide progress report on diversity and participation of people of color in higher education.* Olympia, WA: Higher Education Coordinating Board.

West, C. (1995). Foreword. In K. Crenshaw, N. Gotanda, G. Peller, & K. Thomas (Eds.), *Critical Race Theory: The key writings that formed that movement* (pp. xi–xii). New York: The New Press.

White House. (1996, April 6). *Review of federal government's affirmative action program* [On-line], http://www .whitehouse.gov/WH/EOP/OP/html/aa/aa01.html

Part Four

*Critical Race Research Methodology
in Education*

9

Critical Race Methodology
Counter-Storytelling as an Analytical Framework for Educational Research

Daniel G. Solórzano and Tara J. Yosso

> Necesitamos teorías [we need theories] that will rewrite history using race, class, gender, and ethnicity as categories of analysis, theories that cross borders, that blur boundaries—new kinds of theories with new theorizing methods . . . We are articulating new positions in the "in-between," Borderland worlds of ethnic communities and academies . . . social issues such as race, class, and sexual difference are intertwined with the narrative and poetic elements of a text, elements in which theory is embedded. In our mestizaje theories we create new categories for those of us left out or pushed out of existing ones.
>
> Anzaldúa (1990, pp. xxv–xxvi)

Gloria Anzaldúa's (1990) epigraph challenges us to develop new theories that will help us to better understand those who are at the margins of society. She also suggests that along with new theories, we need new "theorizing methods" to conduct the research that would answer the problems posed by these theories. Research and theory that explicitly address issues of race and racism have the potential to fill this void. In this article, we elaborate on and expand work in critical race theory to include what we call *critical race methodology*. We define critical race methodology as a theoretically grounded approach to research that (a) foregrounds race and racism in all aspects of the research process. However, it also challenges the separate discourses on race, gender, and class by showing how these three elements intersect to affect the experiences of students of color;[1] (b) challenges the traditional research paradigms, texts, and theories used to explain the experiences of students of color; (c) offers a liberatory or transformative solution to racial, gender, and class subordination; and (d) focuses on the racialized, gendered, and classed experiences of students of color. Furthermore, it views these experiences as sources of strength and (e) uses the interdisciplinary knowledge base of ethnic studies, women's studies, sociology, history, humanities, and the law to better understand the experiences of students of color.

This exercise in developing critical race methodology must begin by defining race and racism. According to James Banks (1993), Eurocentric versions of U.S. history reveal race to be a socially constructed category, created to differentiate racial groups and to show the superiority or dominance of one race over another. This definition leads to the question: Does the dominance of a racial group require a rationalizing ideology? One could argue that dominant groups try to legitimate their position through the use of an ideology (i.e., a set of beliefs that explains or justifies some actual or potential social arrangement). Because racism is the ideology that justifies the dominance of one race over another, we must ask, how do we define racism? For our purpose, Audre Lorde (1992) may have produced the most concise definition of racism as "the belief in the inherent superiority of one race over all others and thereby the right to dominance" (p. 496). Manning Marable (1992) also defined racism as "a system of ignorance, exploitation, and power used to oppress African-Americans, Latinos, Asians, Pacific Americans, American Indians and other people on the basis of ethnicity, culture, mannerisms, and color" (p. 5). Marable's definition of racism is important because it shifts the discussion of race and racism from a Black-White discourse to one that includes multiple faces, voices, and experiences. Embedded in the Lorde and Marable definitions of racism are at least three important points: (a) One group deems itself superior to all others, (b) the group that is superior has the power to carry out the racist behavior, and (c) racism benefits the superior group while negatively affecting other racial and/or ethnic groups. These two definitions take the position that racism is about institutional power, and people of color in the United States have never possessed this form of power. These definitions of race and racism are our guides as we embark upon a discussion of critical race theory and critical race methodology.

Critical Race Theory and Critical Race Methodology[2]

To develop critical race methodology, we must define its theoretical foundation, critical race theory. Critical race theory draws from and extends a broad literature base in law, sociology, history, ethnic studies, and women's studies.

Mari Matsuda (1991) views critical race theory as

> the work of progressive legal scholars of color who are attempting to develop a jurisprudence that accounts for the role of racism in American law and that work toward the elimination of racism as part of a larger goal of eliminating all forms of subordination. (p. 1331)

We extend Matsuda's definition and argue that critical race theory advances a strategy to foreground and account for the role of race and racism in education and works toward the elimination of racism as part of a larger goal of opposing or eliminating other forms of subordination based on gender, class, sexual orientation, language, and national origin. Indeed, for our purpose here, critical race theory in education is a framework or set of basic insights, perspectives, methods, and pedagogy that seeks to identify, analyze, and transform those structural and cultural aspects of education that maintain subordinate and dominant racial positions in and out of the classroom (see Crenshaw, Gotanda, Peller, & Thomas, 1995; Matsuda, Lawrence, Delgado, & Crenshaw, 1993; Tierney, 1993).

Critical race theory and methodology in education have at least the following five elements that form their basic insights, perspectives, methodology, and pedagogy (see Solórzano, 1997, 1998; Solórzano & Delgado Bernal, 2001; Solórzano & Yosso, 2000, 2001, in press-a).[3]

The intercentricity of race and racism with other forms of subordination. A critical race theory in education starts from the premise that race and racism are endemic, permanent, and in the words of Margaret Russell (1992), "a central rather than marginal factor in defining and explaining individual experiences of the law" (pp. 762–763). Although race and racism are at the center of a critical race analysis, we also view them at their intersection with other forms of subordination such as gender and class discrimination (Crenshaw, 1989, 1993). As Robin Barnes (1990) has stated, "Critical race scholars have refused to ignore the differences between class and race as a basis for oppression . . . Critical race scholars know that class oppression alone cannot account for racial oppression" (p. 1868). A critical race methodology in education also acknowledges the intercentricity of racialized oppression—the layers of subordination based on race, gender, class, immigration status, surname, pheno-type, accent, and sexuality.[4] Here, in the intersections of racial oppression, we can use critical race methodology to search for some answers to the theoretical, conceptual, methodological, and pedagogical questions related to the experiences of people of color.

The challenge to dominant ideology. A critical race theory challenges the traditional claims that educational institutions make toward objectivity, meritocracy, color-blindness, race neutrality, and equal opportunity. Critical race scholars argue that these traditional claims act as a camouflage for the self-interest, power, and privilege of dominant groups in U.S. society (Calmore, 1992; Solórzano, 1997). A critical race methodology in education challenges White privilege, rejects notions of "neu-tral" research or "objective" researchers, and exposes deficit-informed research that silences and distorts epistemologies of people of color (Delgado Bernal, 1998).

The commitment to social justice. A critical race theory is committed to social justice and offers a liberatory or transformative response to racial, gender, and class oppression (Matsuda, 1991). We envision a social justice research agenda that leads toward the following:

- the elimination of racism, sexism, and poverty and
- the empowering of subordinated minority groups.

Critical race researchers acknowledge that educational institutions operate in contradictory ways, with their potential to oppress and marginalize coexisting with their potential to emancipate and empower. Likewise, a critical race methodology in education recognizes that multiple layers of oppression and discrimination are met with multiple forms of resistance.

The centrality of experiential knowledge. Critical race theory recognizes that the experiential knowledge of people of color is legitimate, appropriate, and critical to understanding, analyzing, and teaching about racial subordination. In fact, critical race theorists view this knowledge as a strength and draw explicitly on the lived experiences of people of color by including such methods as storytelling, family histories, biographies, scenarios, parables, *cuentos, testimonios*, chronicles, and narra-tives (Bell, 1987; Carrasco, 1996; Delgado, 1989, 1993, 1995a, 1995b, 1996; Olivas, 1990). Critical race methodology in education challenges traditional research para-digms, texts, and theories used to explain the experiences of people of color. It exposes deficit-informed research and methods that silence and distort the experiences of people of color and instead focuses on their racialized, gendered, and classed experiences as sources of strength (Solórzano & Solórzano, 1995; Valencia & Solórzano, 1997).

The transdisciplinary perspective. A critical race theory challenges ahistoricism and the unidisciplinary focus of most analyses and insists on analyzing race and racism by placing them in both historical and contemporary contexts (Delgado, 1984, 1992; Garcia, 1995; Harris, 1994; Olivas, 1990). Critical race methodology in education uses the transdisciplinary knowledge and methodological base of ethnic studies, women's studies, sociology, history, law, and other fields to guide research that better understands the effects of racism, sexism, and classism on people of color.

These five themes are not new in and of themselves, but collectively, they represent a challenge to the existing modes of scholarship. Indeed, critical race theory names racist injuries and identifies their origins. In examining the origins, critical race methodology finds that racism is often well disguised in the rhetoric of shared "normative" values and "neutral" social scientific and educational principles and practices (Matsuda et al., 1993). However, when the ideology of racism is examined and racist injuries are named, victims of racism can find their voice. Furthermore, those injured by racism and other forms of oppression discover they are not alone in their marginality. They become empowered participants, hearing their own stories and the stories of others, listening to how the arguments against them are framed, and learning to make the arguments to defend themselves.

Racism, White Privilege, and Storytelling

> The use of a master narrative to represent a group is bound to provide a very narrow depiction of what it means to be Mexican-American, African-American, White, and so on . . . A master narrative essentializes and wipes out the complexities and richness of a group's cultural life . . . A monovocal account will engender not only stereotyping but also curricular choices that result in representations in which fellow members of a group represented cannot recognize themselves.
>
> (Montecinos, 1995, pp. 293–294)

We concur with Carmen Montecinos (1995) and assert that the ideology of racism creates, maintains, and justifies the use of a "master narrative" in storytelling. It is within the context of racism that "monovocal" stories about the low educational achievement and attainment of students of color are told. Unacknowledged White privilege helps maintain racism's stories. As such, we are defining White privilege as a system of opportunities and benefits conferred upon people simply because they are White (Delgado & Stefancic, 1997). Indeed, Whiteness is a category of privilege. Beverly Tatum (1997) writes about the underresearched issue of White privilege as she reminds her readers that "despite the current rhetoric about affirmative action and 'reverse discrimination,' every social indicator, from salary to life expectancy, reveals the advantages of being White" (p. 8). White privilege is often invisible— it is the norm (McIntosh, 1989). Tatum continues, "In very concrete terms, it [White privilege] means if a person of color is the victim of housing discrimination, the apartment that would otherwise have been rented to that person of color is still available for a White person" (p. 9). So while the person of color is still stressed with finding adequate housing, the White person is "knowingly or unknowingly, the beneficiary of racism, a system of advantage based on race" (Tatum, 1997, p. 9).

Because "majoritarian" stories generate from a legacy of racial privilege, they are stories in which racial privilege seems "natural." Indeed, White privilege is often expressed through majoritarian stories; through the "bundle of presuppositions, perceived wisdoms, and shared cultural understandings persons in the dominant race bring to the discussion of race" (Delgado & Stefancic, 1993, p. 462). However, majoritarian stories are not just stories of racial privilege, they are also stories of gender, class, and other forms of privilege. As such, they are stories that carry layers of assumptions that persons in positions of racialized privilege bring with them to discussions of racism, sexism, classism, and other forms of subordination. In other words, a majoritarian story is one that privileges Whites, men, the middle and/ or upper class, and heterosexuals by naming these social locations as natural or normative points of reference.

People of color often buy into and even tell majoritarian stories. Ironically, although Whites most often tell majoritarian stories, people of color can also tell them.[5] In the same way, misogynistic stories are often told by men but can also be told by women. As an example of minority majoritarian storytelling, African American scholar Thomas Sowell (1981) claimed that "the goals and values of Mexican Americans have never centered on education" (p. 266) and that many Mexican Americans find the process of education "distasteful" (p. 267). Another example can be found with a Latino, Lauro Cavazos, who as United States Secretary of Education, stated that Latino parents deserve much of the blame for the high dropout rate among their children because "Hispanics have always valued education . . . but somewhere along the line we've lost that. I really believe that, today, there is not that emphasis" (Snider, 1990, p. 1). Indeed, Linda Chavez (1992), who writes about the necessities of cultural and linguistic assimilation, and Supreme Court Justice Clarence Thomas, whose writings demonstrate his stance against the civil rights of people of color and of women, are two other examples of minority majoritarian storytellers (see Higginbotham, 1992). Whether told by people of color or Whites, majoritarian stories are not often questioned because people do not see them as stories but as "natural" parts of everyday life.

Whether we refer to them as monovocals, master narratives, standard stories, or majoritarian stories, it is important to recognize the power of White privilege in constructing stories about race. For example, as Lisa Ikemoto (1997) challenges the medical profession for forcing women of color to undergo procedures during childbirth without their consent, she reveals the often-unquestioned power of majoritarian stories.

> The act of subordinating occurs first in the mind of those with authority. It is the implicit assumption that women of color, particularly those who live in poverty, are not fit for motherhood. This assumption is rooted in the experience of domination and in the construction of stories—negative stereotypes—about the "Others" to justify the resulting privileged status. (p. 140)

She further explains how this standard blinds and silences the racial discourse through majoritarian storytelling as follows:

> The standard legal story does not expressly speak to race and class. By failing to look to the experience of women who have been raced and impoverished, we let the standard story blind and silence us. The de facto standard then used to identify, prioritize, and address subordination is the experience of White middle class women. This excludes and diminishes women of color, particularly those who live in poverty.
>
> (Ikemoto, 1997, p. 136)

A majoritarian story distorts and silences the experiences of people of color. Using "standard formulae," majoritarian methods purport to be neutral and objective yet implicitly make assumptions according to negative stereotypes about people of color (Ikemoto, 1997). For example, when White middle-class people fall victim to violence in their own neighborhoods and their schools, the shock comes from the standard story: "How could this happen? This is a good neighborhood" or "We never thought this could happen here. This is a good school." The standard story implies that violent crimes such as these are unheard of in White middle-class communities. At the same time, the standard story infers that communities of color and working-class communities may be more accustomed to violence. The silence within statements about "good neighborhoods" and "good schools" indicates racialized and classed dimensions underlying "standard" understandings of these communities and schools. Within the silence, one may note negative stereotypes reinforcing images of "bad neighborhoods" and "bad schools." The unspoken discourse is that White communities are "good" communities that house "good" schools, and these "good" places do not experience such tragedies. "Other" communities, "colored" communities, or those "bad" communities are the ones who experience such events.

The majoritarian story tells us that darker skin and poverty correlate with bad neighborhoods and bad schools. It informs us that limited or Spanish-accented English and Spanish surnames equal bad schools and poor academic performance. It also reminds us that people who may not have the legal documents to "belong" in the United States may be identified by their skin color, hair texture, eye shape, accent, and/or surname. Standard, majoritarian methodology relies on stock stereotypes that covertly and overtly link people of color, women of color, and poverty with "bad," while emphasizing that White, middle- to upper-class people embody all that is "good." Morally, the silence within which assumptions are made about good versus bad describes people of color and working-class people as less intelligent and irresponsible while depicting White middle-class and upper-class people as just the opposite.

Racism and Deficit Social Science Storytelling

Whether explicitly or implicitly, social science theoretical models explaining educational inequality support majoritarian stories. We draw on the work of Valencia and Solórzano (1997) to demonstrate the consistent language of biological and cultural deficit in these majoritarian stories. For example, Valencia and Solórzano outline biological deficiency models, which assume that students of color lack the biological traits necessary for success within the educational system. Using such models, scholars proclaim Mexicans, Blacks, and Native Americans to be biologically deficient compared with Whites. For instance, a majoritarian story told by Lewis Terman in 1916 claimed

> high grade or border-line deficiency ... is very, very common among Spanish-Indian and Mexican families of the Southwest and also among Negroes. Their dullness appears to be racial, or at least inherent in the family stocks from which they come ... Children of this group should be segregated into separate classes ... They cannot master abstractions but they can often be made efficient workers ... There is no possibility at the present of convincing society that they should be allowed to reproduce, although from a eugenic point of view they constitute a grave problem because of their unusually prolific breeding. (pp. 91–92)

In 1994, 78 years later, the debate over *The Bell Curve* (Herrnstein & Murray, 1994) demonstrates that some scholars continue to draw upon the beliefs of eugenicists such as Terman (1916) to tell majoritarian stories about the educational failure of students of color. Arguing over the merits of the Standardized Aptitude Test, social scientists and educators resurrected biological deficiency models to claim that Chicana/Chicano, Latina/Latino, and Black children do not have the mental capacity of their White peers (Dunn, 1987; Jensen, 1969).

Within deficiency models, however, biological explanations for inequity have not been as pervasive as cultural explanations (Coleman et al., 1966; Lewis, 1968). Indeed, what some scholars originally attributed to the biology and genetics of students of color were reclassified and described as cultural deficits. For example, a majoritarian cultural deficit story told by Cecilia Heller (1966) states the following:

> The kind of socialization that Mexican American children generally receive at home is not conducive to the development of the capacities needed for advancement in a dynamic industrialized society. This type of upbringing creates stumbling blocks to future advancement by stressing values that hinder mobility—family ties, honor, masculinity, and living in the present—and by neglecting the values that are conducive to it—achievement, independence, and deferred gratification. (p. 34)

Indeed, culture continues to be cited as the leading cause of the low socioeconomic status and educational failure of students of color. For instance, John Ogbu's (1990) majoritarian story argues, "Involuntary minorities [Blacks, Chicanas/Chicanos, and Native Americans] have not developed a widespread effort optimism or a strong cultural ethic of hard work and perseverance in the pursuit of education" (p. 53). A more recent example of cultural deficit theorizing (i.e., majoritarian storytelling) comes from an African American linguistics professor, John McWhorter. In a *Los Angeles Times* article, McWhorter claims that

> the sad and simple fact is that while there are some excellent Black students ... on average, Black students do not try as hard as other students. The reason they do not try as hard is not because they are inherently lazy, nor is it because they are stupid ... these students belong to a culture infected with an anti-intellectual strain, which subtly but decisively teaches them from birth not to embrace school-work too whole-heartedly.
>
> (George, 2000, p. E3)

Currently, many teacher education programs draw on majoritarian stories to explain educational inequity through a cultural deficit model and thereby pass on beliefs that students of color are culturally deprived (Kretovics & Nussel, 1994; Persell, 1977).

The main solution for the socioacademic failure offered by cultural deficit majoritarian storytellers is cultural assimilation. Specifically, they argue that students of color should assimilate to the dominant White middle-class culture to succeed in school and in life (Banfield, 1970; Bernstein, 1977; Schwartz, 1971). Methods by which this cultural assimilation may take place include learning English at the expense of losing Spanish and becoming an individual "American" success story by loosening or cutting family and community ties. This cultural assimilation solution becomes a major part of the curriculum in teacher education programs and is thereby brought to the schools in communities of color. Therefore, according to cultural deficit storytelling, a successful student of color is an assimilated student of color. Given the current rhetoric of "at-risk" and the resurrection of terms such as *disadvantaged*, it is clear that just as insidiously as racism has changed forms, so has the cultural deficit terminology used by social scientists (Solórzano, 1998; Valencia, 1997; Valencia & Solórzano, 1997).

Some scholars critique our focus on race and racism by telling stories that forefront class-based or gender-based theories and discuss racialization as one of many unfortunate by-products of capitalism. In response, we argue that it is crucial to focus on the intersections of oppression because storytelling is racialized, gendered, and classed and these stories affect racialized, gendered, and classed communities. This means that when examining the experiences of students of color, a class-based theory or even a class-gender theory is insufficient. Methodologies that dismiss or decenter racism and its intersections with other forms of subordination omit and distort the experiences of those whose lives are daily affected by racism—those "at the bottom of society's well" (Bell, 1992, p. vi). In other words, downplaying the intercentricity of race and racism in the discourse helps tell majoritarian stories about the insignificance of race and the notion that racism is something in the past. Such stories are sometimes found in "critical" social science literature.[6] Indeed, these stories can actually serve to reinforce the majoritarian story.

Storytelling Resistance: The Counter-Story

We define the counter-story as a method of telling the stories[7] of those people whose experiences are not often told (i.e., those on the margins of society). The counter-story is also a tool for exposing, analyzing, and challenging the majoritarian stories of racial privilege. Counter-stories can shatter complacency, challenge the dominant discourse on race, and further the struggle for racial reform.[8] Yet, counter-stories need not be created only as a direct response to majoritarian stories. As Ikemoto (1997) reminds us, "By responding only to the standard story, we let it dominate the discourse" (p. 136). Indeed, within the histories and lives of people of color, there are numerous unheard counter-stories. Storytelling and counter-storytelling these experiences can help strengthen traditions of social, political, and cultural survival and resistance.

Types of Counter-Narratives and/or Stories

Storytelling has a rich and continuing tradition in African American (see Bell, 1987, 1992, 1996; Berkeley Art Center, 1982; Lawrence, 1992), Chicana/Chicano (see Delgado, 1989, 1995a, 1996; Olivas, 1990; Paredes, 1977), and Native American (see Deloria, 1969; R. Williams, 1997) communities. Richard Delgado (1989) reminds us that "oppressed groups have known instinctively that stories are an essential tool to their own survival and liberation" (p. 2436). Critical race scholars continue in this tradition and have practiced counter-storytelling in at least three general forms.[9]

Personal Stories or Narratives

Personal stories or narratives recount an individual's experiences with various forms of racism and sexism. Often, these personal counter-stories are autobiographical reflections of the author, juxtaposed with their critical race analysis of legal cases and within the context of a larger sociopolitical critique. The work of Patricia Williams (1991), Margaret Montoya (1994), and Leslie Espinoza (1990) illustrates personal counter-storytelling.

Other People's Stories or Narratives

A narrative that tells another person's story can reveal experiences with and responses to racism and sexism as told in a third person voice. This type of counter-narrative usually offers biographical analysis of the experiences of a person of color, again in relation to U.S. institutions and in a sociohistorical context. Work by Lawrence and Matsuda (1997) as well as Lilia Fernández's (2002 [this issue]) story of Pablo offer examples of telling other people's counter-stories.

Composite Stories or Narratives

Composite stories and narratives draw on various forms of "data" to recount the racialized, sexualized, and classed experiences of people of color. Such counter-stories may offer both biographical and autobiographical analyses because the authors create composite characters and place them in social, historical, and political situations to discuss racism, sexism, classism, and other forms of subordination. The work of Bell (1987, 1992, 1996), Delgado (1995a, 1995b, 1996), Solórzano and Yosso (2000, 2001, in press-a, in press-b), Solórzano and Delgado Bernal (2001), and Solórzano and Villalpando (1998) exemplify composite counter-narratives.

Creating Counter-Stories

To create our counter-stories, we begin by finding and unearthing sources of data. To accomplish this task, we borrow from the works of Strauss and Corbin (1990) and

Dolores Delgado Bernal (1998). Strauss and Corbin (1990) use a concept called *theoretical sensitivity* and refer to it as

> a personal quality of the researcher. It indicates an awareness of the subtleties of meaning of data. One can come to the research situation with varying degrees of sensitivity depending upon previous reading and experience with or relevant to the data. It can also be developed further during the research process. Theoretical sensitivity refers to the attribute of having insight, the ability to give meaning to data, the capacity to understand, and capability to separate the pertinent from that which isn't. (pp. 41–42)

Delgado Bernal's (1998) notion of "cultural intuition" differs from theoretical sensitivity in that it "extends one's personal experience to include collective experience and community memory, and points to the importance of participants' engaging in the analysis of data" (pp. 563–564). She further explains as follows:

> A Chicana researcher's cultural intuition is achieved and can be nurtured through our personal experiences (which are influenced by ancestral wisdom, community memory, and intuition), the literature on and about Chicanas, our professional experiences, and the analytical process we engage in when we are in a central position of our research and our analysis. Thus, cultural intuition is a complex process that is experiential, intuitive, historical, personal, collective, and dynamic. (pp. 567–568)

Using Strauss and Corbin's theoretical sensitivity (1990) and Delgado Bernal's cultural intuition (1998), we created counter-stories from (a) the data gathered from the research process itself, (b) the existing literature on the topic(s), (c) our own professional experiences, and (d) our own personal experiences. For example, in one counter-story we created, the first form of data came from primary sources, namely, focus groups and individual interviews we conducted with Chicana and Chicano undergraduate and graduate students, postdoctoral fellows, and faculty (see Solórzano & Yosso, 2001). We searched and sifted through these data for examples of the concepts we were seeking to illuminate (Glaser & Strauss, 1967). We used the critical lenses of race, gender, and class and the experiences of Chicana and Chicano undergraduate and graduate students, postdoctoral fellows, and faculty to examine the concepts of self-doubt, survivor guilt, impostor syndrome, and invisibility.

Next, we looked to other sources for secondary data analysis related to these concepts in the social sciences, humanities, and legal literature. For the article previously mentioned, we decided to focus on a specific set of manuscripts we had recently read on the theme of women of color and resistance in the academy (see Solórzano & Yosso, 2001). In sifting through this literature, we began to draw connections with previous readings and the relevant focus group and/or individual interview data. Just as in the interview analysis, we listened to the voices of these women as we read and discussed the articles. We often heard varying emotions, even in traditional academic style texts. For us, literary analysis from poetry and short story segments helped tap into these emotions and challenged us to look more deeply into the humanities and social sciences to find these pained yet triumphant voices of experience. Finally, we added our own professional and personal experiences related to the concepts and ideas. Here, we not only shared our own stories and reflections but also drew on the multiple voices of family, friends, colleagues, and acquaintances.

Once these various sources of data were compiled, examined, and analyzed, we created composite characters who helped us tell a story. We attempted to get the characters to engage in a real and critical dialogue about our findings from the interviews, literature, and experiences. This dialogue emerged between the characters much like our own discussions emerged—through sharing, listening, challenging, and reflecting. As the dialogue began to emerge between the characters, we started to insert the various forms of related data from fields such as literature, art, music, theatre, film, social sciences, and the law.

As an example, we offer the following excerpt from the previously mentioned article (Solórzano & Yosso, 2001). Our characters are Professor Leticia Garcia, an untenured sociology professor at a western university, and Esperanza Gonzalez, a 3rd-year graduate student at the same university in the education department. For a moment, we ask you to suspend judgment. We find these two women engaged in dialogue. We begin with Leticia's comments.

> "Olivia Espin (1993) talks about silence being a mode of self preservation. And heaven knows, we need to preserve ourselves. Between 1980 and 1990, all of the graduate schools in the U.S. combined produced only 751 Chicana doctorates in all fields and they represented only 0.7% of all female doctorates (Solórzano, 1994, 1995). Given these facts, I think that both strategic silence and action are strategies we should not overlook."
>
> Esperanza pressed on, "You're right, but there comes a time when I can no longer stay silent."
>
> As I listened to her pained comments, I asked, "Have you read Audre Lorde's (1978) 'Litany of Survival'? She is actually responding to you through poetry. She writes:
>
> > 'and when we speak we are afraid/
> > our words will not be heard/
> > nor welcomed/
> > but when we are silent/
> > we are still afraid/
> > So it is better to speak/
> > remembering/
> > we were never meant to survive.' " (pp. 31–32)
>
> Esperanza put her head in her hands, took in a deep breath, and sighed. "She says it exactly. Those contradictory feelings we have all bundled up inside. So when we do speak out, people often do not understand the depth of emotion welling up in our throats. And if we show any emotion it makes it that much easier to write us off as 'supersensitive,' or 'out of control.' It's exactly like Lorde writes, afraid to speak and afraid to stay silent." Esperanza paused to take a bite of her carrot muffin before she continued, "In my classes, because I didn't have a strong grasp of the many languages of the institution, the challenges I raised against the liberal ideas of social justice that ignore Chicanas/os fell on deaf ears. So at that point, I felt that a silent revolution was better than a clamoring battle cry quickly stifled."
>
> I smirked at the image of myself in a faculty meeting dressed in a suit of armor with a sword, thwarting off blows from my colleagues as if in the midst of a battle. "Often it's hard to know which strategy is most appropriate in which context. Choosing our battles is not easy, but our energies are limited," I said.
>
> "Too bad ignorance isn't!" Esperanza shot back.
>
> (Solórzano & Yosso, 2001, pp. 482–483)

This excerpt of a counter-story demonstrates how we create dialogue that critically illuminates concepts, ideas, and experiences while it tries to use the elements of critical race theory. We hear Esperanza as she expresses her concerns about her experiences as a Chicana being silenced in the classroom. We also listen to Leticia talking about maintaining strategic silence and developing strategies of resistance.

We believe counter-stories serve at least four functions as follows: (a) They can build community among those at the margins of society by putting a human and familiar face to educational theory and practice, (b) they can challenge the perceived wisdom of those at society's center by providing a context to understand and transform established belief systems, (c) they can open new windows into the reality of those at the margins of society by showing possibilities beyond the ones they live and demonstrating that they are not alone in their position, and (d) they can teach others that by combining elements from both the story and the current reality, one can construct another world that is richer than either the story or the reality alone.

Counter-storytelling is different from fictional storytelling. We are not developing imaginary characters that engage in fictional scenarios. Instead, the "composite" characters we develop are grounded in real-life experiences and actual empirical data and are contextualized in social situations that are also grounded in real life, not fiction.

Discussion

Most of our research asserts that U.S. educational institutions marginalize people of color. Often, educational marginalization is justified through research that decenters and even dismisses communities of color—through majoritarian storytelling. We continually ask, "Whose stories are privileged in educational contexts and whose stories are distorted and silenced?" U.S. history reveals that White upper-class and middle-class stories are privileged, whereas the stories of people of color are distorted and silenced. We further ask, "What are the experiences and responses of those whose stories are often distorted and silenced?" In documenting the voices of people of color, our work tells their stories.

Critical race methodology in education offers a way to understand the experiences of people of color along the educational pipeline (see Solórzano & Yosso, 2000). Such a methodology generates knowledge by looking to those who have been epistemologically marginalized, silenced, and disempowered (Denzin & Lincoln, 1994). Critical race theory challenges traditional methodologies because it requires us to develop "theories of social transformation wherein knowledge is generated specifically for the purpose of addressing and ameliorating conditions of oppression, poverty, or deprivation" (Lincoln, 1993, p. 33). Critical race methodology in education focuses research on how students of color experience and respond to the U.S. educational system. From developing research questions to collecting, analyzing, and presenting data, critical race methodology centers on students of color.

Using critical race methodology confirms that we must look to experiences with and responses to racism, sexism, classism, and heterosexism in and out of schools as valid, appropriate, and necessary forms of data. Critical race methodology contextualizes student-of-color experiences in the past, present, and future. It strategically uses multiple methods, often unconventional and creative, to draw on the knowledge of people of color who are traditionally excluded as an official part of the academy. Critical race methodology in education challenges biological and cultural deficit stories through counter-storytelling, oral traditions, historiographies, *corridos*, poetry, films, *actos*, or by other means.

Critical race scholarship concurs with Calmore (1997), noting that what is noticeably missing from the discussion of race is a substantive discussion of racism. We further this claim to assert that substantive discussions of racism are missing from critical discourse in education. We believe critical race methodology can move us toward these discussions. As we work from our own positions in the margins of society, we hold on to the belief that the margin can be "more than a site of deprivation . . . it is also the site of radical possibility, a space of resistance" (hooks, 1990, p. 149). As Anzaldúa (1990) explains:

> Theory, then, is a set of knowledges. Some of these knowledges have been kept from us—entry into some professions and academia denied us. Because we are not allowed to enter discourse, because we are often disqualified and excluded from it, because what passes for theory these days is forbidden territory for us, it is vital that we occupy theorizing space, that we not allow whitemen and women solely to occupy it. By bringing in our own approaches and methodologies, we transform that theorizing space. (p. xxv)

We argue that critical race methodology, with its counter-stories and even poetic modes of expression, articulates a response to Anzaldúa's (1990) challenge that "if we have been gagged and disempowered by theories, we can also be loosened and empowered by theories" (p. xxvi). Our response draws on the strengths of communities of color. If methodologies have been used to silence and marginalize people of color, then methodologies can also give voice and turn the margins into places of transformative resistance (Solórzano & Delgado Bernal, 2001; Solórzano & Yosso, in press-a). We know that many would discount the histories, experiences, and lives of people of color through majoritarian stories. Revealing the deficit discourse in majoritarian stories reveals White privilege, and this often is perceived as a threat to those who benefit from racism. However, as a strategy of survival and a means of resistance, we will continue to work to tell the counter-stories of those "at the bottom of society's well" (Bell, 1992, p. v). We are deeply grateful for those who have shared their counter-stories with us and who continue to struggle, survive, and thrive in the intersections of racial oppression.

Notes

1. For this study, the terms *students, people, persons,* and *communities of color* refer to those persons of African American, Chicana/Chicano, Latina/Latino, Asian American, and Native American ancestry. It should be noted that each of these terms has a political dimension that this article does not discuss.
2. According to Sandra Harding (1987), a research method is a technique for gathering evidence such as interviews, focus groups, participant observation, ethnographies, and surveys. On the other hand, research methodology is "a theory and analysis of how research does or should proceed" (p. 3). We define methods as the specific techniques used in the research process, such as data gathering and analysis. Whether we use quantitative, qualitative, or a combination of methods depends on which techniques of data gathering and analysis will best help us answer our research questions. We define methodology as the overarching theoretical approach guiding the research. For us, methodology is the nexus of theory and method in the way praxis is to theory and practice. In other words, methodology is the place where theory and method meet. Critical race methodology is an

approach to research grounded in critical race theory. We approach our work and engage in various techniques of data gathering and analysis guided by critical race theory and Latino critical race (LatCrit) theory (see note 4). Critical race methodology pushes us to humanize quantitative data and to recognize silenced voices in qualitative data.

3. For three comprehensive annotated bibliographies on critical race and LatCrit theory, see Delgado and Stefancic (1993, 1994) and Stefancic (1998).

4. Our definition of critical race methodology is formulated based on the work of critical race theorists as well as LatCrit theorists. LatCrit theory extends critical race discussions to Chicanas/Chicanos and Latinas/Latinos in education. Our working definition of LatCrit theory informs our definition of critical race methodology. As such, we feel it is important to state the following working definition, which is adapted from the *LatCrit Primer* (2000):

> A LatCrit theory in education is a framework that can be used to theorize and examine the ways in which race and racism explicitly and implicitly impact on the educational structures, processes, and discourses that effect people of color generally and Latinas/os specifically. Important to this critical framework is a challenge to the dominant ideology, which supports deficit notions about students of color while assuming "neutrality" and "objectivity." Utilizing the experiences of Latinas/os, a LatCrit theory in education also theorizes and examines that place where racism intersects with other forms of subordination such as sexism, classism, nativism, monolingualism, and heterosexism. LatCrit theory in education is conceived as a social justice project that attempts to link theory with practice, scholarship with teaching, and the academy with the community. LatCrit acknowledges that educational institutions operate in contradictory ways with their potential to oppress and marginalize co-existing with their potential to emancipate and empower. LatCrit theory in education is transdisciplinary and draws on many other schools of progressive scholarship.

We see LatCrit theory as a natural outgrowth of critical race theory, but we do not see them as mutually exclusive. For us, LatCrit scholarship is evidence of an ongoing process of finding a framework that addresses racism and its accompanying oppressions. LatCrit draws on the strengths outlined in critical race theory, while at the same time, it emphasizes the intersectionality of experience with oppression and resistance and the need to extend conversations about race and racism beyond the Black-White binary. We believe, as we have defined it, critical race methodology is driven by our LatCrit consciousness. This means that our own experiences with the multiplicity of racialized oppression and our responses to and resistance against such oppressions from our positions of multiple marginality inform and shape our research.

5. It is important to note that often, being a "minority" majoritarian storyteller means receiving benefits provided by those with racial, gender, and/or class privilege. For an example, see the character of Professor Gleason Golightly in Derrick Bell's (1992) *Faces at the Bottom of the Well*, chapter 9, "The Space Traders" (pp. 163–164).

6. Often, those who tell these stories dominate the "critical" discourse, and more often than not, they omit the "critical" work of people of color. For example, Delgado (1984, 1992) looked at this phenomenon of "selective citing" in civil rights legal scholarship through his articles titled "The Imperial Scholar" and "The Imperial Scholar Revisited." Delgado exposed a racial citation pattern wherein White authors (imperial scholars) cite each other and are much less likely to cite scholars of color. A similar pattern exists in the social science literature. Just as some Whites do not often venture into communities of color to do research, White scholars do not often venture into ethnic-specific journals or other scholarly writings to read the work of scholars of color (see Graham, 1992; Rosaldo, 1994). We know some may try to excuse this pattern by arguing that scholars of color just do not publish as much as Whites. However, we refute this notion. Instead, we believe there may be at least two reasons for racially selective citing: (a) They either do not know where to go or (b) they know where to go, but they choose to ignore the scholarship.

7. So as not to confuse the reader, we clarify here that a "story" can refer to a majoritarian story or a counter-story. A story becomes a counter-story when it begins to incorporate the five elements of critical race theory. In this article, we refer to people of color who draw on the elements of critical race theory in their writing as telling a story or a counter-story. Storytelling that draws on the elements of critical race theory is synonymous with counter-storytelling.

8. As we speak of this struggle for racial reform, we recognize the work of Gorz (1967), *Strategies for Labor: A Radical Proposal*. Andre Gorz outlines three types of social reforms: reformist, nonreformist, and revolutionary. He explains that reformist reforms are those that maintain the status quo and do not challenge the system of inequality. For example, a reformist reform might work to reform a school bureaucracy, only to make the bureaucracy marginalize students of color more efficiently. According to Gorz, nonreformist reforms move to change the system but keep the system intact. The difference here is that the nonreformist reform works to change the system into something more equitable, but it works within the system to make this happen. As a result, the

system itself is not challenged. Finally, revolutionary reforms work toward a radical transformation of the present system and the creation of an entirely different, more equitable system. Although we concede that at best, much of our work probably falls into the category of nonreformist racial reform, we maintain our hopes for and continue to struggle toward revolutionary racial reform. We believe counter-storytelling in the critical race tradition offers a small but important contribution in this struggle to "advance toward a radical transformation of society" (Gorz, 1967, p. 6).

9. We cite only a few of the many critical race and LatCrit scholars who have written in this counter-storytelling tradition.

References

Anzaldúa, G. (1990). Haciendo caras, una entrada. In G. Anzaldúa (Ed.), *Making face, making soul: Creative and critical perspectives by feminists of color* (pp. xv–xxviii). San Francisco, CA: Aunt Lute Books.

Banfield, E. C. (1970). Schooling versus education. *The unheavenly city: The nature and future of our urban crisis* (pp. 132–157). Boston: Little, Brown.

Banks, J. A. (1993). The canon debate, knowledge construction, and multicultural education. *Educational Researcher, 22*(5), 4–14.

Barnes, R. (1990). Race consciousness: The thematic content of racial distinctiveness in critical race scholarship. *Harvard Law Review, 103*, 1864–1871.

Bell, D. (1987). *And we will not be saved: The elusive quest for racial justice.* New York: Basic Books.

Bell, D. (1992). *Faces at the bottom of the well: The permanence of racism.* New York: Basic Books.

Bell, D. (1996). *Gospel choirs: Psalms of survival for an alien land called home.* New York: Basic Books.

Berkeley Art Center. (1982). *Ethnic notions: Black images in the White mind.* Berkeley, CA: Author.

Bernstein, B. (1977). *Class, codes, and control: Vol. 3: Towards a theory of educational transmission.* Boston: Routledge Kegan Paul.

Calmore, J. (1992). Critical race theory, Archie Shepp, and fire music: Securing an authentic intellectual life in a multicultural world. *Southern California Law Review, 65*, 2129–2231.

Calmore, J. (1997). Exploring Michael Omi's "messy" real world of race: An essay for "naked people longing to swim free." *Law and Inequality, 15*, 25–82.

Carrasco, E. (1996). Collective recognition as a communitarian device: Or, of course we want to be role models! *La Raza Law Journal, 9*, 81–101.

Chavez, L. (1992). *Out of the barrio: Toward a new politics of Hispanic assimilation.* New York: Basic Books.

Coleman, J., Campbell, E., Hobson, C., McPartland, J., Mood, A., Weinfield, F., & York, R. (1966). *Equality of educational opportunity.* Washington, DC: Government Printing Office.

Crenshaw, K. (1989). Demarginalizing the intersection of race and sex: A Black feminist critique of antidiscrimination doctrine, feminist theory and antiracist politics. *University of Chicago Legal Forum, 1989*, 139–167.

Crenshaw, K. (1993). Mapping the margins: Intersectionality, identity politics, and the violence against women of color. *Stanford Law Review, 43*, 1241–1299.

Crenshaw, K., Gotanda, N., Peller, G., & Thomas, K. (Eds.). (1995). *Critical race theory: The key writings that formed the movement.* New York: New Press.

Delgado, R. (1984). The imperial scholar: Reflections on a review of civil rights literature. *University of Pennsylvania Law Review, 132*, 561–578.

Delgado, R. (1989). Storytelling for oppositionists and others: A plea for narrative. *Michigan Law Review, 87*, 2411–2441.

Delgado, R. (1992). The imperial scholar revisited: How to marginalize outsider writing, ten years later. *University of Pennsylvania Law Review, 140*, 1349–1372.

Delgado, R. (1993). On telling stories in school: A reply to Farber and Sherry. *Vanderbilt Law Review, 46*, 665–676.

Delgado, R. (1995a). *The Rodrigo chronicles: Conversations about America and race.* New York: New York University Press.

Delgado, R. (Ed.). (1995b). *Critical race theory: The cutting edge.* Philadelphia, PA: Temple University Press.

Delgado, R. (1996). *The coming race war?: And other apocalyptic tales of America after affirmative action and welfare.* New York: New York University Press.

Delgado, R., & Stefancic, J. (1993). Critical race theory: An annotated bibliography. *Virginia Law Review, 79*, 461–516.

Delgado, R., & Stefancic, J. (1994). Critical race theory: An annotated bibliography 1993, a year of transition. *University of Colorado Law Review, 66*, 159–193.

Delgado, R., & Stefancic, J. (1997). (Eds.). *Critical White studies: Looking behind the mirror.* Philadelphia, PA: Temple University Press.

Delgado Bernal, D. (1998). Using a Chicana feminist epistemology in educational research. *Harvard Educational Review, 68*, 555–582.

Deloria, V. (1969). *Custer died for your sins: An Indian manifesto.* New York: Avon.

Denzin, N., & Lincoln, Y. (1994). Introduction: Entering the field of qualitative research. In N. Denzin & Y. Lincoln (Eds.), *Handbook of qualitative research* (pp. 1–17). Thousand Oaks, CA: Sage.

Dunn, L. (1987). *Bilingual Hispanic children on the mainland: A review of research of their cognitive, linguistic, and scholastic development.* Circle Pines, MN: American Guidance Service.

Espin, O. (1993). Giving voice to silence: The psychologist as witness. *American Psychologist, 48*, 408–414.

Espinoza, L. (1990). Masks and other disguises: Exposing legal academia. *Harvard Law Review, 103*, 1878–1886.

Fernández, L. (2002). Telling stories about school: Using critical race and Latino critical theories to document Latina/Latino education and resistance. *Qualitative Inquiry, 8*, 44–63.

Garcia, R. (1995). Critical race theory and Proposition 187: The racial politics of immigration law. *Chicano-Latino Law Review, 17*, 118–148.

George, L. (2000, October 17). Stirring up a rage in Black America. *Los Angeles Times*, pp. E1, E3.

Glaser, B., & Strauss, A. (1967). *The discovery of grounded theory.* Hawthorne, NY: Aldine.

Gorz, A. (1967). *Strategies for labor: A radical proposal.* Boston: Beacon.

Graham, S. (1992). "Most of the subjects were White and middle class": Trends in published research on African Americans in selected APA journals, 1970–1989. *American Psychologist, 47*, 629–639.

Harding, S. (1987). *Feminism and methodology.* Bloomington, IN: Indiana University Press.

Harris, A. (1994). Forward: The jurisprudence of reconstruction. *California Law Review, 82*, 741–785.

Heller, C. (1966). *Mexican American youth: Forgotten youth at the crossroads.* New York: Random House.

Herrnstein, R., & Murray, C. (1994). *The bell curve: Intelligence and class structure in American life.* New York: Free Press.

Higginbotham, L. (1992). An open letter to Justice Clarence Thomas from a federal judicial colleague. In T. Morrison (Ed.), *Race-ing justice, en-gendering power: Essays on Anita Hill, Clarence Thomas, and the construction of social reality* (pp. 3–39). New York: Random House.

hooks, b. (1990). *Yearning: Race, gender, and cultural politics.* Boston, MA: South End.

Ikemoto, L. (1997). Furthering the inquiry: Race, class, and culture in the forced medical treatment of pregnant women. In A. Wing (Ed.), *Critical race feminism: A reader* (pp. 136–143). New York: New York University Press.

Jensen, A. (1969). How much can we boost I.Q. and scholastic achievement? *Harvard Educational Review, 39*, 1–123.

Kretovics, J., & Nussel, E. (Eds.). (1994). *Transforming urban education.* Boston: Allyn & Bacon.

LatCrit Primer. (2000, May 4–7). Fact sheet: LatCrit. Presented to the 5th annual LatCrit conference titled "Class in LatCrit: Theory and praxis in the world of economic inequality." The Village at Breckenridge Resort, Breckenridge, Colorado.

Lawrence, C. (1992). The word and the river: Pedagogy as scholarship as struggle. *Southern California Law Review, 65*, 2231–2298.

Lawrence, C., & Matsuda, M. (1997). *We won't go back: Making the case for affirmative action.* Boston: Houghton-Mifflin.

Lewis, O. (1968). The culture of poverty. In D. Moynihan (Ed.), *On understanding poverty: Perspectives from the social sciences* (187–200). New York: Basic Books.

Lincoln, Y. (1993). I and thou: Method, voice, and roles in research with the silenced. In D. McLaughlin & W. Tierney (Eds.), *Naming silenced lives* (pp. 29–47). Boston: Routledge Kegan Paul.

Lorde, A. (1978). A litany of survival. In A. Lorde, *The Black unicorn* (pp. 31–32). New York: Norton.

Lorde, A. (1992). Age, race, class, and sex: Women redefining difference. In M. Andersen & P. Hill Collins (Eds.), *Race, class, and gender: An anthology* (pp. 495–502). Belmont, CA: Wadsworth.

Marable, M. (1992). *Black America.* Westfield, NJ: Open Media.

Matsuda, C. (1991). Voices of America: Accent, antidiscrimination law, and a jurisprudence for the last reconstruction. *Yale Law Journal, 100*, 1329–1407.

Matsuda, M., Lawrence, C., Delgado, R., & Crenshaw, K. (1993). *Words that wound: Critical race theory, assaultive speech, and the first amendment.* Boulder, CO: Westview.

McIntosh, P. (1989, July/August). White privilege: Unpacking the invisible knapsack. *Peace and Freedom*, pp. 10–12.

Montecinos, C. (1995). Culture as an ongoing dialogue: Implications for multicultural teacher education. In C. Sleeter & P. McLaren (Eds.), *Multicultural education, critical pedagogy, and the politics of difference* (pp. 269–308). Albany: State University of New York Press.

Montoya, M. (1994). Mascaras, trenzas, y grenas: Un/masking the self while un/braiding Latina stories and legal discourse. *Chicano-Latino Law Review, 15*, 1–37.

Ogbu, J. (1990). Minority education in comparative perspective. *Journal of Negro Education, 59*, 45–57.

Olivas, M. (1990). The chronicles, my grandfather's stories, and immigration law: The slave traders chronicle as racial history. *Saint Louis University Law Journal, 34*, 425–441.

Paredes, A. (1977). On ethnographic work among minority groups: A folklorist's perspective. *New Scholar, 6,* 1–32.

Persell, C. (1977). *Education and inequality: The roots and results of stratification in America's schools.* New York: Free Press.

Rosaldo, R. (1994). Whose cultural studies? *American Anthropologist, 96,* 524–529.

Russell, M. (1992). Entering great America: Reflections on race and the convergence of progressive legal theory and practice. *Hastings Law Journal, 43,* 749–767.

Schwartz, A. (1971). A comparative study of values and achievement: Mexican-American and Anglo-American youth. *Sociology of Education, 44,* 438–462.

Snider, W. (1990, April 18). Outcry follows Cavazos comments on the values of Hispanic parents. *Education Week,* p. 1.

Solórzano, D.G. (1994). The baccalaureate origins of Chicana and Chicano doctorates in the physical, life, and engineering sciences: 1980–1990. *Journal of Women and Minorities in Science and Engineering, 1,* 253–272.

Solórzano, D.G. (1995). The baccalaureate origins of Chicana and Chicano doctorates in the social sciences. *Hispanic Journal of Behavioral Sciences, 17,* 3–32.

Solórzano, D.G. (1997). Images and words that wound: Critical race theory, racial stereotyping, and teacher education. *Teacher Education Quarterly, 24,* 5–19.

Solórzano, D.G. (1998). Critical race theory, racial and gender microaggressions, and the experiences of Chicana and Chicano scholars. *International Journal of Qualitative Studies in Education, 11,* 121–136.

Solórzano, D.G., & Delgado Bernal, D. (2001). Examining transformational resistance through a critical race and LatCrit theory framework: Chicana and Chicano students in an urban context. *Urban Education, 3,* 308–342.

Solórzano, D. G., & Solórzano, R. (1995). The Chicano educational experience: A proposed framework for effective schools in Chicano communities. *Educational Policy, 9,* 293–314.

Solórzano, D. G., & Villalpando, O. (1998). Critical race theory, marginality, and the experience of minority students in higher education. In C. Torres & T. Mitchell (Eds.), *Emerging issues in the sociology of education: Comparative perspectives* (pp. 211–224). New York: State University of New York Press.

Solórzano, D. G., & Yosso, T.J. (2000). Toward a critical race theory of Chicana and Chicano education. In C. Tejeda, C. Martinez, & Z. Leonardo (Eds.), *Charting new terrains of Chicana(o)/Latina(o) education* (pp. 35–65). Cresskill, NJ: Hampton.

Solórzano, D. G., & Yosso, T. J. (2001). Critical race and LatCrit theory and method: Counterstorytelling Chicana and Chicano graduate school experiences. *International Journal of Qualitative Studies in Education, 4,* 471–495.

Solórzano, D. G., & Yosso, T. J. (in press-a). Maintaining social justice hopes within academic realities: A Freirean approach to critical race/LatCrit pedagogy. *Denver Law Review.*

Solórzano, D. G., & Yosso, T. J. (in press-b). A critical race theory counterstory of affirmative action in higher education. *Journal of Equity and Excellence in Education.*

Sowell, T. (1981). *Ethnic America: A history.* New York: Basic Books.

Stefancic, J. (1998). Latino and Latina critical theory: An annotated bibliography. *La Raza Law Journal, 10,* 423–498.

Strauss, A., & Corbin, J. (1990). *Basics of qualitative research: Grounded theory procedures and techniques.* Newbury Park, CA: Sage.

Tatum, B. (1997). *Why are all the Black kids sitting together in the cafeteria? And other conversation about race.* New York: Basic Books.

Terman, L. (1916). *The measurement of intelligence.* Boston, MA: Houghton Mifflin.

Tierney, W. (1993). *Building communities of difference: Higher education in the twenty-first century.* Westport, CT: Bergin & Garvey.

Valencia, R. (Ed.). (1997). *The evolution of deficit thinking in educational thought and practice.* New York: Falmer.

Valencia, R., & Solórzano, D. (1997). Contemporary deficit thinking. In R. Valencia (Ed.), *The evolution of deficit thinking in educational thought and practice* (pp. 160–210). New York: Falmer.

Williams, P. (1991). *The alchemy of race and rights: Diary of a law professor.* Cambridge, MA: Harvard University Press.

Williams, R. (1997). Vampires anonymous and critical race practice. *Michigan Law Review, 95,* 741–765.

10

What's Race Got to Do With It?
Critical Race Theory's Conflicts With and Connections to Qualitative Research Methodology and Epistemology

Laurence Parker and Marvin Lynn

In this special issue titled "Critical Race Theory and Qualitative Research," we not only reflect on the role and status of qualitative research in the lives of people of color but also examine the ways critical race theory (CRT)—a legal theory of race and racism designed to uncover how race and racism operate in the law and in society—can be used as a tool through which to define, expose, and address educational problems. The goal here is to look specifically at how such issues can be addressed through the use of the qualitative research paradigm. Each of the articles contributes toward the goal of completing this important task in different ways. They do this specifically by arguing for the nexus of CRT and qualitative research methodologies to address the particular historical, legal, and contemporary social context of persons of color while discussing how the work informs criticisms of Whiteness and White privilege. This article will provide the theoretical and conceptual grounding for forthcoming discussions regarding the specific ways CRT, as a discourse of liberation, can be used as a methodological tool as well as a greater ontological and epistemological understanding of how race and racism affect the education and lives of the racially disenfranchised. More specifically, we hope to be able to perform three important functions. First, we seek to flesh out, in some detail, the contours of the legal concept of CRT by situating it within a specific socio-historical context and defining some of its broader elements. Second, we seek to present an argument for why there is a need for CRT in educational research and in qualitative inquiry. In doing so, we hope to point out the ways concerns regarding race and racism have or have not been addressed previously in educational research. Finally, we seek to speculate about what lies ahead. As the subsequent articles will more fully illustrate, we will assess the possible points of agreement and conflicts between CRT and qualitative research in education.

Recentering Race and Racism: Defining and Historicizing CRT's Social Justice Agenda

"Just what is [CRT] and what is it doing in a nice field like education," asked Gloria Ladson-Billings (1998) in an article that addressed the ways CRT can be used as a tool to address long-standing educational problems, particularly those experienced by students of color. Although the discussion began a few years ago when Ladson-Billings and Tate (1995) published the first known article to address that very question, the questions still remain: Just what is CRT, and more important, where did it come from? In this section, we hope to provide a brief historical examination of the concept and then talk in more detail about how it has come to be defined.

Where Did CRT Come From?

With roots in African American, Latino/Latina, and Native American critical social thought, CRT was necessarily borne out of a need for people of color to begin to move discussions of race and racism from the realm of the experiential to the realm of the ideological (Ladson-Billings, 2000; Tate, 1997). Whereas African Americans and other people of color have always thought in theoretical terms about their conditions of social, political, and economic subordination in a White supremacist society, racism has not been given full explanatory power in the academy (Feagin, 2000). In other words, because racism has heretofore been understood as a willful act of aggression against a person based on their skin color and other phenotypic characteristics, discussions of race and racism rarely addressed the ways race and racism are deeply embedded within the framework of American society (Omi & Winant, 1994). Because of that, it was difficult to talk about racism as a system of oppression. CRT pioneers such as Derrick Bell (1988) and Richard Delgado (1989) argued that racism should not be viewed as acts of individual prejudice that can simply be eradicated. Rather, it is an endemic part of American life, deeply ingrained through historical consciousness and ideological choices about race, which in turn has directly shaped the U.S. legal system and the ways people think about the law, racial categories, and privilege (C. Harris, 1993). In particular, critical race scholars began publishing extensive critiques of critical legal studies (CLS)—a movement within the law of mostly White Marxist and postmodernist legal scholars who were attempting to uncover the ideological underpinnings of American jurisprudence (Crenshaw, 1988; Matsuda, 1987; Williams, 1987, 1991). Critical race theorists argued that the obsession with deconstructing the nature, role, form, and function of ideology in American society left little room for a discussion about unalienable human rights, which, as Williams (1987) argues, has always been of utmost concern for African Americans. Furthermore, critical legal scholars of color argued that what was left out of CLS critiques of the law was an honest discussion of race and racial oppression (Crenshaw, 1988.)

Critical race theorists claimed that CLS scholars not only failed to address issues of racial inequality directly but also overlooked and underplayed the role that race and racism played in the very construction of the legal foundations upon which our society rests (Crenshaw, 1988; A. P. Harris, 1994). CRT also focused a good deal of attention on the limitations of liberal ideology in the law (Bell, 1992). Ensconced in a liberal integrationist ideal, the former stewards of racial justice proposed legal remedies that operated under the presumption that racial integration on White America's terms, as long as they were accompanied by slow and protracted reforms to the legal system, would ultimately improve social conditions for people of color.

CRT scholars, many of whom had been strongly influenced by civil rights law and CLS law, began to take up seriously the question of race and racism in the law by calling for a complete reinterpretation of civil rights law with regard to its ineffectiveness in addressing racial injustices, particularly institutional racism and structural racism in the political economy (Guinier, 1991, 1994). To that extent, CRT also engages in an "undressing" of the objective nature of the law and legal doctrine. Concepts such as color-blind interpretations of the law or meritocracy are "unmasked" by critical race theorists to be precursors for White, European American hegemonic control of the social and structural arrangements in U.S. society. In this regard, the critical race theorists have developed a body of legal scholarship and alternative and intersecting paradigms based on the perspectives of "outsider" groups who experience racism and sexism in multiple ways.

As a result, CRT has garnered increasing attention from various academic circles and disciplines as an emerging perspective in jurisprudence scholarship that centralizes and foregrounds race and racism (Crenshaw, Gotanda, Peller, & Thomas, 1995; Delgado & Stefancic, 2000; Symposium, 1994). CRT is a discourse generated by legal scholars of color devoted to uncovering the often hidden subtext of race in society (Crenshaw et al., 1995; Delgado & Stefancic, 2000; Matsuda, 1987). CRT seeks to expose the historical, ideological, psychological, and social contexts in which racism has been declared virtually eradicated while racially subordinated peoples have been chastised for relying too much on racial "victimology" (McWhorter, 2000). The CRT position challenged the dominant racial ideology through law (and other political and social forces) and initially sought to use the power of the courts to "further the goal of eradicating the effects of racial oppression" (Crenshaw, 1988, p. 134). In that sense, CRT has three main goals: (a) to present storytelling and narratives as valid approaches through which to examine race and racism in the law and in society; (b) to argue for the eradication of racial subjugation while simultaneously recognizing that race is a social construct; and (c) to draw important relationships between race and other axes of domination.

Narratives and Storytelling

CRT evolved not only through alternative interpretations of traditional legal doctrine (A. P. Harris, 1994) but also through the legitimating of narrative and storytelling that present a different interpretation of how the law has been used to justify an ideology of racism against persons of color (Delgado, 1989). The theory serves an important role because the storytelling constitutes an integral part of historical and current legal evidence gathering and findings of fact in racial discrimination litigation. The federal courts and the White European American majority should be interested in these "stories" because, as Delgado asserts, only through listening can the conviction of seeing the world one way be challenged and "one can acquire the ability to see the world through others' eyes" (p. 2439). Matsuda (1987) argued for the legitimization of stories about discrimination from the perspective of people of color because too often, the law has not "looked to the needs of the bottom which recognizes economic as well as racial injustice and views reparations awards as a step forward in the long journey toward substantive equality" (p. 397). Matsuda used the example of Japanese American interment camps and reparations for World War II confinement: Those who argued against reparations for groups such as Japanese Americans asserted that legal facts cannot be specifically traced to victims of groups and that their voices lack sufficient connection between past wrong and present assertions of discrimination. However, Matsuda argued that the stories of victims were useful under CRT because these experiences were real and that connections from the past have to be understood to see how the hierarchical relationships of power protect the legal interest of White European Americans over persons of color. Some critical race theorists, such as Williams (1991) in *The Alchemy of Race and Rights*, have examined the possibility of racial justice by exposing White European Americans to racism through personal narratives and have theorized that perceptions about race and the law can be transformed by these narratives to truly achieve justice.

CRT narratives and storytelling provide readers with a challenging account of preconceived notions of race, and the stories are sometimes integral to developing cases that consist of legal narratives of racial discrimination. The thick descriptions and interviews, characteristic of case study research, not only serve illuminative purposes but also can be used to document institutional as well as overt racism. The interviewing process can be pulled together to create narratives that can be used to build a case against racially biased officials or discriminatory practices. For example, CRT was used as a lens to see and act on discriminatory educational policy practices (e.g., tracking, operating virtually dual school systems based on race, and not providing bilingual services) of administrators and White Mormon community leaders in southern Utah in the Navajo's civil rights case against the district (Deyhle, 1995; *Meyers v. the Board of Education of San Juan County*, 1995; Villenas, Deyhle, & Parker, 1999). The use of narrative in CRT added a different dimension to the purpose of educational research by taking on a different potential dimension as an integral part of legal testimony. In this case, expert witness testimony and personal narratives of discrimination played a key role in proving the school district's intent to discriminate and neglect the legal rights of Navajo children with respect to equal educational opportunity through an inequitable distribution of educational services. Deyhle (Villenas et al., 1999) connected this testimony to *social justice validity*, a term used by Deyhle and Swisher (1997) in their review of research on Native American tribal nations and education. Social justice validity posits a research validity that is seriously grounded in social justice and commitment on tribal nation terms and long-term involvement in challenging White supremacy over tribal nation affairs.

The Social Construction of Race

Critical race theorists have also called for a reexamination of the concept of race, recognizing that it is not a fixed term. Rather, race has fluid, decentered social meanings that are continually shaped by political pressures (Calmore, 1992). Hayman (1995) has also posited that CRT has postmodern threads in that both reject traditional legal realist and conceptualist epistemologies and rely instead on the importance of perspective and context in assessing truth claims. He saw similarities in that both the postmodernists and critical race theorists reject the assertion that established doctrine and texts have objective truth and universal meanings. Instead, race goes through "relentless, deconstruction and reconstruction" (Hayman, 1995, p. 70), and race, like other aspects of identity, is indeed a sociopolitical construction. However, CRT deviates from postmodern legal critique in the

> insistence that justice can not [sic] be merely theoretical. Furthermore, it must be informed by and realized in lived experiences, and while the struggle for racial justice may offer no prospects for immediate or ultimate success, the struggle has to be continuous.
>
> (Hayman, 1995, p. 70)

CRT and Intersectionality

A third emerging expansion of CRT is in the area of key intersections of other areas of difference, such as feminism. Crenshaw et al. (1995) have sought to combine feminist legal theory with CRT to uncover the patterns of disempowerment on gender and racial lines in the areas of law as well as popular discourse. Crenshaw et al.'s work specifically seeks to (a) expose the concept of Whiteness to legal critique and for its association with unspoken acceptance of power and authority in U.S. society; (b) bring issues that affect women, such as domestic violence, gender role socialization, child care, and so forth, into the public discourse to expose how these issues are excluded from public debate because they are seen as private issues or family issues; and (c) address the marginalization of African American women in public discourse and the law and eventually seek ways in which connections can be made with other women on common issues. According to Crenshaw (1988), "The experiences of women of color are frequently the product of intersecting patterns of racism and sexism . . . Because of their intersectional identity as both women and of color, . . . women of color are marginalized" along the lines of gender and race at the same time. Although race and gender epistemologies have attempted to bifurcate and thereby essentialize identity into frozen fixed frames, an intersectional analysis forces us to see the relationship between sexism and racism as symbiotic. In other words, racism sustains and rearticulates sexism. Moreover, in the case of Black women, race does not exist outside of gender and gender does not exist outside of race.

In sum, CRT has emerged from the legal arena to uncover the deep patterns of racial exclusion. As illustrated, there are many emerging strands from which CRT borrows to expand itself to include other critical epistemologies and to seek intersections and conjunctions with other areas of difference to push a social justice agenda into the legal and public discourse on race and gender. The critical race theorists seek to break the dominance of storytelling about success of merit, equality, the market, and objectivity that is so deeply entrenched and accepted unquestioningly by larger society through the legitimating of legal narratives of racial discrimination and the power of the law used against persons of color. Thus, CRT has important implications for qualitative research, particularly in education and youth culture.

Exploring the Utility of CRT in Educational Research

Traditionally, educational research has (a) ignored historically marginalized groups by simply not addressing their concerns, (b) relied heavily on genetic or biological determinist perspectives to explain away complex social educational problems, or (c) epiphenomenized or de-emphasized race by arguing that the problems minority students experience in schools can be understood via class or gender analyses that do not fully take race, culture, language, and immigrant status into account (McCarthy & Crichlow, 1993; Solórzano, 1997; Solórzano & Villapando, 1998). This is even more important because research that has attempted to call attention to the concerns of disenfranchised groups has relied heavily on antediluvian and sometimes culturally inappropriate methods of investigation and exploration (Stanfield, 1999). Moreover, questions regarding methodology—what approaches we take to help us understand specific populations—and epistemology—what counts as knowledge about a particular group—have often remained unaddressed or become shrouded in a language that fails to address important questions regarding the origins, uses, and abuses of social scientific inquiry and the importance of minority representation in this enterprise. For example, after conducting a review of educational research that focuses on Chicano students, Pizarro (1998) found that by and large, educational research has tended to undervalue the voices of Chicano students by focusing too much attention on Chicano school failure without exploring how these students make sense of their own lived realities. Stanfield (1999) and Foster (1994) have noted how qualitative research used to describe various aspects of Black life and the African American community was typically fraught with problems of participant exploitation by White European American researchers who failed to honestly address the power struggles between researchers and their participants of color. Some of these issues have been addressed in more recently published studies—many of them published in this very journal—that examine the intersection of race and qualitative research.

Race as Discussed in Recent Qualitative Research

Lincoln's (1995) discussion of criteria for quality in interpretive research revealed major questions for qualitative researchers and now CRT legal scholars to address as they use qualitative research methods and methodologies. For example, Lincoln discusses the importance of the positionality or standpoint judgment of the researcher as well as the community as judge of the research study's ability to meet validity standards. Other central questions surrounding voice(s) and who speaks for whom are critical issues that have already been discussed in qualitative research and will become even more critical to explore through CRT in qualitative research circles.

For example, Ellis (1995), in *Qualitative Inquiry*, described the role of her own position and storytelling as she recalled her past relationship with an African American young man in a small southern town in the 1960s. She discussed how the narrative structure allowed her to tell the story to readers while also giving freedom and responsibility to others to peel off the layers of complexity in everyday life. This resulted in critical questions regarding Ellis's self-critique of her White privilege and her appearance as the authority on issues of race as opposed to the others in her narrative. Nebeker (1998) also took this a step further by linking but still questioning CRT in relation to her positionality as a White female writing in a racialized space to challenge White "colorblindness." The positionality and privilege of Whiteness in terms of who gets to tell the critical race story has also been discussed in the legal area: in particular, the assumed notion of Whiteness as property, which has been recognized in the law as upholding the rights and legal narratives of White European Americans over persons of color regarding property rights, land treaties, slavery, reverse discrimination in university admissions, and denial of equal protection of the laws (Delgado & Stefancic, 1997; C. Harris, 1993). In a *Qualitative Inquiry* article by Wong (1998), the author discussed the dangers of researcher closeness to African American and Latina welfare mothers and how this leads to problematic relationships in terms of who the research is for, what purpose it serves, and why the research is even being conducted. Wong's own narrative regarding these respondents was insightful in its attempt to trace and critique, for social justice purposes, the impact of new conservative restrictions in welfare policy and what it has done to the women's lives in terms of race, gender, and social class discrimination. Wong was hoping for more of a social justice critique from these mothers, but instead, what she got through her interviews was more narratives based on personal concerns about family life and relationships as well as a concern for money and the paid interview process. Wong warns about expecting too much from narratives in terms of interviewer expectations for critical perspectives and insights. This may be a question for future exploration in CRT as it is more widely used as a framework of analysis for narratives, as some have already questioned the use of CRT as another theory to "box in" the voices of native-indigenous people and what they want from education. Hermes (1998) spoke to this by partially using CRT as a way to analyze the legal tribal history with the Ojinwe reservations and Whites, revealing how CRT was not useful as an interview interpretive framework for what the tribe wanted for education in their communities. Therefore, community standards for qualitative research become crucial for purposes of social justice validity. It should also come as no surprise that, for example, African American evaluators who have used qualitative inquiry methodologies have made this same social justice validity point for quite some time now, yet it has been ignored by Whites in the academy until recently when other current African American scholars have seen it as important scholarship in the evaluation arena (Hood, 1998; personal communication, Stafford Hood, Arizona State University, March 7, 2001;[1] Stanfield, 1999).

The issue of subjectivity has also been widely discussed in *Qualitative Inquiry*, and we seek to build on this discussion with the set of articles in this special issue. Geertz (1983), Peshkin (1988), Guba (1990), Denzin (2000), Schwandt (2000), and a host of others have discussed subjectivity in qualitative research through myriad informed perspectives, ranging from narrow definitions of personal interest and values as a nemesis of scientific validity, to more nuanced definitions of the overt and covert thoughts and emotions of the individual and their worldviews, to a critique of the pretense of distancing the informants from the interviewer. Bloom (1996) pulls these criticisms together by focusing on nonunitary subjectivity, how it is produced, and how we can interpret it in narrative self-representations. Bloom used her oral histories and personal narratives with Olivia, who was a second-year assistant professor when she started the interviews. In the process of the interviews, she uncovered Olivia's story about being in the corporate world, being married and being seen as a wife, and now facing academic and/or faculty expectations. Bloom found that Olivia's multiple positions in her life led to a fragmented subjectivity, so that even as she (and other women) made choices in her life, the choices are truncated by other more powerful forces that set constraints on these choices based on either chosen or imposed roles. Bloom calls for an understanding of these different subject positions based on situated responses that individuals make relevant to the complexities of specific situations. This is very similar to articles by Solórzano (1998), Gonzalez (1998), Tanaka and Cruz (1998), and others in this issue (for example, Fernandez, 2002 [this issue]). CRT's evolution in the law review journals and other areas (for example, education) has mirrored the discussions in qualitative research on the positionality and subjectivity of respondents. The emergence of critical race feminism and Latino critical theory (LatCrit) and its emphasis on race, ethnicity, nationality, and language have made an impact in terms of sharpening and simultaneously blurring nonsychronist positions of where persons of color are at racially and in certain racial situations (McCarthy, 1988; McCarthy & Crichlow, 1993). For example, the use of polyphonic text by Tanaka and Cruz (1998) shows the conflicts and societal constraints around race, gender, and homosexuality regarding straight male discomfort in White gay space, silence, and understanding of the positions of African American upper middle-class women versus Asian American male administrators with respect to racial separatism on predominantly White campuses. Similarly, Fernandez (2002) gives us the story of Pablo and his struggle to succeed as a Latino student in a Chicago school system that has statistically structured him and other Latino students to fail. We hear the story of how Pablo has to negotiate the low expectations for students like him and how he rises above them but at the same time resists completely buying into this form of total acceptance of "Whiteness." The role of Whiteness and how it plays out in the subjectivity of the respondents in the Duncan article (2002 [this issue]) and the Smith-Maddox and Solórzano (2002 [this issue]) article also speak to the complexities of situations when White teacher education candidates and urban education students at both sites in the respective studies engage in reflexive thinking about what it means to be White in a field such as education and its impact on practice (Thompson, 1999; Young & Laible, 2000). To be sure, as Ulichny (1997) and Fine and Weis (1996) have pointed out earlier in *Qualitative Inquiry* that we cannot expect researched accounts to radically transform institutions, particularly around complex issues of race as qualitative researchers conduct urban ethnographies. But as Solórzano and Yosso (2002 [this issue]) argue, critical race methodology, which has epistemological grounding in other fields and disciplines (sociology, Marxism, feminism, cultural studies, gender studies; Torres, Miron, & Inda, 1999; University of California, Los Angeles, Law Review Symposium, 2000; Villalpando, 2000), recognizes the intersections and conflicts that can emerge from data narratives and seeks to place those narratives at the center of legal and political social change and justice. For the critical race qualitative researcher, therefore, it is also important not only to deal with issues of nonunitary subjectivity in narrative representation but also to document how this plays out in various settings such as schools, where expectations of different groups of students based on race can lead to fluid but fixed notions of racial identity and responses by school officials to the achievement or failure of students of color (Mirón, 1996).

We also feature an article on CRT, LatCrit, and Chicana feminist epistemology by Delgado Bernal (2002 [this issue]). She discusses the importance of an epistemology that centers on the Chicana experience and how previous research traditions have either ignored Chicanas or have subsumed them under other forms of analysis (such as feminism). Delgado Bernal (1998) posits that this Chicana feminist epistemology originates from the lived experiences of Chicana women themselves. Furthermore, researchers and interviewees are seen more as conversational partners, and there is a shared understanding of the cultural interview process with Chicanas in particular settings. The article by Delgado Bernal (2002) is similar to previous articles in *Qualitative Inquiry* by Carspecken and Cordeiro (1995), Madriz (1998), and Rodriguez (1998). Carspecken and Cordeiro's article focuses on interviews with 20 high-achieving Latino/Latina students. In this study, Carspecken and Cordeiro looked at how the patterns of student success through the data also gave insights into cultural systems and cultural text. Rodriguez (1998) examined how anthropology silences the identities of Chicanas and elevates the narrative interpretations of the researchers. In her article, she called for a fundamental inclusion of Chicana voices to disrupt the demands of anthropology as a discipline. Madriz's (1998) article in *Qualitative Inquiry* also called for a serious undertaking of incorporating Latina interest in the research process by focusing on their experiences with crime through the use of focus groups. Madriz found that the focus group served to narrow the gap between the researcher and the Latina women as they discussed the impact of crime on their lives and families and acted as a collective form of testimony, which can also be seen in CRT.

Finally, the use of fiction, artistic expression and/or aesthetics, and narrative story to paint a portrait of racialized life has been featured in *Qualitative Inquiry* articles and is also linked to CRT. Kotarba (1998) and Dimitriadis and McCarthy (2000) showed how Black music and artistic expression contributed to performance ethnography. This performance ethnography relied on a Black aesthetic as a form of political artistic expressions and literary presentations of racial data that challenge the way race is discussed to provide new avenues of conceptualizing race and connecting with cultural rituals. Dimitriadis and McCarthy used the work of James Baldwin in citing the importance of fiction as it connects to youth culture and popular culture. The importance of narrative has also been a part of *Qualitative Inquiry* in recent articles by Diversi (1998), Dunbar (1999), and Pifer (1999). All of these accounts are short story descriptions of race and racial incidents that take place in Illinois and Brazil, and the intent of the narratives is to highlight racial categorizations of individuals and how racism plays out in youth experiences. For example, Dunbar's article shows how young African American boys in an alternative school setting are supposed to be rehabilitated but are racialized in these school settings as Black predators who live out a self-fulfilling prophesy of crime and Black male incarceration that is partly fueled by White expectations and fears of crime by African American youth. The importance of these stories is to, hopefully, provide the reader with a better understanding of race and racial context. Denzin (2000) spoke to the utility of CRT in combination with alternative forms of textual expressions in qualitative research, which is more affirming of a racial humanity that is grounded in the experiences and expressions of various groups and individuals.

Conclusion: The Future of CRT in Qualitative Research

Given the conservative nature of the federal court rulings on questions of race, as exemplified in the bevy of anti-affirmative action decisions and laws that have sprung up around the country in recent years, CRT in education will come under the same attack it is facing in the legal arena. Therefore, the future of CRT and its place in qualitative research will partially depend on the efforts made by researchers and scholars to explore its possible connections to life in schools and communities of color. For example, the emerging broader theoretical framework related to race and the widening of the lens to take into account other perspectives besides the Black-White paradigm would be very useful in terms of developing a more multi-layered research discussion about life in racially diverse schools with different populations of students. Connections can be made in educational research through the use of narrative in CRT, which has already been a part of literature and commentary on racism, and feminist research that uses narrative with regard to women's lives and activist scholarship, as discussed previously by Casey (1995) and Weis (1995) in their respective reviews of how narrative and life-story research has added depth and complexity to qualitative research, particularly in education.

   In this introduction, we have pointed to ways in which qualitative research, action, and CRT can be seen as a way to link theory and understanding about race from critical perspectives to actual practice and actions going on in education for activist social justice and change. One of the limitations expressed about CRT is its lack of connection to the "real world" of practice, law use, and other forces (e.g., media and grass-roots campaigns) used by activist scholars to engage in activism with persons of color (Yamamoto, 1997). We contend that linking CRT to education can indeed foster the connections of theory to practice and activism on issues related to race. The key is (according to Tate, 1999) specifically defining how one is using CRT in qualitative research at the epistemological or methodological levels of analysis and its connection with the law and racism. This special issue will facilitate an understanding of how CRT can be a valuable tool with which to view and analyze issues related to race-based epistemology as well as earlier works on race and racism and/or ethnicity and their intersections and conflicts with social class analysis, gender analysis, and so forth. We will also attempt to show how the legal tools and framework of CRT combined with qualitative research methodology can be helpful in linking practice to ongoing legal struggles for equal educational opportunity and equity. This special issue will hopefully give readers a sense of not only what CRT is but also what and/or how struggles for education equity and social justice can form the basis of critical race praxis, in this way demonstrating what the field of qualitative studies and education has to offer to the field of law and CRT. Employing multidisciplinary frameworks, the articles in this special issue will address a variety of historical, methodological, and epistemological issues as they relate to the scope and trajectory of educational research in the 21st century.

Note

1. The e-mail discussion concerned his research exploring the leading African Americans in educational evaluation. One of them, Leander Boykin (Stanford University), was published in the *Journal of Educational Research* on the importance of qualitative and quantitative measures for evaluation as well as connecting evaluation to African American communities.

References

Bell, D. A. (1988). White superiority in America: Its legal legacy, its economic costs. *Villanova Law Review, 33,* 767–779.

Bell, D. A. (1992). *Faces at the bottom of the well: The permanence of racism.* New York: Basic Books.

Bloom, L. R. (1996). Stories of one's own: Nonunitary subjectivity in narrative representation. *Qualitative Inquiry, 2,* 176–197.

Calmore, J. O. (1992). Critical race theory, Archie Shepp, and firemusic: Securing an authentic intellectual life in a multicultural world. *Southern California Law Review, 65,* 2129–2230.

Carspecken, P. F., & Cordeiro, P. A. (1995). Being, doing, and becoming: Textual interpretations of social identity and a case study. *Qualitative Inquiry, 1,* 87–109.

Casey, K. (1995). The new narrative research in education. In M. Apple (Ed.), *Review of research in education* (Vol. 21, pp. 211–254). Washington, DC: American Educational Research Association.

Crenshaw, K. W. (1988). Race, reform and retrenchment: Transformation and anti-discrimination law. *Harvard Law Review, 101,* 1331–1387.

Crenshaw, K. W., Gotanda, N., Peller, G., & Thomas, K. (Eds.). (1995). *Critical race theory: Key writings that formed the movement.* New York: New Press.

Delgado, R. (1989). Storytelling for oppositionists and others: A plea for narrative. *Michigan Law Review, 87,* 2411–2441.

Delgado, R., & Stefancic, J. (Eds.). (1997). *Critical White studies: Looking behind the mirror.* Philadelphia, PA: Temple University Press.

Delgado, R., & Stefancic, J. (Eds.). (2000). *Critical race theory: The cutting edge* (2nd ed.). Philadelphia, PA: Temple University Press.

Delgado Bernal, D. (1998). Using a Chicana feminist epistemology in educational research. *Harvard Educational Review, 68,* 555–579.

Delgado Bernal, D. (2002). Critical race theory, Latino critical theory, and critical raced-gendered epistemologies: Recognizing students of color as holders and creators of knowledge. *Qualitative Inquiry, 8,* 103–124.

Denzin, N. K. (2000). The practices and politics of interpretation. In N. K. Denzin & Y.S. Lincoln (Eds.), *Handbook of qualitative research* (2nd ed., pp. 897–922). Thousand Oaks, CA: Sage.

Deyhle, D. (1995). Navajo youth and anglo racism: Cultural integrity and resistance. *Harvard Educational Review, 65,* 23–67.

Deyhle, D., & Swisher, K. (1997). Research in American Indian, Alaskan, Native American education: From assimilation to self-determination. In M. Apple (Ed.), *Review of research in education* (pp. 113–147). Washington, DC: American Educational Research Association.

Dimitriadis, G., & McCarthy, C. (2000). Stranger in the village: James Baldwin, popular culture, and the ties that bind. *Qualitative Inquiry, 6,* 171–187.

Diversi, M. (1998). Glimpses of street life: Representing lived experience through short stories. *Qualitative Inquiry, 2,* 131–147.

Dunbar, C., Jr. (1999). Three short stories. *Qualitative Inquiry, 5,* 130–140.

Duncan, G. A. (2002). Critical race theory and method: Rendering race in urban ethnographic research. *Qualitative Inquiry, 8,* 83–102.

Ellis, C. (1995). The other side of the fence: Seeing Black and White in a small southern town. *Qualitative Inquiry, 1,* 147–167.

Feagin, J. (2000). *Racist America.* Boston: Routledge Kegan Paul.

Fernández, L. (2002). Telling stories about school: Using critical race and Latino critical theories to document Latina/ Latino education and resistance. *Qualitative Inquiry, 8,* 44–63.

Fine, M., & Weis, L. (1996). Writing the "wrongs" of fieldwork: Confronting our own research/writing dilemmas in urban ethnographies. *Qualitative Inquiry, 2,* 251–274.

Foster, M. (1994). The power to know one thing is never the power to know all things: Methodological notes on two studies of Black American teachers. In A. Gitlin (Ed.), *Power and method: Political activism and educational research* (pp. 129–146). Boston: Routledge Kegan Paul.

Geertz, C. (1983). *Local knowledge: Further essays on interpretive methodology.* New York: Basic Books.

Gonzalez, F. E. (1998). Formations of Mexicanness: Trenzas de identidades multiples/growing up Mexican: Braid of multiple identities. *International Journal of Qualitative Studies in Education, 11,* 81–102.

Guba, E. G. (1990). Subjectivity and objectivity. In E. W. Eisner & A. Peshkin (Eds.), *Qualitative inquiry in education: The continuing debate* (pp. 74–91). New York: Teachers College Press.

Guinier, L. (1991). The triumph of tokenism: The Voting Rights Act and the theory of Black electoral success. *Michigan Law Review, 89,* 1077–1154.

Guinier, L. (1994). *The tyranny of the majority: Fundamental fairness in representative democracy.* New York: Free Press.

Harris, A. P. (1994). Forward: The jurisprudence of reconstruction. *California Law Review, 82,* 741–785.

Harris, C. (1993). Whiteness as property. *Harvard Law Review, 106,* 1701–1791.

Hayman, R. L. (1995). The color of tradition: Critical race theory and postmodern constitutional traditionalism. *Harvard Civil Rights and Civil Liberties Law Review, 30,* 57–108.

Hermes, M. (1998). Research methods as a situated response: Towards a First Nation's methodology. *International Journal of Qualitative Studies in Education, 11,* 155–168.

Hood, S. (1998). Culturally responsive performance-based assessment: Conceptual and psychometric considerations. *Journal of Negro Education, 67,* 187–197.

Kotarba, J. A. (1998). Black men, Black voices: The role of the producer in synthetic performance ethnography. *Qualitative Inquiry, 4,* 398–404.

Ladson-Billings, G. (1998). Just what is critical race theory and what's it doing in a nice field like education? *International Journal of Qualitative Studies in Education, 11,* 7–24.

Ladson-Billings, G. (2000). Racialized discourses and ethnic epistemologies. In N. K. Denzin & Y.S. Lincoln (Eds.), *Handbook of qualitative research* (2nd ed., pp. 257–278). Thousand Oaks, CA: Sage.

Ladson-Billings, G., & Tate, W. F., IV. (1995). Toward a critical race theory of education. *Teachers College Record, 97,* 47–63.

Lincoln, Y. S. (1995). Emerging criteria for quality in qualitative and interpretive research. *Qualitative Inquiry, 3,* 275–289.

Madriz, E. I. (1998). Using focus groups with lower socioeconomic status Latina women. *Qualitative Inquiry, 4,* 144–128.

Matsuda, M. J. (1987). Looking to the bottom: Critical legal studies and reparations. *Harvard Civil Rights–Civil Liberties Review, 72,* 30–164.

McCarthy, C. (1988). Rethinking liberal and radical perspectives on racial inequality in schooling: Making the case for nonsynchrony. *Harvard Educational Review, 58,* 265–279.

McCarthy, C., & Crichlow, W. (Eds.). (1993). *Race, identity and representation in education.* Boston: Routledge Kegan Paul.

McWhorter, J. (2000). *Losing the race: Self-sabotage in Black America.* New York: Free Press.

Meyers v. the Board of Education of San Juan County, 905 F. Supp. 1544(D. Utah 1995).

Miron, L. F. (1996). *The social construction of urban schooling: Situating the crisis.* Cresskill, NJ: Hampton.

Nebeker, K. C. (1998). Critical race theory: A White graduate student's struggle with this growing area of scholarship. *International Journal of Qualitative Studies in Education, 11,* 25–42.

Omi, M., & Winant, H. (1994). *Racial formation in the United States: From the 1960s to the 1990s* (2nd ed.). Boston: Routledge Kegan Paul.

Peshkin, A. (1988). In search of subjectivity—One's own. *Educational Researcher, 17,* 17–22.

Pifer, D. A. (1999). Small town race: A performance text. *Qualitative Inquiry, 4,* 541–562.

Pizarro, M. (1998). "Chicana/ o power!" Epistemology and methodology for social justice and empowerment in Chicana/o communities. *International Journal of Qualitative Studies in Education, 11,* 57–80.

Rodriguez, M. R. y (1998). Confronting anthropology's silencing praxis: Speaking of/from a Chicana consciousness. *Qualitative Inquiry, 4,* 15–40.

Schwandt, T. A. (2000). Three epistemological stances for qualitative inquiry: Interpretivism, hermeneutics, and social constructionism. In N. K. Denzin & Y. S. Lincoln (Eds.), *Handbook of qualitative research* (2nd ed., pp. 189–214). Thousand Oaks, CA: Sage.

Smith-Maddox, R., & Solórzano, D. G. (2002). Using critical theory, Paulo Freire's problem-posing method, and case study research to confront race and racism in education. *Qualitative Inquiry, 8,* 64–82.

Solórzano, D. G. (1997). Images and words that wound: Critical race theory, racial stereotyping and teacher education. *Teacher Education Quarterly, 24,* 5–19.

Solórzano, D. G. (1998). Critical race theory, race and gender microaggressions, and the experience of Chicana and Chicano scholars. *International Journal of Qualitative Studies in Education, 11,* 121–136.

Solórzano, D. G., & Villalpando, O. (1998). Critical race theory, marginality, and the experience of minority students in higher education. In C. Torres & T. Mitchell (Eds.), *Emerging issues in the sociology of education: Comparative perspectives* (pp. 211–224). Albany: SUNY Press.

Solórzano, D. G., & Yosso, T. J. (2002). Critical race methodology: Counter-storytelling as an analytical framework for education research. *Qualitative Inquiry, 8,* 22–43.

Stanfield, J. H., II. (1999). Slipping through the front door: Relevant social scientific evaluation in the people of color century. *American Journal of Evaluation, 20,* 415–431.

Symposium. (1994). Critical race theory [Special issue]. *California Law Review, 82* (4).

Tanaka, G., & Cruz, C. (1998). The locker room: Eroticism and exoticism in a polyphonic text. *International Journal of Qualitative Studies in Education, 11,* 137–154.

Tate, W. F., IV. (1997). Critical race theory and education: History, theory and implications. In M. Apple (Ed.), *Review of research in education* (pp. 191–243). Washington, DC: American Educational Research Association.

Tate, W. F., IV. (1999). Conclusion. In L. Parker, D. Deyhle, & S. Villenas (Eds.), *Race is . . . race isn't. Critical race theory and qualitative studies in education* (pp. 251–272). Boulder, CO: Westview.

Thompson, A. (1999). Colortalk: Whiteness and off white. *Educational Studies, 30,* 141–160.

Torres, R. D., Mirón, L. F., & Inda, J. X. (Eds.). (1999). *Race, identity, and citizenship: A reader.* Oxford, UK: Basil Blackwell.

University of California, Los Angeles, Law Review Symposium. (2000). Race and the law at the turn of the century [Special issue]. *UCLA Law Review, 47* (6).

Ulichny, P. (1997). When critical ethnography and action collide. *Qualitative Inquiry, 3,* 139–168.

Villalpando, O. (2000, November 4). *Critical race theory, LatCrit and Latino-Latina student persistence: A study of higher education barriers and possibilities.* Paper presented at the meeting of the American Educational Studies Association, Vancouver, Canada.

Villenas, S., Deyhle, D., & Parker, L. (1999). Critical race theory and praxis: Chicano(a)/Latino(a) and Navajo struggles for dignity, educational equity and social justice. In L. Parker, D. Deyhle, & S. Villenas (Eds.), *Race is . . . Race isn't: Critical race theory and qualitative studies in education* (pp. 31–52). Boulder, CO: Westview.

Weis, L. (1995). Qualitative research in sociology of education: Reflections on the 1970s and beyond. In W. T. Pink & G. W. Noblit (Eds.), *Continuity and contradiction: The futures of the sociology of education* (pp. 157–173). Creekskill, NJ: Hampton.

Williams, P. (1987). Alchemical notes: Reconstructing ideals from deconstructed rights. *Harvard Civil Rights–Civil Liberties Law Review, 22,* 401–433.

Williams, P.J. (1991). *The alchemy of race and rights.* Cambridge, MA: Harvard University Press.

Wong, L. M. (1998). The ethics of rapport: Institutional safeguards, resistance, and betrayal. *Qualitative Inquiry, 4,* 178–199.

Yamamoto, E. K. (1997). Critical race praxis: Race theory and political lawyering practice in post-Civil Rights America. *Michigan Law Review, 95,* 821–900.

Young, M., & Laible, J. (2000). White racism, antiracism, and school leadership preparation. *Journal of School Leadership, 10,* 374–414.

Part Five

Race in the Classroom

11

A Threat in the Air
How Stereotypes Shape Intellectual Identity and Performance
Claude M. Steele

From an observer's standpoint, the situations of a boy and a girl in a math classroom or of a Black student and a White student in any classroom are essentially the same. The teacher is the same; the textbooks are the same; and in better classrooms, these students are treated the same. Is it possible, then, that they could still experience the classroom differently, so differently in fact as to significantly affect their performance and achievement there? This is the central question of this article, and in seeking an answer, it has both a practical and a theoretical focus. The practical focus is on the perhaps obvious need to better understand the processes that can hamper a group's school performance and on what can be done to improve that performance. The theoretical focus is on how societal stereotypes about groups can influence the intellectual functioning and identity development of individual group members. To show the generality of these processes and their relevance to important outcomes, this theory is applied to two groups: African Americans, who must contend with negative stereotypes about their abilities in many scholastic domains, and women, who must do so primarily in math and the physical sciences. In trying to understand the schooling outcomes of these two groups, the theory has a distinct perspective, that of viewing people, in Sartre's (1946/1965) words, as "first of all beings in a situation" such that if one wants to understand them, one "must inquire first into the situation surrounding [them]" (p. 60).

The theory begins with an assumption: that to sustain school success one must be identified with school achievement in the sense of its being a part of one's self-definition, a personal identity to which one is self-evaluatively accountable. This accountability—that good self-feelings depend in some part on good achievement—translates into sustained achievement motivation. For such an identification to form, this reasoning continues, one must perceive good prospects in the domain, that is, that one has the interests, skills, resources, and opportunities to prosper there, as well as that one belongs there, in the sense of being accepted and valued in the domain. If this relationship to schooling does not form or gets broken, achievement may suffer. Thus, in trying to understand what imperils achievement among women and African Americans, this logic points to a basic question: What in the experience of these groups might frustrate their identification with all or certain aspects of school achievement?

One must surely turn first to social structure: limits on educational access that have been imposed on these groups by socioeconomic disadvantage, segregating social practices, and restrictive cultural orientations, limits of both historical and ongoing effect. By diminishing one's educational prospects, these limitations (e.g., inadequate resources, few role models, preparational disadvantages) should make it more difficult to identify with academic domains. To continue in math, for example, a woman might have to buck the low expectations of teachers, family, and societal gender roles in which math is seen as unfeminine as well as anticipate spending her entire professional life in a male-dominated world. These realities, imposed on her by societal structure, could so reduce her sense of good prospects in math as to make identifying with it difficult.

But this article focuses on a further barrier, one that has its effect on the already identified, those members of these groups who, having survived structural obstacles, have achieved identification with the domain (of the present groups, school-identified African Americans and math-identified women). It is the social—psychological threat that arises when one is in a situation or doing something for which a negative stereotype about one's group applies. This predicament threatens one with being negatively stereotyped, with being judged or treated stereotypically, or with the prospect of conforming to the stereotype. Called *stereotype threat*, it is a situational threat—a threat in the air—that, in general form, can affect the members of any group about whom a negative stereotype exists (e.g., skateboarders, older adults, White men, gang members). Where bad stereotypes about these groups apply, members of these groups can fear being reduced to that stereotype. And for those who identify with the domain to which the stereotype is relevant, this predicament can be self-threatening.

Negative stereotypes about women and African Americans bear on important academic abilities. Thus, for members of these groups who are identified with domains in which these stereotypes apply, the threat of these stereotypes can be sharply felt and, in several ways, hampers their achievement.

First, if the threat is experienced in the midst of a domain performance—classroom presentation or test-taking, for example—the emotional reaction it causes could directly interfere with performance. My colleagues and I (Spencer, Steele, & Quinn, 1997; C. M. Steele & Aronson, 1995) have tested this possibility with women taking standardized math tests and African Americans taking standardized verbal tests. Second, when this threat becomes chronic in a situation, as for the woman who spends considerable time in a competitive, male-oriented math environment, it can pressure *disidentification*, a reconceptualization of the self and of one's values so as to remove the domain as a self-identity, as a basis of self-evaluation. Disidentification offers the retreat of not caring about the domain in relation to the self. But as it protects in this way, it can undermine sustained motivation in the domain, an adaptation that can be costly when the domain is as important as schooling.

Stereotype threat is especially frustrating because, at each level of schooling, it affects the vanguard of these groups, those with the skills and self-confidence to have identified with the domain. Ironically, their susceptibility to this threat derives not from internal doubts about their ability (e.g., their internalization of the stereotype) but from their identification with the domain and the resulting concern they have about being stereotyped in it. (This argument has the hopeful implication that to improve the domain performance of these students, one should focus on the feasible task of lifting this situational threat rather than on altering their internal psychology.) Yet, as schooling progresses and the obstacles of structure and stereotype threat take their cumulative toll, more of this vanguard will likely be pressured into the ranks of the unidentified. These students, by not caring about the domain vis-à-vis the self, are likely to underperform in it regardless of whether they are stereotype threatened there. Thus, although the identified among these groups are likely to underperform only under stereotype threat, the unidentified (casualties of sociocultural disadvantage or prior internalization of stereotype threat) are likely to underperform and not persist in the domain even when stereotype threat has been removed.

In these ways, then, the present analysis sees social structure and stereotypes as shaping the academic identities and performance outcomes of large segments of society. But first, for the two groups under consideration, what are these outcomes?

As is much discussed, these outcomes are in a crisis state for African Americans. Although Black students begin school with standardized test scores that are not too far behind those of their White counterparts, almost immediately a gap begins to appear (e.g., Alexander & Entwistle, 1988; Burton & Jones, 1982; Coleman et al., 1966) that, by the sixth grade in most school districts, is two full grade levels (Gerard, 1983). There have been encouraging increases in the number of African Americans completing high school or its equivalence in recent years: 77% for Black students versus 83% for White students (American Council on Education, 1995–1996). And there have been modest advances in the number of African American high school graduates enrolling in college, although these have not been as substantial as in other groups (American Council on Education, 1995–1996). Perhaps most discouraging has been the high dropout rate for African American college students: Those who do not finish college within six years is 62%, compared with a national dropout rate of 41% (American Council on Education, 1995–1996). And there is evidence of lower grade performance among those who do graduate of, on average, two thirds of a letter grade lower than those of other graduating students (Nettles, 1988). On predominantly White campuses, Black students are also underrepresented in math and the natural sciences. Although historically Black colleges and universities now enroll only 17% of the nation's Black college students, they produce 42% of all Black BS degrees in natural science (Culotta & Gibbons, 1992). At the graduate level, although Black women have recently shown modest gains in PhDs received, the number awarded to Black men has declined over the past decade more than for any other subgroup in society (American Council on Education, 1995–1996).

Women clearly thrive in many areas of schooling. But in math, engineering, and the physical sciences, they often endure lesser outcomes than men. In a meta-analysis involving over 3 million participants, Hyde, Fennema, and Lamon (1990), for example, found that through elementary and middle school, there are virtually no differences between boys and girls in performance on standardized math tests but that a trend toward men doing better steadily increases from high school ($SD = .29$) through college ($SD = .41$) and into adulthood ($SD = .59$). And, as their college careers begin, women leave these fields at a rate two and a half times that of men (Hewitt & Seymour, 1991). Although White women constitute 43% of the U.S. population, they earn only 22% of the BS degrees and 13% of the PhDs and occupy only

10% of the jobs in physical science, math, and engineering, where they earn only 75% of the salary paid to men (Hewitt & Seymour, 1991).

These inequities have compelled explanations ranging from the sociocultural to the genetic. In the case of African Americans, for example, past and ongoing socioeconomic disadvantage, cultural orientations (e.g., Ogbu, 1986), and genetic differences (e.g., Herrnstein & Murray, 1994; Jensen, 1969) have all been proposed as factors that, through singular and accumulated effect, could undermine their performance. In the case of women's performance in math and the physical sciences, there are parallel arguments: structural and cultural gender role constraints that shunt women away from these areas; culturally rooted expectations (e.g., Eccles, 1987; Eccles-Parsons et al., 1983); and, again, genetic limitations (Benbow & Stanley, 1980, 1983). But, like crumbs along the forest floor, several findings lead away from these analyses as fully sufficient.

For one thing, minority student achievement gaps persist even in the middle and upper socioeconomic classes. Using data from the Coleman report (Coleman et al., 1966) and a more recent College Board study of Scholastic Assessment Test (SAT) scores, Miller (1995, 1996) found that the gaps in academic performance (grades as well as standardized test scores) between Whites and non-Asian minorities (e.g., African Americans, Hispanics, and Native Americans) were as large, or larger, in the upper and middle classes (as measured by parental education and occupation) than in the lower classes. Group differences in socioeconomic status (SES), then, cannot fully explain group differences in academic performance.

Another point is that these differences are not even fully explained by group differences in skills. This is shown in the well-known *overprediction* or *underperformance* phenomenon of the test bias literature. Overprediction occurs when, at each level of performance on a test of preparation for some level of schooling (e.g., the SAT), students from one group wind up achieving less—getting lower college grades, for example—than other students with the same beginning scores. In this sense, the test scores of the low-performing group overpredict how well they will actually achieve, or, stated another way, the low-performing group underperforms in relation to the test's prediction. But the point here is that because the students at each test-score level have comparable initial skills, the lower eventual performance of one group must be due to something other than skill deficits they brought with them.

In the case of African Americans, overprediction across the academic spectrum has been so reliably observed as to be almost a lawful phenomenon in American society (e.g., Jensen, 1980; Vars & Bowen, 1997). Perhaps the most extensive single demonstration of it comes from a recent Educational Testing Service study (Ramist, Lewis, & McCamley-Jenkins, 1994) that examined the predictiveness of the SAT on 38 representative college and university campuses. As is typically the case, the study found that the predictive validity to the SAT—its correlation with subsequent grades—was as good for African American, Hispanic, and Native American students as for White and Asian students. But for the three non-Asian minority groups, there was sizable overprediction (underperformance) in virtually all academic areas. That is, at each level of preparation as measured by the SAT, something further depressed the grades of these groups once they arrived on campus.

As important, the same study found evidence of SAT overprediction for female students (i.e., women performing less well than men at comparable SAT levels) in technical and physical science courses such as engineering, economics, and computer science but not in non-technical areas such as English. It is interesting though that women in this study were not overpredicted in math per se, a seeming exception to this pattern. The overprediction of women's college math performance has generally been unreliable, with some studies showing it (e.g., Benbow & Arjmand, 1990; Levin & Wyckoff, 1988; Lovely, 1987; Ware, Steckler, & Leserman, 1985) and others not (e.g., Adelman, 1991; DeBoer, 1984; Ware & Dill, 1986). However, a recent study (Strenta, Elliott, Adair, Scott, & Matier, 1993) involving over 5,000 students at four prestigious northeastern colleges identified a pattern of effects that suggests why these different results occur: Underperformance reliably occurred among women who were talented in math and science and who, perhaps for that reason, took courses in these areas that were intended for majors, whereas it did not occur among women with less math and science preparation who took courses in these areas intended for nonmajors. Thus, women may be reliably overpredicted in math and the physical sciences, just as Black students are more generally, but only when the curriculum is more advanced and only among women who are more identified with the domain. Among this vanguard, though, something other than skill deficits depresses their performance. What are these further processes?

Social and Stereotype Structure as Obstacles to Achievement Identification

The proposed answer is that at least one of these processes is a set of social psychological phenomena that obstructs these groups' identification with domains of schooling.[1] I turn first to school identification.

Academic Identification

As noted, this analysis assumes that sustained school achievement depends, most centrally, on identifying with school, that is, forming a relationship between oneself and the domains of schooling such that one's self-regard significantly depends on achievement in those domains. Extrinsic rewards such as better career outcomes, personal security, parental exhortation, and so on, can also motivate school achievement. But it is presumed that sustaining motivation through the ebb and flow of these other rewards requires school identification. How, then, is this identification formed?

Not a great deal is known about the process. But several models (e.g., Schlenker & Weigold, 1989; C. M. Steele, 1988; Tesser, 1988) share an implicit reasoning, the first assumption of which is that people need positive self-regard, a self-perception of "adaptive and moral adequacy" (C. M. Steele, 1988, p. 289). Then, the argument goes, identification with a given domain of life depends, in large part, on the self-evaluative prospects it offers. James (1890/1950) described the development of the self as a process of picking from the many, often incompatible, possible selves, those "on which to stake one's salvation" (p. 310). This choice and the assessment of prospects that goes into it are, of course, multifaceted: Are the rewards of the domain attractive or important? Is an adequate opportunity structure available? Do I have the requisite skills, talents, and interests? Have others like me succeeded in the domain? Will I be seen as belonging in the domain? Will I be prejudiced against in the domain? Can I envision wanting what this domain has to offer? and so on. Some of these assessments undergird a sense of efficacy in the domain (e.g., Bandura, 1977, 1986). Others have to do with the rewards, importance, and attractiveness of the domain itself. And still others have to do with the feasibility and receptiveness of the domain. The point here is that students tacitly assess their prospects in school and its subdomains, and, roughly speaking, their identifications follow these assessments: increasing when they are favorable and decreasing when they are unfavorable. As for the two groups under consideration, then, this analysis suggests that something systematically downgrades their assessments of, and thus their identification with, critical domains of schooling.

Threats to Academic Identification

Structural and cultural threats. Both groups have endured and continue to endure sociocultural influences that could have such effects. Among the most replicable facts in the schooling literature is that SES is strongly related to school success and cognitive performance (e.g., Coleman et al., 1966; Miller, 1996). And because African Americans have long been disproportionately represented in lower socioeconomic classes, this factor surely contributes to their achievement patterns in school, both through the material limitations associated with lower SES (poor schools, lack of resources for school persistence, etc.) and through the ability of these limitations, by downgrading school-related prospects, to undermine identification with school. And beyond socioeconomic structure, there are cultural patterns within these groups or in the relation between these groups and the larger society that may also frustrate their identification with school or some part of it, for example, Ogbu's (1986) notion of a lower-class Black culture that is "oppositional" to school achievement or traditional feminine gender roles that eschew math-related fields (e.g., Eccles-Parsons et al., 1983; Linn, 1994).

Stereotype threat. Beyond these threats, waiting for those in these groups who have identified with school, is yet another threat to their identification, more subtle perhaps but nonetheless profound: that of stereotype threat. I define it as follows: the event of a negative stereotype about a group to which one belongs becoming self-relevant, usually as a plausible interpretation for something one is doing, for an experience one is having, or for a situation one is in, that has relevance to one's self-definition. It happens when one is in the *field* of the stereotype, what Cross (1991) called a "spotlight anxiety" (p. 195), such that one can be judged or treated in terms of a racial stereotype. Many analysts have referred to this predicament and the pressure it causes (e.g., Allport, 1954; Carter, 1991; Cose, 1993; Goffman, 1963; Howard & Hammond, 1985; E. E. Jones et al., 1984; Sartre, 1946/1965; C. M. Steele, 1975; C. M. Steele & Aronson, 1995; S. Steele, 1990). The present definition stresses that for a negative stereotype to be threatening, it must be self-relevant. Then, the situational contingency it establishes—the possibility of conforming to the stereotype or of being treated and judged in terms of it—becomes self-threatening. It means that one could be limited or diminished in a domain that is self-definitional. For students from groups in which abilities are negatively stereotyped in all or some school domains and yet who remain identified with those domains, this threat may be keenly felt, felt enough, I argue, to become a further barrier to their identification with the domain.

There is, however, a more standard explanation of how negative stereotypes affect their targets. Beginning with Freud (as cited in Brill, 1938) in psychology and Cooley (1956) and Mead (1934) in sociology, treatises on the experience of oppression have depicted a fairly standard sequence of events: Through long exposure to negative stereotypes about their group, members of prejudiced-against groups often internalize the stereotypes, and the resulting sense of inadequacy becomes part of their personality (e.g., Allport, 1954; Bettelheim, 1943; Clark, 1965; Grier & Coobs, 1968; Erikson, 1956; Fanon, 1952/1967; Kardiner & Ovesey, 1951; Lewin, 1941).

In recent years, the tone of this argument has constructively lightened, replacing the notion of a broad self-hatred with the idea of an inferiority anxiety or low expectations and suggesting how situational factors contribute to this experience. S. Steele's (1990) essays on *racial vulnerability* (i.e., a vulnerability of both Blacks and Whites that stems, in part, from the situational pressures of reputations about their groups) offered an example. This work depicts the workings of this anxiety among African Americans in an interconnected set of ideas: *integration shock* that, like Goffman (1963), points to settings that integrate Blacks and Whites as particularly anxiety arousing; *objective correlatives* or race-related situational cues that can trigger this anxiety; and the inherent sense of risk, stemming from an internalized *inferiority anxiety* and from a *myth of inferiority* pervading integrated settings, of being judged inferior or of confirming one's own feared inferiority. Howard and Hammond (1985) earlier made this argument specifically in relation to the school achievement of Black students. They argued that once "rumors of inferiority" (stereotypes; p. 18) about Black students' abilities pervade the environment—through, for example, national debates over the genetic basis of racial differences in IQ—they can intimidate Black students; become internalized by them; and, in turn, lead to a low sense of self-efficacy, demotivation, and underperformance in school. Analogous arguments have been applied to women interested in math-related areas (cf. Eccles-Parsons et al., 1983).

These models recognize the situational influence of negative stereotypes (e.g., Allport, 1954; Howard & Hammond, 1985; S. Steele, 1990) but most often describe it as a process in which the stereotype, or more precisely the possibility of being stereotyped, triggers an internalized inferiority doubt or low expectancy. And because this anxiety is born of a socialization presumed to influence all members of the stereotyped group, virtually all members of the group are presumed to have this anxiety, to one degree or another.

Stereotype threat, in contrast, refers to the strictly situational threat of negative stereotypes, the threat that does not depend on cuing an internalized anxiety or expectancy. It is cued by the mere recognition that a negative group stereotype could apply to oneself in a given situation. How threatening this recognition becomes depends on the person's identification with the stereotype-relevant domain. For the domain identified, the situational relevance of the stereotype is threatening because it threatens diminishment in a domain that is self-definitional. For the less domain identified, this recognition is less threatening or not threatening at all, because it threatens something that is less self-definitional.

Stereotype threat, then, as a situational pressure "in the air" so to speak, affects only a subportion of the stereotyped group and, in the area of schooling, probably affects confident students more than unconfident ones. Recall that to be identified with schooling in general, or math in particular, one must have confidence in one's domain-related abilities, enough to perceive good prospects in the domain. This means that stereotype threat should have its greatest effect on the better, more confident students in stereotyped groups, those who have not internalized the group stereotype to the point of doubting their own ability and have thus remained identified with the domain—those who are in the academic vanguard of their group.[2]

Several general features of stereotype threat follow:

1. Stereotype threat is a general threat not tied to the psychology of particular stigmatized groups. It affects the members of any group about whom there exists some generally known negative stereotype (e.g., a grandfather who fears that any faltering of memory will confirm or expose him to stereotypes about the aged). Stereotype threat can be thought of as a subtype of the threat posed by negative reputations in general.

2. That which turns stereotype threat on and off, the controlling "mechanism" so to speak, is a particular concurrence: whether a negative stereotype about one's group becomes relevant to interpreting oneself or one's behavior in an identified-with setting. When such a setting integrates stereotyped and nonstereotyped people, it may make the stereotype, as a dimension of difference, more salient and thus more strongly felt (e.g., Frable, Blackstone, & Sherbaum, 1990; Goffman, 1963; Kleck & Strenta, 1980; Sartre, 1946/1965; S. Steele, 1990). But such integration is neither necessary nor sufficient for this threat to occur. It can occur even when the person is alone, as for a woman taking an important math test alone in a cubicle but under the threat of confirming a stereotyped limitation of ability. And, in integrated settings, it need not occur. Reducing the interpretive relevance of a stereotype in the setting, say in a classroom or on a standardized test, may reduce this threat and its detrimental effects even when the setting is integrated.[3]

3. This mechanism also explains the variabilities of stereotype threat: the fact that the type and degree of this threat vary from group to group and, for any group, across settings. For example, the type and degree of stereotype threat experienced by White men, Black people, and people who are overweight differ considerably, bearing on sensitivity and fairness in the first group, on school performance in the second, and on self-control in the third. Moreover, for any of these groups, this threat will vary across settings (e.g., Goffman, 1963; S. Steele, 1990). For example, women may reduce their stereotype threat substantially by moving across the hall from math to English class. The explanation of this model is straightforward: Different groups experience different forms and degrees of stereotype threat because the stereotypes about them differ in content, in scope, and in the situations to which they apply.

4. To experience stereotype threat, one need not believe the stereotype nor even be

worried that it is true of oneself. The well-known African American social psychologist James M. Jones (1997) wrote,

> When I go to the ATM machine and a woman is making a transaction, I think about whether she will fear I may rob her. Since I have no such intention, how do I put her at ease? Maybe I can't . . . and maybe she has no such expectation. But it goes through my mind. (p. 262)

Jones felt stereotype threat in this situation even though he did not believe that the stereotype characterized him. Of course, this made it no less a life-shaping force. One's daily life can be filled with recurrent situations in which this threat pressures adaptive responses.

5. The effort to overcome stereotype threat by disproving the stereotype—for example, by outperforming it in the case of academic work—can be daunting. Because these stereotypes are widely disseminated throughout society, a personal exemption from them earned in one setting does not generalize to a new setting where either one's reputation is not known or where it has to be renegotiated against a new challenge. Thus, even when the stereotype can be disproven, the need to do so can seem Sisyphean, everlastingly recurrent. And in some critical situations, it may not be disprovable. The stereotypes considered in this work allege group-based limitations of ability that are often reinforced by the structural reality of increasingly small group representations at more advanced levels of the schooling domain. Thus, for group members working at these advanced levels, no amount of success up to that point can disprove the stereotype's relevance to their next, more advanced performance. For the advanced female math student who has been brilliant up to that point, any frustration she has at the frontier of her skills could confirm the gender-based limitation alleged in the stereotype, making this frontier, because she is so invested in it, a more threatening place than it is for the nonstereotyped. Thus, the work of dispelling stereotype threat through performance probably increases with the difficulty of work in the domain, and whatever exemption is gained has to be rewon at the next new proving ground.

Empirical Support for a Theory of Stereotype Threat and Disidentification

In testing these ideas, the research of my colleagues and I has had two foci: The first is on intellectual performance in the domain in which negative group stereotypes apply. Here, the analysis has two testable implications. One is that for domain-identified students, stereotype threat may interfere with their domain-related intellectual performance. Analysts have long argued that behaving in a situation in which one is at risk of confirming a negative stereotype about one's group, or of being seen or treated stereotypically, causes emotional distress and pressure (e.g., Cross, 1991; Fanon, 1952/1967; Goffman, 1963; Howard & Hammond, 1985; Sartre, 1946/1965; C. M. Steele & Aronson, 1995; S. Steele, 1990). The argument here is that for those who identify with the domain enough to experience this threat, the pressure it causes may undermine their domain performance. Disruptive pressures such as evaluation apprehension, test anxiety, choking, and token status have long been shown to disrupt performance through a variety of mediating mechanisms: interfering anxiety, reticence to respond, distracting thoughts, self-consciousness, and so on (Baumeister & Showers, 1984; Geen, 1991; Lord & Saenz, 1985; Sarason, 1980; Wine, 1971). The assumption of this model is that stereotype threat is another such interfering pressure. The other testable implication is that reducing this threat in the performance setting, by reducing its interfering pressure, should improve the performance of otherwise stereotype-threatened students.

The second research focus is the model's implication that stereotype threat, and the anticipation of having to contend with it unceasingly in school or some domain of schooling, should deter members of these groups from identifying with these domains, and, for group members already identified, it should pressure their disidentification.[4]

Stereotype Threat and Intellectual Performance

Steven Spencer, Diane Quinn, and I (Spencer et al., 1997) first tested the effect of stereotype threat on intellectual performance by testing its effect on the standardized math test performance of women who were strong in math.

The stereotype threat of women performing math. At base, of course, the stereotype threat that women experience in math-performance settings derives from a negative stereotype about their math ability that is disseminated throughout society. But whether this threat impaired their performance, we reasoned, would depend on two things. First, the performance would have to be construed so that any faltering would imply the limitation of ability alleged in the stereotype. This means that the performance would have to be difficult enough so that faltering at it would imply having reached an ability limit but not so difficult as to be nondiagnostic of ability. And second, as has been much emphasized, the women in question would have to be identified with math, so that faltering and its stereotype-confirming implication would threaten something they care about, their belongingness and acceptance in a domain they identify with. Of course, men too (at least those of equal skill and identification with math) could be threatened in this situation; faltering would reflect on their ability too. But their faltering would not carry the extra threat of confirming a stereotyped limitation in math ability or of causing them to be seen that way. Thus, the threat that women experience, through the interfering pressure it causes, should worsen their performance in comparison to equally qualified men. Interestingly, though, these otherwise confident women should perform equally as well as equally qualified men when this situational threat is lessened.

To explore these questions, Spencer, Quinn, and I (Spencer et al., 1997) designed a basic research paradigm: We recruited female and male students, mostly college sophomores, who were both good at math and strongly identified with it in the sense of seeing themselves as strong math students and seeing math as important to their self-definition. We then gave them a very difficult math test one at a time. The items were taken from the advanced math General Records Examination (GRE) and we assumed would frustrate the skills of these students without totally exceeding them. As expected, and presumably reflecting the impairing effects of stereotype threat, women significantly underperformed in relation to equally qualified men on this difficult math test. But more important, in another condition of this experiment in which the test was an advanced literature test rather than a math test and in which participants had been selected and matched for their strong literature skills and identification, women performed just as well as equally qualified men. This happened, we reasoned, because women are not stereotype threatened in this area.

A second experiment replicated women's underperformance on the difficult math test and showed that it did not happen when the test was easier, that is when the items, taken from the regular quantitative section of the GRE, were more within the skills of these strong math students. The lack of performance frustration on this easier test, presumably, reduced women's stereotype threat by making the stereotype less relevant as an interpretation of their performance.

Stereotype threat versus genes. So went our interpretation. But an alternative was possible: The biological limits of women's math ability do not emerge until the material tested is difficult. It is this very pattern of evidence that Benbow and Stanley (1980, 1983) used to suggest a genetic limitation in women's math ability. Thus, the first two experiments reproduced the gender effects on math performance reported in the literature: that women underperform primarily in math and mainly when the material is difficult. But they fall short of establishing our interpretation.

To do this, we would need to give women and men a difficult math test (one capable of producing women's underperformance) but then experimentally vary stereotype threat, that is, vary how much women were at risk of confirming the stereotype while taking the test. A third experiment did this by varying how the test (the same difficult one used in the earlier experiments) was represented. Participants were told either that the test generally showed gender differences, implying that the stereotype of women's limitations in math was relevant to interpreting their own frustration, or that it showed no gender differences, implying that the gender stereotype was not relevant to their performance and thus could not be confirmed by it on this particular test. The no-gender-differences representation did not challenge the validity of the stereotype; it simply eliminated the risk that the stereotype could be fulfilled on this test. In the gender-differences condition, we expected women (still stereotype threatened) to underperform in relation to equally qualified men, but in the no-gender-differences condition, we expected women (with stereotype threat reduced) to perform equal to such men. The genetic interpretation, of course, predicts that women will underperform on this difficult test regardless of how it is represented.

In dramatic support of our reasoning, women performed worse than men when they were told that the test produced gender differences, which replicated women's underperformance observed in the earlier experiments, but they performed equal to men when the test was represented as insensitive to gender differences, even though, of course, the same difficult "ability" test was used in both conditions (see Figure 11.1). Genetic limitation did not cap the performance of women in these experiments. A fourth experiment showed that reducing stereotype threat (through the no-gender-differences treatment) raised women's performance to that of equally qualified men, even when participants' specific performance expectancies were set low, that is, when participants were led to expect poor test performance. Also, a fifth

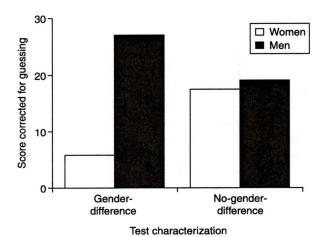

Figure 11.1 Mean Performance on a Difficult Math Test as a Function of Gender and Test Characterization.

experiment (that again replicated the treatment effects of the third experiment) found that participants' posttreatment anxiety, not their expectancies or efficacy, predicted their performance. Thus, the disruptive effect of stereotype threat was mediated more by the self-evaluative anxiety it caused than by its lowering of performance expectations or self-efficacy.

Internal or situational threat. These findings make an important theoretical and practical point: The gender-differences conditions (including those in which the possibility of gender differences was left to inference rather than stated directly) did not impair women's performance by triggering doubts they had about their math ability. For one thing, these women had no special doubts of this sort; they were selected for being very good at math and for reporting high confidence in their ability. Nor was this doubt a factor in their test performance. Recall that the math test was represented as an ability test in all conditions of these experiments. This means that in the no-gender-differences conditions, women were still at risk of showing their own math ability to be weak—the same risk that men had in these conditions. Under this risk (when their own math ability was on the line), they performed just as well as men. Whatever performance-impairing anxiety they had, it was no greater than that of equally qualified men. Thus, the gender-differences conditions (the normal condition under which people take these tests) could not have impaired their performance by triggering some greater internalized anxiety that women have about their own math ability—an anxiety acquired, for example, through prior socialization. Rather, this condition had its effect through situational pressure. It set up an interpretive frame such that any performance frustration signaled the possible gender-based ability limitation alleged in the stereotype. For these women, this signal challenged their belongingness in a domain they cared about and, as a possibly newly met limit to their ability, could not be disproven by their prior achievements, thus its interfering threat.

The stereotype threat of African Americans on standardized tests. Joshua Aronson and I (C. M. Steele & Aronson, 1995) examined these processes among African

American students. In these studies, Black and White Stanford University students took a test composed of the most difficult items on the verbal GRE exam. Because the participants were students admitted to a highly selective university, we assumed that they were identified with the verbal skills represented on standardized tests. The first study varied whether or not the stereotype about Black persons' intellectual ability was relevant to their performance by varying whether the test was presented as *ability-diagnostic*, that is, as a test of intellectual ability, or as *ability-nondiagnostic*, that is, as a laboratory problem-solving task unrelated to ability and thus to the stereotype about ability. Analysis of covariance was used to remove the influence of participants' initial skills, measured by their verbal SAT scores, on their test performance. This done, the results showed strong evidence of stereotype threat: Black participants greatly underperformed White participants in the diagnostic condition but equaled them in the nondiagnostic condition (see Figure 11.2). A second experiment produced the same pattern of results with an even more slight manipulation of stereotype threat: whether or not participants recorded their race on a demographic questionnaire just before taking the test (described as nondiagnostic in all conditions). Salience of the racial stereotype alone was enough to depress the performance of identified Black students (see Figure 11.3).

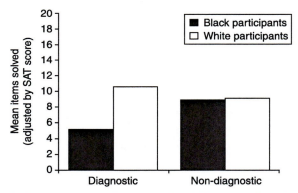

Figure 11.2 Mean Performance on a Difficult Verbal Test as a Function of Race and Test Characterization.

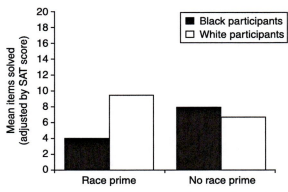

Figure 11.3 Mean Performance on a Difficult Verbal Test as a Function of Whether Race Was Primed.

The cognitive mediation of stereotype threat. Stereotype threat, then, can impair the standardized test performance of domain-identified students; this effect generalizes to several ability-stereotyped groups, and its mediation seems to involve anxiety more than expectancies. But do these manipulations cause a specific state of stereotype threat, that is, a sensed threat specifically about being stereotyped or fitting the stereotype? To address this question, Aronson and I (C. M. Steele & Aronson, 1995) tested two things: whether manipulating stereotype threat actually activates the racial stereotype in the thinking and information processing of stereotype-threatened test takers and whether it produces in them a specific motivation to avoid being seen stereotypically. Again, Black and White participants were run in either an ability-diagnostic or ability-nondiagnostic condition, except that just after the condition instructions and completion of the sample test items (so that participants could see how difficult the items were) and just before participants expected to take the test, they completed measures of stereotype activation and avoidance. The stereotype-activation measure asked them to complete 80 word fragments, 10 of which we knew from pretesting could be completed with, among other words, words symbolic of African American stereotypes (e.g., _ _ ce[race], la_ _ [lazy],or _ _ or [poor]) and 5 of which could be completed with, among other words, words signifying self-doubts (e.g., lo_ _ _ [loser], du_ _ [dumb], or sha_ _ [shame]). The measure of participants' motivation to avoid being seen stereotypically simply asked them how much they preferred various types of music, activities, sports, and personality traits, some of which a pretest sample had rated as stereotypic of African Americans.[5]

If expecting to take a difficult ability-diagnostic test is enough to activate the racial stereotype in the thinking of Black participants and to motivate them to avoid being stereotyped, then these participants, more than those in the other conditions, should show more stereotype and self-doubt word completions and fewer preferences for things that are African American. This is precisely what happened. Black participants in the diagnostic condition completed more word fragments with stereotype- and self-doubt-related words and had fewer preferences for things related to African American experience (e.g., jazz, basketball, hip-hop) than Black participants in the nondiagnostic condition or White participants in either condition, all of whom were essentially the same (see Figure 11.4). Also, as a last item before participants expected to begin the test, they were given the option of recording their race, a measure we thought might further tap into an apprehension about being viewed stereotypically. Interestingly, then, all of the Black participants in the nondiagnostic condition and all of the White participants in both conditions listed their race, whereas only 25% of the Black participants in the diagnostic condition did so.

Self-rejection or self-presentation? A troubling implication of the earlier mentioned internalization models (e.g., Allport, 1954; Bettelheim, 1943; Clark, 1965; Grier & Coobs, 1968; Erikson, 1956; Fanon, 1952/1967; Kardiner & Ovesey, 1951) is that negative stereotypes about one's group eventually become internalized and cause rejection of one's own group, even of oneself—*self-hating* preferences. The famous finding of Clark and Clark (1939) that Black children preferred White dolls over Black dolls has been interpreted this way. The preferences of Black participants in the diagnostic condition fit this pattern; with negative stereotypes about their group cognitively activated, they valued things that were African American less than any

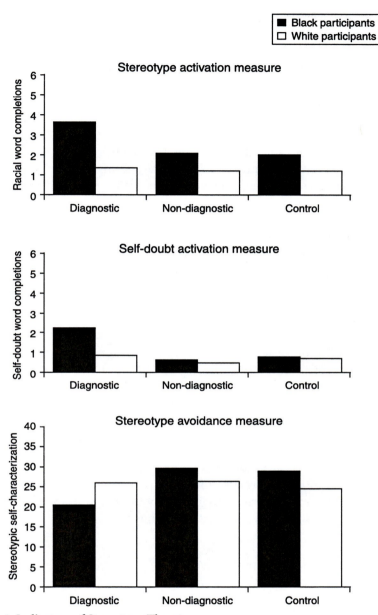

Figure 11.4 Indicators of Stereotype Threat.

other group. But the full set of results suggests a different interpretation. In those conditions in which Black participants did not have to worry about tripping a stereotypic perception of themselves, they valued things that were African American more strongly than did other participants. Thus, rather than reflecting self- or own-group rejection, their devaluing of things that were African American in the diagnostic condition was apparently a strategic self-presentation aimed at cracking the stereotypic lens through which they could be seen. So it could be, then, in the general case, rather than reflecting real self-concepts, behavior that appears group rejecting or self-rejecting may reflect situation-bound, self-presentational strategies.

Stereotype threat and domain identification. Not being identified with a domain, our (C. M. Steele & Aronson, 1995) theory reasons, means that one's experience of stereotype threat in the domain is less self-threatening. Although we have yet to complete a satisfactory test of this prediction, partially completed experiments and pretests show that stereotype threat has very little, if any, effect on participants not identified with the domain of relevance. Most typically, these participants give up and underperform on the difficult test regardless of whether they are under stereotype threat. Although not yet constituting a complete test of this implication of the theory, these data do emphasize that the above results generalize only to domain-identified students.

Stereotype threat and the interpretation of group differences in standardized test performance. Inherent to the science of quantifying human intelligence is the unsavory possibility of ranking societal groups as to their aggregated intelligence. It is from this corner of psychology that the greatest controversy has arisen, a controversy that has lasted throughout this century and that is less about the fact of these group differences than about their interpretation (cf. Hernstein & Murray, 1994; Kamin, 1974). To the set of possible causes for these group differences, our (C. M. Steele & Aronson, 1995) findings add a new one: the differential impact of stereotype threat on groups in the testing situation itself. Thus, stereotype threat may be a possible source of bias in standardized tests, a bias that arises not from item content but from group differences in the threat that societal stereotypes attach to test performance. Of course, not every member of an ability-stereotyped group is going to be affected by stereotype threat every time they take a test. As our research has shown, the experience of success as one takes the test can dispel the relevance of the stereotype. Nonetheless, among the most identified test takers in the stereotype-threatened group—those in its academic vanguard who have the greatest confidence and skills—this threat can substantially depress performance on more difficult parts of the exam. And this depression could contribute significantly to the group's underperformance in comparison with nonstereotype-threatened groups.[6]

Reaction of Disidentification

Stereotype threat is assumed to have an abiding effect on school achievement—an effect beyond its impairment of immediate performance—by preventing or breaking a person's identification with school, in particular, those domains of schooling in which the stereotype applies. This reasoning has several implications for which empirical evidence can be brought to bear: the resilience of self-esteem to stigmatization; the relationship between stigmatized status and school achievement; and, among ability-stigmatized people, the relationship between their school performance and self-esteem.

Self-esteem's resilience to stigmatization. In a recent review, Crocker and Major (1989) were able to make a strong case for the lack of something that common sense suggests should exist: a negative effect of stigmatization on self-esteem. Following the logic of the internalization models described above and viewing stigmatization as, among other things, an assault to self-esteem, one might expect that people who are stigmatized would have lower self-esteem than people who are not. Yet, as Crocker and Major reported, when the self-esteem of stigmatized groups (e.g., Blacks, Chicanos, the facially disfigured, obese people, etc.) is actually measured, one finds that their self-esteem is as high as that of the nonstigmatized.

Crocker and Major (1989) offered the intriguing argument that stigma itself offers esteem-protective strategies. For example, the stigmatized can blame their failures on the prejudice of out-group members, they can limit their self-evaluative social comparisons to the ingroup of other stigmatized people, and they can devalue the domains in which they feel devalued. Other models have also described esteem-saving adaptations to stigma. For example, models that assume internalization of stereotype-related anxieties often posit compensatory personality traits (e.g., grandiosity) that protect self-esteem but leave one poorly adapted to the mainstream (e.g., Allport, 1954; Clark, 1965; Grier & Coobs, 1968; Kardiner & Ovesey, 1951; S. Steele, 1990). In the present reasoning, stigmatization stems from stereotype threat in specific domains. Thus, it adds to the list of stigma adaptations the possibility of simple domain disidentification, the rescuing of self-esteem by rendering as self-evaluatively irrelevant the domain in which the stereotype applies. Herein may lie a significant source of the self-esteem resilience shown in stigmatized groups. This idea also implies that once domain disidentification is achieved, the pressure for adaptations of attribution and personality may be reduced.

A universal connection between stigmatization and poor school achievement. If disidentification with school, and the resulting underachievement, can be a reaction to ability-stigmatizing stereotypes in society, then it might be expected that ability stigmatization would be associated with poor school performance wherever it occurs in the world. Finding such a relationship would not definitively prove the present theory; the direction of causality could be quarreled with, as could the mediation of such a relationship. Still, it would be suggestive, and, in that respect, Ogbu (1986) reported an interesting fact: Among the caste-like minorities in industrial and non-industrial nations throughout the world (e.g., the Maoris of New Zealand, the Baraku of Japan, the Harijans of India, the Oriental Jews of Israel, and the West Indians of Great Britain), there exists the same 15-point IQ gap between them and the nonstigmatized members of their society as exists between Black and White Americans. These groups also suffer poorer school performance, higher dropout rates, and related behavior problems. Moreover, these gaps appear even when the stigmatized and nonstigmatized are of the same race, as in the case of the Baraku and other Japanese. What these groups share that is capable of explaining their deficits is a caste-like status that, through stereotypes in their societies, stigmatizes their intellectual abilities—sowing the seeds, I suggest, of their school disidentification.

The disassociation of self-esteem and school achievement. If the poor school achievement of ability-stigmatized groups is mediated by disidentification, then it might be expected that among the ability stigmatized, there would be a disassociation between school outcomes and overall self-esteem. Several kinds of evidence suggest this process among African Americans. First, there is the persistent finding that although Black students underperform in relation to White students on school outcomes from grades to standardized tests (e.g., Demo & Parker, 1987; Simmons, Brown, Bush, & Blyth, 1978; C. M. Steele, 1992), their global self-esteem is as high or higher than that of White students (e.g., Porter & Washington, 1979; Rosenberg, 1979; Wylie, 1979). For both of these facts to be true, some portion of Black students must have acquired an imperviousness to poor school performance.

Several further studies suggest that this imperviousness is rooted in disidentification. In a study of desegregated schools in Champaign, Illinois, Hare and Costenell (1985) measured students' school achievement; overall self-esteem; and self-esteem in the specific domains of home life, school, and peer-group relations. Like others, they found that although Black students performed less well than White students, they still had comparable levels of overall self-esteem. Their domain-specific measures suggested why: Although Black students were lower than White students in school and home-life self-esteem, Blacks slightly exceeded Whites in peer-group self-esteem. Here then, perhaps, was the source of their overall self-regard: disidentification with domains in which their evaluative prospects were poor (in this case, school and home life) and identification with domains in which their prospects were better (i.e., their peers).

A recent study suggests that this may be a not uncommon phenomenon. Analyzing data available from the National Educational Longitudinal Survey (National Center for Educational Statistics, 1992; a nationally representative longitudinal survey begun in 1988), Osborne (1994) found that from the 8th through 10th grades, Black students had lower achievement and somewhat higher self-esteem than White students, which replicated the general pattern of findings described above. But more than this, he found evidence of increasing Black students' disidentification over this period: The correlation between their school achievement and self-esteem for this period decreased significantly more for Black than for White students. Also, using a scale measure of school disidentification, Major, Spencer, Schmader, Wolfe, and Crocker (in press) found that Black students were more disidentified than White students in several college samples and that for disidentified students of both races, negative feedback about an intellectual task had less effect on their self-esteem than it did for identified students. Major et al. further showed that when racial stereotypes were primed, neither negative nor positive feedback affected Black students' self-esteem, whereas the self-esteem of White students followed the direction of the feedback. Ability stigmatization of the sort experienced by African Americans, then, can be associated with a protective "disconnect" between performance and self-regard, a disconnect of the sort that is consistent with disidentification theory.

Can stereotype threat directly cause this disconnect? To test this question, Kirsten Stoutemeyer and I varied the strength of stereotype threat that female test takers (Stanford students) were under by varying whether societal differences between women and men in math performance were attributed to small but stable differences in innate ability (suggesting an inherent, gender-based limit in math ability) or to social causes such as sex-role prescriptions and discrimination (suggesting no inherent, gender-based limit in math ability). We then measured their identification with math and math-related careers, either before or after they took a difficult math test. Regardless of when identification was measured, women under stronger stereotype threat disidentified with math and math-related careers more than women under weaker stereotype threat. Although domain identification has several determinants, these findings suggest that stereotype threat is an important one of them.

"Wise" Schooling: Practice and Policy

As a different diagnosis, the present analysis comes to a different prescription: The schooling of stereotype-threatened groups may be improved through situational changes (analogous to those manipulated in our experiments) that reduce the stereotype threat these students might otherwise be under. As noted, psychological diagnoses have more typically ascribed the problems of these students to internal processes ranging from genes to internalized stereotypes. On the face of it, at least, internal states are more difficult to modify than situational factors. Thus, the hope of the present analysis, encouraged by our research, is that these problems might be more tractable through the situational design of schooling, in particular, design that secures these students in the belief that they will not be held under the suspicion of negative stereotypes about their group. Schooling that does this, I have called *wise*, a term borrowed from Irving Goffman (1963), who borrowed it from gay men and lesbians of the 1950s. They used it to designate heterosexuals who understood their full humanity despite the stigma attached to their sexual orientation: family and friends, usually, who knew the person beneath the stigma. So it must be, I argue, for the effective schooling of stereotype-threatened groups.

Although "wisdom" may be necessary for the effective schooling of such students, it may not always be sufficient. The chief distinction made in this analysis (between those of these groups who are identified with the relevant school domain and those who are not) raises a caution. As noted, stereotype threat is not keenly felt by those who identify little with the stereotype-threatening domain. Thus, although reducing this threat in the domain may be necessary to encourage their identification, it may not be sufficient to build an identification that is not there. For this to occur, more far-reaching strategies that develop the building blocks of domain identification may be required: better skills, greater domain self-efficacy, feelings of social and cultural comfort in the domain, a lack of social pressure to disidentify, and so on.

But for the identified of these groups, who are quite numerous on college campuses, the news may be better than is typically appreciated. For these students, feasible changes in the conditions of schooling that make threatening stereotypes less applicable to their behavior (i.e., wisdom) may be enough. They are already identified with the relevant domain, they have skills and confidence in the domain, and they have survived other barriers to identification. Their remaining problem is stereotype threat. Reducing that problem, then, may be enough to bring their performance on par with that of nonstereotyped persons in the domain.

This distinction raises an important and often overlooked issue in the design of schooling for stereotype-threatened students, that of *triage*, the issue of rendering onto the right students the right intervention. Mistakes can easily be made. For example, applying a strategy to school-identified students (on the basis of their membership in a stereotype-threatened group) that assumes weak identification, poor skills, and little confidence could backfire. It could increase stereotype threat and underperformance by signaling that their abilities are held under suspicion because of their group membership. But the opposite mistake could be made by applying a strategy that assumes strong identification, skills, and confidence to those who are actually unidentified with the relevant domain. Merely reducing stereotype threat may not accomplish much when the more primary need of these students is to gain the interests, resources, skills, confidences, and values that are needed to identify with the domain.

Some wise strategies, then, may work for both identified and unidentified students from these groups, but others may have to be appropriately targeted to be effective. I offer some examples of both types.

For both domain-identified and domain-unidentified students:

1. Optimistic teacher-student relationships. The prevailing stereotypes make it plausible for ability-stigmatized students to worry that people in their schooling environment will doubt their abilities. Thus, one wise strategy, seemingly suitable for all students, is to discredit this assumption through the authority of potential-affirming adult relationships. The Comer (1988) Schools Project has used this strategy with great success at the elementary school level, and Johnides, von Hippel, Lerner, and Nagda (1992) have used it in designing a mentoring program for incoming minority and other students at the University of Michigan. In analogous laboratory experiments, Geoffrey Cohen, Lee Ross, and I (Cohen, Steele, & Ross, 1997) found that critical feedback to African American students was strongly motivating when it was coupled with optimism about their potential.
2. Challenge over remediation. Giving challenging work to students conveys respect for their potential and thus shows them that they are not regarded through the lens of an ability-demeaning stereotype. Urie Treisman (1985) used this strategy explicitly in designing his successful group-study workshops in math for college-aged women and minorities. Taking students where they are skillwise, all students can be given challenging work at a challenging, not overwhelming, pace, especially in the context of supportive adult–student relationships. In contrast, remedial work reinforces in these students the possibility that they are being viewed stereotypically. And this, by increasing stereotype threat in the domain, can undermine their performance.
3. Stressing the expandability of intelligence. The threat of negative-ability stereotypes is that one could confirm or be seen as having a fixed limitation inherent to one's group. To the extent that schooling can stress what Carol Dweck (1986) called the *incremental* nature of human intelligence—its expandability in response to experience and training—it should help to deflect this meanest implication of the stereotype. Aronson (1996) recently found, for example, that having African American college students repeatedly advocate the expandability of intelligence to their elementary school tutees significantly improved their own grades.

For domain-identified students:

1. Affirming domain belongingness. Negative-ability stereotypes raise the threat that one does not belong in the domain. They cast doubt on the extent of one's abilities, on how well one will be accepted, on one's social compatibility with the domain, and so on. Thus, for students whose primary barrier to school identification is stereotype threat, direct affirmation of their belongingness in the domain may be effective. But it is important to base this affirmation on the students' intellectual potential. Affirming social belonging alone, for those under the threat of an ability stereotype, could be taken as begging the question.

2. Valuing multiple perspectives. This refers to strategies that explicitly value a variety of approaches to both academic substance and the larger academic culture in which that substance is considered. Making such a value public tells stereotype-threatened students that this is an environment in which the stereotype is less likely to be used.

3. Role models. People from the stereotype-threatened group who have been successful in the domain carry the message that stereotype threat is not an insurmountable barrier there.

For domain-unidentified students:

1. Nonjudgmental responsiveness. Research by Lepper, Woolverton, Mumme, and Gurtner (1993) has identified a distinct strategy that expert tutors use with especially poor students: little direct praise, Socratic direction of students' work, and minimal attention to right and wrong answers. For students weakly identified with the domain, who are threatened by a poor reputation and who probably hold internalized doubts about their ability, this Socratic strategy has the wisdom of securing a safe teacher–student relationship in which there is little cost of failure and the gradual building of domain efficacy from small gains.

2. Building self-efficacy. Based on Bandura's (1977, 1986) theory of self-efficacy, this strategy attempts to build the student's sense of competence and self-efficacy in the schooling domain. Howard and Hammond (1985) have developed a powerful implementation of this strategy for African American and other minority students, especially in inner-city public schools.

Existence Proof: A Wise Schooling Intervention

Providing a definitive test of wise schooling theory will require, of course, an extensive research program. But as a first step, something might be learned from what Urie Treisman (1985) called an existence proof, in this case, a demonstration that an intervention derived from the theory could stop or reverse a tenacious negative trajectory in the school performance of stereotype-threatened students. Such an intervention would of necessity confound things: different wise practices as well as other practices and structures, peculiar to that setting, that could also affect academic outcomes. It could not stand as a test of the psychological theory per se. But if a particular architecture of wise strategies succeeded, it would encourage their applicability to the real-world schooling of these students.

With this rationale, my colleagues and I (Steven Spencer, Richard Nisbett, Mary Hummel, David Schoem, Kent Harber, Ken Carter) implemented a freshman-year program at the University of Michigan aimed at the underachievement and low retention rates of African American students. Each year, the program included approximately 250 freshmen in the ethnic proportions of the larger campus but with an oversampling of approximately 20% Black students and 20% non-Black minority students (i.e., Asian, Hispanic, and Native American students as a single group). Program students were randomly selected from the students admitted to Michigan and then recruited by phone to participate. All program participants lived together in the wing of a large, 1,200-student dormitory throughout their freshman year.

In this context, we implemented several wise strategies. The program was presented as a transition program aimed at helping students maximize the advantages of university life. We also recruited students honorifically; they were told that, as Michigan admittees, they had survived a very competitive selection process and that our program was designed to help them maximize their strong potential. These practices represented the program as nonremediational and represented the university as having acknowledged their intellectual potential and as having high expectations for them—all things that signal the irrelevance of negative group stereotypes. Once the students were in the program, these expectations were reinforced by their being offered a "challenge" workshop, modeled on those developed by Treisman (1985) for calculus, in either freshman calculus, chemistry, physics, or writing. These were taken on a voluntary basis in the dormitory. Students also participated in small weekly discussion groups, centered on brief readings, that allowed discussion of adjustment-relevant social and even personal issues. This activity has the wisdom of letting students know that they, or other members of their group, are not the only ones with concerns about adjusting to university life—an insight that can deflect the relevance of negative group stereotypes. These formal program components lasted for the first 10 weeks of the school year, and, as voluntary activities, approximately half of the students regularly participated in either one or both of them.

The first-semester grades averaged over the first two years of this ongoing project give a reliable picture of the program's initial impact. To show the size of the program's effect on students at different levels of preparation, Figure 11.5 graphs first-semester grades, using regression lines, for the different student groups as a function of standardized test scores on entry into the university (they are presented as standard deviation units in this figure to provide a common scale for students who took either the SAT or American College Test exam). The first thing to notice is the two essentially parallel lines for White and Black students outside of any program at Michigan. They replicate the standard overprediction–underperformance of Black students alluded to earlier, and it is against this pattern that the effects of the program can be evaluated. Looking first at the line for White students in our program, there is a modest tendency for these students to do better than the White control students (i.e., those outside the program), but given our accumulation of n throughout these first two years, this difference is not significant. It is the results for Black students in our program (but who were not also in the campus minority program) that are most

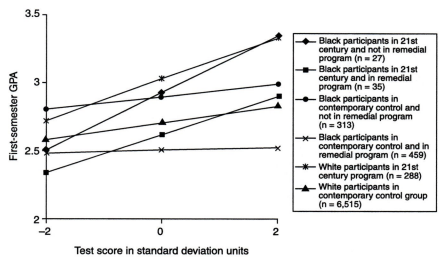

Figure 11.5 First-Semester Grade Point Average (GPA) as a Function of Program and Race Controlling for High School GPA.

promising. Their line is considerably above that for Black control students (i.e., Black students outside any program) and, even with the modest sample size ($n = 27$), is significantly higher than this control line in the top one third of the standardized test distribution, $t = 2.72$, $p < .05$. It is important that this group of Black students showed almost no underperformance; in the top two thirds of the test distribution, they had essentially the same grades as White students. We also know from follow-up data that their higher grade performance continued at least through their sophomore year and that as long as four years later, only one of them had dropped out.

Theoretically just as important, is the bottom line in Figure 11.5, depicting the results for Black students in a large minority remediation program. Despite getting considerable attention, they performed worse than the other groups at nearly every level of preparation. The difference between Black students in the minority program and Black students not in any program becomes significant at 1.76 standard deviations below the mean for test performance and is significant from that point on, $ps < .05$. Also, by the beginning of their junior year, 25% of these students had failed to register, and among those who entered with test scores in the top one third of the test distribution, this figure was 40%. Some selection factor possibly contributed to this. Despite our having controlled for test scores and high school grade point averages in these analyses, some portion of these students may have been assigned to this program because they evidenced other risk factors. Still, these results suggest that the good intentions of the minority–remediation framework for schooling African American students can backfire by, in our terms, institutionalizing the racial stereotype by which they are already threatened.

Although these findings are preliminary and we do not know that they were mediated as our theory claims, they are a step toward an existence proof; they show that wise practices can reduce Black students' underachievement in a real-school context and, as important, that unwise practices seem to worsen it.

Conclusion

In social psychology, we know that as observers looking at a person or group, we tend to stress internal, dispositional causes of their behavior, whereas when we take the perspective of the actor, now facing the circumstances they face, we stress more situational causes (e.g., E. E. Jones & Nisbett, 1972; Ross, 1977). If there is a system to the present research, it is that of taking the actor's perspective in trying to understand the intellectual performance of African American and female students. It is this perspective that brings to light the broadly encompassing condition of having these groups' identification with domains of schooling threatened by societal stereotypes. This is a threat that in the short run can depress their intellectual performance and, over the long run, undermine the identity itself, a predicament of serious consequence. But it is a predicament—something in the interaction between a group's social identity and its social psychological context, rather than something essential to the group itself. Predicaments can be treated, intervened on, and it is in this respect that I hope the perspective taken in this analysis and the early evidence offer encouragement.

Notes

1. Other factors may also contribute. For example, there are persistent reports of women and minorities being treated differently in the classroom and in other aspects of schooling (e.g., Hewitt & Seymour, 1991). This treatment includes both the "chilly-climate" sins of omission—the failure to call on them in class or to recognize and encourage their talents, and so on—and, in the case of low-income minorities, sins of commission—disproportionate expulsion from school, assignment to special education classes, and administration or corporal punishment ("National Coalition of Advocates for Students Report," 1988).
2. The point is not that negative stereotypes are never internalized as low self-expectancies and self-doubts. It is that in such internalization, disidentification is the more primary adaptation. That is, once the stereotype-relevant domain (e.g., math) is dropped as a self-definition, the negative stereotype (e.g., that women are limited in math) can be accepted as more self-descriptive (i.e., internalized) without it much affecting one's self-regard (as for the woman who, not caring about math, says she is lousy at it). But this internalization is probably resisted (e.g., Crocker & Major, 1989) until disidentification makes it less self-threatening. Once this has happened, the person is likely to avoid the domain because of both disinterest and low confidence regardless of whether stereotype threat is present.
3. As a process of social devaluation, stereotype threat is both a subform of stigmatization and something more general. It is that form of stigmatization that is mediated by collectively held, devaluing group stereotypes. This means that it does not include stigmatization that derives from nonstereotyped features such as a facial disfigurement or, for example, what Goffman (1963) called abominations of the body. Stereotype threat is a situational predicament. And, in this sense, it is also more general than stigmatization. It is a threat that can befall anyone about whom a negative reputation or group stereotype exists.
4. Moreover, a protective avoidance of identification can become a group norm. In reaction to a shared sense of threat in school, for example, it can become a shared reaction that is transmitted to group members as the normative relation to school. Both research (e.g., Ogbu, 1986; Solomon, 1992) and the media have documented this reaction in minority students from inner-city high schools to Harvard University's campus. Thus, disidentification can be sustained by normative pressure from the in-group as well as by stereotype threat in the setting.
5. Participants did not actually take the test in this experiment, as completing these measures would likely have activated the stereotype in all conditions.
6. Those who are less domain identified in the stereotype-threatened group may also underperform on standardized tests. Because they care less about the domain it represents, they may be undermotivated or they may withdraw effort in the face of frustration. And for all of the reasons I have discussed, the greater portion of the stereotype-threatened group may be academically unidentified. This fact too, then, may contribute to the group's overall weaker performance on these tests in comparison with nonstereotype-threatened groups.

References

Adelman, C. (1991). *Women at thirty-something: Paradoxes of attainment*. Washington, DC: U.S. Department of Education, Office of Research and Development.

Alexander, K. L., & Entwistle, D. R. (1988). Achievement in the first two years of school: Patterns and processes. *Monographs of the Society for Research in Child Development, 53*(2).

Allport, G. (1954). *The nature of prejudice*. New York: Doubleday.

American Council on Education. (1995–1996). *Minorities in higher education*. Washington, DC: Office of Minority Concerns.

Aronson, J. (1996). *Advocating the malleability of intelligence as an intervention to increase college grade performance*. Unpublished manuscript, University of Texas.

Bandura, A. (1977). Self-efficacy: Toward a unifying theory of behavior change. *Psychological Review, 84*, 191–215.

Bandura, A. (1986). *Social foundations of action: A social-cognitive theory*. Englewood Cliffs, NJ: Prentice Hall.

Baumeister, R. F., & Showers, C. J. (1984). A review of paradoxical performance effects: Choking under pressure in sports and mental tests. *European Journal of Social Psychology, 16*, 361–383.

Benbow, C. P., & Arjmand, O. (1990). Predictions of high academic achievement in mathematics and science by mathematically talented students: A longitudinal study. *Journal of Educational Psychology, 82*, 430–441.

Benbow, C. P., & Stanley, J. C. (1980). Sex differences in mathematical ability: Fact or artifact? *Science, 210*, 1262–1264.

Benbow, C. P., & Stanley, J. C. (1983). Sex differences in mathematical reasoning ability: More facts. *Science, 222*, 1029–1031.

Bettelheim, B. (1943). Individual and mass behavior in extreme situations. *Journal of Abnormal and Social Psychology, 38*, 417–452.

Brill, A. A. (Ed.). (1938). *The basic writings of Sigmund Freud*. New York: Random House.

Burton, N. W., & Jones, L. V. (1982). Recent trends in achievement levels of Black and White youth. *Educational Researcher, 11*, 10–17.

Carter, S. (1991). *Reflections of an affirmative action baby*. New York: Basic Books.

Clark, K. B. (1965). *Dark ghetto: Dilemmas of social power*. New York: Harper & Row.

Clark, K. B., & Clark, M. K. (1939). The development of consciousness of self and the emergence of racial identification of Negro school children. *Journal of Social Psychology, 10*, 591–599.

Cohen, G., Steele, C. M., & Ross, L. (1997). *Giving feedback across the racial divide: Overcoming the effects of stereotypes*. Unpublished manuscript, Stanford University.

Coleman, J. S., Campbell, E. Q., Hobson, C. J., McPartland, J., Mood, A. M., Weinfield, F. D., & York, R. L. (1966). *Equality of educational opportunity*. Washington, DC: U.S. Government Printing Office.

Comer, J. (1988, November). Educating poor minority children. *Scientific American, 259*, 42.

Cooley, C. H. (1956). *Human nature and the social order*. New York: Free Press.

Cose, E. (1993). *The rage of a privileged class*. New York: Harper Collins.

Crocker, J., & Major, B. (1989). Social stigma and self-esteem: The self-protective properties of stigma. *Psychological Review, 96*, 608–630.

Cross, W. E., Jr. (1991). *Shades of black: Diversity in African-American identity*. Philadelphia: Temple University Press.

Culotta, E., & Gibbons, A. (Eds.). (1992, November 13). Minorities in science [Special section]. *Science, 258*, 1176–1232.

DeBoer, G. (1984). A study of gender effects in science and mathematics course-taking behavior among students who graduated from college in the late 1970's. *Journal of Research in Science Teaching, 21*, 95–103.

Demo, D. H., & Parker, K. D. (1987). Academic achievement and self-esteem among Black and White college students. *Journal of Social Psychology, 4*, 345–355.

Dweck, C. (1986). Motivational processes affecting learning. *American Psychologist, 41*, 1040–1048.

Eccles, J. S. (1987). Gender roles and women's achievement-related decisions. *Psychology of Women Quarterly, 11*, 135–172.

Eccles-Parsons, J. S., Adler, T. F., Futterman, R., Goff, S. B., Kaczala, C. M., Meece, J. L., & Midgley, C. (1983). Expectations, values, and academic behaviors. In J. T. Spence (Ed.), *Achievement and achievement motivation* (pp. 75–146). New York: Freeman.

Erikson, E. (1956). The problem of ego-identity. *Journal of the American Analytical Association, 4*, 56–121.

Fanon, F. (1967). *Black skins, white masks*. New York: Grove Press. (Original work published 1952)

Frable, D., Blackstone, T., & Sherbaum, C. (1990). Marginal and mindful: Deviants in social interaction. *Journal of Personality and Social Behavior, 59*, 140–149.

Geen, R. G. (1991). Social motivation. *Annual Review of Psychology, 42*, 377–399.

Gerard, H. (1983). School desegregation: The social science role. *American Psychologist, 38*, 869–878.

Goffman, E. (1963). *Stigma: Notes on the management of spoiled identity*. New York: Touchstone.

Grier, W. H., & Coobs, P. M. (1968). *Black rage.* New York: Basic Books.

Hare, B. R., & Costenell, L. A. (1985). No place to run, no place to hide: Comparative status and future prospects of Black boys. In M. B. Spencer, G. K. Brookins, & W. Allen (Eds.), *Beginnings: The social and affective development of Black children* (pp. 201–214). Hillsdale, NJ: Erlbaum.

Herrnstein, R. A., & Murray, C. (1994). *The bell curve.* New York: Grove Press.

Hewitt, N. M., & Seymour, E. (1991). *Factors contributing to high attrition rates among science and engineering undergraduate majors.* Unpublished report to the Alfred P. Sloan Foundation.

Howard, J., & Hammond, R. (1985, September 9). Rumors of inferiority. *New Republic, 72,* 18–23.

Hyde, J. S., Fennema, E., & Lamon, S. J. (1990). Gender differences in mathematics performance: A meta-analysis. *Psychological Bulletin, 107,* 139–155.

James, W. (1950). *The principles of psychology* (Vol. 1). New York: Dover. (Original work published 1890)

Jensen, A. R. (1969). How much can we boost IQ and scholastic achievement? *Harvard Educational Review, 39,* 1–123.

Jensen, A. R. (1980). *Bias in mental testing.* New York: Free Press.

Johnides, J., von Hippel, W., Lerner, J. S., & Nagda, B. (1992, August). *Evaluation of minority retention programs: The undergraduate research opportunities program at the University of Michigan.* Paper presented at the 100th Annual Convention of the American Psychological Association, Washington, DC.

Jones, E. E., Farina, A., Hastorf, A. H., Markus, H., Miller, O. T., & Scott, R. A. (1984). *Social stigma: The psychology of marked relationships.* New York: Freeman.

Jones, E. E., & Nisbett, R. E. (1972). The actor and the observer: Divergent perceptions of the causes of behavior. In E. E. Jones, D. E. Kanouse, H. H. Kelley, R. E. Nisbett, S. Valins, & B. Weiner (Eds.), *Attribution: Perceiving the causes of behavior* (pp. 79–94). Morristown, NJ: General Learning Press.

Jones, J. M. (1997). *Prejudice and racism* (2nd ed.). New York: McGraw-Hill.

Kamin, L. (1974). *The science and politics of I.Q.* Hillsdale, NJ: Erlbaum.

Kardiner, A., & Ovesey, L. (1951). *The mark of oppression: Explorations in the personality of the American Negro.* New York: Norton.

Kleck, R. E., & Strenta, A. (1980). Perceptions of the impact of negatively valued physical characteristics on social interactions. *Journal of Personality and Social Psychology, 39,* 861–873.

Lepper, M. R., Woolverton, M., Mumme, D. L., & Gurtner, J.-L. (1993). Motivational techniques of expert human tutors: Lessons for the design of computer-based tutors. In S. P. Lajoie & S. J. Derry (Eds.), *Computers as cognitive tools* (pp. 75–104). Hillsdale, NJ: Erlbaum.

Levin, J., & Wyckoff, J. (1988). Effective advising: Identifying students most likely to persist and succeed in engineering. *Engineering Education, 78,* 178–182.

Lewin, K. (1941). *Resolving social conflict.* New York: Harper & Row.

Linn, M.C. (1994). The tyranny of the mean: Gender and expectations. *Notices of the American Mathematical Society, 41,* 766–769.

Lord, C. G., & Saenz, D. S. (1985). Memory deficits and memory surfeits: Differential cognitive consequences of tokenism for tokens and observers. *Journal of Personality and Social Psychology, 49,* 918–926.

Lovely, R. (1987, February). *Selection of undergraduate majors by high ability students: Sex difference and attrition of science majors.* Paper presented at the annual meeting of the Association for the Study of Higher Education, San Diego, CA.

Major, B., Spencer, S., Schmader, T., Wolfe, C., & Crocker, J. (in press). Coping with negative stereotypes about intellectual performance: The role of psychological disengagement. *Personality and Social Psychology Bulletin.*

Mead, G. H. (1934). *Mind, self, and society.* Chicago: University of Chicago Press.

Miller, L. S. (1995). *An American imperative: Accelerating minority educational advancement.* New Haven, CT: Yale University Press.

Miller, L. S. (1996, March). *Promoting high academic achievement among non-Asian minorities.* Paper presented at the Princeton University Conference on Higher Education, Princeton, NJ.

National Center for Educational Statistics. (1992). *National Educational Longitudinal Study of 1988: First follow-up. Student component data file user's manual.* Washington, DC: U.S. Department of Education, Office of Educational Research and Improvement.

National Coalition of Advocates for Students Report. (1988, December 12). *The Ann Arbor News,* pp. A1, A4.

Nettles, M. T. (1988). *Toward undergraduate student equality in American higher education.* New York: Greenwood.

Ogbu, J. (1986). The consequences of the American caste system. In U. Neisser (Ed.), *The school achievement of minority children: New perspectives* (pp. 19–56). Hillsdale, NJ: Erlbaum.

Osborne, J. (1994). Academics, self-esteem, and race: A look at the underlying assumption of the disidentification hypothesis. *Personality and Social Psychology Bulletin, 21,* 449–455.

Porter, J. R., & Washington, R. E. (1979). Black identity and self-esteem: A review of the studies of Black self-concept, 1968–1978. *Annual Review of Sociology, 5,* 53–74.

Ramist, L., Lewis, C., & McCamley-Jenkins, L. (1994). *Student group differences in predicting college grades: Sex, language, and ethnic groups* (College Board Report No. 93–1, ETS No. 94.27). New York: College Entrance Examination Board.

Rosenberg, M. (1979). *Conceiving self.* New York: Basic Books.

Ross, L. (1977). The intuitive psychologist and his shortcomings: Distortions in the attribution process. In L. Berkowitz (Ed.), *Advances in experimental social psychology* (Vol. 10, pp. 337–384). New York: Academic Press.

Sarason, I. G. (1980). Introduction to the study of test anxiety. In I. G. Sarason (Ed.), *Test anxiety: Theory, research, and applications* (pp. 57–78). Hillsdale, NJ: Erlbaum.

Sartre, J. P. (1965). *Anti-Semite and Jew.* New York: Schocken Books. (Original work published 1946)

Schlenker, B. R., & Weigold, M. F. (1989). Goals and the self-identification process: Constructing desired identities. In L. A. Pervin (Ed.), *Goals concepts in personality and social psychology* (pp. 243–290). Hillsdale, NJ: Erlbaum.

Simmons, R. G., Brown, L., Bush, D. M., & Blyth, D. A. (1978). Self-esteem and achievement of Black and White adolescents. *Social Problems, 26*, 86–96.

Solomon, R. P. (1992). *Forging a separatist culture.* Albany: State University of New York Press.

Spencer, S., Steele, C. M., & Quinn, D. (1997). *Under suspicion of inability: Stereotype threat and women's math performance.* Manuscript submitted for publication.

Steele, C. M. (1975). Name-calling and compliance. *Journal of Personality and Social Psychology, 31*, 361–369.

Steele, C. M. (1988). The psychology of self-affirmation: Sustaining the integrity of the self. In L. Berkowitz (Ed.), *Advances in experimental social psychology* (Vol. 21, pp. 261–302). New York: Academic Press.

Steele, C. M. (1992, April). Race and the schooling of Black Americans. *The Atlantic Monthly*, pp. 68–78.

Steele, C. M., & Aronson, J. (1995). Stereotype threat and the intellectual test performance of African Americans. *Journal of Personality and Social Psychology, 69*, 797–811.

Steele, S. (1990). *The content of our character.* New York: St. Martin's Press.

Strenta, A. C., Elliott, R., Adair, R., Scott, J., & Matier, M. (1993). *Choosing and leaving science in highly selective institutions.* Unpublished report to the Alfred P. Sloan Foundation.

Tesser, A. (1988). Toward a self-evaluation maintenance model of social behavior. In L. Berkowitz (Ed.), *Advances in experimental social psychology* (Vol. 21, pp. 181–227). New York: Academic Press.

Treisman, U. (1985). *A study of mathematics performance of Black students at the University of California, Berkeley.* Unpublished report.

Vars, F. E., & Bowen, W. G. (1997). *SAT scores, race, and academic performance: New evidence from academically successful colleges.* Unpublished manuscript.

Ware, N. C., & Dill, D. (1986, March). *Persistence in science among mathematically able male and female college students with pre-college plans for a scientific major.* Paper presented at the annual meeting of the American Educational Research Association, San Francisco.

Ware, N. C., Steckler, N. A., & Leserman, J. (1985). Undergraduate women: Who chooses a science major? *Journal of Higher Education, 56*, 73–84.

Wine, J. (1971). Test anxiety and direction of attention. *Psychological Bulletin, 76*, 92–104.

Wylie, R. (1979). *The self-concept* (Vol. 2). Lincoln: University of Nebraska Press.

12

Peer Networks of African American Students in Independent Schools
Affirming Academic Success and Racial Identity
*Amanda Datnow and Robert Cooper**

Introduction

A plethora of research documents the educational experiences of African American students. Early research in this area primarily focused on the failures of African American students to achieve at the same academic level as their White counterparts (Coleman et al., 1969; Jencks et al., 1972). More recently, the emphasis in research has shifted from studies of academic failure to studies of the factors that contribute to African American student success (Ladson-Billings, 1990; Lee, Winfield, & Wilson, 1991). Since the 1960s, increasing numbers of African American students have been enrolling in predominantly White elite independent schools known to prepare students for positions of power and leadership (Cookson & Persell, 1985). Much of the increase in enrollment can be attributed to the efforts of a number of organizations, including A Better Chance (ABC), Prep for Prep, Black Student Fund (BSF), and the Baltimore Educational Scholarship Trust (BEST), that have initiated and maintained the presence and participation of African American students in these schools (Cookson & Persell, 1991; Johnson & Anderson, 1992). Additionally, the majority of these schools have enacted policies of nondiscrimination, and a growing number actively recruit minority students in their efforts to create more diverse student bodies on their campuses (Speede-Franklin, 1988).

Despite these efforts, research shows that predominantly White elite independent schools, with their history of racial exclusion, are often places where African American students find it difficult to fit in (Brookins, 1988; Zweigenhaft & Domhoff, 1991). Moreover, African American students in such institutions have frequently reported that they feel caught between two cultures and consequently doubly marginalized.[1] They have also indicated that often they feel alienated from the culture of the school and from their own parents and friends, particularly in boarding school environments (Cookson & Persell, 1991). This is not surprising, as NELS:88 data indicate that African American students at predominantly White elite independent schools have substantially fewer family economic resources relative to the school populations as a whole (Schneider & Shouse, 1992). Research also suggests that African American students at these institutions may have weaker social relationships with their teachers than do their peers at the schools, and that this lack of connection may affect their motivation and academic performance (Schneider & Shouse, 1992).

Given these findings, it appears that the social bonds that African American students at predominantly White elite independent schools develop with each other may provide an important but as yet unexplored support network that could potentially contribute to their academic performance and sense of identity and belonging. Although African American students in such settings often form their own cliques and clubs (Cookson & Persell, 1991), the functions served by these peer networks are not clearly understood. Thus, the study presented here used qualitative interview data to explore the peer networks developed by African American students enrolled in predominantly White elite independent schools through the Baltimore Educational Scholarship Trust (BEST).

BEST is a program that helps to place and fund economically disadvantaged, academically talented African American students from the Baltimore (Maryland) metropolitan area in 20 local independent schools. Over five hundred African American families seek out BEST's services each year, applying for independent school admission at all grade levels. Approximately 70 new BEST students are placed in these schools each year.

Peer Group Influence on Academic and Cultural Identities: The Contribution of Ethnographic Studies

Ethnographic studies provide a promising avenue for assessing the role of peer culture in the formation of students' academic and cultural identities. In particular, studies of resistance, which emerged as a response to the neo-Marxian perspective represented in the work of Bowles and Gintis (1976), have argued that students actively make choices in life rather than passively respond to structural demands (Fine, 1991; Fordham & Obgu, 1986; Labov, 1982; MacLeod, 1987; Willis, 1977). A central focus of these studies is peer group ideology. Typically, they characterize the low-income and minority students in their samples as having a peer group ideology that is resistant to school success. Instead of "buying into" the dominant ideology of a meritocratic system in which rewards are fairly distributed on the basis of hard work, these students chose to resist the dominant ideology, believing that no matter how hard they work, they would not rise up in the social system, or alternately, that success in school was equal to failure within their peer group.

Willis's (1977) study of male secondary school students in an industrial town in England is a frequently cited example of resistance theory. Willis identified two low-income peer groups: the "lads" and the " 'earholes." The 'earholes were studious, hard-working students who adhered to the dominant ideology: hard work in school will ensure success in later life. The lads, on the other hand, engaged in disruptive activities in classes, saw little purpose in school, and used drugs and alcohol. Instead of buying into the dominant ideology, the lads resisted school and created their own standards for measuring success. They equated the masculinity of manual labor with success and the mental labor of an office job with failure. In sum, Willis's study revealed that different peer groups of boys from the same social class had very different experiences in school, depending upon whether they chose to see school as a legitimate institution.

Fine's (1991) study of dropouts in New York City produced similar but more striking findings about student resistance. Fine interviewed one hundred low-income African American and Latino students who had dropped out of high school. She discovered that not only did these dropouts formulate a sophisticated critique of the failings of the educational system, they were also nonconformists who resisted schools for teaching a curriculum entirely focused on Anglo Americans. The students also recognized the hidden curriculum of schools and the illusion of meritocracy that existed within them. Like the lads in Willis's study, Fine's dropouts attempted to assess the potential rewards of staying in school, only to determine that those rewards did not outweigh the costs of dropping out. Interestingly, the dropouts in Fine's study were not low-achieving students when they attended school; rather, they were academically average.

MacLeod's (1987) ethnography of two groups of high school boys living in a low-income housing project in Boston further reinforces the role of peer groups in mediating students' aspirations and academic identities. MacLeod characterized the "Hallway Hangers" as a peer group of White, ethnically identified, resistant teenage boys. These boys were mostly dropouts, substance abusers, and described by others in their school setting as "hoodlums." Their unique peer subculture was diametrically opposed to the dominant culture. The second peer group in MacLeod's study was the "Brothers," a group of African American boys also living in the projects. The picture was quite different for the Brothers, who attended school regularly and had high aspirations for school and career success. Unlike the Hallway Hangers, the Brothers did not form a distinctive subculture; instead, they bought into the achievement ideology and adhered to the norms of society. Both the Brothers and their parents agreed that the opportunity structure was much more open for them due to the gains of the civil rights movement and affirmative action policies. Further, some of the Brothers had older siblings who had graduated from high school. Although MacLeod indicated that the Brothers and the Hallway Hangers might end up in similar positions, he showed that the way the two groups responded to the structures of domination was not predetermined or uniform.

The above-noted studies are helpful in that they advance our understanding about how peer group associations and ideological ties can influence academic identities. However, Fordham and Ogbu (1986) offer a more pointed explanation of the school-resistance phenomenon as it relates to African American students. In their ethno-graphic study of successful and unsuccessful students in a predominantly Black high school, these two authors argue that Black students' underachievement can be explained in terms of the sense of collective oppositional identity Black develop in response to racial stigmatization by Whites. They maintain that African Americans have defined an oppositional cultural frame such that certain behaviors, activities, or values are seen as inappropriate because they characterize White culture. They further argue that the ambivalence the Black students in their sample felt about school success arose because Whites did not acknowledge that Blacks were intellectually capable, thereby leading the students to question their own ability. The students subsequently defined academic success as "White people's prerogative" and discouraged their peers who were striving for academic success from doing so on the grounds that they were "acting White." Fordham and Ogbu subsequently maintained that some Black students, for fear of betraying the collective group identity, resisted or opposed the idea of working hard in school. Success in these students' view was measured by how one behaves and works within the Black culture. This finding has powerful consequences, given that group membership is very important insofar as peer relationships are concerned, especially among the young. For the students in Fordham and Ogbu's study, the net effect of the "burden of acting White" is detrimental to Black students' future opportunities.

Similarly, in his study of the linguistic codes developed by Black students, Labov (1982) found that although the students' use of the Black English Vernacular (BEV) contributed to the maintenance of group solidarity, it also contributed to the students' academic demise because White teachers perceived the use of BEV as oppositional behavior. However, the Black peer culture shunned students who spoke "school English." Because students valued acceptance by their peers, they opted out of conforming to school norms and instead resisted authority and used the linguistic code accepted by the peer culture.

The ethnographic studies reviewed here reveal that peer group cultures can have a powerful effect on students' academic identities; indeed, peer groups often define what counts as success. These studies also show that for low-income and minority students, success within the peer culture is often not defined in terms of success in school. Rather, success within the peer culture is defined in terms of resistance to institutional structures that are characterized by White, middle-class domination.

In striking contrast to Fordham and Ogbu's and Labov's findings, Mehan and his colleagues found that groups of African American and Latino students in an untracking program affirmed their cultural identities while simultaneously recognizing the importance of academic achievement for their success in the mainstream culture (Mehan, Villanueva, Hubbard, & Lintz, 1996). The Mehan et al. study pointed to the important role of peer group influences in the formation of students' academic identities. Instead of finding tension between the academic demands of the untracking program and the oppositional demands of peer groups, Mehan and his colleagues discovered that the African American and Latino students formed new, academically oriented peer groups that also promoted a respect for cultural maintenance. These students' ideology was neither oppositional nor conformist, the authors concluded. Moreover, the institutional scaffolds of the untracking program formed an intellectual space for students to develop academic identities without feeling as though they were diminishing their cultural identities.

Like the African American and Latino students in the Mehan et al. study, the African American students in the present study were also found to develop criteria for success within their peer group that rewarded an academic orientation yet reaffirmed the students' cultural identity as African Americans. Before explaining this important finding in greater detail, an overview of our research methods and a description of the school context are presented.

Method

Study Design

Because it allows educational researchers to examine a contemporary phenomenon within its real life context (Yin, 1989), case study methodology was deemed the best strategy available for exploring situations in which the intervention being evaluated (i.e., BEST) has no clear, single set of outcomes (Yin, 1989). This methodology relies on a triangulation of multiple sources of evidence including interviews, relevant documents, and observations to establish construct validity. As such, for the present study, interviews were conducted with students, admissions directors, teachers, and parents to explore the peer networks developed and utilized by African American students to succeed in predominantly White elite independent schools. In the context of this study, success is defined as a student's ability to maintain satisfactory academic progress at an independent school for at least three years. Additionally, this research involved classroom observations and review of documents produced by BEST and each of the schools in which BEST students were placed. We (the authors) conducted all of the data collection and analysis ourselves and did not employ the use of research assistants. Although there are only two of us, we comprise a research team that is diverse in terms of race, gender, and disciplinary background.

Sample

Data for the present study were drawn from year one (1996) of a three-year longitudinal case study of African American students enrolled in predominantly White elite independent schools in the Baltimore area with the assistance of BEST. In that year, there were a total of 380 students enrolled in 20 independent schools through BEST. A total of 42 African American students in grades 10 through 12 in eight different schools were interviewed about their experiences. With the exception of a few, all of the students in this sample had been enrolled in their schools for two or more years. In most schools, we were able to interview the entire population of African American students that fit this criteria.

The sample was comprised of students from a range of social-class backgrounds. Most students lived in predominantly African American neighborhoods and would attend predominantly African American public schools if they were not enrolled in independent schools. The majority of BEST students receive financial assistance, but there are a few who do not. Some students receive full financial aid to attend their recipient schools, and some receive much less than the average. The approximate annual tuition cost at the eight schools is $11,000 per year; the average financial award to a BEST student is approximately $6,500. Although BEST provides funding assistance for some students, most of the financial aid comes directly from the schools.

School Settings

This study and case study research in general employs replication rather than sampling logic, as application of a statistical sampling logic is inappropriate for case study research in which the goal is to study both a phenomenon of interest and its context (Yin, 1989). For external validity, case studies rely on analytical instead of statistical generalizability, aiming toward generalization of results to a broader theory rather than to the larger universe. In other words, cases (in this case, schools) are included because they are likely to produce either similar results, or contrary results but for predictable reasons, not because they represent the entire set of available cases (Yin, 1989). Therefore, to obtain a more in-depth picture of what the independent school experience is like for the BEST program's African American students, the present study focused on a subset of recipient schools selected after reviewing the relevant literature on the factors that are likely to produce contrary results. Specifically, the eight schools from which data were collected varied somewhat in terms of their selectivity in admissions, size, single-sex versus coed status, day versus boarding structure, and religious affiliation (see Table 12.1).

The eight schools selected for the present study are located in and around the city of Baltimore. All are members of the National Association of Independent Schools (NAIS) and the Association of Independent Maryland Schools (AIMS).[2] NAIS member schools are nonprofit, tax-exempt, and maintain fiscal independence from government and church entities. Each is governed by a board of trustees and subscribes to policies of nondiscrimination (Speede-Franklin, 1988). Although obvious size and architectural differences exist across schools, all of the campuses are physically beautiful—often serene—ideal environments for scholarly pursuits. Grounds are well-manicured and buildings are in excellent repair. Each offers special facilities of some type or other; most have superb athletic and fine arts facilities, high-tech libraries, and several even offer horse-riding facilities.

The schools range in size from a total enrollment of 180 to 945 students. All but two offer schooling in grades kindergarten, or pre-first, through twelve. The total percentage of African American students ranges from a high of approximately 15% to a low of 5% (and possibly less, given that some of the schools did not reveal exactly

Table 12.1 School Characteristics

	Single-sex or coed	Day or boarding
The Franklin School	All boys	Day
Highlands School	All boys	Day
The Garland School	All girls	Day
The Brookline School	All girls	Day
Simmons Academy	All girls	Day
The Orwell School	Coed	Day and boarding
The Lake School	Coed	Day
The Bennett School	All girls	Day and boarding

how many Black students they enrolled). These figures are slightly skewed in K-12 settings because lower schools (K–5) tend to have far smaller African American enrollments than do the middle and upper schools (grades 9–12), the latter of which may be as much as 25% African American in a school that is 15% African American overall.

Procedures

Most of the interviews were conducted in small groups; some were conducted individually. Semi-structured interview protocols, which involved asking open-ended questions of respondents, were used. These protocols included questions about students' backgrounds, home lives, and interests; their academic course work and progress; their social adjustment and peer groups; and their perceptions of the school climate and faculty. Interviews lasted an average of one hour, although many were longer. Most were jointly conducted by the authors. All were audiotaped and transcribed at the completion of each school site visit. To encourage participants to respond honestly to our questions, we promised confidentiality throughout the study.

Data Analysis

As Eisenhardt (1989) contends, data analysis is the most difficult and least codified part of the case study process. Though there is flexibility, the goal of the analysis is to become intimately familiar with each case under study and with patterns across cases. In analyzing our data—drawn from interview transcripts, field notes, and relevant documents—we drew upon advice and methods detailed by several qualitative methodologists, including Miles and Huberman (1984), Yin (1989), and Strauss and Corbin (1990). We followed Miles and Huberman's outline of very specific methods for analyzing qualitative data acquired in a case study, including constructing a matrix of categories and placing the evidence within such categories and creating data displays. We were also mindful of Yin's admonishment that the ultimate goal of case study data analysis is to treat evidence fairly, to produce compelling conclusions, and to rule out alternative interpretations. Thus, in the process of coding and sorting our data for analysis, we made every effort to bring our findings into an ongoing conversation with a theoretical framework that brought together literature in education and sociology.

Results

Hangin' with the Crew: Peer Networks Among African American Students

Despite the schools' efforts to integrate students of diverse backgrounds into their school communities, many BEST students reported having difficulty acclimating to their school environment. Several reported initial feelings of alienation, a lack of belonging, and difficulty fitting in. Although most indicated that they believed their schooling experience was providing them with the academic training required to be successful, they often described feeling like the "outsiders within"—a term coined by Collins (1986) to describe African American students' participation in the activities of institutions yet their incomplete acceptance in the minds of those within them.

Many of the students identified their African American peer group networks, both formal and informal, as one of the most important factors in helping them cope in the predominantly White environments of their schools and lessen the feelings of alienation. They indicated that these peer networks functioned in important ways to simultaneously foster school success and provide a mental space for them to reaffirm their racial identities.

For the majority of the students in the sample, their informal peer group associations were with other Black students, although most indicated that they had some White friends. Typically, the students noted that they felt close bonds with other Black students and seldom had close bonds with White students.[3] As Tanika, a student at Bennett School, stated: "There is a very strong Black unit here." Moreover, although she claimed that her friends at school were of all races, those she identified as her "better friends" were Black. This latter sentiment is one that was shared by all of the students in our sample. Many of the students qualified their assertion that their peer group was majority Black by explaining that they simply shared similar values and life experiences with other Black students. According to Michael, a sophomore at Lake School: "People tend to associate with other people who believe what they believe in, and who talk about the same things they do. . . . It's not really like I don't sit with them just because they're White."

Three African American seniors at Highlands School attributed their strong bond with each other to the conclusion that they "just have things in common." They further maintained that their friendship went beyond being Black. As Jamal noted: "We have White friends, but the bonds are not as strong." None of the three indicated the existence of any animosity between the African American and White students on their campus. However, they avowed feeling that some of the White students were ignorant about the history, culture, and life experiences of African Americans.

Although the African American independent school students we interviewed found their peer associations with other African American students to be of utmost importance, many also recognized the importance of creating friendships with White students. Peer associations with Whites were seen as helpful in later life. As one of the students at Orwell School explained:

> I can come here and interact with people of different races. They do have a lot of different races here, and I still get along with them, and they get along with me. And I understand what they're talking about. You make friends and get those connections with a lot of rich people.

The students in this sample also referred to the identifiable cliques on the campuses of several of the eight schools: the "preppy" clique, the "jocks" (athletes), the "artsy" students, and, of course, "the Black students." Though they indicated that they did not necessarily feel excluded from the other cliques, they described their peer associations with other African American students as simply "normal gravitation" to people of their own kind. For example, Jason, a student at Lake School, indicated that he and his best friend developed their relationship because they were the only Black males in their class. Cherise, a student at Simmons, expressed a similar affiliation and sentiments: "It's kind of like a bond . . . the fact that we're Black and in this school, which is an occasion in itself, brought us together."

Several of the African American students in our sample who had been attending independent schools since a young age maintained that more racial clustering was evident at the upper school levels than in the lower grades. According to Michael, a sophomore at Lake School:

> [In] middle school, everyone was tighter, you know, I went over to friends' houses all the time. Ninth grade, that was probably the biggest transition, because you still have friends, but in the upper school you have your identity. . . . that's where you become a person, I guess.

Mary, a student at Orwell, shared a similar experience, stating: "In sixth grade, I remember when I came, everyone was just a happy-go-lucky family, and they wanted me to be the new Black kid in the family." Yet, by high school, she noted, the Black students tended to separate themselves from the White students insofar as social activities were concerned.

According to the students interviewed, formal associations between African American students at predominantly White elite independent schools were fostered through Black Student Unions, Black Awareness Clubs, gospel choirs, and multi-cultural alliances. They maintained that these organizations were critical to sustaining African American students' ability to negotiate their outsider-within status at the schools. Though they were quick to point out that those who participated in these organized structures were not all close friends and that each organization was different and tailored to meet the needs of its members, the students stressed that the formal structure of these groups gave them the opportunity to connect with each other in very important ways. The existence of Black student associations at the various schools also facilitated the formation of peer networks of Black students across the schools. Most of the students talked about attending dances sponsored by other schools' Black Awareness Clubs and about forming friendships with Black students from other schools this way. For example, students at Bennett discussed attending Black Awareness Club meetings at Orwell and vice-versa.

"If You're Not Smart, You're Not Cool": Forming Academic Identities

The strength of the informal networks forged by this sampling of African American students at predominantly White elite independent schools not only helped the students to cope with social and psychological challenges but also to succeed academically. The most striking feature of these networks was the social value their members placed upon high academic achievement and hard work in school. They allowed students to be "smart" without feeling as though they were "selling out" or "acting White." For example, Michael, a sophomore at Lake School, claimed that one of the two major differences between his school and a public school was that students at the former were rewarded by their peer groups for exhibiting intelligence. In his words:

> It's just like . . . public schools, it's not really cool to be smart, you know. And here, if you're not smart, you're not cool. Like, the complete opposite.

An Orwell student offered similar remarks:

> In the public high schools . . . you have a good time and you don't really pay attention and these people are the popular ones, the ones that most people want to hang around with. But here it's like the smart ones are the ones that you go to. I have more respect for a person who gets good grades.

Jennifer, a Simmons student, also recognized the importance of peer networks in creating a culture in which academic success is either rewarded or discredited. "If you are at a school where everyone else is not doing their homework," she stated, "then you will not want to succeed, either." She was aware, however, that while academic success was rewarded within the Black peer culture of her independent school, it was not as readily accepted in some peer cultures outside the school. Conceding that she does not fit in with the students in her Black church youth group, she explained: "I'm different. I do well in school. . . . We don't have a lot of things in common, and we have different aspirations."

For students at Bennett, the mantra "if you're not smart, you're not cool" played out a little differently. Not only did academic successfulness determine who was seen as "cool" among the informal peer group of Black students, it also extended to impressions that some faculty had about Black students. As 10th-grader Antoinette explained, "You're on scholarship, you're Black, you're supposed to be smart. . . . If you're average, you get shunned." She commented that Camilla and Kelly, two high-achieving Black students at Bennett, were always being recognized and were seen as "good Black folk," whereas average Black students were seen as "bad apples," especially if they did not "kiss up [and] voice their opinions" and refused to "get walked on."

Several students noted that the socialization process with which African American students at predominantly White elite independent schools are confronted makes it hard for Blacks to fit in, sometimes even with their own families. Consequently, the students explained, they turn to their friends as role models. When asked about support for his academic success, a Franklin student stated: "A lot of it has come from my friends, just seeing what they're doing and wanting to be part of that, too." The Black peer group's promotion of strong academic identities begins when new students arrive at the schools, with the older students serving as role models for the new entrants. For example, study participants from Simmons Academy recalled that when a new African American student who had won a full academic scholarship was introduced in an assembly, the older African American students quickly approached and welcomed her, stating: "We really need your accomplishment." A senior explained: "We were all, like, this is my little sister now, fighting over her!" Clearly, it was seen as positive, and even "cool," for African American students to succeed in these school contexts.

Other students spoke of junior and senior students who took them under their wings to acclimate them to the academic and social demands of their new schools. Jeff, a senior at Franklin, recounted his experiences as a new student:

> When I first came here it was all new to me and I wasn't sure who was a friend and who was the enemy. When I came here all the Black students were, like, "What's up, man? How you doing? Hey, come on, join in, join in. Come do this." They made me feel great, and they did not discourage me from doing things. They encouraged me to go out there and try everything.

Jeff added that while his newfound friends encouraged him to get involved in extracurricular activities, they did not allow him to forget that his academic work took priority. He noted that they also expressed confidence that he was capable of handling the workload and that he belonged at the school.

The Black Awareness Club at Orwell had a formal Big Brother/Big Sister program, in which upper-school African American students mentor lower- and middle-school African American students. This mentoring was common to Simmons and Highlands as well. A Highlands student reported that although there was no formalized process of mentoring younger students at his school, one of the goals of its Black Awareness Club was to "look out for the younger guys" and serve as role models for them. In turn, he stated: "It makes you feel good when the younger guys look up to you."

Students in the upper grades also looked to each other for positive academic role models. A Franklin student explained:

> So I'm just hanging around playing and stuff and I notice that William—he's like our group scholar—William's in the library studying. And we're playing basketball and it's the end of the week. He's still sitting on the computer at five o'clock. So it makes the rest of us think.

Study participants also indicated that their teachers capitalized on the positive attributes of the informal social networks among African American students to foster these students' academic identities. For example, seniors at Franklin recalled that teachers had enlisted their support in helping a younger student learn appropriate study skills and mastery of subject matter. As one student explained: "One of the teachers might come to us, me or another senior, and [say], 'Go out and study with them. Let them know that they need to get on top of something.' " An extreme case of teachers' use of students' informal networks was recounted by a senior, who explained that a teacher once showed him some of the younger Black students' grades in hopes that the senior would help them improve academically:

> He showed me everybody's grade. He shouldn't have, but still. He didn't give me time to look at all of them, he just said, "Look over these grades and try to make sure that everybody's doing their thing." We did that, and we offered anybody who needed help to come to a junior or senior.

Students at some schools were even rather boastful about their academic accomplishments in front of their peers in their group interviews with us. During the interview, students at Garland boasted about high college admissions test scores, about the several brochures they had received from prospective colleges, and about special academic programs they were involved in. For example, when discussing her combined SAT (Scholastic Aptitude Test) score of 1,340, Janie stated: "I did pretty well on them, which means that I've got colleges pouring down my throat." Another student quickly interrupted with: "Yeah, I got over a hundred colleges [inviting me to apply.]"

Creating a Space for the Affirmation of Racial Identity

In addition to promoting academic success, both formal and informal peer networks created opportunities for Black students in predominantly White elite independent schools to affirm their racial identities. Black student organizations were the most important formal networks in this regard. Many students indicated that these organizations created a "space" for them to express and affirm their racial identity. Study participants described Black student organization meetings and activities as forums in which students could address and raise their own and others' awareness about issues pertinent to African Americans. As a Garland student explained: "If we have a racial problem, you can go to the [Black Awareness] club."

Bennett students explained that the goals of their Black Awareness Club were to "bring more Black authors into the library" and "make people aware of the accomplishments of African Americans." The impetus for forming the organization, one student declared, was the Black students' realization that "no attention [was being paid] to multicultural issues at the school." "We felt that there was a need for one in order to dispel stereotypes," a Bennett student maintained. Others noted that, "Teachers deliberately avoid discussing race and are afraid that we'll bring up racial issues in classes," and "Teachers are afraid of debates and confrontations." Still others recalled that the name "Black Awareness Club" was chosen over "Black Student Union" by the school's faculty and administration because they found the latter name too "threatening" and "united." They noted that the fact that the group is open to everyone is "stressed greatly" by school personnel.

African American students who did not participate in these formal networks were not necessarily ostracized. For example, not all of the African American students at Simmons chose to be part of its Cultural Awareness Club (essentially a Black club), but those who were members did not disparage the strength of non-members' racial identity. As a member explained, "I don't think whether you're in the club identifies you as acting White. It's all about how you act in the hallway, whether you want to speak to us, whether you acknowledge the fact that you are a Black person." She noted, however, that there were some Black students at her school "who just forget [that they're Black]."

Although the respondents indicated that Black students who chose not to participate in formal Black peer networks were not ostracized, these students were frequently ostracized for having informal peer connections that did not include any Blacks. Affecting a "valley girl" [White suburban affluent] accent, Cherise, a senior, stated: "If you talk like *this*, like, all the time, and you don't want to hang out with us, I mean, like, at *all*, [then you would be ostracized for] 'acting White.'" Referring to one student specifically, she added: "I guess when she finds her identity, then she'll be okay, but I think she needs to go somewhere like Howard [an historically Black university] for college." Cherise qualified her statements by noting that style of speech was not always indicative of Black cultural identity; rather, "It's all in how you act" toward other Blacks. She admitted that she too has been accused by Blacks outside her school setting of "talking White" because "*Yo'* is not [her] every other word."

Study participants from the Orwell School claimed that they too were wary of other African American students who chose to associate with White students to the exclusion of other Blacks both in and outside school. As one student explained:

> You have to have bonds. When I first came here in sixth grade, I was so happy that I had my friends in my community to go back to and my church to go back to. I see Black students here who are just so into Orwell that they have forgotten who they are.

Apparently, Black students' informal peer networks also created a space for the affirmation of their racial identity in the predominantly White setting of their elite independent schools. Several noted that groups of African American male students gather together every day for lunch as a way for them to assert their racial identity on campus. As a Highlands student stated, "the big thing for us is sitting together." However, another Highlands student recalled that a group of African American students seated together in the lunchroom was once approached by a teacher, who emphatically stated, "Segregation ended in the sixties," and asked the boys to split up and integrate with the White students in the lunchroom. He noted that this incident greatly frustrated the Black youth because it suggested that the burden of integration was to be borne by the African American students, not the White students.

The BEST organization also functioned to promote peer networks and cultural identity among African American students across and within schools by offering a variety of activities for the African American students in its member schools. These activities have included a Black engineering conference, a people of color conference, and a Kwanzaa celebration, which several students in each of the schools reported attending and enjoying. As an Orwell student confirmed, these programs indicated that BEST was "really trying to get [Black students] to participate in as much stuff as they can to help [us] succeed." The former director of BEST also occasionally attended Black Awareness Club meetings at various schools. Many students mentioned in their interviews that they knew him personally and regarded him as a positive African American role model.

The informal and formal peer networks among this group of African American students were also seen as providing places of refuge and emotional support in environments in which students indicated they sometimes felt like "outsiders within." Gender differences were apparent in the students' perceptions of the function of peer networks as sources of emotional support. For example, female students were much more likely than male students to identify their peer networks as serving this function. This was true of young women in both single-sex and coed schools. As a Bennett sophomore explained: "We go to each other with problems. It is an outlet where you can go to plug up and get the energy you need to face the world." Mary, a junior at Orwell, concurred: "I guess we just strive to be there for one another, like an outlet where we can just set a time when we can come and see all faces, in case you did not pass someone [another Black student] that day." A young woman at Brookline offered a poignant explanation of the importance of her school's Black Awareness Club:

> Although everybody's friendly most of the time, sometimes you can still feel like just not a part of [the school], like, when you are in the classroom with all White people. They might be nice to you, but they are talking about something you do not know about, you're just not in sync with what they are talking about. . . . But, if you have a problem with another student in the school from a different race you have about 37 people you can chose from to go talk to. . . . They are your friends, no matter what grade or whatever.

Only one African American male student interviewed described peer networks as sources of emotional support. As he stated: "It seems like the track team is one big Black Awareness Club, because the team is mostly Black people and I guess a couple of White people." The student noted that the Black track team members had developed a strong sense of mutual support and encouragement for each other, and that the African American male coach of the team provided a source of emotional support as well.

Caught Between Two Peer Cultures

Our interviews revealed further that this group of Black students struggled with the challenge of being accepted by their African American peers outside the school and, of course, their White peers inside the school. As a Franklin student stated: "If I meet somebody who goes to [a local public school] . . . they think I have sold out to the point that I'm not like them." An Orwell student reiterated: "A lot of people thought that I thought that I was better than them because I was going to a private school. I lost a lot of friends." Similarly, a student at Brookline was also shunned by her neighborhood peers for enrolling at the predominantly White elite independent school. However, she explained that she eventually regained acceptance by these peers:

> Initially, when I went to Brookline, people seemed to have a problem with it, but since then people have decided not to care because it has not changed me. They thought I was going to turn into some valley girl. It just has not happened. If anything, I swear that I am more . . . you could say "ghetto" than I would be if I was in a [public school].

By contrast, another Brookline student admitted that she had changed "a little bit" due to her independent school experience. Moreover, Justin, a junior at Lake School, explained that the small African American population at his school tended to compel him and another African American schoolmate to adopt the practices and behaviors of the majority White students:

> In the sixth grade, Devon and I raised all kinds of trouble together because there was just the two of us and we came from a public school. In the seventh grade, they split us up. We had different classes. We kind of changed. We went to hanging with all of these White brothers doing stupid stuff, like throwing food at lunch time, just stuff we did not used to do . . . that we would not usually do.

Justin stated that his friend Devon's musical tastes also changed over time: he now listened to rock and roll, a musical preference more commonly associated with White teenagers. As explanation, he added:

> When you change your surroundings, eventually you will change. Well, the reason I haven't changed is because most of my friends go to public schools, so I am usually around them, and I guess they keep me in line.

Unlike Justin, some Black students at predominantly White elite independent schools did not believe that connections to African American peers outside the school were essential to affirming their racial identity. Tanika, a Simmons student, claimed to have very loose associations with her peers from her former public school, and maintained that she had reconciled this issue for herself. As she confidently stated:

> A lot of people say since I go to a predominantly White school, I'm missing something by not being around Black people, but, I mean, I've been Black my whole life! Nothing will ever change that, no matter where I go. I will never wake up White. I won't wake up Puerto Rican. I won't wake up anything but Black. So the Black experience, I've been getting it.

Most of the students interviewed agreed that attending a predominantly White elite independent school did change them to some degree, but they argued that style of dress or speaking proper English did not constitute "acting White." Lisa, a Brookline student, recounted her experience with this issue:

> I did not say "Yo" in the beginning. . . . I was resented that I did not dress a certain way and I did not do my hair all up. It is a racial thing. . . . They [Black students] would be, like, "Why are you trying to be White? Why are you trying to act like a White girl?" I don't think you need to act that way to be successful.

Most of the students indicated that they too had encountered situations in which they had being caught between two peer cultures and had been forced to defend their behaviors outside school and even sometimes within school. A Franklin student found a unique solution to this dilemma. As he explained, he incorporated the values of the institution, yet still maintained his connections to peers outside the school who shared similar values but did not necessarily attend Franklin:

> Gradually I began to spend more time here. School here, sports here, summer job here, weekends here. People in the neighborhood, they know me, but I don't know them. I'm still kind of in touch. You know, I have friends. Most of my friends that don't go to private school are not necessarily from my neighborhood. I met them some other way. And I keep in touch with them and do the same things.

Several students talked about making the conscious but difficult decision to distance themselves from old neighborhood friends in order to achieve academic success. According to Jason, a sophomore at Lake School:

> The friends I had when I was younger, I would say four out of the ten of them are in trouble. Two are in jail, and one just got caught stealing a car. They are always hanging on the street

corner. I used to be like that, but now I am too busy for that. . . . It seemed like that was not the right thing. Now you see all them in trouble, and I know it was not.

Students indicated that they worked hard to maintain friendships with Black peers outside their schools. Some achieved this by working part-time jobs in their neighborhoods. Students boarding at their schools claimed that they had difficulty maintaining their friendships with African American students from their neighborhoods because they spend so much time at school. As one such student stated: "You don't really speak to them that much because you don't see them anymore." By contrast, those Black students who did not board at their schools found it easier to maintain ties with peers and others in their neighborhoods.

Three young men talked about how their relationships with neighborhood peers faded since they began attending the Highlands School. They explained that the distance between them and their neighborhood friends developed, not because they had changed, but because of their restrictive time schedules. Jamal, a senior, maintained that Highlands "was like a boarding school, because the students are there for so many hours a day and they spend so much time together." However, because of the enormous amount of time these three spent together, they had become very close friends.

The strength of peer associations outside the school also appears to be related to the length of time students attend their independent school. That is, the longer students are enrolled in such schools, the less likely they are to have friendships outside. For example, a Garland senior who had attended the school since fifth grade explained: "I don't know them anymore. Since I've been here, I have no life outside of school."

Discussion

The findings of the present study seem to indicate that for many African American students in predominantly White elite independent school environments, "cool" has been redefined to include academic success. At the eight schools included in our study, Black students who were high-achieving were revered by their peers and held up as role models. Moreover, these students helped socialize new Black peer group members toward academic striving. These findings are consistent with those of Zweigenhaft and Domhoff (1991) in their study of Black students in enrolled in boarding schools through the ABC (A Better Chance) program:

> What the ABC program did very simply was to negate the usual social psychological dialectic between the powerful and the powerless by initiating its Black students into a new social and psychological identity that overcame the effects of stigmatization and any inclination toward an oppositional identity. (p. 162)

Apparently, what Fordham and Ogbu (1986) describe as an oppositional identity does not evolve in the atypical predominantly White elite independent school setting. Instead, these schools appear to offer African American students an alternative identity, one with an emphasis on doing well in school.

The African American students at the predominantly White elite independent schools focused upon in the present study agreed that one of the main factors contributing to their academic success was their strong bonds with each other. Indeed, their formal and informal peer networks supported academic success while simultaneously creating opportunities for them to reaffirm their racial identities and seek refuge from what could otherwise be difficult places for them to fit in. In contrast to Fordham and Ogbu's (1986) finding that adopting academically successful behaviors leads Black students to be labeled as acting White, these students actually made social gains within the school when they were academically successful. Their Black peer groups allowed for the development of an identity that was not oppositional and that promoted academic success. This did not mean, however, that these students were fully accepted by African American peers outside the school; subsequently, many of the students developed a variety of strategies to address the dilemma of being caught between the worlds of their African American peers in and outside of school.

Why do the findings of this study differ from those of Fordham and Ogbu? Several hypotheses emerge: One possibility is that within the context of college preparatory independent schools that hold high expectations for students and have positive school climates, African American students are more inclined toward academic success. Another possibility points to selection bias—namely, that the students in the present study comprise a select group, given that they attend elite independent schools. Most of these students are likely to have parents who are highly involved in their education, at least to the point of making choices about where they attend school, and who value the reward structure inherent in the educational system.

Though plausible, these hypotheses emphasize the importance of structural and cultural forces in fostering the academic identities of African American students rather than recognizing that the students themselves are active agents in creating a peer group ideology that fosters academic success. Structural and cultural factors are likely to interact with agency, but they do not predetermine ideology or actions (Datnow, 1995). As our research has shown, and consistent with studies of resistance cited earlier (e.g., Fine, 1991; Fordham & Ogbu, 1986; Willis, 1977), students are indeed actively engaged in the creation of their own academic success. Moreover, instead of resisting the dominant culture, the students in the present study were successful at helping to elevate each other. Unlike the students in Willis's and Fine's studies, who, by resisting, contributed to their own demise and were thus complicitors in the reproduction of the social order, our study participants were active agents who challenged the social order through their success-oriented behaviors.

Consistent with Mehan et al.'s (1996) findings, this study reveals that the dynamics and ideologies of Black peer groups are more complex and varied than prior research has suggested. Certainly the African American peer group ideology is not monolithic, nor is acting White universally defined. Ideology has an active quality; it is defined through the processes in which meaning is constructed (McLaren, 1989). Consequently, one must question the assumptions that guide studies of Black student ideology and achievement, as these studies often portray African American students stereotypically. Only by moving beyond such characterizations can researchers and educators gain a better understanding of the factors influencing the achievement and engagement of African American students in both in public and private schools.

The formal and informal peer networks developed by these African American students functioned in powerful ways to help shape their academic and social experiences in the predominantly White elite independent school setting. Most notably, these networks promoted academic success among African American students, created a space for the affirmation of their racial identity, and served as sources of emotional support. Moreover, they functioned to heighten the awareness of the larger school communities about issues pertinent to African Americans. Informal peer networks were found to be critical in helping African American students develop the necessary skills to negotiate their new schooling environments. Formal peer networks served additional functions. Although the structure, purpose, importance, and names of these organizations varied across the different schools, the common denominator for them all was that they allowed African American students to remain grounded in the culture, history, and struggle of their people. Interestingly, it was not the activities of the organization, but rather their symbolic representation, that signaled to students that they had a place in the school culture and that their individual voices could be heard collectively. The strong social bonds among African American students fostered within these organizations created opportunities for dialogue about race issues and helped maintain an identifiable, unified African American presence on campus.

Overall, the frequent mismatch between the African American peer culture inside the school and that outside the school created dilemmas for some students. Cookson and Persell (1991) argue that the double marginalization of race and class accounts for this mismatch. The data from our study suggest this as well. Consequently, for African American students in predominantly White elite independent school settings, finding one's niche often means searching out and associating with other African Americans students. Some students dealt with this dilemma by managing dual identities, one inside and one outside. More often, however, students reconciled the fact that African American peer group acceptance inside the school was sufficient. Notwithstanding, the issues encountered by these students point to the difficulty of being both an outsider within the independent school and an insider-without in their neighborhood peer cultures.

Conclusion

Despite the culture shock experienced by many African American students when they first enter predominantly White elite independent institutions, many have developed strong peer networks that allow them to overcome the unique academic, social, emotional, and psychological challenges they encounter in these environments. Our data suggest that these peer networks help African American students to be both academically and socially successful in independent schools, while also providing a space for them to express and affirm their racial identities.

Although independent schools are making strides toward becoming places where African American students can succeed and feel a part of the school community, they would be advised to continue and expand their efforts in this area. In addition to sponsoring Black student associations and increasing the enrollment of African

American students in order to facilitate the development of strong peer groups, these institutions should recruit more African American faculty, increasingly reflect cultural diversity in their curricula, and more openly confront racial issues in their communities. By doing so, they can more effectively acknowledge and bridge the gap between the double lives that some of their African American students lead in and outside of schools.

Notes

* An earlier draft of this article was presented at the 1996 annual meeting of the American Sociological Association, New York, NY. Our thanks to Will Jordan, Steve Plank, Mavis Sanders, Wendy Winters, Erin Horvat, Anthony Antonio, Richard Zweigenhaft, and William Domhoff for their comments and direction in preparing this article. This study was funded by the Abell Foundation as part of a larger evaluation of the Baltimore Educational Scholarship Trust (BEST). Support was also provided by a grant from the Office of Educational Research and Improvement, U.S. Department of Education, to the Center for Research on the Education of Students Placed At Risk (CRESPAR) (Grant No. R-117D-40005). However, any opinions expressed by the authors are our own and do not represent the policies or positions of the funders.

1. An extreme and isolated case of this marginalization is represented in Anson's (1987) journalistic account of a Black male in the ABC program who committed suicide.
2. For purposes of confidentiality, pseudonyms are used for the schools and participants in the study.
3. These findings contradict Zweigenhaft and Domhoff's (1991) earlier research on Black students in boarding schools. Due to the nature of the isolated boarding school environment and the very small Black enrollments at the schools, they found that some Black students formed strong bonds with their White peers. However, our findings are consistent with Cooper's (1996) study of students in racially mixed public schools. Cooper found that even in some of the most racially diverse public schools, the vast majority of students associate with students of their same racial/ethnic group.

References

Anson, R. (1987). *Best intentions: The education and killing of Edmund Perry*. New York: Random House.

Bowles, S., & Gintis, H. (1976). *Schooling in capitalist America*. New York: Basic Books.

Brookins, G. (1988). Making the honor roll: A Black parent's perspective on private education. In D. Slaughter & D. Johnson (Eds.), *Visible now: Blacks in private schools* (pp. 12–20). Westport, CT: Greenwood Press.

Coleman, J. S., Campbell, E. Q., Hobson, C. J., McPartland, J., Mood, A. M., Weinfeld, F. D., & York, R. L. (1966). *Equality of educational opportunity*. Washington, DC: U.S. Government Printing Office

Collins, P. H. (1986). Learning from the outsider within: The sociological significance of Black feminist thought. *Social Problems, 33*, S14–S32.

Cookson, P. W., & Persell, C. H. (1985). *Preparing for power: America's elite boarding schools*. New York: Basic Books.

Cookson, P. W., & Persell, C. H. (1991). Race and class in America's elite boarding schools: African Americans as the outsiders within. *Journal of Negro Education, 60*(2), 219–228.

Cooper, R. (1996, April). *The politics of change: Racial tension and conflict on school campuses—Strategies to improve intergroup relations*. Paper presented at the annual meeting of the American Educational Research Association, New York, NY.

Datnow, A. (1995). *Making sense of teacher agency: Linking theory to school reform policy*. Unpublished doctoral dissertation, University of California-Los Angeles.

Fine, M. (1991). *Framing dropouts*. Albany: State University of New York Press.

Fordham, S., & Ogbu, J. (1986). Black students' school success: Coping with the burden of acting White." *Urban Review, 18*(3), 176–206.

Jencks, C., Smith, M., Acland, H., Bane, M. J., Cohen, D., Gintis, H., Heyns, B., & Michelson, S. (1972). *Inequality: A reassessment of the effects of family and schooling in America*. New York: Basic Books.

Johnson, S., & Anderson, D. K. (1992). Legacies and lessons from independent schools. *Journal of Negro Education, 61*(2), 121–124.

Labov, W. (1982). Competing value systems in inner city schools. In P. Gilmore & A. Glathorn (Eds.), *Children in and out of school: Ethnography and Education* (pp. 148–171). Washington, DC: Center for Applied Linguistics.

Ladson-Billings, G. (1990, Spring). Culturally relevant teaching: Effective instruction for Black students. *College Board Review, 155,* 20–25.

Lee, V. E., Winfield, L. F., & Wilson, T. C. (1991). Academic behaviors among high-achieving African American students. *Education and Urban Society, 24*(1), 65–86.

MacLeod, J. (1987). *Ain't no makin it.* Boulder, CO: Westview Press.

McLaren, P. (1989). *Life in schools.* New York: Longman.

Mehan, H., Villanueva, I., Hubbard, L., & Lintz, A. (1996). *Constructing school success: The consequence of untracking low-achieving students.* Cambridge: Cambridge University Press.

Miles, M., & Huberman, M. (1984). *Qualitative data analysis.* Beverly Hills, CA: Sage.

Schneider, B., & Shouse, R. (1992). Children of color in independent schools: An analysis of the eighth grade cohort from the National Education Longitudinal Study of 1988. *Journal of Negro Education, 61*(2), 223–234.

Speede-Franklin, W. (1988). Ethnic diversity: Patterns and implications of minorities in independent schools. In D. Slaughter & D. Johnson (Eds.), *Visible now: Blacks in private schools.* (pp. 21–31). Westport, CT: Greenwood Press.

Strauss, A., & Corbin, J. (1990). *Basics of qualitative research: Grounded theory procedures and techniques.* Newbury Park, CA: Sage.

Willis, P. (1977). *Learning to labor.* New York: Columbia University Press.

Yin, R. (1989). *Case study research.* Newbury Park, CA: Sage.

Zweigenhaft, R. L., & Domhoff, G. W. (1991). *Blacks in the White establishment.* New Haven, CT: Yale University Press.

Part Six

Intersections: Gender, Class, and Culture

13

Mapping the Margins
Intersectionality, Identity Politics, and Violence Against Women of Color

Kimberle Crenshaw

Introduction

Over the last two decades, women have organized against the almost routine violence that shapes their lives. Drawing from the strength of shared experience, women have recognized that the political demands of millions speak more powerfully than the pleas of a few isolated voices. This politicization in turn has transformed the way we understand violence against women. For example, battering and rape, once seen as private (family matters) and aberrational (errant sexual aggression), are now largely recognized as part of a broad-scale system of domination that affects women as a class. This process of recognizing as social and systemic what was formerly perceived as isolated and individual has also characterized the identity politics of African Americans, other people of color, and gays and lesbians, among others. For all these groups, identity-based politics has been a source of strength, community, and intellectual development.

The embrace of identity politics, however, has been in tension with dominant conceptions of social justice. Race, gender, and other identity categories are most often treated in mainstream liberal discourse as vestiges of bias or domination—that is, as intrinsically negative frameworks in which social power works to exclude or marginalize those who are different. According to this understanding, our liberatory objective should be to empty such categories of any social significance. Yet implicit in certain strands of feminist and racial liberation movements, for example is the view that the social power in delineating difference need not be the power of domination; it can instead be the source of social empowerment and reconstruction.

The problem with identity politics is not that it fails to transcend difference, as some critics charge, but rather the opposite—that it frequently conflates or ignores intragroup differences. In the context of violence against women, this elision of difference in identity politics is problematic, fundamentally because the violence that many women experience is often shaped by other dimensions of their identities, such as race and class. Moreover, ignoring difference *within* groups contributes to tension *among* groups, another problem of identity politics that bears on efforts to politicize violence against women. Feminist efforts to politicize experiences of women and antiracist efforts to politicize experiences of people of color have frequently proceeded as though the issues and experiences they each detail occur on mutually exclusive terrains. Although racism and sexism readily intersect in the lives of real people, they seldom do in feminist and antiracist practices. And so, when the practices expound identity as woman or person of color as an either/or proposition, they relegate the identity of women of color to a location that resists telling.

My objective in this article is to advance the telling of that location by exploring the race and gender dimensions of violence against women of color. Contemporary feminist and antiracist discourses have failed to consider intersectional identities such as women of color. Focusing on two dimensions of male violence against women—battering and rape—I consider how the experiences of women of color are frequently the product of intersecting patterns of racism and sexism, and how these experiences tend not to be represented within the discourses of either feminism or antiracism. Because of their intersectional identity as both women *and* of color within discourses that are shaped to respond to one *or* the other, women of color are marginalized within both.

In an earlier article, I used the concept of intersectionality to denote the various ways in which race and gender interact to shape the multiple dimensions of Black women's employment experiences. My objective there was to illustrate that many of the experiences Black women face are not subsumed within the traditional boundaries of race or gender discrimination as these boundaries are currently understood, and that the intersection of racism and sexism factors into Black women's lives in ways that cannot be captured wholly by looking at the race or gender dimensions of those experiences separately. I build on those observations here by exploring the various ways in which race and gender intersect in shaping structural, political, and representational aspects of violence against women of color.

I should say at the outset that intersectionality is not being offered here as some new, totalizing theory of identity. Nor do I mean to suggest that violence against women of color can be explained only through the specific frameworks of race and gender considered here. Indeed, factors I address only in part or not at all, such as class or sexuality, are often as critical in shaping the experiences of women of color. My focus on the intersections of race and gender only highlights the need to account for multiple grounds of identity when considering how the social world is constructed.

I have divided the issues presented in this article into three categories. In Part I, I discuss structural intersectionality, the ways in which the location of women of color at the intersection of race and gender makes our actual experience of domestic violence, rape, and remedial reform qualitatively different than that of white women. I shift the focus in Part II to political intersectionality, where I analyze how both feminist and antiracist politics have, paradoxically, often helped to marginalize the issue of violence against women of color. Then in Part III, I discuss representational intersectionality, by which I mean the cultural construction of women of color. I consider how controversies over the representation of women of color in popular culture can also elide the particular location of women of color, and thus become yet another source of intersectional disempowerment. Finally, I address the implications of the intersectional approach within the broader scope of contemporary identity politics.

I. Structural Intersectionality

A. Structural Intersectionality and Battering

I observed the dynamics of structural intersectionality during a brief field study of battered women's shelters located in minority communities in Los Angeles. In most cases, the physical assault that leads women to these shelters is merely the most immediate manifestation of the subordination they experience. Many women who seek protection are unemployed or underemployed, and a good number of them are poor. Shelters serving these women cannot afford to address only the violence inflicted by the batterer; they must also confront the other multilayered and routinized forms of domination that often converge in these women's lives, hindering their ability to create alternatives to the abusive relationships that brought them to shelters in the first place. Many women of color, for example, are burdened by poverty, child care responsibilities, and the lack of job skills. These burdens, largely the consequence of gender and class oppression, are then compounded by the racially discriminatory employment and housing practices women of color often face, as well as by the disproportionately high unemployment among people of color that makes battered women of color less able to depend on the support of friends and relatives for temporary shelter.

Where systems of race, gender, and class domination converge, as they do in the experiences of battered women of color, intervention strategies based solely on the experiences of women who do not share the same class or race backgrounds will be of limited help to women who because of race and class face different obstacles. Such was the case in 1990 when Congress amended the marriage fraud provisions of the Immigration and Nationality Act to protect immigrant women who were battered or exposed to extreme cruelty by the United States citizens or permanent residents these women immigrated to the United States to marry. Under the marriage fraud provisions of the Act, a person who immigrated to the United States to marry a United States citizen or permanent resident had to remain "properly" married for two years before even applying for permanent resident status, at which time applications for the immigrant's permanent status were required of both spouses. Predictably, under these circumstances, many immigrant women were reluctant to leave even the most abusive of partners for fear of being deported. When faced with the choice between protection from their batterers and protection against deportation, many immigrant women chose the latter. Reports of the tragic consequences of this double subordination put pressure on Congress to include in the Immigration Act of 1990 a provision amending the marriage fraud rules to allow for an explicit waiver for hardship caused by domestic violence. Yet many immigrant women, particularly immigrant women of color, have remained vulnerable to battering because they are unable to meet the conditions established for a waiver. The evidence required to support a waiver "can include, but is not limited to, reports and affidavits from police, medical personnel, psychologists, school officials, and social service agencies." For many immigrant women, limited access to these resources can make it difficult for them to obtain the evidence needed for a waiver. And cultural barriers often further discourage immigrant women from reporting or escaping battering situations. Tina Shum, a family counselor at a social service agency, points out that "[t]his law sounds so easy to apply, but there are cultural complications in the Asian community that make even these requirements difficult. . . . Just to find the opportunity and courage to call us is an accomplishment for many." The typical immigrant spouse, she suggests, may live "[i]n an extended family where several generations live together, there may be no privacy on the telephone, no opportunity to leave the house and no understanding of public phones." As a consequence, many immigrant women are wholly dependent on their husbands as their link to the world outside their homes.

Immigrant women are also vulnerable to spousal violence because so many of them depend on their husbands for information regarding their legal status. Many women who are now permanent residents continue to suffer abuse under threats of deportation by their husbands. Even if the threats are unfounded, women who have no independent access to information will still be intimidated by such threats. And even though the domestic violence waiver focuses on immigrant women whose husbands are United States citizens or permanent residents, there are countless women married to undocumented workers (or who are themselves undocumented) who suffer in silence for fear that the security of their entire families will be jeopardized should they seek help or otherwise call attention to themselves.

Language barriers present another structural problem that often limits opportunities of non-English-speaking women to take advantage of existing support services. Such barriers not only limit access to information about shelters, but also limit access to the security shelters provide. Some shelters turn non-English-speaking women away for lack of bilingual personnel and resources.

These examples illustrate how patterns of subordination intersect in women's experience of domestic violence. Intersectional subordination need not be intentionally produced; in fact, it is frequently the consequence of the imposition of one burden that interacts with preexisting vulnerabilities to create yet another dimension of disempowerment. In the case of the marriage fraud provisions of the Immigration and Nationality Act, the imposition of a policy specifically designed to burden one class—immigrant spouses seeking permanent resident status—exacerbated the disempowerment of those already subordinated by other structures of domination. By failing to take into account the vulnerability of immigrant spouses to domestic violence, Congress positioned these women to absorb the simultaneous impact of its anti-immigration policy and their spouses' abuse.

The enactment of the domestic violence waiver of the marriage fraud provisions similarly illustrates how modest attempts to respond to certain problems can be ineffective when the intersectional location of women of color is not considered in fashioning the remedy. Cultural identity and class affect the likelihood that a battered spouse could take advantage of the waiver. Although the waiver is formally available to all women, the terms of the waiver make it inaccessible to some. Immigrant women who are socially, culturally, or economically privileged are more likely to be able to marshall the resources needed to satisfy the waiver requirements. Those immigrant women least able to take advantage of the waiver—women who are socially or economically the most marginal—are the ones most likely to be women of color.

B. Structural Intersectionality and Rape

Women of color are differently situated in the economic, social, and political worlds. When reform efforts undertaken on behalf of women neglect this fact, women of color are less likely to have their needs met than women who are racially privileged. For example, counselors who provide rape crisis services to women of color report that a significant proportion of the resources allocated to them must be spent handling problems other than rape itself. Meeting these needs often places these counselors at odds with their funding agencies, which allocate funds according to standards of need that are largely white and middle-class. These uniform standards of need ignore the fact that different needs often demand different priorities in terms of resource allocation, and consequently, these standards hinder the ability of counselors to address the needs of nonwhite and poor women. A case in point: women of color occupy positions both physically and culturally marginalized within dominant society, and so information must be targeted directly to them in order to reach them. Accordingly, rape crisis centers must earmark more resources for basic information dissemination in communities of color than in white ones.

Increased costs are but one consequence of serving people who cannot be reached by mainstream channels of information. As noted earlier, counselors in minority communities report spending hours locating resources and contacts to meet the housing and other immediate needs of women who have been assaulted. Yet this work is only considered "information and referral" by funding agencies and as such, is typically underfunded, notwithstanding the magnitude of need for these services in minority communities. The problem is compounded by expectations that rape crisis centers will use a significant portion of resources allocated to them on counselors to accompany victims to court, even though women of color are less likely to have their cases pursued in the criminal justice system. The resources expected to be set aside for court services are misdirected in these communities.

The fact that minority women suffer from the effects of multiple subordination, coupled with institutional expectations based on inappropriate nonintersectional contexts, shapes and ultimately limits the opportunities for meaningful intervention on their behalf. Recognizing the failure to consider intersectional dynamics may go far toward explaining the high levels of failure, frustration, and burn-out experienced by counselors who attempt to meet the needs of minority women victims.

II. Political Intersectionality

The concept of political intersectionality highlights the fact that women of color are situated within at least two subordinated groups that frequently pursue conflicting political agendas. The need to split one's political energies between two sometimes opposing groups is a dimension of intersectional disempowerment that men of color and white women seldom confront. Indeed, their specific raced *and* gendered experiences, although intersectional, often define as well as confine the interests of the entire group. For example, racism as experienced by people of color who are of a particular gender—male—tends to determine the parameters of antiracist strategies, just as sexism as experienced by women who are of a particular race—white—tends to ground the women's movement. The problem is not simply that both discourses fail women of color by not acknowledging the "additional" issue of race or of patriarchy but that the discourses are often inadequate even to the discrete tasks of articulating the full dimensions of racism and sexism. Because women of color experience racism in ways not always the same as those experienced by men of color and sexism in ways not always parallel to experiences of white women, antiracism and feminism are limited, even on their own terms.

Among the most troubling political consequences of the failure of antiracist and feminist discourses to address the intersections of race and gender is the fact that, to the extent they can forward the interest of "people of color" and "women," respectively, one analysis often implicitly denies the validity of the other. The failure of feminism to interrogate race means that the resistance strategies of feminism will often replicate and reinforce the subordination of people of color, and the failure of antiracism to interrogate patriarchy means that antiracism will frequently reproduce the subordination of women. These mutual elisions present a particularly difficult political dilemma for women of color. Adopting either analysis constitutes a denial of a fundamental dimension of our subordination and precludes the development of a political discourse that more fully empowers women of color.

A. The Politicization of Domestic Violence

That the political interests of women of color are obscured and sometimes jeopardized by political strategies that ignore or suppress intersectional issues is illustrated by my experiences in gathering information for this article. I attempted to review Los Angeles Police Department statistics reflecting the rate of domestic violence interventions by precinct because such statistics can provide a rough picture of arrests by racial group, given the degree of racial segregation in Los Angeles. L.A.P.D., however, would not release the statistics. A representative explained that one reason the statistics were not released was that domestic violence activists both within and outside the Department feared that statistics reflecting the extent of domestic violence in minority communities might be selectively interpreted and publicized so as to undermine long-term efforts to force the Department to address domestic violence as a serious problem. I was told that activists were worried that the statistics might permit opponents to dismiss domestic violence as a minoirty problem and, therefore, not deserving of aggressive action.

The informant also claimed that representatives from various minority communities opposed the release of these statistics. They were concerned, apparently, that the data would unfairly represent Black and Brown communities as unusually violent, potentially reinforcing stereotypes that might be used in attempts to justify oppressive police tactics and other discriminatory practices. These misgivings are based on the familiar and not unfounded premise that certain minority groups—especially Black men—have already been stereotyped as uncontrollably violent. Some worry that attempts to make domestic violence an object of political action may only serve to confirm such stereotypes and undermine efforts to combat negative beliefs about the Black community.

This account sharply illustrates how women of color can be erased by the strategic silences of antiracism and feminism. The political priorities of both were defined in ways that suppressed information that could have facilitated attempts to confront the problem of domestic violence in communities of color.

1. Domestic Violence and Antiracist Politics

Within communities of color, efforts to stem the politicization of domestic violence are often grounded in attempts to maintain the integrity of the community. The articulation of this perspective takes different forms. Some critics allege that feminism has no place within communities of color, that the issues are internally divisive, and that they represent the migration of white women's concerns into a context in which they are not only irrelevant but also harmful. At its most extreme, this rhetoric denies that gender violence is a problem in the community and characterizes any effort to politicize gender subordination as itself a community problem. This is the position taken by Shahrazad Ali in her controversial book, *The Blackman's Guide to Understanding the Blackwoman*. In this stridently antifeminist tract, Ali draws a positive correlation between domestic violence and the liberation of African Americans. Ali blames the deteriorating conditions within the Black community on the insubordination of Black women and on the failure of Black men to control them. Ali goes so far as to advise Black men to physically chastise Black women when they are "disrespectful." While she cautions that Black men must use moderation in disciplining "their" women, she argues that Black men must sometimes resort to physical force to reestablish the authority over Black women that racism has disrupted.

Ali's premise is that patriarchy is beneficial for the Black community, and that it must be strengthened through coercive means if necessary. Yet the violence that accompanies this will to control is devastating, not only for the Black women who are victimized, but also for the entire Black community. The recourse to violence to resolve conflicts establishes a dangerous pattern for children raised in such environments and contributes to many other pressing problems. It has been estimated that nearly forty percent of all homeless women and children have fled violence in the home, and an estimated sixty-three percent of young men between the ages of eleven and twenty who are imprisoned for homicide have killed their mothers' batterers. And yet, while gang violence, homicide, and other forms of Black-on-Black crime have increasingly been discussed within African-American politics, patriarchal ideas about gender and power preclude the recognition of domestic violence as yet another compelling incidence of Black-on-Black crime.

Efforts such as Ali's to justify violence against women in the name of Black liberation are indeed extreme. The more common problem is that the political or cultural interests of the community are interpreted in a way that precludes full public recognition of the problem of domestic violence. While it would be misleading to suggest that white Americans have come to terms with the degree of violence in their own homes, it is nonetheless the case that race adds yet another dimension to why the problem of domestic violence is suppressed within nonwhite communities. People of color often must weigh their interests in avoiding issues that might reinforce distorted public perceptions against the need to acknowledge and address intracommunity problems. Yet the cost of suppression is seldom recognized in part because the failure to discuss the issue shapes perceptions of how serious the problem is in the first place.

The controversy over Alice Walker's novel *The Color Purple* can be understood as an intracommunity debate about the political costs of exposing gender violence within the Black community. Some critics chastised Walker for portraying Black men as violent brutes. One critic lambasted Walker's portrayal of Celie, the emotionally and physically abused protagonist who finally triumphs in the end. Walker, the critic contended, had created in Celie a Black woman whom she couldn't imagine existing in any Black community she knew or could conceive of.

The claim that Celie was somehow an unauthentic character might be read as a consequence of silencing discussion of intracommunity violence. Celie may be unlike any Black woman we know because the real terror experienced daily by minority women is routinely concealed in a misguided (though perhaps understandable) attempt to forestall racial stereotyping. Of course, it is true that representations of Black violence—whether statistical or fictional—are often written into a larger script that consistently portrays Black and other minority communities as pathologically violent. The problem, however, is not so much the portrayal of violence itself as it is the absence of other narratives and images portraying a fuller range of Black experience. Suppression of some of these issues in the name of antiracism imposes real costs. Where information about violence in minority communities is not available, domestic violence is unlikely to be addressed as a serious issue.

The political imperatives of a narrowly focused antiracist strategy support other practices that isolate women of color. For example, activists who have attempted to provide support services to Asian- and African-American women report intense resistance from those communities. At other times, cultural and social factors contribute to suppression. Nilda Rimonte, director of Everywoman's Shelter in Los Angeles, points out that in the Asian community, saving the honor of the family from shame is a priority. Unfortunately, this priority tends to be interpreted as obliging women not to scream rather than obliging men not to hit.

Race and culture contribute to the suppression of domestic violence in other ways as well. Women of color are often reluctant to call the police, a hesitancy likely due to a general unwillingness among people of color to subject their private lives to the scrutiny and control of a police force that is frequently hostile. There is also a more generalized community ethic against public intervention, the product of a desire to create a private world free from the diverse assaults on the public lives of racially subordinated people. The home is not simply a man's castle in the patriarchal sense, but may also function as a safe haven from the indignities of life in a racist society. However, but for this "safe haven" in many cases, women of color victimized by violence might otherwise seek help.

There is also a general tendency within antiracist discourse to regard the problem of violence against women of color as just another manifestation of racism. In this sense, the relevance of gender domination within the community is reconfigured as a consequence of discrimination against men. Of course, it is probably true that racism contributes to the cycle of violence, given the stress that men of color experience in dominant society. It is therefore more than reasonable to explore the links between racism and domestic violence. But the chain of violence is more complex and extends beyond this single link. Racism is linked to patriarchy to the extent that racism denies men of color the power and privilege that dominant men enjoy. When violence is understood as an acting-out of being denied male power in other spheres, it seems counterproductive to embrace constructs that implicitly link the solution to domestic violence to the acquisition of greater male power. The more promising political imperative is to challenge the legitimacy of such power expectations by exposing their dysfunctional and debilitating effect on families and communities of color. Moreover, while understanding links between racism and domestic violence is an important component of any effective intervention strategy, it is also clear that women of color need not await the ultimate triumph over racism before they can expect to live violence-free lives.

2. Race and the Domestic Violence Lobby

Not only do race-based priorities function to obscure the problem of violence suffered by women of color; feminist concerns often suppress minority experiences as well. Strategies for increasing awareness of domestic violence within the white community tend to begin by citing the commonly shared assumption that battering is a minority problem. The strategy then focuses on demolishing this strawman, stressing that spousal abuse also occurs in the white community. Countless first-person stories begin with a statement like, "I was not supposed to be a battered wife." That battering occurs in families of all races and all classes seems to be an ever-present theme of anti-abuse campaigns. First-person anecdotes and studies, for example, consistently assert that battering cuts across racial, ethnic, economic, educational, and religious lines. Such disclaimers seem relevant only in the presence of an initial, widely held belief that domestic violence occurs primarily in minority or poor families. Indeed some authorities explicitly renounce the "stereotypical myths" about battered women. A few commentators have even transformed the message that battering is not *exclusively* a problem of the poor or minority communities into a claim that it *equally* affects all races and classes. Yet these comments seem less concerned with exploring domestic abuse within "stereotyped" communities than with removing the stereotype as an obstacle to exposing battering within white middle- and upper-class communities.

Efforts to politicize the issue of violence against women challenge beliefs that violence occurs only in homes of "others." While it is unlikely that advocates and others who adopt this rhetorical strategy intend to exclude or ignore the needs of poor and colored women, the underlying premise of this seemingly univeralistic appeal is to keep the sensibilities of dominant social groups focused on the experiences of those groups. Indeed, as subtly suggested by the opening comments of Senator David Boren (D-Okla.) in support of the Violence Against Women Act of 1991, the displacement of the "other" as the presumed victim of domestic violence works primarily as a political appeal to rally white elites. Boren said,

> Violent crimes against women are not limited to the streets of the inner cities, but also occur in homes in the urban and rural areas across the country.
>
> Violence against women affects not only those who are actually beaten and brutalized, but indirectly affects all women. Today, our wives, mothers, daughters, sisters, and colleagues are held captive by fear generated from these violent crimes—held captive not for what they do or who they are, but solely because of gender.

Rather than focusing on and illuminating how violence is disregarded when the home is "othered," the strategy implicit in Senator Boren's remarks functions instead to politicize the problem only in the dominant community. This strategy permits white women victims to come into focus, but does little to disrupt the patterns of neglect that permitted the problem to continue as long as it was imagined to be a minority problem. The experience of violence by minority women is ignored, except to the extent it gains white support for domestic violence programs in the white community.

Senator Boren and his colleagues no doubt believe that they have provided legislation and resources that will address the problems of all women victimized by domestic violence. Yet despite their universalizing rhetoric of "all" women, they were able to empathize with female victims of domestic violence only by looking past the plight of "other" women and by recognizing the familiar faces of their own. The strength of the appeal to "protect our women" must be its race and class specificity. After all, it has always been someone's wife, mother, sister, or daughter that has been abused, even when the violence was stereotypically Black or Brown, and poor. The point here is not that the Violence Against Women Act is particularistic on its own terms, but that unless the Senators and other policymakers ask why violence remained insignificant as long as it was understood as a minority problem, it is unlikely that women of color will share equally in the distribution of resources and concern. It is even more unlikely, however, that those in power will be forced to confront this issue. As long as attempts to politicize domestic violence focus on convincing whites that this is not a "minority" problem but *their* problem, any authentic and sensitive attention to the experiences of Black and other minority women probably will continue to be regarded as jeopardizing the movement.

While Senator Boren's statement reflects a self-consciously political presentation of domestic violence, an episode of the CBS news program *48 Hours* shows how similar patterns of othering nonwhite women are apparent in journalistic accounts of domestic violence as well. The program presented seven women who were victims of abuse. Six were interviewed at some length along with their family members, friends, supporters, and even detractors. The viewer got to know something about each of these women. These victims were humanized. Yet the seventh woman, the only nonwhite one, never came into focus. She was literally unrecognizable throughout the segment, first introduced by photographs showing her face badly beaten and later shown with her face electronically altered in the videotape of a hearing at which she was forced to testify. Other images associated with this woman included shots of a bloodstained room and blood-soaked pillows. Her boyfriend was pictured handcuffed while the camera zoomed in for a close-up of his bloodied sneakers. Of all the presentations in the episode, hers was the most graphic and impersonal. The overall point of the segment "featuring" this woman was that battering might not escalate into homicide if battered women would only cooperate with prosecutors. In focusing on its own agenda and failing to explore why this woman refused to cooperate, the program diminished this woman, communicating, however subtly, that she was responsible for her own victimization.

Unlike the other women, all of whom, again, were white, this Black woman had no name, no family, no context. The viewer sees her only as victimized and uncooperative. She cries when shown pictures. She pleads not to be forced to view the blood-stained room and her disfigured face. The program does not help the viewer to understand her predicament. The possible reasons she did not want to testify—fear, love, or possibly both—are never suggested. Most unfortunately, she, unlike the other six, is given no epilogue. While the fates of the other women are revealed at the end of the episode, we discover nothing about the Black woman. She, like the "others" she represents, is simply left to herself and soon forgotten.

I offer this description to suggest that "other" women are silenced as much by being relegated to the margin of experience as by total exclusion. Tokenistic, objectifying, voyeuristic inclusion is at least as disempowering as complete exclusion. The effort to politicize violence against women will do little to address Black and other minority women if their images are retained simply to magnify the problem rather than to humanize their experiences. Similarly, the antiracist agenda will not be advanced significantly by forcibly suppressing the reality of battering in minority communities. As the *48 Hours* episode makes clear, the images and stereotypes we fear are readily available and are frequently deployed in ways that do not generate sensitive understanding of the nature of domestic violence in minority communities.

3. Race and Domestic Violence Support Services

Women working in the field of domestic violence have sometimes reproduced the subordination and marginalization of women of color by adopting policies, priorities, or strategies of empowerment that either elide or wholly disregard the particular intersectional needs of women of color. While gender, race, and class intersect to create the particular context in which women of color experience violence, certain choices made by "allies" can reproduce intersectional subordination within the very resistance strategies designed to respond to the problem.

This problem is starkly illustrated by the inaccessibility of domestic violence support services to many non-English-speaking women. In a letter written to the deputy commissioner of the New York State Department of Social Services, Diana Campos, Director of Human Services for Programas de Ocupaciones y Desarrollo Económico Real, Inc. (PODER), detailed the case of a Latina in crisis who was repeatedly denied accomodation at a shelter because she could not prove that she was English-proficient. The woman had fled her home with her teenaged son, believing her husband's threats to kill them both. She called the domestic violence hotline administered by PODER seeking shelter for herself and her son. Because most shelters would not accommodate the woman with her son, they were forced to live on the streets for two days. The hotline counselor was finally able to find an agency that would take both the mother and the son, but when the counselor told the intake coordinator at the shelter that the woman spoke limited English, the coordinator told her that they could not take anyone who was not English-proficient. When the woman in crisis called back and was told of the shelter's "rule," she replied that she could understand English if spoken to her slowly. As Campos explains, Mildred, the hotline counselor, told Wendy, the intake coordinator

> that the woman said that she could communicate a little in English. Wendy told Mildred that they could not provide services to this woman because they have house rules that the woman must agree to follow. Mildred asked her, "What if the woman agrees to follow your rules? Will you still not take her?" Wendy responded that all of the women at the shelter are required to attend [a] support group and they would not be able to have her in the group if she could not communicate. Mildred mentioned the severity of this woman's case. She told Wendy that the woman had been wandering the streets at night while her husband is home, and she had been mugged twice. She also reiterated the fact that this woman was in danger of being killed by either her husband or a mugger. Mildred expressed that the woman's safety was a priority at this point, and that once in a safe place, receiving counseling in a support group could be dealt with.

The intake coordinator restated the shelter's policy of taking only English-speaking women, and stated further that the woman would have to call the shelter herself for screening. If the woman could communicate with them in English, she might be accepted. When the woman called the PODER hotline later that day, she was in such a state of fear that the hotline counselor who had been working with her had difficulty understanding her in Spanish. Campos directly intervened at this point, calling the executive director of the shelter. A counselor called back from the shelter. As Campos reports,

> Marie [the counselor] told me that they did not want to take the woman in the shelter because they felt that the woman would feel isolated. I explained that the son agreed to translate for his mother during the intake process. Furthermore, that we would assist them in locating a Spanish-speaking battered women's advocate to assist in counseling her. Marie stated that utilizing the son was not an acceptable means of communication for them, *since it further victimized the victim*. In addition, she stated that they had similar experiences with women who were non-English-speaking, and that the women eventually just left because they were not able to communicate with anyone. I expressed my extreme concern for her safety and reiterated that we would assist them in providing her with the necessary services until we could get her placed someplace where they had bilingual staff.

After several more calls, the shelter finally agreed to take the woman. The woman called once more during the negotiation; however, after a plan was in place, the woman never called back. Said Campos, "After so many calls, we are now left to wonder if she is alive and well, and if she will ever have enough faith in our ability to help her to call us again the next time she is in crisis."

Despite this woman's desperate need, she was unable to receive the protection afforded English-speaking women, due to the shelter's rigid commitment to exclusionary policies. Perhaps even more troubling than the shelter's lack of bilingual resources was its refusal to allow a friend or relative to translate for the woman. This story illustrates the absurdity of a feminist approach that would make the ability to attend a support group without a translator a more significant consideration in the distribution of resources than the risk of physical harm on the street. The point is not that the shelter's image of empowerment is empty, but rather that it was imposed without regard to the disempowering consequences for women who didn't match the kind of client the shelter's administrators imagined. And thus they failed to accomplish the basic priority of the shelter movement—to get the woman out of danger.

Here the woman in crisis was made to bear the burden of the shelter's refusal to anticipate and provide for the needs of non-English-speaking women. Said Campos, "It is unfair to impose more stress on victims by placing them in the position of having to demonstrate their proficiency in English in order to receive services that are readily available to other battered women." The problem is not easily dismissed as one of well-intentioned ignorance. The specific issue of monolingualism and the monistic view of women's experience that set the stage for this tragedy were not new issues in New York. Indeed, several women of color reported that they had repeatedly struggled with the New York State Coalition Against Domestic Violence over language exclusion and other practices that marginalized the interests of women of color. Yet despite repeated lobbying, the Coalition did not act to incorporate the specific needs of nonwhite women into its central organizing vision.

Some critics have linked the Coalition's failure to address these issues to the narrow vision of coalition that animated its interaction with women of color in the first place. The very location of the Coalition's headquarters in Woodstock, New York—an area where few people of color live—seemed to guarantee that women of color would play a limited role in formulating policy. Moreover, efforts to include women of color came, it seems, as something of an afterthought. Many were invited to participate only after the Coalition was awarded a grant by the state to recruit women of color. However, as one "recruit" said, "they were not really prepared to deal with us or our issues. They thought that they could simply incorporate us into their organization without rethinking any of their beliefs or priorities and that we would be happy." Even the most formal gestures of inclusion were not to be taken for granted. On one occasion when several women of color attended a meeting to discuss a special task force on women of color, the group debated all day over including the issue on the agenda.

The relationship between the white women and the women of color on the Board was a rocky one from beginning to end. Other conflicts developed over differing definitions of feminism. For example, the Board decided to hire a Latina staffperson to manage outreach programs to the Latino community, but the white members of the hiring committee rejected candidates favored by Latina committee members who did not have recognized feminist credentials. As Campos pointed out, by measuring Latinas against their own biographies, the white members of the Board failed to recognize the different circumstances under which feminist consciousness develops and manifests itself within minority communities. Many of the women who interviewed for the position were established activists and leaders within their own community, a fact in itself suggesting that these women were probably familiar with the specific gender dynamics in their communities and were accordingly better qualified to handle outreach than other candidates with more conventional feminist credentials.

The Coalition ended a few months later when the women of color walked out. Many of these women returned to community-based organizations, preferring to struggle over women's issues within their communities rather than struggle over race and class issues with white middle-class women. Yet as illustrated by the case of the Latina who could find no shelter, the dominance of a particular perspective and set of priorities within the shelter community continues to marginalize the needs of women of color.

The struggle over which differences matter and which do not is neither an abstract nor an insignificant debate among women. Indeed, these conflicts are about more than difference as such; they raise critical issues of power. The problem is not simply that women who dominate the antiviolence movement are different from women of color but that they frequently have power to determine, either through material or rhetorical resources, whether the intersectional differences of women of color will be incorporated at all into the basic formulation of policy. Thus, the struggle over incorporating these differences is not a petty or superficial conflict about who gets to sit at the head of the table. In the context of violence, it is sometimes a deadly serious matter of who will survive—and who will not.

B. Political Intersectionalities in Rape

In the previous sections, I have used intersectionality to describe or frame various relationships between race and gender. I have used intersectionality as a way to articulate the interaction of racism and patriarchy generally. I have also used intersectionality to describe the location of women of color both within overlapping systems of subordination and at the margins of feminism and antiracism. When race and gender factors are examined in the context of rape, intersectionality can be used to map the ways in which racism and patriarchy have shaped conceptualizations of rape, to describe the unique vulnerability of women of color to these converging systems of domination, and to track the marginalization of women of color within antiracist and antirape discourses.

1. Racism and Sexism in Dominant Conceptualizations of Rape

Generations of critics and activists have criticized dominant conceptualizations of rape as racist and sexist. These efforts have been important in revealing the way in which representations of rape both reflect and reproduce race and gender hierarchies in American society. Black women, as both women and people of color, are situated within both groups, each of which has benefitted from challenges to sexism and racism, respectively, and yet the particular dynamics of gender and race relating to the rape of Black women have received scant attention. Although antiracist and antisexist assaults on rape have been politically useful to Black women, at some level, the monofocal antiracist and feminist critiques have also produced a political discourse that disserves Black women.

Historically, the dominant conceptualization of rape as quintessentially Black offender/white victim has left Black men subject to legal and extralegal violence. The use of rape to legitimize efforts to control and discipline the Black community is well established, and the casting of all Black men as potential threats to the sanctity of white womanhood was a familiar construct that antiracists confronted and attempted to dispel over a century ago.

Feminists have attacked other dominant, essentially patriarchal, conceptions of rape, particularly as represented through law. The early emphasis of rape law on the property-like aspect of women's chastity resulted in less solicitude for rape victims whose chastity had been in some way devalued. Some of the most insidious assumptions were written into the law, including the early common-law notion that a woman alleging rape must be able to show that she resisted to the utmost in order to prove that she was raped, rather than seduced. Women themselves were put on trial, as judge and jury scrutinized their lives to determine whether they were innocent victims or women who essentially got what they were asking for. Legal rules thus functioned to legitimize a good woman/bad woman dichotomy in which women who lead sexually autonomous lives were usually least likely to be vindicated if they were raped.

Today, long after the most egregious discriminatory laws have been eradicated, constructions of rape in popular discourse and in criminal law continue to manifest vestiges of these racist and sexist themes. As Valerie Smith notes, "a variety of cultural narratives that historically have linked sexual violence with racial oppression continue to determine the nature of public response to [interracial rapes]." Smith reviews the well-publicized case of a jogger who was raped in New York's Central Park to expose how the public discourse on the assault "made the story of sexual victimization inseparable from the rhetoric of racism." Smith contends that in dehumanizing the rapists as "savages," "wolves," and "beasts," the press "shaped the discourse around the event in ways that inflamed pervasive fears about black men." Given the chilling parallels between the media representations of the Central Park rape and the sensationalized coverage of similar allegations that in the past frequently culminated in lynchings, one could hardly be surprised when Donald Trump took out a full page ad in four New York newspapers demanding that New York "Bring Back the Death Penalty, Bring Back Our Police."

Other media spectacles suggest that traditional gender-based stereotypes that are oppressive to women continue to figure in the popular construction of rape. In Florida, for example, a controversy was sparked by a jury's acquittal of a man accused of a brutal rape because, in the jurors' view, the woman's attire suggested that she was asking for sex. Even the press coverage of William Kennedy Smith's rape trial involved a considerable degree of speculation regarding the sexual history of his accuser.

The racism and sexism written into the social construction of rape are merely contemporary manifestations of rape narratives emanating from a historical period when race and sex hierarchies were more explicitly policed. Yet another is the devaluation of Black women and the marginalization of their sexual victimizations. This was dramatically shown in the special attention given to the rape of the Central Park jogger during a week in which twenty-eight other cases of first-degree rape or attempted rape were reported in New York. Many of these rapes were as horrific as the rape in Central Park, yet all were virtually ignored by the media. Some were gang rapes, and in a case that prosecutors described as was "one of the most brutal in recent years," a woman was raped, sodomized and thrown fifty feet off the top of a four-story building in Brooklyn. Witnesses testified that the victim "screamed as she plunged down the air shaft. . . . She suffered fractures of both ankles and legs, her pelvis was shattered and she suffered extensive internal injuries." This rape survivor, like most of the other forgotten victims that week, was a woman of color.

In short, during the period when the Central Park jogger dominated the headlines, many equally horrifying rapes occurred. None, however, elicited the public expressions of horror and outrage that attended the Central Park rape. To account for these different responses, Professor Smith suggests a sexual hierarchy in operation that holds certain female bodies in higher regard than others. Statistics from prosecution of rape cases suggest that this hierarchy is at least one significant, albeit often overlooked factor in evaluating attitudes toward rape. A study of rape dispositions in Dallas, for example, showed that the average prison term for a man convicted of raping a Black woman was two years, as compared to five years for the rape of a Latina and ten years for the rape of an Anglo woman. A related issue is the fact that African-American victims of rape are the least likely to be believed. The Dallas study and others like it also point to a more subtle problem: neither the antirape nor the antiracist political agenda has focused on the Black rape victim. This inattention stems from the way the problem of rape is conceptualized within antiracist and antirape reform discourses. Although the rhetoric of both agendas formally includes Black women, racism is generally not problematized in feminism, and sexism, not problematized in antiracist discourses. Consequently, the plight of Black women is relegated to a secondary importance: The primary beneficiaries of policies supported by feminists and others concerned about rape tend to be white women; the primary beneficiaries of the Black community's concern over racism and rape, Black men. Ultimately, the reformist and rhetorical strategies that have grown out of antiracist and feminist rape reform movements have been ineffective in politicizing the treatment of Black women.

2. Race and the Antirape Lobby

Feminist critiques of rape have focused on the way rape law has reflected dominant rules and expectations that tightly regulate the sexuality of women. In the context of the rape trial, the formal definition of rape as well as the evidentiary rules applicable in a rape trial discriminate against women by measuring the rape victim against a narrow norm of acceptable sexual conduct for women. Deviation from that norm tends to turn women into illegitimate rape victims, leading to rejection of their claims.

Historically, legal rules dictated, for example, that rape victims had to have resisted their assailants in order for their claims to be accepted. Any abatement of struggle was interpreted as the woman's consent to the intercourse under the logic that a real rape victim would protect her honor virtually to the death. While utmost resistance is not formally required anymore, rape law continues to weigh the credibility of women against narrow normative standards of female behavior. A woman's sexual history, for example, is frequently explored by defense attorneys as a way of suggesting that a woman who consented to sex on other occasions was likely to have consented in the case at issue. Past sexual conduct as well as the specific circumstances leading up to the rape are often used to distinguish the moral character of the legitimate rape victim from women who are regarded as morally debased or in some other way responsible for their own victimization.

This type of feminist critique of rape law has informed many of the fundamental reform measures enacted in antirape legislation, including increased penalties for convicted rapists and changes in evidentiary rules to preclude attacks on the woman's moral character. These reforms limit the tactics attorneys might use to tarnish the image of the rape victim, but they operate within preexisting social constructs that distinguish victims from nonvictims on the basis of their sexual character. And so these reforms, while beneficial, do not challenge the background cultural narratives that undermine the credibility of Black women.

Because Black women face subordination based on both race and gender, reforms of rape law and judicial procedures that are premised on narrow conceptions of gender subordination may not address the devaluation of Black women. Much of the problem results from the way certain gender expectations for women intersect with certain sexualized notions of race, notions that are deeply entrenched in American culture. Sexualized images of African Americans go all the way back to Europeans' first engagement with Africans. Blacks have long been portrayed as more sexual, more earthy, more gratification-oriented. These sexualized images of race intersect with norms of women's sexuality, norms that are used to distinguish good women from bad, the madonnas from the whores. Thus Black women are essentially pre-packaged as bad women within cultural narratives about good women who can be raped and bad women who cannot. The discrediting of Black women's claims is the consequence of a complex intersection of a gendered sexual system, one that con-structs rules appropriate for good and bad women, and a race code that provides images defining the allegedly essential nature of Black women. If these sexual images form even part of the cultural imagery of Black women, then the very representation of a Black female body at least suggests certain narratives that may make Black women's rape either less believable or less important. These narratives may explain why rapes of Black women are less likely to result in convictions and long prison terms than rapes of white women.

Rape law reform measures that do not in some way engage and challenge the narratives that are read onto Black women's bodies are unlikely to affect the way cultural beliefs oppress Black women in rape trials. While the degree to which legal reform can directly challenge cultural beliefs that shape rape trials is limited, the very effort to mobilize political resources toward addressing the sexual oppression of Black women can be an important first step in drawing greater attention to the problem. One obstacle to such an effort has been the failure of most antirape activists to analyze specifically the consequences of racism in the context of rape. In the absence of a direct attempt to address the racial dimensions of rape, Black women are simply presumed to be represented in and benefitted by prevailing feminist critiques.

3. Antiracism and Rape

Antiracist critiques of rape law focus on how the law operates primarily to condemn rapes of white women by Black men. While the heightened concern with protecting white women against Black men has been primarily criticized as a form of discrimination against Black men, it just as surely reflects devaluation of Black women. This disregard for Black women results from an exclusive focus on the consequences of the problem for Black men. Of course, rape accusations historically have provided a justification for white terrorism against the Black community, generating a legitimating power of such strength that it created a veil virtually impenetrable to appeals based on either humanity or fact. Ironically, while the fear of the Black rapist was exploited to legitimate the practice of lynching, rape was not even alleged in most cases. The well-developed fear of Black sexuality served primarily to increase white tolerance for racial terrorism as a prophylactic measure to keep Blacks under control. Within the African-American community, cases involving race-based accusations against Black men have stood as hallmarks of racial injustice. The prosecution of the Scottsboro boys and the Emmett Till tragedy, for example, triggered African-American resistance to the rigid social codes of white supremacy. To the extent rape of Black women is thought to dramatize racism, it is usually cast as an assault on Black manhood, demonstrating his inability to protect Black women. The direct assault on Black womanhood is less frequently seen as an assault on the Black community.

The sexual politics that this limited reading of racism and rape engenders continues to play out today, as illustrated by the Mike Tyson rape trial. The use of antiracist rhetoric to mobilize support for Tyson represented an ongoing practice of viewing with considerable suspicion rape accusations against Black men and interpreting sexual racism through a male-centered frame. The historical experience of Black men has so completely occupied the dominant conceptions of racism and rape that there is little room to squeeze in the experiences of Black women. Consequently, racial solidarity was continually raised as a rallying point on behalf of Tyson, but never on behalf of Desiree Washington, Tyson's Black accuser. Leaders ranging from Benjamin Hooks to Louis Farrakhan expressed their support for Tyson, yet no established Black leader voiced any concern for Washington. The fact that Black men have often been falsely accused of raping white women underlies the antiracist defense of Black men accused of rape even when the accuser herself is a Black woman.

As a result of this continual emphasis on Black male sexuality as the core issue in antiracist critiques of rape, Black women who raise claims of rape against Black men are not only disregarded but also sometimes vilified within the African-American community. One can only imagine the alienation experienced by a Black rape survivor such as Desiree Washington when the accused rapist is embraced and defended as a victim of racism while she is, at best, disregarded, and at worst, ostracized and ridiculed. In contrast, Tyson was the beneficiary of the longstanding practice of using antiracist rhetoric to deflect the injury suffered by Black women victimized by Black men. Some defended the support given to Tyson on the ground that all African Americans can readily imagine their sons, fathers, brothers, or uncles being wrongly accused of rape. Yet daughters, mothers, sisters, and aunts also deserve at least a similar concern, since statistics show that Black women are more likely to be raped than Black men are to be falsely accused of it. Given the magnitude of Black women's vulnerability to sexual violence, it is not unreasonable to expect as much concern for Black women who are raped as is expressed for the men who are accused of raping them.

Black leaders are not alone in their failure to empathize with or rally around Black rape victims. Indeed, some Black women were among Tyson's staunchest supporters and Washington's harshest critics. The media widely noted the lack of sympathy Black women had for Washington; Barbara Walters used the observation as a way of challenging Washington's credibility, going so far as to press Washington for a reaction. The most troubling revelation was that many of the women who did not support Washington also doubted Tyson's story. These women did not sympathize with Washington because they believed that Washington had no business in Tyson's hotel room at 2:00 a.m. A typical response was offered by one young Black woman who stated, "She asked for it, she got it, it's not fair to cry rape."

Indeed, some of the women who expressed their disdain for Washington acknowledged that they encountered the threat of sexual assault almost daily. Yet it may be precisely this threat—along with the relative absence of rhetorical strategies challenging the sexual subordination of Black women—that animated their harsh criticism. In this regard, Black women who condemned Washington were quite like all other women who seek to distance themselves from rape victims as a way of denying their own vulnerability. Prosecutors who handle sexual assault cases acknowledge that they often exclude women as potential jurors because women tend to empathize the least with the victim. To identify too closely with victimization may reveal their own vulnerability. Consequently, women often look for evidence that the victim brought the rape on herself, usually by breaking social rules that are generally held applicable only to women. And when the rules classify women as dumb, loose, or weak on the one hand, and smart, discriminating, and strong on the other, it is not surprising that women who cannot step outside the rules to critique them attempt to validate themselves within them. The position of most Black women on this issue is particularly problematic, first, because of the extent to which they are consistently reminded that they are the group most vulnerable to sexual victimization, and second, because most Black women share the African-American community's general resistance to explicitly feminist analysis when it appears to run up against long-standing narratives that construct Black men as the primary victims of sexual racism.

C. Rape and Intersectionality in Social Science

The marginalization of Black women's experiences within the antiracist and feminist critiques of rape law are facilitated by social science studies that fail to examine the ways in which racism and sexism converge. Gary LaFree's *Rape and Criminal Justice: The Social Construction of Sexual Assault* is a classic example. Through a study of rape prosecutions in Minneapolis, LaFree attempts to determine the validity of two prevailing claims regarding rape prosecutions. The first claim is that Black defendants face significant racial discrimination. The second is that rape laws serve to regulate the sexual conduct of women by withholding from rape victims the ability to invoke sexual assault law when they have engaged in nontraditional behavior. LaFree's compelling study concludes that law constructs rape in ways that continue to manifest both racial and gender domination. Although Black women are positioned as victims of both the racism and the sexism that LaFree so persuasively details, his analysis is less illuminating than might be expected because Black women fall through the cracks of his dichotomized theoretical framework.

1. Racial Domination and Rape

LaFree confirms the findings of earlier studies that show that race is a significant determinant in the ultimate disposition of rape cases. He finds that Black men accused of raping white women were treated most harshly, while Black offenders accused of raping Black women were treated most leniently. These effects held true even after controlling for other factors such as injury to the victim and acquaintance between victim and assailant.

> Compared to other defendants, blacks who were suspected of assaulting white women received more serious charges, were more likely to have their cases filed as felonies, were more likely to receive prison sentences if convicted, were more likely to be incarcerated in the state penitentiary (as opposed to a jail or minimum-security facility), and received longer sentences on the average.

LaFree's conclusions that Black men are differentially punished depending on the race of the victim do not, however, contribute much to understanding the plight of Black rape victims. Part of the problem lies in the author's use of "sexual stratification" theory, which posits both that women are differently valued according to their race and that there are certain "rules of sexual access" governing who may have sexual contact with whom in this sexually stratified market. According to the theory, Black men are discriminated against in that their forced "access" to white women is more harshly penalized than their forced "access" to Black women. LaFree's analysis focuses on the harsh regulation of access by Black men to white women, but is silent about the relative subordination of Black women to white women. The emphasis on differential access to women is consistent with analytical perspectives that view racism primarily in terms of the inequality between men. From this prevailing viewpoint, the problem of discrimination is that white men can rape Black women with relative impunity while Black men cannot do the same with white women. Black women are considered victims of discrimination only to the extent that white men can rape them without fear of significant punishment. Rather than being viewed as victims of discrimination in their own right, they become merely the means by which discrimination against Black men can be recognized. The inevitable result of this orientation is that efforts to fight discrimination tend to ignore the particularly vulnerable position of Black women, who must both confront racial bias *and* challenge their status as instruments, rather than beneficiaries, of the civil rights struggle.

Where racial discrimination is framed by LaFree primarily in terms of a contest between Black and white men over women, the racism experienced by Black women will only be seen in terms of white male access to them. When rape of Black women by white men is eliminated as a factor in the analysis, whether for statistical or other reasons, racial discrimination against Black women no longer matters, since LaFree's analysis involves comparing the "access" of white and Black men to white women. Yet Black women are not discriminated against simply because white men can rape them with little sanction and be punished less than Black men who rape white women, or because white men who rape them are not punished the same as white men who rape white women. Black women are also discriminated against because intraracial rape of white women is treated more seriously than intraracial rape of Black women. But the differential protection that Black and white women receive against intraracial rape is not seen as racist because intraracial rape does not involve a contest between Black and white men. In other words, the way the criminal justice system treats rapes of Black women by Black men and rapes of white women by white men is not seen as raising issues of racism because Black and white men are not involved with each other's women.

In sum, Black women who are raped are racially discriminated against because their rapists, whether Black or white, are less likely to be charged with rape, and when charged and convicted, are less likely to receive significant jail time than the rapists of white women. And while sexual stratification theory does posit that women are stratified sexually by race, most applications of the theory focus on the inequality of male agents of rape rather than on the inequality of rape victims, thus marginalizing the racist treatment of Black women by consistently portraying racism in terms of the relative power of Black and white men.

In order to understand and treat the victimization of Black women as a consequence of racism and sexism, it is necessary to shift the analysis away from the differential access of men and more toward the differential protection of women. Throughout his analysis, LaFree fails to do so. His sexual stratification thesis—in particular, its focus on the comparative power of male agents of rape—illustrates how the marginalization of Black women in antiracist politics is replicated in social science research. Indeed, the thesis leaves unproblematized the racist subordination of less valuable objects (Black women) to more valuable objects (white women), and it perpetuates the sexist treatment of women as property extensions of "their" men.

2. Rape and Gender Subordination

Although LaFree does attempt to address gender-related concerns of women in his discussion of rape and the social control of women, his theory of sexual stratification fails to focus sufficiently on the effects of stratification on women. LaFree quite explicitly uses a framework that treats race and gender as separate categories, giving no indication that he understands that Black women may fall in between or within both. The problem with LaFree's analysis lies not in its individual observations, which can be insightful and accurate, but in his failure to connect them and develop a broader, deeper perspective. His two-track framework makes for a narrow interpretation of the data because it leaves untouched the possibility that these two tracks may intersect. And it is those who reside at the intersection of gender and race discrimination—Black women—that suffer from this fundamental oversight.

LaFree attempts to test the feminist hypothesis that "the application of law to nonconformist women in rape cases may serve to control the behavior of all women." This inquiry is important, he explains, because "if women who violate traditional sex roles and are raped are unable to obtain justice through the legal system, then the law may be interpreted as an institutional arrangement for reinforcing women's gender-role conformity." He finds that "acquittals were more common and final sentences were shorter when nontraditional victim behavior was alleged." Thus LaFree concludes that the victim's moral character was more important than victim injury, and was second only to the defendant's character. Overall, 82.3 percent of the traditional victim cases resulted in convictions and average sentences of 43.38 months. Only 50 percent of nontraditional victim cases led to convictions, with an average term of 27.83 months. The effects of traditional and nontraditional behavior by Black women are difficult to determine from the information given and must be inferred from LaFree's passing comments. For example, LaFree notes that Black victims were evenly divided between traditional and nontraditional gender roles. This observation, together with the lower rate of conviction for men accused of raping Blacks, suggests that gender role behavior was not as significant in determining case disposition as it was in cases involving white victims. Indeed, LaFree explicitly notes that "the victim's *race* was . . . an important predictor of jurors' case evaluations."

> Jurors were less likely to believe in a defendant's guilt when the victim was black. Our interviews with jurors suggested that part of the explanation for this effect was that jurors . . . were influenced by stereotypes of black women as more likely to consent to sex or as more sexually experienced and hence less harmed by the assault. In a case involving the rape of a young black girl, one juror argued for acquittal on the grounds that a girl her age from "that kind of neighborhood" probably wasn't a virgin anyway.

LaFree also notes that "[o]ther jurors were simply less willing to believe the testimony of black complainants." One white juror is quoted as saying, "Negroes have a way of not telling the truth. They've a knack for coloring the story. So you know you can't believe everything they say."

Despite explicit evidence that the race of the victim is significant in determining the disposition of rape cases, LaFree concludes that rape law functions to penalize nontraditional behavior in women. LaFree fails to note that racial identification may itself serve as a proxy for nontraditional behavior. Rape law, that is, serves not only to penalize actual examples of nontraditional behavior but also to diminish and devalue women who belong to groups in which nontraditional behavior is perceived as common. For the Black rape victim, the disposition of her case may often turn less on her behavior than on her identity. LaFree misses the point that although white and Black women have shared interests in resisting the madonna/whore dichotomy altogether, they nevertheless experience its oppressive power differently. Black women continue to be judged by who they are, not by what they do.

3. Compounding the Marginalizations of Rape

LaFree offers clear evidence that the race/sex hierarchy subordinates Black women to white women, as well as to men—both Black and white. However, the different effects of rape law on Black women are scarcely mentioned in LaFree's conclusions. In a final section, LaFree treats the devaluation of Black women as an aside—one without apparent ramifications for rape law. He concludes: "The more severe treatment of black offenders who rape white women *(or, for that matter, the milder treatment of black offenders who rape black women)* is probably best explained in terms of racial discrimination within a broader context of continuing social and physical segregation between blacks and whites." Implicit throughout LaFree's study is the assumption that Blacks who are subjected to social control are Black *men*. Moreover, the social control to which he refers is limited to securing the boundaries between Black males and white females. His conclusion that race differentials are best understood within the context of social segregation as well as his emphasis on the interracial implications of boundary enforcement overlook the intraracial dynamics of race and gender subordination. When Black men are leniently punished for raping Black women, the problem is *not* "best explained" in terms of social segregation but in terms of both the race- and gender-based devaluation of Black women. By failing to examine the sexist roots of such lenient punishment, LaFree and other writers sensitive to racism ironically repeat the mistakes of those who ignore race as a factor in such cases. Both groups fail to consider directly the situation of Black women.

Studies like LaFree's do little to illuminate how the interaction of race, class and nontraditional behavior affects the disposition of rape cases involving Black women. Such an oversight is especially troubling given evidence that many cases involving Black women are dismissed outright. Over 20 percent of rape complaints were recently dismissed as "unfounded" by the Oakland Police Department, which did not even interview many, if not most, of the women involved. Not coincidentally, the vast majority of the complainants were Black and poor; many of them were substance abusers or prostitutes. Explaining their failure to pursue these complaints, the police remarked that "those cases were hopelessly tainted by women who are transient, uncooperative, untruthful or not credible as witnesses in court."

The effort to politicize violence against women will do little to address the experiences of Black and other nonwhite women until the ramifications of racial stratification among women are acknowledged. At the same time, the antiracist agenda will not be furthered by suppressing the reality of intraracial violence against women of color. The effect of both these marginalizations is that women of color have no ready means to link their experiences with those of other women. This sense of isolation compounds efforts to politicize sexual violence within communities of color and permits the deadly silence surrounding these issues.

D. Implications

With respect to the rape of Black women, race and gender converge in ways that are only vaguely understood. Unfortunately, the analytical frameworks that have traditionally informed both antirape and antiracist agendas tend to focus only on single issues. They are thus incapable of developing solutions to the compound marginalization of Black women victims, who, yet again, fall into the void between concerns about women's issues and concerns about racism. This dilemma is complicated by the role that cultural images play in the treatment of Black women victims. That is, the most critical aspects of these problems may revolve less around the political agendas of separate race- and gender-sensitive groups, and more around the social and cultural devaluation of women of color. The stories our culture tells about the experience of women of color present another challenge—and a further opportunity—to apply and evaluate the usefulness of the intersectional critique.

III. Representational Intersectionality

With respect to the rape of Black women, race and gender converge so that the concerns of minority women fall into the void between concerns about women's issues and concerns about racism. But when one discourse fails to acknowledge the significance of the other, the power relations that each attempts to challenge are strengthened. For example, when feminists fail to acknowledge the role that race played in the public response to the rape of the Central Park jogger, feminism contributes to the forces that produce disproportionate punishment for Black men who rape white women, and when antiracists represent the case solely in terms of racial domination, they belittle the fact that women particularly, and all people generally, should be outraged by the gender violence the case represented.

Perhaps the devaluation of women of color implicit here is linked to how women of color are represented in cultural imagery. Scholars in a wide range of fields are increasingly coming to acknowledge the centrality of issues of representation in the reproduction of racial and gender hierarchy in the United States. Yet current debates over representation continually elide the intersection of race and gender in the popular culture's construction of images of women of color. Accordingly, an analysis of what may be termed "representational intersectionality" would include both the ways in which these images are produced through a confluence of prevalent narratives of race and gender, as well as a recognition of how contemporary critiques of racist and sexist representation marginalize women of color.

In this section I explore the problem of representational intersectionality—in particular, how the production of images of women of color and the contestations over those images tend to ignore the intersectional interests of women of color—in the context of the controversy over 2 Live Crew, the Black rap group that was the subject of an obscenity prosecution in Florida in 1990. I oppose the obscenity prosecution of 2 Live Crew, but not for the same reasons as those generally offered in support of 2 Live Crew, and not without a sense of sharp internal division, of dissatisfaction with the idea that the "real issue" is race or gender, inertly juxtaposed. An intersectional analysis offers both an intellectual and political response to this dilemma. Aiming to bring together the different aspects of an otherwise divided sensibility, an intersectional analysis argues that racial and sexual subordination are mutually reinforcing, that Black women are commonly marginalized by a politics of race alone or gender alone, and that a political response to each form of subordination must at the same time be a political response to both.

A. The 2 Live Crew Controversy

In June 1990, the members of 2 Live Crew were arrested and charged under a Florida obscenity statute for their performance in an adults-only club in Hollywood, Florida.

The arrests came just two days after a federal court judge ruled that the sexually explicit lyrics in 2 Live Crew's album, *As Nasty As They Wanna Be*, were obscene. Although the members of 2 Live Crew were eventually acquitted of charges stemming from the live performance, the federal court determination that *Nasty* is obscene still stands. This obscenity judgment, along with the arrests and subsequent trial, prompted an intense public controversy about rap music, a controversy that merged with a broader debate about the representation of sex and violence in popular music, about cultural diversity, and about the meaning of freedom of expression.

Two positions dominated the debate over 2 Live Crew. Writing in *Newsweek*, political columnist George Will staked out a case for the prosecution. Will argued that *Nasty* was misogynistic filth and characterized 2 Live Crew's performance as a profoundly repugnant "combination of extreme infantilism and menace" that objectified Black women and represented them as suitable targets of sexual violence. The most prominent defense of 2 Live Crew was advanced by Henry Louis Gates, Jr., Harvard professor and expert on African-American literature. In a *New York Times* op-ed piece and in testimony at the criminal trial, Gates contended that 2 Live Crew's members were important artists operating within and inventively elaborating upon distinctively African-American forms of cultural expression. According to Gates, the characteristic exaggeration featured in 2 Live Crew's lyrics served a political end: to explode popular racist stereotypes in a comically extreme form. Where Will saw a misogynistic assault on Black women by social degenerates, Gates found a form of "sexual carnivalesque" with the promise to free us from the pathologies of racism.

Unlike Gates, there are many who do not simply "bust out laughing" upon first hearing 2 Live Crew. One does a disservice to the issue to describe the images of women in *Nasty* as simply "sexually explicit." Listening to *Nasty*, we hear about "cunts" being "fucked" until backbones are cracked, "asses" being "busted," "dicks" rammed down throats, and semen splattered across faces. Black women are "cunts," "bitches," and all-purpose "hos."

This is no mere braggadocio. Those who are concerned about high rates of gender violence in our communities must be troubled by the possible connections between these images and the tolerance for violence against women. Children and teenagers are listening to this music, and one cannot but be concerned that the range of acceptable behavior is being broadened by the constant propagation of misogynistic imagery. One must worry as well about young Black women who, like young men, are learning that their value lies between their legs. But the sexual value of women, unlike that of men, is a depletable commodity; boys become men by expending theirs, while girls become whores.

Nasty is misogynist, and an intersectional analysis of the case against 2 Live Crew should not depart from a full acknowledgement of that misogyny. But such an analysis must also consider whether an exclusive focus on issues of gender risks overlooking aspects of the prosecution of 2 Live Crew that raise serious questions of racism.

B. The Obscenity Prosecution of 2 Live Crew

An initial problem with the obscenity prosecution of 2 Live Crew was its apparent selectivity. Even the most superficial comparison between 2 Live Crew and other mass-marketed sexual representations suggests the likelihood that race played some role in distinguishing 2 Live Crew as the first group ever to be prosecuted for obscenity in connection with a musical recording, and one of a handful of recording artists to be prosecuted for a live performance. Recent controversies about sexism, racism, and violence in popular culture point to a vast range of expression that might have provided targets for censorship, but was left untouched. Madonna has acted out masturbation, portrayed the seduction of a priest, and insinuated group sex on stage, but she has never been prosecuted for obscenity. While 2 Live Crew was performing in Hollywood, Florida, Andrew Dice Clay's recordings were being sold in stores and he was performing nationwide on HBO. Well-known for his racist "humor," Clay is also comparable to 2 Live Crew in sexual explicitness and misogyny. In his show, for example, Clay offers, "Eenie, meenie, minee, mo / Suck my [expletive] and swallow slow," and "Lose the bra, bitch." Moreover, graphic sexual images—many of them violent—were widely available in Broward County where the performance and trial took place. According to the testimony of a Broward County vice detective, "nude dance shows and adult bookstores are scattered throughout the county where 2 Live Crew performed." Given the availability of other forms of sexually explicit "entertainment" in Broward County, Florida, one might wonder how 2 Live Crew could have been seen as uniquely obscene by the lights of the "community standards" of the county. After all, patrons of certain Broward County clubs "can see women dancing with at least their breasts exposed," and bookstore patrons can "view and purchase films and magazines that depict vaginal, oral and anal sex, homo-sexual sex and group sex." In arriving at its finding of obscenity, the court placed little weight on the available range of films, magazines, and live shows as evidence of the community's sensibilities. Instead, the court apparently accepted the sheriff's testimony that the decision to single out *Nasty* was based on the number of complaints against 2 Live Crew "communicated by telephone calls, anonymous messages, or letters to the police."

Evidence of this popular outcry was never substantiated. But even if it were, the case for selectivity would remain. The history of social repression of Black male sexuality is long, often violent, and all too familiar. Negative reactions to the sexual conduct of Black men have traditionally had racist overtones, especially where that conduct threatens to "cross over" into the mainstream community. So even if the decision to prosecute did reflect a widespread community perception of the purely prurient character of 2 Live Crew's music, that perception itself might reflect an established pattern of vigilante attitudes directed toward the sexual expression of Black men. In short, the appeal to community standards does not undercut a concern about racism; rather, it underscores that concern.

A second troubling dimension of the case brought against 2 Live Crew was the court's apparent disregard for the culturally rooted aspects of 2 Live Crew's music. Such disregard was essential to a finding of obscenity given the third prong of the *Miller* test requiring that material judged obscene must, taken as a whole, lack literary, artistic, or political value. 2 Live Crew argued that this criterion of the *Miller* test was not met in the case of *Nasty* since the recording exemplified such African-American cultural modes as "playing the dozens," "call and response," and "signifying." The court denied each of the group's claims of cultural specificity, recharacterizing in more generic terms what 2 Live Crew contended was distinctly African American. According to the court, "playing the dozens" is "commonly seen in adolescents, especially boys, of all ages"; "boasting" appears to be "part of the universal human condition"; and the cultural origins of "call and response"—featured in a song on *Nasty* about fellatio in which competing groups chanted "less filling" and "tastes great"—were to be found in a Miller beer commercial, not in African-American cultural tradition. The possibility that the Miller beer commercial may have itself evolved from an African-American cultural tradition was apparently lost on the court.

In disregarding the arguments made on behalf of 2 Live Crew, the court denied that the form and style of *Nasty* and, by implication, rap music in general had any artistic merit. This disturbing dismissal of the cultural attributes of rap and the effort to universalize African-American modes of expression are a form of color-blindness that presumes to level all significant racial and ethnic differences in order to pass judgment on intergroup conflicts. The court's analysis here also manifests a frequently encountered strategy of cultural appropriation. African-American contributions that have been accepted by the mainstream culture are eventually absorbed as simply "American" or found to be "universal." Other modes associated with African-American culture that resist absorption remain distinctive and are either neglected or dismissed as "deviant."

The court apparently rejected as well the possibility that even the most misogynistic rap may have political value as a discourse of resistance. The element of resistance found in some rap is in making people uncomfortable, thereby challenging received habits of thought and action. Such challenges are potentially political, as are more subversive attempts to contest traditional rules by becoming what is most feared. Against a historical backdrop in which the Black male as social outlaw is a prominent theme, "gangsta' rap" might be taken as a rejection of a conciliatory stance aimed at undermining fear through reassurance, in favor of a more subversive form of opposition that attempts to challenge the rules precisely by becoming the very social outlaw that society fears and attempts to proscribe. Rap representations celebrating an aggressive Black male sexuality can be easily construed as discomforting and oppositional. Not only does reading rap in this way preclude a finding that *Nasty* lacks political value, it also defeats the court's assumption that the group's intent was to appeal solely to prurient interests. To be sure, these considerations carry greater force in the case of other rap artists, such as N.W.A., Too Short, Ice Cube, and The Geto Boys, all of whose standard fare includes depictions of violent assault, rape, rapemurder, and mutilation. In fact, had these other groups been targeted rather than the comparatively less offensive 2 Live Crew, they might have successfully defeated prosecution. The graphic violence in their representations militate against a finding of obscenity by suggesting an intent not to appeal to prurient interests but instead to more expressly political ones. So long as violence is seen as distinct from sexuality, the prurient interest requirement may provide a shield for the more violent rap artists.

However, even this somewhat formalistic dichotomy may provide little solace to such rap artists given the historical linkages that have been made between Black male sexuality and violence. Indeed, it has been the specter of violence that surrounds images of Black male sexuality that presented 2 Live Crew as an acceptable target of an obscenity prosecution in a field that included Andrew Dice Clay and countless others.

The point here is not that the distinction between sex and violence should be rigorously maintained in determining what is obscene or, more specifically, that rap artists whose standard fare is more violent ought to be protected. To the contrary, these more violent groups should be much more troubling than 2 Live Crew. My point instead is to suggest that obscenity prosecutions of rap artists do nothing to protect the interests of those most directly implicated in rap—Black women. On the one hand, prevailing notions of obscenity separate out sexuality from violence, which has the effect of shielding the more violently misogynistic groups from prosecution; on the other, historical linkages between images of Black male sexuality and violence permit the singling out of "lightweight" rappers for prosecution among all other purveyors of explicit sexual imagery.

C. Addressing the Intersectionality

Although Black women's interests were quite obviously irrelevant in the 2 Live Crew obscenity judgment, their images figured prominently in the public case supporting the prosecution. George Will's *Newsweek* essay provides a striking example of how Black women's bodies were appropriated and deployed in the broader attack against 2 Live Crew. Commenting on "America's Slide into the Sewers," Will laments that

> America today is capable of terrific intolerance about smoking, or toxic waste that threatens trout. But only a deeply confused society is more concerned about protecting lungs than minds, trout than black women. We legislate against smoking in restaurants; singing "Me So Horny" is a constitutional right. Secondary smoke is carcinogenic; celebration of torn vaginas is "mere words."

Lest one be misled into thinking that Will has become an ally of Black women, Will's real concern is suggested by his repeated references to the Central Park jogger assault. Will writes, "Her face was so disfigured a friend took 15 minutes to identify her. 'I recognized her ring.' Do you recognize the relevance of 2 Live Crew?" While the connection between the threat of 2 Live Crew and the image of the Black male rapist was suggested subtly in the public debate, it is blatant throughout Will's discussion. Indeed, it bids to be the central theme of the essay. "Fact: Some members of a particular age and societal cohort—the one making 2 Live Crew rich—stomped and raped the jogger to the razor edge of death, for the fun of it." Will directly indicts 2 Live Crew in the Central Park jogger rape through a fictional dialogue between himself and the defendants. Responding to one defendant's alleged confession that the rape was fun, Will asks, "Where can you get the idea that sexual violence against women is fun? From a music store, through Walkman earphones, from boom boxes blaring forth the rap lyrics of 2 Live Crew." Since the rapists were young Black males and *Nasty* presents Black men celebrating sexual violence, 2 Live Crew was in Central Park that night, providing the underlying accompaniment to a vicious assault. Ironically, Will rejected precisely this kind of argument in the context of racist speech on the ground that efforts to link racist speech to racist violence presume that those who hear racist speech will mindlessly act on what they hear. Apparently, the certain "social cohort" that produces and consumes racist speech is fundamentally different from the one that produces and consumes rap music.

Will invokes Black women—twice—as victims of this music. But if he were really concerned with the threat of 2 Live Crew to Black women, why does the Central Park jogger figure so prominently in his argument? Why not the Black woman in Brooklyn who was gang-raped and then thrown down an airshaft? In fact, Will fails even to mention Black victims of sexual violence, which suggests that Black women simply function for Will as stand-ins for white women. Will's use of the Black female body to press the case against 2 Live Crew recalls the strategy of the prosecutor in Richard Wright's novel *Native Son*. Bigger Thomas, Wright's Black male protagonist, is on trial for killing Mary Dalton, a white woman. Because Bigger burned her body, it cannot be established whether Bigger had sexually assaulted her, so the prosecutor brings in the body of Bessie, a Black woman raped by Bigger and left to die, in order to establish that Bigger had raped Mary Dalton.

These considerations about selectivity, about the denial of cultural specificity, and about the manipulation of Black women's bodies convince me that race played a significant, if not determining, role in the shaping of the case against 2 Live Crew. While using antisexist rhetoric to suggest a concern for women, the attack on 2 Live Crew simultaneously endorses traditional readings of Black male sexuality. The fact that the objects of these violent sexual images are Black women becomes irrelevant in the representation of the threat in terms of the Black rapist/white victim dyad. The Black male becomes the agent of sexual violence and the white community becomes his potential victim. The subtext of the 2 Live Crew prosecution thus becomes a re-reading of the sexualized racial politics of the past.

While concerns about racism fuel my opposition to the obscenity prosecution of 2 Live Crew, the uncritical support for, and indeed celebration of, 2 Live Crew by other opponents of the prosecution is extremely troubling as well. If the rhetoric of antisexism provided an occasion for racism, so, too, the rhetoric of antiracism provided an occasion for defending the misogyny of 2 Live Crew. That defense took two forms, one political, the other cultural, both advanced prominently by Henry Louis Gates. Gates's political defense argues that 2 Live Crew advances the antiracist agenda by exaggerating stereotypes of Black male sexuality "to show how ridiculous [they] are." The defense contends that by highlighting to the extreme the sexism, misogyny, and violence stereotypically associated with Black male sexuality, 2 Live Crew represents a postmodern effort to "liberate" us from the racism that perpetuates these stereotypes.

Gates is right to contend that the reactions of Will and others confirm that the racial stereotypes still exist, but even if 2 Live Crew intended to explode these stereotypes, their strategy was misguided. Certainly, the group wholly miscalculated the reaction of their white audience, as Will's polemic amply illustrates. Rather than exploding stereotypes, as Gates suggests, 2 Live Crew, it seems most reasonable to argue, was simply (and unsuccessfully) trying to be funny. After all, trading in sexual stereotypes has long been a means to a cheap laugh, and Gates's cultural defense of 2 Live Crew recognizes as much in arguing the identification of the group with a distinctly African-American cultural tradition of the "dozens" and other forms of verbal boasting, raunchy jokes, and insinuations of sexual prowess, all of which were meant to be laughed at and to gain for the speaker respect for his word wizardry, and not to disrupt conventional myths of Black sexuality. Gates's cultural defense of 2 Live Crew, however, recalls similar efforts on behalf of racist humor, which has sometimes been defended as antiracist—an effort to poke fun at or to show the ridiculousness of racism. More simply, racist humor has often been excused as "just joking"—even racially motivated assaults have been defended as simple pranks. Thus the racism of an Andrew Dice Clay could be defended in either mode as an attempt to explode racist stereotypes or as simple humor not meant to be taken seriously. Implicit in these defenses is the assumption that racist representations are injurious only if they are intended to injure, or to be taken literally, or are devoid of some other nonracist objective. It is highly unlikely that this rationale would be accepted by Blacks as a persuasive defense of Andrew Dice Clay. Indeed, the Black community's historical and ongoing criticism of such humor suggests widespread rejection of these arguments.

The claim that a representation is meant simply as a joke may be true, but the joke functions as humor within a specific social context in which it frequently reinforces patterns of social power. Though racial humor may sometimes be intended to ridicule racism, the close relationship between the stereotypes and the prevailing images of marginalized people complicates this strategy. And certainly, the humorist's positioning vis-á-vis a targeted group colors how the group interprets a potentially derisive stereotype or gesture. Although one could argue that Black comedians have broader license to market stereotypically racist images, that argument has no force here. 2 Live Crew cannot claim an in-group privilege to perpetuate misogynist humor against Black women: the members of 2 Live Crew are not Black women, and more importantly, they enjoy a power relationship over them.

Humor in which women are objectified as packages of bodily parts to serve whatever male-bonding/male-competition needs men please subordinates women in much the same way that racist humor subordinates African Americans. Claims that incidences of such humor are just jokes and are not meant to injure or to be taken literally do little to blunt their demeaning quality—nor, for that matter, does the fact that the jokes are told within an intragroup cultural tradition.

The notion that sexism can serve antiracist ends has proponents ranging from Eldridge Cleaver to Shahrazad Ali, all of whom seem to expect Black women to serve as vehicles for the achievement of a "liberation" that functions to perpetuate their own subordination. Claims of cultural specificity similarly fail to justify toleration of misogyny. While the cultural defense of 2 Live Crew has the virtue of recognizing merit in a form of music common to the Black community, something George Will and the court that convicted 2 Live Crew were all too glib in dismissing, it does not eliminate the need to question both the sexism within the tradition it defends and the objectives to which the tradition has been pressed. The fact that playing the dozens, say, is rooted in the Black cultural tradition, or that themes represented by mythic folk heroes such as "Stackolee" are African American does not settle the question of whether such practices oppress Black women. Whether these practices are a distinctive part of the African-American cultural tradition is decidedly beside the point. The real question is how subordinating aspects of these practices play out in the lives of people in the community, people who share the benefits as well as the burdens of a common culture. With regard to 2 Live Crew, while it may be true that the Black community has accepted the cultural forms that have evolved into rap, that acceptance should not preclude discussion of whether the misogyny within rap is itself acceptable.

With respect to Gates's political and cultural defenses of 2 Live Crew, then, little turns on whether the "word play" performed by the Crew is a postmodern challenge to racist sexual mythology or simply an internal group practice that crossed over into mainstream America. Both defenses are problematic because they require Black women to accept misogyny and its attendant disrespect and exploitation in the service of some broader group objective, whether it be pursuing an antiracist political agenda or maintaining the cultural integrity of the Black community. Neither objective obligates Black women to tolerate such misogyny.

Likewise, the superficial efforts of the anti-2 Live Crew movement to link the prosecution of the Crew to the victimization of Black women had little to do with Black women's lives. Those who deployed Black women in the service of condemning 2 Live Crew's misogynist representations did not do so in the interest of empowering Black women; rather, they had other interests in mind, the pursuit of which was racially subordinating. The implication here is not that Black feminists should stand in solidarity with the supporters of 2 Live Crew. The spirited defense of 2 Live Crew was no more about defending the entire Black community than the prosecution was about defending Black women. After all, Black women whose very assault is the subject of the representation can hardly regard the right to be represented as bitches and whores as essential to their interest. Instead, the defense primarily functions to protect 2 Live Crew's prerogative to be as misogynistic as they want to be.

Within the African-American political community, Black women will have to make it clear that patriarchy is a critical issue that negatively affects the lives not only of Black women, but of Black men as well. Doing so would help reshape traditional practices so that evidence of racism would not constitute sufficient justification for uncritical rallying around misogynistic politics and patriarchal values. Although collective opposition to racist practice has been and continues to be crucially important in protecting Black interests, an empowered Black feminist sensibility would require that the terms of unity no longer reflect priorities premised upon the continued marginalization of Black women.

Conclusion

This article has presented intersectionality as a way of framing the various interactions of race and gender in the context of violence against women of color. Yet intersectionality might be more broadly useful as a way of mediating the tension between assertions of multiple identity and the ongoing necessity of group politics. It

is helpful in this regard to distinguish intersectionality from the closely related perspective of antiessentialism, from which women of color have critically engaged
white feminism for the absence of women of color on the one hand, and for speaking
for women of color on the other. One rendition of this antiessentialist critique—that
feminism essentializes the category woman—owes a great deal to the postmodernist
idea that categories we consider natural or merely representational are actually
socially constructed in a linguistic economy of difference. While the descriptive
project of postmodernism of questioning the ways in which meaning is socially
constructed is generally sound, this critique sometimes misreads the meaning of
social construction and distorts its political relevance.

One version of antiessentialism, embodying what might be called the vulgarized
social construction thesis, is that since all categories are socially constructed, there is
no such thing as, say, Blacks or women, and thus it makes no sense to continue
reproducing those categories by organizing around them. Even the Supreme Court
has gotten into this act. In *Metro Broad-casting, Inc. v. FCC*, the Court conservatives,
in rhetoric that oozes vulgar constructionist smugness, proclaimed that any set-aside
designed to increase the voices of minorities on the air waves was itself based on a
racist assumption that skin color is in some way connected to the likely content of
one's broadcast.

But to say that a category such as race or gender is socially constructed is not to say
that that category has no significance in our world. On the contrary, a large and
continuing project for subordinated people—and indeed, one of the projects for
which postmodern theories have been very helpful—is thinking about the way power
has clustered around certain categories and is exercised against others. This project
attempts to unveil the processes of subordination and the various ways those processes are experienced by people who are subordinated and people who are privileged
by them. It is, then, a project that presumes that categories have meaning and consequences. And this project's most pressing problem, in many if not most cases, is not
the existence of the categories, but rather the particular values attached to them and
the way those values foster and create social hierarchies.

This is not to deny that the process of categorization is itself an exercise of power,
but the story is much more complicated and nuanced than that. First, the process of
categorizing—or, in identity terms, naming—is not unilateral. Subordinated people
can and do participate, sometimes even subverting the naming process in empowering ways. One need only think about the historical subversion of the category "Black"
or the current transformation of "queer" to understand that categorization is not a
one-way street. Clearly, there is unequal power, but there is nonetheless some degree
of agency that people can and do exert in the politics of naming. And it is important
to note that identity continues to be a site of resistance for members of different
subordinated groups. We all can recognize the distinction between the claims "I am
Black" and the claim "I am a person who happens to be Black." "I am Black" takes
the socially imposed identity and empowers it as an anchor of subjectivity. "I am
Black" becomes not simply a statement of resistance but also a positive discourse of
self-identification, intimately linked to celebratory statements like the Black nationalist "Black is beautiful." "I am a person who happens to be Black," on the other hand,
achieves self-identification by straining for a certain universality (in effect, "I am first

a person") and for a concommitant dismissal of the imposed category ("Black") as contingent, circumstantial, nondeterminant. There is truth in both characterizations, of course, but they function quite differently depending on the political context. At this point in history, a strong case can be made that the most critical resistance strategy for disempowered groups is to occupy and defend a politics of social location rather than to vacate and destroy it.

Vulgar constructionism thus distorts the possibilities for meaningful identity politics by conflating at least two separate but closely linked manifestations of power. One is the power exercised simply through the process of categorization; the other, the power to cause that categorization to have social and material consequences. While the former power facilitates the latter, the political implications of challenging one over the other matter greatly. We can look at debates over racial subordination throughout history and see that in each instance, there was a possibility of challenging either the construction of identity or the system of subordination based on that identity. Consider, for example, the segregation system in *Plessy v. Ferguson*. At issue were multiple dimensions of domination, including categorization, the sign of race, and the subordination of those so labeled. There were at least two targets for Plessy to challenge: the construction of identity ("What is a Black?"), and the system of subordination based on that identity ("Can Blacks and whites sit together on a train?"). Plessy actually made both arguments, one against the coherence of race as a category, the other against the subordination of those deemed to be Black. In his attack on the former, Plessy argued that the segregation statute's application to him, given his mixed race status, was inappropriate. The Court refused to see this as an attack on the coherence of the race system and instead responded in a way that simply reproduced the Black/white dichotomy that Plessy was challenging. As we know, Plessy's challenge to the segregation system was not successful either. In evaluating various resistance strategies today, it is useful to ask which of Plessy's challenges would have been best for him to have won—the challenge against the coherence of the racial categorization system or the challenge to the practice of segregation?

The same question can be posed for *Brown v. Board of Education*. Which of two possible arguments was politically more empowering—that segregation was unconstitutional because the racial categorization system on which it was based was incoherent, or that segregation was unconstitutional because it was injurious to Black children and oppressive to their communities? While it might strike some as a difficult question, for the most part, the dimension of racial domination that has been most vexing to African Americans has not been the social categorization as such, but the myriad ways in which those of us so defined have been systematically subordinated. With particular regard to problems confronting women of color, when identity politics fail us, as they frequently do, it is not primarily because those politics take as natural certain categories that are socially constructed but rather because the descriptive content of those categories and the narratives on which they are based have privileged some experiences and excluded others.

Along these lines, consider the Clarence Thomas/Anita Hill controversy. During the Senate hearings for the confirmation of Clarence Thomas to the Supreme Court, Anita Hill, in bringing allegations of sexual harassment against Thomas, was rhetorically disempowered in part because she fell between the dominant interpretations of feminism and antiracism. Caught between the competing narrative tropes of rape (advanced by feminists) on the one hand and lynching (advanced by Thomas and his antiracist supporters) on the other, the race and gender dimensions of her position could not be told. This dilemma could be described as the consequence of antiracism's essentializing Blackness and feminism's essentializing womanhood. But recognizing as much does not take us far enough, for the problem is not simply linguistic or philosophical in nature. It is specifically political: the narratives of gender are based on the experience of white, middle-class women, and the narratives of race are based on the experience of Black men. The solution does not merely entail arguing for the multiplicity of identities or challenging essentialism generally. Instead, in Hill's case, for example, it would have been necessary to assert those crucial aspects of her location that were erased, even by many of her advocates—that is, to state what difference her difference made.

If, as this analysis asserts, history and context determine the utility of identity politics, how then do we understand identity politics today, especially in light of our recognition of multiple dimensions of identity? More specifically, what does it mean to argue that gender identities have been obscured in antiracist discourses, just as race identities have been obscured in feminist discourses? Does that mean we cannot talk about identity? Or instead, that any discourse about identity has to acknowledge how our identities are constructed through the intersection of multiple dimensions? A beginning response to these questions requires that we first recognize that the organized identity groups in which we find ourselves in are in fact coalitions, or at least potential coalitions waiting to be formed.

In the context of antiracism, recognizing the ways in which the intersectional experiences of women of color are marginalized in prevailing conceptions of identity politics does not require that we give up attempts to organize as communities of color. Rather, intersectionality provides a basis for reconceptualizing race as a coalition between men and women of color. For example, in the area of rape, intersectionality provides a way of explaining why women of color have to abandon the general argument that the interests of the community require the suppression of any confrontation around intraracial rape. Intersectionality may provide the means for dealing with other marginalizations as well. For example, race can also be a coalition of straight and gay people of color, and thus serve as a basis for critique of churches and other cultural institutions that reproduce heterosexism.

With identity thus reconceptualized, it may be easier to understand the need for and to summon the courage to challenge groups that are after all, in one sense, "home" to us, in the name of the parts of us that are not made at home. This takes a great deal of energy and arouses intense anxiety. The most one could expect is that we will dare to speak against internal exclusions and marginalizations, that we might call attention to how the identity of "the group" has been centered on the intersectional identities of a few. Recognizing that identity politics takes place at the site where categories intersect thus seems more fruitful than challenging the possibility of talking about categories at all. Through an awareness of intersectionality, we can better acknowledge and ground the differences among us and negotiate the means by which these differences will find expression in constructing group politics.

14

Ain't I a Woman? Revisiting Intersectionality

Avtar Brah and Ann Phoenix

Introduction

At the time of the 1991 war against Iraq, feminist critiques of the then familiar discourse of "global sisterhood" were a commonplace. As American and British bombs fell over Iraq once again in March 2003, many of the "old" questions that we have debated about the category "woman" assume critical urgency once again, albeit they now bear the weight of global circumstances of the early twenty first century.

This paper aims briefly to discuss some "old" issues that continue to be central to making feminist agenda currently relevant. In order to do so, it revisits debates on "intersectionality" that helped to take forward feminisms in previous decades. The first part of the paper discusses some long-standing internal conversations among different strands of feminisms which have already furnished important insights into contemporary problems. By revisiting these historical developments, we do not wish to suggest that the past unproblematically provides an answer to the present. On the contrary, we would wish to learn from and build upon these insights through critique so that they can shed new light on current predicaments. Hence, when we start with the 19th century debates, it is not because there is a direct correspondence between slavery and 21st century forms of governmentality, but rather to indicate that some issues that emerged then can help illuminate and elucidate our current entanglements with similar problematics.

The second part of the paper comments on intersections as they have been analysed in some autobiographical and empirical research based texts. We argue that the need for understanding complexities posed by intersections of different axis of differentiation is as pressing today as it has always been. In the final section we briefly examine the contribution of recent theoretical developments to the analysis of "intersectionality" which could potentially nurture fruitful new feminist agendas.

Ain't I a Woman? Sojourner's "Truth"

One critical thematic of feminism that is perennially relevant is the important question of what it means to be a woman under different historical circumstances. Throughout the 1970s and the 1980s, this concern was the subject of major debate as the concept of "global sisterhood" was critiqued for its failure to fully take on board the power relations that divided us (Haraway, 1991, Davis 1981, Feminist Review, 1984, Talpade Mohanty 1988). A century earlier, contestations among feminists involved in anti-slavery struggles and campaigns for women's suffrage also foregrounded similar conflicts. Their memory still resonates with us because the interrelationships between racism, gender, sexuality, and social class were at the heart of these contestations. Indeed, we begin this paper with the 19th century political locution "*Ain't I a Woman?*" precisely because – by fundamentally challenging all ahistoric or essentialist notions of "woman" – it neatly captures all the main elements of the debate on "intersectionality". We regard the concept of "intersectionality" as signifying the complex, irreducible, varied, and variable effects which ensue when multiple axis of differentiation – economic, political, cultural, psychic, subjective and experiential – intersect in historically specific contexts. The concept emphasizes that different dimensions of social life cannot be separated out into discrete and pure strands.

It is worth bearing in mind that the phrase, "Ain't I a Woman?" was first introduced into North American and British feminist lexicon by an enslaved woman Sojourner Truth (the name she took, instead of her original name Isabella, when she became a travelling preacher). It predates by a century some of our more recent feminist texts on the subject such as Denise Riley's (2003/1988) "Am I that name?" or Judith Butler's "Gender Trouble" (Butler, 1990). It is as well to remember in this regard, that the first women's antislavery society was formed in 1832 by black women in Salem, Massachusetts in the USA. Yet, black women were conspicuous by their absence at the Seneca Falls Anti-Slavery Convention of 1848 where the mainly middle class white delegates debated the motion for women's suffrage. Several questions arise when we reflect on black women's absence at the Convention. What, for instance, are the implications of an event which occludes the black female subject from the political imaginary of a feminism designed to campaign for the abolition of slavery? What consequences did such disavowals have for the constitution of gendered forms of "whiteness" as the normative subject of western imagination? How did events like these mark black and white women's relational sense of themselves? Importantly, what happens when the subaltern subject – black woman in this case – repudiates such silencing gestures?

We know from the biographies of black women such as Sojourner Truth that many of them spoke loud and clear. They would not be caged by the violence of slavery even as they were violently marked by it. Sojourner Truth's 1851 speech at the Women's Rights Convention in Akron, Ohio, very well demonstrates the historical power of a political subject who challenges imperatives of subordination and thereby creates new visions. This power (which, according to Foucault, simultaneously disciplines and creates new subjects) and its consequences are much bigger than the gains or losses of an individual life who articulates a particular political subject position. Sojourner Truth was born into enslavement (to a wealthy Dutch slave-owner living in New York). She campaigned for both the abolition of slavery and for equal rights for women. Since she was illiterate throughout her life, no formal record of the speech exists and, indeed, two different versions of it are in existence (Gates and McKay, 1997). The first was published in *The Anti-Slavery Bugle*, Salem, Ohio, on June 21,

1851. However, it is the more dramatic account, recounted in 1863 by the abolitionist and president of the Convention, Frances Gage, which is in common circulation. What is clear is that the words of Sojourner Truth had an enormous impact at the Convention and that the challenge they express foreshadowed campaigns by black feminists more than a century later:

> Well, children, where there is so much racket, there must be something out of kilter, I think between the Negroes of the South and the women of the North – all talking about rights – the white men will be in a fix pretty soon. But what's all this talking about? That man over there says that women need to be helped into carriages, and lifted over ditches, and to have the best place everywhere. Nobody helps me any best place. And ain't I a woman? Look at me! Look at my arm. I have plowed (sic), I have planted and I have gathered into barns. And no man could head me. And ain't I a woman? I could work as much, and eat as much as any man – when I could get it – and bear the lash as well! And ain't I a woman? I have borne children and seen most of them sold into slavery, and when I cried out with a mother's grief, none but Jesus heard me. And ain't I a woman? . . .

This cutting edge speech (in all senses of the term) deconstructs every single major truth-claim about gender in a patriarchal slave social formation. More generally, the discourse offers a devastating critique of socio-political, economic and cultural processes of "othering" whilst drawing attention to the simultaneous importance of subjectivity – of subjective pain and violence that the inflictors do not often wish to hear about or acknowledge. Simultaneously, the discourse foregrounds the importance of spirituality to this form of political activism when existential grief touches ground with its unconscious and finds affirmation through a belief in the figure of a Jesus who listens. Political identity here is never taken as a given but is performed through rhetoric and narration. Sojourner Truth's identity claims are thus relational, constructed in relation to white women and all men and clearly demonstrate that what we call "identities" are not objects but processes constituted in and through power relations.

It is in this sense of critique, practice and inspiration that this discourse holds crucial lessons for us today. Part lament, but defiant, articulating razor sharp politics but with the sensibility of a poet, the discourse performs the analytic moves of a "decolonised mind", to use Wa Thiongo's (1986) critical insight. It refuses all final closures. We are all in dire need of decolonised open minds today. Furthermore, Sojourner Truth powerfully challenges essentialist thinking that a particular category of woman is essentially this or essentially that (e.g. that women are necessarily weaker than men or that enslaved black women were not real women). This point holds critical importance today when the allure of new Orientalisms and their concomitant desire to "unveil" Muslim women has proved to be attractive even to some feminists in a "post September 11" world.

There are millions of women today who remain marginalized, treated as a "problem", or construed as the focal point of a moral panic – women suffering poverty, disease, lack of water, proper sanitation; women who themselves or their households are scattered across the globe as economic migrants, undocumented workers, as refugees and asylum seekers; women whose bodies and sexualities are commodified, fetishised, criminalized, racialised, disciplined and regulated through a myriad of representational regimes and social practices. So many of us, indeed, perhaps, all of us one way or another, continue to be "hailed" as subjects within Sojourner Truth's diasporic imagination with its massive potential for un-doing the hegemonic moves of social orders confronting us today. She enacts dispersal and dissemination both in terms of being members of a historical diaspora but equally, in the sense of disarticulating, rupturing and de-centring the precariously sutured complacency and self-importance of certain feminisms.

Late Modern Decentrings

Since Sojourner Truth many feminists have consistently argued for the importance of examining "intersectionality". A key feature of feminist analysis of "intersectionality" is that they are concerned with "decentring" of the "normative subject" of feminism. Such decentring activities scaled new heights when fuelled by political energies generated by the social movements of the second half of the last century – anti-colonial movements for independence, Civil Rights and the Black Power movements, the Peace movement, student protests and the Workers' movements, the Women's Movement or the Gay and Lesbian Movement. Whichever set of hegemonic moves became the focus of contestation in a specific debate – whether it was the plight of subordinated sexualities, class injustices, or other subaltern realities – the concept of a self-referencing, unified subject of modernity now became the subject of overt and explicit political critique. Political projects such as that of the Combahee River Collective, the black lesbian feminist organisation from Boston, pointed, as early as 1977, to the futility of privileging a single dimension of experience as if it constituted the whole of life. Instead, they spoke of being "actively committed to struggling against racial, sexual, heterosexual and class oppression" and advocated "the development of integrated analysis and practice based upon the fact that the major systems of oppression are interlocking" (ibid: 272).

The concept of "simultaneously interlocking oppressions" that were local at the same time as they were global was one of the earliest and most productive formulations of the subsequent theorisation of a "decentred subject" (see, e.g. hooks, 1981). As Norma Alacorn, in her analysis of the book "The Bridge Called My Back" – a North American collection of political writings by women of colour – later suggested, the theoretical subject of "Bridge" is a figure of multiplicity, representing consciousness as a "site of multiple voicings" seen "not as necessarily originating with the subject but as discourses that traverse consciousness and which the subject must struggle with constantly". This figure is the bearer of modes of subjectivity that are deeply marked by "psychic and material violence" and it demands a thorough "reconfiguration of feminist theory" (Alacorn in Anzaldua 1990: 359–365).

In Britain, we were making similar claims when women of African, Caribbean, and South Asian background came to be figured as "black" through political coalitions, challenging the essentialist connotations of racism (Grewal et al., 1988, Brah 1996, Mirza 1997). This particular project of Black British feminism was forged through the work of local women's organisations around issues such as wages and conditions of work, immigration law, fascist violence, reproductive rights, and domestic violence. By 1978, local groups had combined to form a national body called the Organisation of Women of Asian and African Descent (OWAAD). This network held annual conferences, published a newsletter, and served as an active conduit for inform-ation, intellectual conversations and political mobilisation. The ensuing dialogue entailed sustained analysis of racism, class, and gender with much debate as to the best means of confronting their outcomes whilst remaining alive to <u>cultural specificities</u>:

> Our group organises on the basis of Afro-Asian unity, and although that principle is main-tained, we don't deal with it by avoiding the problems this might present, but by having on-going discussions. . . . . Obviously, we have to take into account our cultural differences, and that has affected the way we are able to organise.
>
> (OWAAD cited in Mirza 1997: 43)

This careful attention to working within, through and across cultural differences is a highly significant heritage of this feminism and it is one that can be used as a resource for working with the question of cultural difference in the present moment when, for example, differences between Muslim and non-Muslim women are con-structed as posing insurmountable cultural differences. Internal conflicts within OWAAD, as amongst white women's groups, especially around homophobia, proved salutary so that, even as British "black feminism" assumed a distinctive political identity separate from "white feminism", engaging the latter in critical theoretical and political debate, it was not immune to the contradictions of its own internal heterogeneity. These internal conflicts within and between different feminisms prefigured later theories of "difference"

Gender, Race, Class and Sexuality

During the 1980s, there was much controversy about the best way to theorise the relationship between the above dimensions. The main differences in feminist approaches tended to be understood broadly in terms of socialist, liberal and radical feminisms, with the question of racism forming a point of conflict across all three. We do not wish to rehearse that debate here. Instead, this section discusses the importance of an intersectional approach by first addressing the contributions made by feminist work on gender and class, followed by an exploration of the gains made when the focus shifted to encompass other dimensions. We are aware that social class remains a contested category with its meaning varying with different theoretical and political perspectives. Our focus is somewhat different. We are primarily con-cerned with the ways in which class and its intersections are narrated in some autobiographical and empirical studies.

In the introduction to a now classic book *Truth, Dare or Promise: Girls Growing-Up in the Fifties*, Liz Heron (1985) discusses how the provision of free orange juice gave working class children the sense that they had a right to exist. The implication of this – that social class produces entitlement/lack of entitlement to exist and that social policy decisions affect this – is vividly demonstrated in this example. In the same book, Valerie Walkerdine (who has consistently discussed social class over the last 20 years), describes walking with a middle class friend on a seaside pier and seeing a working class family adding brown sauce to their chips. When her friend asks, "how could they do that?" Walkerdine is immediately interpellated as working class, drawn into recognising the "othering" of her working class background in this class inflected discourse on culinary habits. In later work. Walkerdine also discusses middle class tendencies to view working classes as "animals in a zoo" (with Helen Lucey, 1989) and with Helen Lucey and June Melody (2002) she considers the ways in which social class is lived in everyday practices and the emotional investments and issues it produces. Some of the middle class young women, for example, were subjected to expectations that meant that they could never perform sufficiently well to please their parents.

While the intersection of "race" with social class is not analysed in Walkerdine's example, it is a silent presence in that it is white, working class practices that are subject, in the 1985 example, to the fascinated scopophilic gaze. In a similar way, Beverley Skeggs' (1997) work on young, white, working class women in North-West England showed their struggle for respectability and their often painful awareness of being judged more severely than middle class women. In these examples, social class (and its intersections with gender) are simultaneously subjective, structural, about social positioning and everyday practices. If we consider the intersections of "race" and gender with social class, however, the picture becomes even more complex and dynamic.

> Race matters writes the African American philosopher Cornel West (1993). Actually, class, gender and race matter, and they matter because they structure interactions, opportunities, consciousness, ideology and the forms of resistance that characterize American life . . . They matter in shaping the social location of different groups in contemporary society.
>
> (Andersen, 1996: ix)

Anne McClintock (1995) uses an intersectional analysis to argue that to understand colonialism and postcolonialism, one must first recognize that "race", gender and class are not distinct and isolated realms of experience. Instead, they come into existence in and through contradictory and conflictual relations to each other. In keeping with Catherine Hall's (1992, 2002) argument, McClintock shows that the Victorians connected "race", class, and gender in ways that promoted imperialism abroad and class distinction in Britain.

> Imperialism . . . is not something that happened elsewhere – a disagreeable fact of history external to Western identity. Rather, imperialism and the invention of race were fundamental aspects of Western, industrial modernity. The invention of race in the urban metropoles . . . became central not only to the self-definition of the middle class but also to the policing of the "dangerous classes": the working class, the Irish, Jews, prostitutes, feminists, gays and lesbians, criminals, the militant crowd and so on. At the same time, the cult of domesticity was not simply a trivial and fleeting irrelevance, belonging properly in the private, "natural" realm of the family. Rather, I argue that the cult of domesticity was a crucial, if concealed, dimension of male as well as female identities – shifting and unstable as these were.
>
> (Mclintock, 1995: 5)

At the level of everyday practices and subjectivity, Gail Lewis (1985) demonstrates how "race" and gender intersected with the working class positioning of her parents so that their shifting power relations were only understandable as locally situated, albeit with global underpinnings. Her mother (a white woman) was responsible for dealing with public officials because of her parents' experiences of racism in relation to her father (a black man). In these instances, mother's "whiteness" (Frankenberg, 1993), becomes a signifier of superiority over her black husband. On the other hand, since both parents – marked by patriarchal conventions of the time surrounding heteronormativity – believed that men ought to deal with the outside world, this had implications for their relationship at home, where her father prevailed. Lewis (2000) develops her analysis of the intersections of "race", gender and class in studying the diverse everyday practices of black women social workers in relation to black and white clients and colleagues and white line managers. She demonstrates that the intersection of "race", gender and class is subjectively lived, that it is part of social structure and involves differential (and sometimes discriminatory) treatment (see also Dill, 1993).

Other autobiographical pieces of work also demonstrate these intersections. For example, bell hooks (1994) writes of how she quickly learned that working class black people around Yale University greeted her on the street, while middle class ones ignored her. Using her own experience as a white, Jewish, middle class woman, Paula Rothenberg (2000) examines the intersections of "race", gender and social class. She argues that people generally do not see the ways in which they are privileged, and so well-intentioned, middle class, white liberals often strive to maintain privilege for their children, while denying that they are doing so. Yet, the dynamics of power and privilege shape the key experiences of their lives. From a different class position, Nancie Caraway (1991) argues that a simplistically racialised notion of privilege is highly unsatisfactory for analysing the experiences of working class white women living in poverty.

Over the last twenty years, the manner in which class is discussed in political, popular and academic discourse has radically changed to the point that, as Sayer (2002) notes, some sociologists have found it embarrassing to talk to research participants about class. This tendency is also evident in government circles as when the discourse on child poverty comes to substitute analysis of wider inequalities of class. While the current government does not wish to use the language of class inequality, it has pledged itself to eradicate child poverty within twenty years. However, it is important to ask whether a commitment to eradicating poverty in children can ever be fully achieved without the eradication of poverty among their parents. For example, a study by Middleton et al. (1997) found that one per cent of children do not have a bed and mattress to themselves, five per cent live in damp housing and do not have access to fresh fruit each day or new shoes that fit. More than ten per cent of children over the age of 10 share a bedroom with a sibling of the opposite sex. Yet, counter-intuitively, over half the children who were defined as "not poor" had parents who were defined as "poor". Their parents reported that they sometimes went without clothes, shoes and entertainment in order to make sure that their children are provided for. One in twenty mothers reported that they sometimes go without food in order to provide for their children. Lone mothers were particularly likely to report this. In Britain and the USA, recent studies by Ehrenreich (2002) and Toynbee (2003) provide another timely reminder of how grinding, poorly-paid, working class jobs continue to differentiate women's experiences.

From their analyses of data from 118 British Local Education Authorities, Gillborn and Mirza (2000) found that social class makes the biggest difference to educational attainment, followed by "race" and then by gender – although they recognised that class outcomes are always intertwined with gender and "race". The processes by which social class continues to operate (for the middle as well as the working classes) require more attention if processes of social inclusion and exclusion are to be taken seriously. As Diane Reay (1998) points out in relation to education, this is not because different social classes view the importance of education differently – middle class position is commonly seen by both sections as central to social mobility and success. However, middle class mothers can draw upon more success-related cultural capital than their working class peers – e.g. they are better positioned to provide their children with "compensatory education" (help with school work, for example) and having the status (and confidence) to confront teachers when they feel their children are not being pushed hard enough or taught well enough.

Similarly, The Social Class and Widening Participation in HE Project, based at the then University of North London (Archer and Hutchings, 2000; Archer et al., 2001), found that class has an enormous impact on participation in higher education. However, "working class" people do not constitute a unitary, homogeneous category, and participation in higher education varies between different working class groups. Participation is lowest amongst those from unskilled occupational backgrounds and for inner-city working class groups. These class factors articulate with "race" and ethnicity to produce complex patterns of participation in higher education (CVCP, 1998; Modood, 1993).

Recognition of the importance of intersectionality has impelled new ways of thinking about complexity and multiplicity in power relations as well as emotional investments (e.g. Arrighi, 2001; Kenny, 2000; Pattillo-McCoy, 1999). In particular, recognition that "race", social class and sexuality differentiated women's experiences has disrupted notions of a homogeneous category "woman" with its attendant assumptions of universality that served to maintain the status quo in relation to "race", social class and sexuality, while challenging gendered assumptions. As such, intersectionality fits with the disruption of modernist thinking produced by postcolonial and poststructuralist theoretical ideas.

Postcoloniality, Poststructuralism, Diaspora and Difference

Feminist theories of the 1970s and 1980 were informed by conceptual repertoires drawn largely from "modernist" theoretical and philosophical traditions of European Enlightenment such as liberalism and Marxism. The "postmodernist" critique of these perspectives, including their claims to universal applicability, had precursors, within anticolonial, antiracist, and feminist critical practice. Postmodern theoretical approaches found sporadic expression in Anglophone feminist works from the late 1970s. But, during the 1990s they became a significant influence, in particular their poststructuralist variant. The work of scholars who found poststructuralist insights productive traversed theoretical ground that ranged from discourse theory, deconstruction, psychoanalysis, queer theory, and postcolonial criticism. Contrary to analysis where process may be reified and understood as personified in some essential way in the bodies of individuals, different feminisms could now be viewed as representing historically contingent relationships, contesting fields of discourses, and sites of multiple subject positions. The concept of "agency" was substantially reconfigured, especially through poststructuralist appropriations of psychoanalysis. New theories of subjectivity attempted to take account of psychic and emotional life without recourse to the idea of an inner/outer divide. Whilst all this intellectual flux led to a reassessment of the notion of experiential "authenticity", highlighting the limitations of "identity politics", the debate also demonstrated that experience itself could not become a redundant category. Indeed, it remains crucial in analysis as a "signifying practice" at the heart of the way we make sense of the world symbolically and narratively.

Overall, critical but productive conversations with poststructuralism have resulted in new theories for refashioning the analysis of "difference" (Butler, 1990; Grewal and Kaplan 1994; Weedon 1996; Spivak, 1999). One distinctive strand of this work is concerned with the potential of combining strengths of modern theory with postmodern insights. This approach has taken several forms. Some developments, especially in the field of literary criticism have led to "postcolonial" studies with their particular emphasis upon the insight that both the "metropolis" and the "colony" were deeply altered by the colonial process and that these articulating histories have a mutually constitutive role in the present. Postcolonial feminist studies foreground processes underlying colonial and postcolonial discourses of gender. Frequently, such work uses poststructuralist frameworks, especially Foucauldian discourse analysis or Derridean deconstruction. Some scholars have attempted to combine poststructualist approaches with neo-Marxist or psychoanalytic theories. Others have transformed "border theory" (Anzaldua 1987; Young, 1994, Lewis 1996; Alexander and Mohanty-Talpade 1997; Gedalof, 1999; Mani, 1999; Lewis, 2000). A related development is associated with valorisation of the term diaspora. The concept of diaspora is increasingly used in analysing the mobility of peoples, commodities, capital and cultures in the context of globalisaton and transnationalism. The concept is designed to analyse configurations of power – both productive and coercive – in "local" and "global" encounters in specific spaces and historical moments. In her work, Brah (1996, 2002) addresses the concept of "diaspora" alongside that of Gloria Anzaldua's theorisation of "border" and the widely debated feminist concept of "politics of home". The intersection of these three terms is understood through the concept of "diaspora space" which covers the entanglements of genealogies of dispersal with those of "staying put". The term "homing desire" is used to think through the question of home and belonging; and, both power and time are viewed as multidimensional processes. Importantly, the concept of "diaspora space" embraces the intersection of "difference" in its variable forms, placing emphasis upon emotional and psychic dynamics as much as socio-economic, political and cultural differences. Difference is thus conceptualised as social relation; experience; subjectivity; and, identity. Home and belonging is also a theme of emerging literature on "mixed-race" identities which interrogates the concept of "race" as an essentialist discourse with racist effects (Tizard and Phoenix 2002/1993; Zack, 1993; Ifekwunige 1999; Dalmage, 2000). Accordingly, the idea that you are mixed-race if you have black and white parents is problematised. Instead the analytical focus is upon varying and variable subjectivities, identities, and the specific meanings attached to "differences".

Raising New and Pressing Questions

In 2003, the second war against Iraq has brought into relief many continuing feminist concerns such as the growing militarization of the world, the critical role of the military industrial complex as a technology of imperial governance, the feminisation of global labour markets and migration flows, the reconstitution of differentially racialised forms of sexuality as a constitutive part of developing regimes of "globalisation", and the deepening inequalities of power and wealth across different regions of the world. A historically-rooted and forward looking consideration of intersectionality raises many pressing questions. For example: What are the implications for feminisms of the latest forms of postmodern imperialisms that stalk the globe? What kinds of subjects, subjectivities, and political identities are produced by this juncture when the fantasy of the veiled Muslim woman "in need of rescue", the rhetoric of the "terrorist", and the ubiquitous discourse of democracy becomes an alibi for constructing new global hegemonies? How do we challenge simplistic binaries which posit secularism and fundamentalism as mutually exclusive polar opposites? What is the impact of these new modes of governmentality on the lives of differentially exploited, racialised, ethnicised, sexualised, and religionised humans living in different parts of the world? What do these lived experiences say to us – living as we do in this space called the west – about our own positionalities, responsibilities, politics, and ethics? We have tried to indicate that feminist dialogues and dialogic imaginations provide powerful tools for challenging the power games currently played out on the world stage.

References

Alexander Jacqi & Mohanty, Chandra Talpade (1997) *Feminist Genealogies, Colonial legacies, Democratic Futures*, London & New York: Routledge

Andersen, Margaret (1996) "Introduction", in Esther Ngan-Ling Chow, Doris Wilkinson and Maxine Baca Zinn (eds) *Race, Class & Gender: Common Bonds, Different Voices*, Thousand Oaks, CA: Sage

Anzaldua, Gloria (1990) *Making Face, Making Soul*, San Francisco: Aunt Lute Foundation Books

Archer, Louise and Hutchings, Merryn (2000) " 'Bettering Yourself'? Discourses of Risk, Cost and Benefit in Ethnically Diverse, Young Working Class Non-Participants' Constructions of HE", *British Journal of Sociology of Education*, 21(4), 553–572

Archer, Louise; Pratt, Simon and Phillips, Dave (2001) "Working class men's constructions of masculinity and negotiations of (non)participation in higher education" in *Gender and Education*, 13, (4), pp. 431–449

Arrighi, Barbara. (2001) *Understanding Inequality: the intersection of race/ethnicity, class, and gender*, New York: Rowman and Littlefield.

Brah, Avtar (1996) *Cartographies of Diaspora, Contesting Identities*, London & New York: Routledge

Brah, Avtar (2002) Global mobilities, local predicaments: globalization and the critical imagination, *Feminist Review*, 70, pp. 30–45

Butler, Judith (1990) *Gender Trouble*, New York: Routledge

Caraway, Nancie (1991) *Segregated Sisterhood*, Knoxville, TN: The University of Tennessee Press

Collins-Hill Patricia (1990) *Black Feminist Thought*, Boston: Unwin Hyam

Combahee River Collective (1977) "A black feminist statement" Reprinted in Linda Nicolson (ed.) (1997) *The Second Wave: A Reader in Feminist Theory*, New York: Routledge

Committee of Vice Chancellors and Principals (1998) *From Elitism to Inclusion: good practice in widening access to higher education Main Report*, London: CVCP

Dalmage, Heather (2000), *Tripping on the Color Line: Black-White Multiracial Families in a Racially Divided World*, New Brunswick, NJ: Rutgers University Press

Davis, Angela (1981) *Women, Race and Class*, London: Women's Press

Dill, Barbara Thornton (1993) *Across the Boundaries of Race and Class: An Exploration of Work and Family among Black Female Domestic Servants*, USA: Garland

Ehrenreich, Barbara (2002), *Nickel and Dimed: On (Not) Getting by in America*, USA: Granta

Feminist Review (1984) "Many Voices, One Chant: Black feminist perspectives", *Feminist Review, 17*

Frankenberg, Ruth (1993) *White Women Race Matters: The construction of whiteness* London: Routledge

Gates, Henry Louis and Mckay, Nelly (1997) *The Norton Anthology of African American Literature*, New York: Norton

Gedalof, Irene (1999) *Against Purity*, London: Routledge

Gillborn, David & Mirza, Heidi Safia (2000) *Educational Inequality: mapping race, class and gender. A synthesis of evidence*, London: Ofsted

Grewal, Inderpal and Kaplan, Caren (ed) (1994) *Scattered Hegemonies*, Minnesota: University of Minnesota Press

Grewal, Shabnam, Kay, Jackie, Landor, Lilianne, Lewis, Gail and Parmar, Pratibha (eds) (1988) *Charting the Journey*, London: Sheba

Hall, Catherine (1992) *White, Male and Middle-Class: Explorations in Feminism and History* London: Routledge

Hall, Catherine (2002) *Civilising Subjects: Colony and Metropole in the English Imagination, 1830–1867*, Chicago: University of Chicago Press

Haraway, Donna (1991) *Simians, Cyborgs and Women: the reinvention of nature* London Free Association Books

Heron, Liz (1985) "Introduction" in Liz Heron (ed.) *Truth, Dare or Promise: Girls Growing-Up in the Fifties*, London: Virago

hooks, bell (1981) *Ain't I a Woman: Black Women and Feminism*, Boston: South End Press

hooks, bell (1994) *Teaching to Transgress: Education as the Practice of Freedom*, New York: Routledge

Ifekwunige Jayne (1999) *Scattered Belongings*, London & New York: Routledge

Kenny, Lorraine Delia (2000) *Daughters of Suburbia: Growing Up White, Middle Class, and Female*, New Brunswick, New Jersey: Rutgers University Press

Lewis, Gail (1985) "From deepest Kilburn" in L. Heron (ed.) *Truth, Dare or Promise: Girls Growing-Up in the Fifties*, London: Virago

Lewis, Gail (2000) *Race, Gender, Social Welfare*, Cambridge: Polity

Lewis, Reina (1996) *Gendering Orientalism*, London: Routledge

Mani, Lata (1998) *Contentious Traditions*, Indiana: Indiana University Press

Mclintock, Ann (1995) *Imperial Leather: Race, Gender, and Sexuality in the Colonial Contex*, New York: Routledge

Middleton, S., Ashworth, Karl and Braithwaite, Ian (1997) *Small Fortunes: spending on children, childhood poverty and parental sacrifice*, York: Joseph Rowntree Foundation

Mirza, Heidi Safia (ed.) (1997) *Black British Feminism*, London & New York: Routledge

Modood, Tariq (1993) "The number of ethnic minority students in British Higher Education: some grounds for optimism," *Oxford Review of Education, 19*, 2, pp 167–182

Mohanty, Chandra Talpade (1988) "Under Western Eyes: feminist scholarships and colonial discourses", *Feminist Review 30*, pp 61–88

Pattillo-McCoy, Mary (1999) *Black Picket Fences: privilege and peril among the Black middle class*, Chicago: University of Chicago Press

Reay, Diane (1998) " 'Always knowing' and 'never being sure': Familial and institutional habituses and higher education choice", *Journal of Education Policy, 13*, 4, 519–529

Riley Denise (2003/1988) " 'Am I That Name?' Feminism and the Category of Women" in History. 2nd edition, Minnesota: University of Minnesota Press

Rothenberg, Paula (2000) *Invisible Privilege*, Lawrence, KS: University of Kansas Press

Sayer, Andrew (2002) "What Are You Worth?: Why Class is an Embarrassing Subject". *Sociological Research Online, vol. 7, no. 3*, http://www.socresonline.org.uk/7/3/sayer.html

Skeggs, Beverly (1997) *Formations of Class and Gender*, London, Sage

Spivak, Gayatri Chakravorty (1999) *A Critique of Postcolonial Reason*, Harvard University Press

Sudbury Julia (1998) *Other Kinds of Dreams*, New York & London: Routledge

Tizard, Barbara and Phoenix Ann (1993/2002) *Black, White or Mixed Race?* 2nd edition, London: Routledge

Toynbee, Polly (2003) *Hard Work: Life in Low-pay Britain*, London: Bloomsbury

Wa Thiongo, Ngugi (1986) *Decolonizing the Mind: The Politics of Language in African Literature*, London: Currey

Walkerdine, Valerie (1985) "Dreams from an ordinary childhood' in Heron L (ed.) *Truth, Dare or Promise: Girls Growing-Up in the Fifties*, London: Virago

Walkerdine, Valerie and Lucey, Helen (1989) *Demrocacy in the Kitchen*, London: Virago

Walkerdine, Valerie, Lucey, Helen and Melody, June (2002) *Growing Up Girl*, London: Palgrave

Weedon, Chris (1996) *Feminist Practice and Poststructuralist Theory. 2nd edition*, Oxford: Blackwell

Young, Iris Marion (1990) *Justice and the Politics of Difference*, Princeton: Princeton University Press

Young, Lola (1994) *Fear of the Dark*, London: Routledge

Zack, Naomi (1993) *Race and Mixed Race*, USA: Temple University Press

Part Seven

Intersections: White Supremacy and White Allies

15

The Color of Supremacy
Beyond the Discourse of "White Privilege"

Zeus Leonardo

In the last decade, the study of white privilege has reached currency in the educational and social science literature. In April 2002, the city of Pella, Iowa, hosted the Third Annual Conference on White Privilege. Concerned with the circuits and meanings of whiteness in everyday life, scholars have exposed the codes of white culture, worldview of the white imaginary, and assumptions of the invisible marker that depends on the racial other for its own identity (Frankenberg, 1993, 1997; Hurtado, 1996; Kidder, 1997; Rothenberg, 2002). In particular, authors like Peggy McIntosh (1992) have helped educators understand the taken for granted, daily aspects of white privilege: from the convenience of matching one's skin color with bandages, to opening up a textbook to discover one's racial identity affirmed in history, literature, and civilization in general. In all, the study of white privilege has pushed critical pedagogy into directions that account for the experiences of the "oppressor" identity (Hurtado, 1999).

This essay takes a different approach toward the study of whiteness. It argues that a critical look at white privilege, or the analysis of white racial hegemony, must be complemented by an equally rigorous examination of white supremacy, or the analysis of white racial domination. This is a necessary departure because, although the two processes are related, the conditions of white supremacy make white privilege possible. In order for white racial hegemony to saturate everyday life, it has to be secured by a process of domination, or those acts, decisions, and policies that white subjects perpetrate on people of color. As such, a critical pedagogy of white racial supremacy revolves less around the issue of unearned advantages, or the *state* of being dominant, and more around direct processes that secure domination and the privileges associated with it.

Racial privilege is the notion that white subjects accrue advantages by virtue of being constructed as whites. Usually, this occurs through the valuation of white skin color, although this is not the only criterion for racial distinction. Hair texture, nose shapes, culture, and language also multiply the privileges of whites or those who *approximate* them (Hunter, 2002). Privilege is granted even without a subject's (re)cognition that life is made a bit easier for her. Privilege is also granted despite a subject's attempt to dis-identify with the white race. "Race treason" or the renunciation of whiteness is definitely a choice for many whites (Ignatiev & Garvey, 1996), but without the accompanying structural changes, it does not choke off the flow of institutional privileges that subjects who are constructed as white enjoy.

During his summative comments about racial privilege at a 1998 American Educational Research Association panel, James Scheurich described being white as akin to walking down the street with money being put into your pant pocket without your knowledge. At the end of the day, we can imagine that whites have a generous purse without having worked for it. Scheurich's description is helpful because it captures an accurate portrayal of the unearned advantages that whites, by virtue of their race, have over people of color; in addition, it is symptomatic of the utter sense of oblivion that many whites engender toward their privilege. However, there is the cost here of downplaying the active role of whites who take resources from people of color all over the world, appropriate their labor, and construct policies that deny minorities' full participation in society. These are processes that students rarely appreciate because their textbooks reinforce the innocence of whiteness. As a result, the theme of privilege obscures the subject of domination, or the agent of actions, because the situation is described as happening almost without the knowledge of whites. It conjures up images of domination happening behind the backs of whites, rather than on the backs of people of color. The study of white privilege begins to take on an image of domination without agents. It obfuscates the historical process of domination in exchange for a state of dominance *in medias res*.

Describing white privilege as the process of having money put in your pocket comes with certain discursive consequences. First, it begs the question: if money is being placed in white pockets, who places it there? If we insert the subject of actions, we would conclude that racial minorities put the money in white pockets. It does not take long to realize that this maneuver has the unfortunate consequence of inverting the real process of racial accumulation, whereby whites take resources from people of color; often they also build a case for having earned such resources. Second, we can invoke the opposite case. This is where Scheurich's narrative gives us some direction, but only if we put the logic back onto its feet and reinsert the subject of domination. It might sound something like this. The experience of people of color is akin to walking down the street having your money taken from your pocket. Historically, if "money" represents material, and even cultural, possessions of people of color then the agent of such taking is the white race, real and imagined. The discourse on privilege comes with the unfortunate consequence of masking history, obfuscating agents of domination, and removing the actions that make it clear who is doing what to whom. Instead of emphasizing the process of appropriation, the discourse of privilege centers the discussion on the advantages that whites receive. It mistakes the symptoms for causes. Racial advantages can be explained through a more primary history of exclusions and ideological practices.

At the annual meeting of the National Association of Multicultural Education (NAME) in 2001 in Las Vegas, Nevada, "privilege" was a hot topic. During a workshop led by Victor Lewis, Hugh Vasquez, Catherine Wong, and Peggy McIntosh, the audience was treated to poignant personal histories of people coming to terms with their male, heterosexual, adult, and white privilege, respectively. We might recall that Lewis and Vasquez were two central figures in the excellent film on race, *Color of Fear*. Known for her work in whiteness studies and anthologized in multiple books for having produced the essay with a list of forty-six privileges whites enjoy (see McIntosh, 1992), at the workshop McIntosh spoke clearly about her coming to terms with white skin advantage. Admitting that the gender lens was at first more convenient for her academic work and teaching, she describes her own engagement with race as seeing fin-like figures dancing out of the water before submerging and disappearing from sight, a scene taken from Virginia Woolf's *To the Lighthouse*. Speaking personally about her process of becoming conscious of white skin privilege, McIntosh describes the process as similar to having glimpsed a fin, not sure what to make of it but knowing that beneath the surface something great was attached to it. In short, McIntosh had seen something significant and it became the work of a critical scholar to make sense of it.

Ostensibly addressing a white audience at the NAME workshop, McIntosh continued by saying that coming to terms with white privilege is "not about blame, shame, or guilt" regarding actions and atrocities committed by other whites in their name. Likewise, in a recent invited lecture, titled "Race, Class, and Gender: The problem of domination," I was tempted to begin my talk with the same sentiment. Upon reflection, I decided against the strategy because I wanted my audience to understand that despite the fact that white racial domination procedes us, whites daily recreate it on both the individual and institutional level. On this last point, there are several issues that I want to bring up, which I believe are coterminous with the discourse on privilege.

Domination is a relation of power that subjects enter into and is forged in the historical process. It does not form out of random acts of hatred, although these are condemnable, but rather out of a patterned and enduring treatment of social groups. Ultimately, it is secured through a series of actions, the ontological meaning of which is not always transparent to its subjects and objects. When early Americans, or what patriots fondly refer to as "founding fathers," drafted the Constitution, they proclaimed that people were created equal. Of course, slavery, patriarchy, and industrial capitalism were inscribing forces surrounding their discourse of freedom. In short, "humanity" meant male, white, and propertied. For this reason, any of their claims to universal humanity were betrayed by the inhumanity and violation of the "inalienable rights" of people of color, women, and the working class. In this case, domination means that the referents of discourse are particulars dressed up as universals, of the white race speaking for the human race.

In another instance, the case of African slaves in the U.S. literally reduced them to a fraction of a human being when the government reduced slave representation to three-fifths of a person. Fearing a northern-controlled Congress, the south struck the "Great Compromise", thereby effectively increasing their population while controlling the taxation on importation of slaves. We bracket this process of reduction as a reminder that claims to literation always contain a process of figuration, that is, a representation. The literal reduction of blacks to three-fifths invokes the parasitic figure of whites, the representation of masculinity, and the specter of the bourgeois class. It is easy to see that the white supermacist, patriarchal, capitalist subject represents the standard for human, or the figure of a whole person, and everyone else is a fragment. In this way, policies of domination are betrayed by their accompanying contradictions and tropes.

Although McIntosh's essay enters its second decade since first appearing, it is worthwhile to re-examine it because of its currency. In fact, I include it in one of my course syllabi. To the extent that domination represents a process that establishes the supremacy of a racial group, its resulting everyday politics is understood as "dominance." McIntosh superbly maps this state of privilege by citing the many forms of racial advantage whites enjoy in daily life. However, domination can be distinguished from dominance where the former connotes a process and the latter a state of being, the first a material precondition that makes possible the second as a social condition. It is possible to discuss conferred dominance (McIntosh, 1992, pp. 77–78) because there are existing structures of domination that recognize such benefits, albeit unearned as McIntosh correctly points out. Otherwise, it is meaningless to construct perceived notions of advantage when social structures do not recognize them.

Although they clearly benefit from racism in different ways, whites as a racial group secure supremacy in almost all facets of social life. The concept of race does not just divide the working class along racial lines and compromise proletarian unity. Racism divides the white bourgeoisie from the black bourgeoisie (a mythical group, according to Marable, 1983), and white women from women of color (hooks, 1984). In other words, race is an organizing principle that cuts across class, gender, and other imaginable social identities. This condition does not come about through an innocent process, let alone the innocence of whiteness.

When educators advise white students to avoid feelings of guilt, we are attempting to allay their fears of personal responsibility for slavery and its legacies, housing and job discrimination, and colonialism and other generalized crimes against racial minorities. Indeed, white guilt can be a paralyzing sentiment that helps neither whites nor people of color. White guilt blocks critical reflection because whites end up feeling individually blameworthy for racism. In fact, they become overconcerned with whether or not they "look racist" and forsake the more central project of understanding the contours of structural racism. Anyone who has taught racial themes has witnessed this situation. Many whites subvert a structural study of racism with personalistic concerns over how they are perceived as individuals. In a society that denies whites access to a sociological and critical understanding of racism, this is not a surprising outcome. Stephen Small (1999) advises,

> it is not useful to approach ideologies by asking whether they are "racist" or "non-racist." It is more useful to acknowledge the varied ideologies, and to examine them for their "racialized" intentions, content and consequences. In other words, it is more useful to consider all ideologies and the outcomes they have or are likely to have, for different "racialized" groups. (p. 56)

Looking racist has very little to do with whites' unearned advantages and more to do with white treatment of racial minorities. Said another way, the discourse on privilege comes with the psychological effect of personalizing racism rather than understanding its structural origins in interracial relations. Whites have been able to develop discourses of anti-racism in the face of their unearned advantages. Whites today did not participate in slavery but they surely recreate white supremacy on a daily basis. They may not have supported South African apartheid, but many whites refuse interracial marriage (see Alcoff, 2000), housing integration (Massey & Denton, 1993), and fully desegregated schools (Kozol, 1991).

Teaching, addressing, and writing for a white audience is necessary insofar as whites require inroads into discourses about race and racism. Certain slices of the literature on whiteness, for example, are an attempt to create a discourse that centers on white subjectivity, psychology, and everyday life. Frequently employing ideological critique of white worldview, whiteness studies expose white lies, maneuvers, and pathologies that contribute to the avoidance of a critical understanding of race and racism. As these authors correctly point out, none of these strategies of whiteness is innocent or harmless. They frequently serve to perpetuate white racial supremacy through color-blindness, ahistorical justifications, and sleights-of-mind. However, we arrive at one of the limitations of writings or teachings based on an imagined white audience.

Countless authors from Freire to Fanon have suggested that oppression is best apprehended from the experiences or vantage point of the oppressed. This is not to suggest that oppressed people, as individual subjects of domination, somehow possess the correct or true understanding of racial oppression. Many of them are just as confused as whites when it comes to an organic understanding of racism. Many people of color have shown their inability to perform critical analyses of the causes of their own oppression (Leonardo, 2000). That said, critical analysis begins from the objective experiences of the oppressed in order to understand the dynamics of structural power relations. It also makes sense to say that it is not in the interest of racially dominated groups to mystify the process of their own dehumanization. Yet the case is ostensibly the opposite for whites, who consistently mystify the process of racial accumulation through occlusion of history and forsaking structural analysis for a focus on the individual. This is not to go down the road of essentialized racial subjects, be they black or otherwise, and an equally essentialized white subject, as Stuart Hall (1996a) has pointed out. The advantage of beginning our analysis of domination from the objective position of those who receive policies of domination puts educators on the side of the oppressed, or at least an understanding of history from their conditions. Even when critical analysis takes white experience as its unit of analysis, this must be subjected to the rigors of the analytics of the oppressed. That is, there is a difference between analyzing whiteness with an imagined white audience against an imagined audience of color.

When scholars and educators address an imagined white audience, they cater their analysis to a worldview that refuses certain truths about race relations. As a result, racial understanding proceeds at the snail's pace of the white imaginary (Leonardo, 2002). When McIntosh listed her privileges as a white woman, she came to terms with unearned advantages. White confessionals are helpful insofar as they represent a discursive strategy to recognize the insidiousness of structural privileges. They also articulate an attempt to side with racial minorities through their sympathetic appeal to undo the said privileges. Tim Wise (2002) is insistent on pointing out the pathologies and flights from reason in white rationalizations of the American race situation. Wise's Center at Fiske University links our current assault on whiteness with the avatar of Du Bois, who taught at the same university. However, we must also recognize that recent white attacks on whiteness appeal mainly to a liberal white audience, the content of which has been previously articulated by scholars and activists of color, as Cornel West (1999a) is quick to remind us.

Ruminations on whiteness are not new to many people of color and have been available for white readership. Black women know that their skin color does not match store-bought bandages, Latinos know their language is not spoken by management in most business places, and Asians know that their history rarely achieves the status of what Apple (2000) calls "official knowledge" in schools. White audiences have had access to these traditions of criticism for over a century. As such, radical writings on the topic of white privilege are new to white audiences *who read mainly white authors*. Much like the popularization of black R & B music by Elvis and Pat Boone, critiques of white privilege are given credence by white authors whose consumers are white readers. Rap music has now reached mainstream U.S.A. through its all-time best selling artist, white rapper Eminem. None of this disregards their contributions, which are helpful for students interested in "pedagogies of whiteness" (Kincheloe & Steinberg, 1997). When Roediger (1991) launched his critique of the "wages of whiteness," he expressed his debt to scholars of color, such as Du Bois. That said, the literature on white privilege is indicative of the lag in white uptake of radical racial thought.

Ultimately this same lag limits the racial analysis in the popular film, *Color of Fear*. Although it is one of the most graphic films on the topic of race relations, it suffers from the tethers of white imagination. Throughout much of the ninety minutes, the men of color labor to convince a white participant, David, that white supremacy exists. After a while, one senses that it is a bit like convincing neo-Nazis that the Jewish holocaust happened. Despite the great and memorable lines from the film participants, race conscious viewers are frustrated by David's discourse of refusals when he discredits black people's fear of white rage as "unfounded," and claims that individual hard work (or lack thereof) explains the history of groups, and that being white is essentially like being black. When I have shown the film to my class, students of color felt a sense of vindication when Victor, an assertive black man, lashes out at David. They experience their history articulated with a rage they have often felt toward white supremacy and white people. However, the discourses of color expressed in the film are familiar to my students of color; the information is not new to them.

The newness comes in the form of its publicity, of its coming to voice for them through the film participants. Victor, Hugh, and the other men of color become surrogates for the centuries of oppression experienced by many people of color, which rarely gets articulated in public life. By contrast, the same information is new to many of my white students, some of whom feel attacked, others enlightened. Thus, the majority of the film's discourse is spent on the question, "What does it mean to be white?" and forsakes a deeper engagement with "What does it mean to be black, Latino, or Asian?" David's consciousness drives the discussion and frames the issues because he needs to be convinced of the first fact of racial analysis: mainly, that white domination is a reality. In short, even the progressive discourse of *Color of Fear* caters to the white imagination. It is inscribed by the rudimentary aspects of racial analysis incarnated through David.

There is a double bind at work here. Although it is crucial that whites "buy into" racial justice since they arguably possess the strongest form of investment in race (Lipsitz, 1998), they also have the most to give up in terms of material resources.

Consequently, convincing them to appropriate racial analysis for their own lives runs into difficulties. This is what McIntosh inevitably attempts with her honest appraisal of her own privilege. However, she is led to construct her narrative in such a way as to obscure some of the real processes of racial domination. This strategy might be necessary insofar as she avoids threatening her (white) audience to the point that they discredit her message. Anyone who has performed a radical racial analysis has faced a similar scenario where the messenger is dismissed because the message produces psychological dissonance between a white subject's desire for racial justice and her inability to accept radical change. Nevertheless, there are certain discursive costs.

Throughout her essay, McIntosh repeats her experience of having been taught to ignore her privilege, to consider her worldview as normal, and to treat race as the problem of the other. Deserving to be quoted at length, she writes,

> whites are carefully taught not to recognize white privilege . . . about which I was "meant" to remain oblivious . . . My schooling gave me no training in seeing myself as an oppressor . . . I was taught to see myself as an individual whose moral state depended on her individual moral will . . . [A] pattern of assumptions that were passed on to me as a white person . . . I was taught to recognize racism only in individual acts of meanness by members of my group, never in invisible systems conferring racial dominance on my group from birth. (pp. 71, 72, 77, 81)

First, notice the passage's passive tone. White racist thoughts are disembodied, omnipresent but belonging to no one. White racist teachings, life lessons, and values are depicted as actions done or passed on to a white subject, almost unbeknownst to him, rather than something in which he invests. Second, the passage is consistent with McIntosh's advice for whites to avoid feelings of personal blame for racism. But white domination is never settled once and for all; it is constantly reestablished and reconstructed by whites *from all walks of life*. It is not a relation of power secured by slavery, Jim Crow, or job discrimination alone. It is not a process with a clear beginning or a foreseeable end (Bell, 1992). Last, it is not solely the domain of white supremacist groups. It is rather the domain of average, tolerant people, of lovers of diversity, and of believers in justice.

If racist relations were created only by people in the past, then racism would not be as formidable as it is today. It could be regarded as part of the historical dustbin and a relic of a cruel society. If racism were only problems promulgated by "bad whites," then bad whites today either outnumber "good whites" or overpower them. The question becomes: Who are these bad whites? It must be the position of a good white person to declare that racism is always about "other whites," perhaps "those working-class whites." This is a general alibi to create the "racist" as always other, the self being an exception. Since very few whites exist who actually believe they are racist, then basically no one is racist and racism disappears more quickly than we can describe it. We live in a condition where racism thrives absent of racists (Bonilla-Silva, 2003). There must be an alternative explanation: in general, whites recreate their own racial supremacy, despite good intentions.

There is the other half of domination that needs our attention: white investment. To the extent that racial supremacy is taught to white students, it is pedagogical. Insofar as it is pedagogical, there is the possibility of critically reflecting on its flows in order to disrupt them. The hidden curriculum of whiteness saturates everyday school life and one of the first steps to articulating its features is coming to terms with its specific modes of discourse. In an interview with Grossberg, Stuart Hall (1996b) defines "articulation" as "the connection that *can* make a unity of two different elements, under certain conditions. It is a linkage which is not necessary, determined, absolute, and essential for all time" (p. 141; italics in original). Articulating the possibility of "universal" white supremacy necessitates strategies that unpack discourses in particular school places. One of its features that critical educators confront is the notion of investment. The forces of racial amnesia daily threaten both white and non-white students. School curricula are able to describe racial disparities but are often limited to their testable forms and standardized lessons. Critical discourse on the continuity between past and present, institutional arrangements, and the problems of color-blind discourses are forsaken for "correct" forms of knowledge.

Communities of color have constructed counter-discourses in the home, church, and informal school cultures in order to maintain their sense of humanity. They know too well that their sanity and development, both as individuals and as a collective, depend on alternative (unofficial) knowledge of the racial formation. By contrast, white subjects do not forge these same counter-hegemonic racial understandings because their lives also depend on a certain development; that is, colorblind strategies that maintain their supremacy as a group. Like their non-white counterparts, white students are not taught anti-racist understandings in schools; but, unlike non-whites, whites invest in practices that obscure racial processes. State sponsored curricula fail to encourage students of all racial backgrounds to critique white domination. In other words, schools may teach white students to naturalize their unearned privileges, but they also willingly participate in such discourses, which maintains *their* sense of humanity. White humanity is just that: humanity of whites. So it is not only the case that whites are taught to normalize their dominant position in society; they are susceptible to these forms of teachings because they benefit from them. It is not a process that is somehow done to them, as if they were duped, are victims of manipulation, or lacked certain learning opportunities. Rather, the color-blind discourse is one that they fully endorse.

White domination is the responsibility of every white subject because her very being depends on it. A discourse of absolution misses the mark on the actual processes of white supremacy, a process that benefits every white individual, albeit in different degrees. Poor or working class whites may be beneficiaries of white supremacy, but they are not signatories of it (Miils, 1997). That said, if whites do not assume responsibility for the history of white supremacy, then who can? The strategy of race treason asks whites to take personal and group responsibility for the predicament we know as structural racism (Ignatiev & Garvey, 1996). This is undoubtedly an unpopular option because the situation is admittedly "more complex" than that. It is true that people of color add to or participate in their own oppression, but at most this is annoying, not oppressive, to whites. Often, it is a psycho-social result of the degradation of a whole race of people and the way it compromises their self-confidence and produces apoliticized forms of resistance. We can also speak of maltreatment between minorities, or what I call "inter-minoritarian politics," which is different from white racism. It is even possible that non-whites act or speak in ways that rearticulate and reinforce racist relations.

When Stephen Steinberg (1998) criticizes William Julius Wilson for his "retreat from race," Steinberg, who brands Wilson as former New York Senator Patrick Moynihan's academic reincarnation, calls into question any universal or color-blind social policy as a backlash of liberal thought since the 1960s. Wilson's (1987) popular and generalist proposals for raising black educational skills and credentials puts the onus on blacks to disrupt the cycle or culture of poverty, rather than centering the problem of white racism and its legacy of school segregation and Eurocentric curricula, just to name a few. Steinberg also takes Cornel West to task when the otherwise insurgent philosopher attempts to uplift the spirit of the race by noting its nihilistic tendencies and rampant materialism (see West, 1994), thus deflecting the focus away from white supremacy. One should not confuse Steinberg for suggesting that these afflictions, as West describes them, are not real or that the black community does not have its *own* problems. It also may sound strange to pair two scholars with seemingly divergent political commitments, Wilson being a social democrat of a Weberian persuasion and West (1999b) a self-proclaimed "democratic and libertarian socialist" (p. 256). Wilson and West's political similarity ends with the alliteration of their names. In fact, one senses West discursively distancing himself from his former Harvard colleague who advocates a "bourgeois perspective" with respect to Afro-American oppression (West, 1988, p. 21).

Steinberg interrogates West, like Wilson and Moynihan before him, for a "politics of conversion" that announces black nihilism as "a problem *sui generis*, with an existence and momentum independent of the forces that gave rise to it in the first place" (p. 37), a cultural politics with a life of its own independent of political economy and white domination. Is this a return to the culture of poverty argument? Indeed, it is a bit telling that the trade book *Race Matters*, arguably West's least radical compendium on race and racism, should strike such an enchanting chord with the public. Because *Race Matters* resonates with a white audience's imagery of blacks as pathological and nihilistic, its discursive consequences are such that the text becomes coffee table reading for the white imagination, despite its best intentions. This is the power of discourse to be inserted into the historical flow out of the hands of its creator. West also receives added criticism from Miles and Torres (1999) who question if "race matters," preferring a return to class struggle. On this note, West (1999a) does not negate the importance of class struggle in tandem with race struggle. That said, he seems less concerned that the economy assume a determining effect on race and other relations, let alone an originary point of struggle.

The sheer amount of acts of violence or terror by whites toward racial minorities is overwhelming. However, following the format used by McIntosh, it is helpful to create a selective list of acts, laws, and decisions, if only to capture a reliable portrait of white supremacy.

1. In order to promote the "purity" of the white race, anti-miscegenation laws prevent diversification of the gene pool (Davis, 2001; Alcoff, 2000). White racism's claims to purity are an instance of its problematic humanist essentialism (Balibar, 1990).
2. Housing segregation limits black mobility and access to jobs and other

kinds of networks. Abandoned in inner cities, blacks suffer the most enduring and complete ghettoization in American history (Massey & Denton,
1993).

3. The rule of hypodescent, or the "one drop rule," allows the creation of more
    blacks and hence more slaves, increases scarcity of white identity, and pro-
    vides an "out" for white rapists of black women to disclaim responsibility for
    their children (Davis, 2001; hooks, 1981).

4. Segregated education for students of color creates substandard schools, lack
    of resources, and inferior education (Spring, 2000). Even after the 1954 deci-
    sion following Brown vs. Board of Education in Topeka, Kansas ruled that
    "separate is inherently unequal," second generation, or *de facto*, segregation
    still mars the educational experience of many students of color in the U.S.
    (Kozol, 1991).

5. Anti-immigrant Laws and Exclusion Acts curtail the rights of many Asian
    immigrants on U.S. soil and place limitations or quotas on immigration from
    their home nation (Takaki, 1993). These laws negatively affect family devel-
    opment and life, psychological wellness, and increase experiences of exile in
    Asian immigrants.

6. Colonization of third world nations establishes white global supremacy and
    perceived white superiority (Fanon, 1963; Memmi, 1965). Much of the con-
    tinents of Africa, South America, North America, Australia, frigid Greenland
    and New Zealand, and large chunks of tropical Asia and the Pacific Islands
    succumbed to the expansion of the white race (see Jordan, 1968).

7. The Occident creates its infantilized other through methods of cultural
    imperialism whereby the other is constructed, controlled, and written into
    inferiority (Said, 1979, 1994). Through cultural imperialism, ideologies of
    the West make their way to the shores of the "heart of darkness" (Conrad's
    terminology), where the culture of the white race is consolidated into a
    dominant frame of reference for civilization, moral development, and
    rationality.

8. Job discrimination limits the upward mobility of workers of color and their
    access to productive networks (Feagin & Vera, 1995; Feagin, 2000).

9. Whites' genocidal efforts against Native Americans facilitated takeover of
    Northern American soil and the attempt to eliminate its indigenous popula-
    tion. Where a policy of elimination was not possible, whites produced a form
    of education violent to Native Americans (Dog & Erdoes, 1999).

10. Global enslavement of Africans produced profit for white slave owners, com-
    promised African collective development, and established centuries of the
    master–slave relationship between whites and blacks (Jordan, 1968; Fanon,
    1967).

11. U.S. internment camps for Japanese target an Asian group as "traitors" of
    the nation state and brand them as "forever foreigners" on American soil.
    The same treatment did not fall on other "enemies of the state" during World
    War II, such as Germans or Italians (Houston & Houston, 1973).

12. Exoticization of the other, which masks the colonial policy of the degradation
    of indigenous culture, has turned colonial posts into commercial artifacts to

be enjoyed by the white imagination. Colonized lands, like Hawaii, are now places thoroughly "tourified" for the pleasure of visitors to partake in its stereotypical, prostituted, cultural forms (Trask, 1999).

13. California's Proposition 227, and others like it, impose English as the only legitimate language in schools and the workplace, thereby devaluing non-white cultures (Nieto, 2000). Although other European languages, such as French and German, are also unofficial, groups associated with them are not conveniently constructed as "aliens," or the common insult for Mexicans and other Latinos.

14. Appropriation of third world labor exploits the global work force for the profit of (post)industrial first world nations and the benefit of the white global bourgeoisie. This increases alienation for both groups, with the third world suffering the brutal structures of exploitation, unsafe work conditions, and an imbalance in relations of power between nations (Davis, 1997).

15. Military installation of naval and army bases to "protect" third world nations from external aggression promotes a condescending and patronizing relationship between the protectorate first world nation and third world nation whose sovereignty is compromised (Enloe, 2001).

16. Welfare reform legislation in the U.S., reaching its height during the Clinton era, works against the interests of people of color (Neubeck & Cazenave, 2001).

17. Forced sterilization of women of color continues the curtailment of their human and reproduction rights (Roberts, 1999).

18. The Tuskegee syphilis study, and other unethical medical research projects like it, use minority bodies for medical experimentations without the participants' full awareness and consent. In this case, the U.S. government deceived 400 blacks by promising free treatment for their syphilis. Between 1932 and 1972, the researchers conducted their disguised study of *untreated* syphilis, from which 100 black men died (Spina, 2000).

19. Jim Crow laws create American apartheid whereby blacks and whites are treated unequally under the auspices of the judicial system (Morris, 1984).

20. Inheritance laws favor whites, whose families benefited from free black labor during slavery. Centuries later, their children retain their parents' wealth. In general, whites bequeath wealth onto their children, whereas blacks often bequeath debt to theirs (Oliver & Shapiro, 1997).

21. IQ-intelligence testing, eugenics, and phrenology construct the genetic inferiority of people of color (Stepan, 1990). Herrstein and Murray's recent popular book, *The Bell Curve* (1994), revisits and reasserts eugenics assumptions.

22. Tracking practices in schools limit the educational mobility, curricular offerings, and positive interactions with teachers of black and Latino students (Oakes, 1985).

23. The systematic lynching of African Americans served as a tool of social control. Often couched in the fears of miscegenation, lynching was thought to be justified because African Americans violated the racial and social etiquettes of the South or in order to deter their civil rights activism, such as registering to vote (Davis, 1981).

24. Race riots against blacks were used as tools by whites to destroy black property and business districts, especially when they were flourishing. Riots were also used to enforce neighborhood boundaries that maintained racial segregation. Reparations to blacks, who lost their property during the riots, were never made. Moreover, city governments often never officially acknowledged that the riots occurred (Massey & Denton, 1993; Roediger, 1991).

25. Women of color are more likely to be raped than white women, but less likely to be believed. The U.S. has a long history of sexual abuse of women of color, largely because of their lack of power and whites' hypersexualization of them. Sexual abuse and rape of women of color create a culture of violence (Davis, 1981).

26. Imposition of Christian religion and forceful conversion of non-Christian peoples (Spring, 2000).

27. Whites subverted community reading programs and other educational practices by blacks, forcing them to create clandestine literacy programs (Holt, 1990).

28. Union exclusion of blacks from the working-class movement or from leadership positions in proletarian groups (West, 1999b).

29. Many blacks and Latinos live in forsaken neighborhoods with high levels of toxic pollution. As a result, they suffer from diseases related to these forms of environmental racism (Lipsitz, 1998).

Privilege is the daily cognate of structural domination. Without securing the latter, the former is not activated. A few examples should suffice. Whites have "neighbors . . . [who] are neutral or pleasant" (McIntosh, 1992, p. 73) to them because redlining and other real estate practices, with the help of the Federal Housing Agency, secure the ejection of the black and brown body from white spaces. Whites can enter a business establishment and expect the " 'person in charge' to be white" (McIntosh, 1992, p. 74) because of a long history of job discrimination. Whites are relatively free from racial harassment from police officers because racial profiling strategies train U.S. police officers that people of color are potential criminals. Finally, whites "can choose blemish cover or bandages in 'flesh' color" to match their skin (McIntosh, 1992, p. 75) because of centuries of denigration of darker peoples and images associated with them, fetishism of the color line, and the cultivation of the politics of pigmentation. We can condense the list under a general theme: whites enjoy privileges largely because they have created a system of domination under which they can thrive as a group. The volumes of writing on the issue of domination testify that the process is complex and multi-causal. But the enactment is quite simple: set up a system that benefits the group, mystify the system, remove the agents of actions from discourse, and when interrogated about it, stifle the discussion with inane comments about the "reality" of the charges being made.

When it comes to official history, there is no paucity of representation of whites as its creator. From civil society, to science, to art, whites represent the subject for what Matthew Arnold once called the best that a culture has produced. In other words, white imprint is everywhere. However, when it concerns domination, whites suddenly disappear, as if history were purely a positive sense of contribution.

Their previous omnipresence becomes a position of nowhere, a certain politics of undetectability. When it comes to culture, our students learn a benign form of multiculturalism, as if culture were a purely constructive notion free of imperialist histories and examples of imposition. Encouraging white students to reinsert themselves into the underbelly of history does not always have to occur in a self-destructive context. There are ways to address domination that require very little from people who benefit from it.

A white student in one of my courses admitted that whites possess the ultimate power in the U.S. and it does not threaten him much as an individual to recognize this fact. He explained that he can take this first step and often wonders why other whites find it so hard to join him. After all, admission does not necessarily mean ending domination; yet, many whites find even this act of enunciation impossible. In a brave attempt to ameliorate historical wounds between Japan and the Philippines, Professor Tsuyoshi Amemiya of Aoyama Gakuin University in Tokyo, Japan, works with his students to accept personal responsibility for Japan's imperialist past (Walfish, 2001). None of these students occupied the Philippines during World War II; none of them were involved in the killings during this military invasion; and none of them appropriated the Filipinos' labor. But they all have one thing in common: an inherited sense of history that belongs to, rather than is taken from, them. These students are not admitting that they created Japan's imperialist past and current Asian hegemony. Far from it. However, they recognize that their daily taken-for-granted benefits are legacies from the decades of Japanese imperialist policies.

Likewise, Australians have discussed instituting a national day of grieving, a day of atonement for crimes against the aboriginal population. White Australians are encouraged to sign a "sorry book" to apologize to indigenous people and acknowledge responsibility for the history of colonization and its continuing legacies, like the lost generation of aboriginal people whom the Australian government took from their families and tried to assimilate into white culture. Such a gesture does not represent a radical solution but an official attempt to recognize white racial domination. In the United States, the effort to provide former slaves "forty acres and a mule" failed during Reconstruction. Whites resisted this expression of atonement, one that would have changed the landscape of race relations. Free blacks would have come closer to Booker T. Washington's (1986) dream of economic independence and a rebuilding of black America. In the new millennium, the U.S. government is no closer to an official apology or plans for reparations.

The discourse on privilege has pushed critical pedagogy to ask crucial questions about the nature of "white experience" and the psychological and material benefits from an unearned position in society. To the extent that white audiences need a discursive space they can negotiate as safe participants in race critique, discourses on privilege provide the entry. However, insofar as white feelings of safety perpetuate a legacy of white refusal to engage racial domination, or acts of terror toward people of color, such discourses rearticulate the privilege that whites already enjoy when they are able to evade confronting white supremacy. As long as whites ultimately feel a sense of comfort with racial analysis, they will not sympathize with the pain and discomfort they have unleashed on racial minorities for centuries. Solidarity between whites and non-whites will proceed at the reluctant pace of the white imagination, whose subjects accept the problem of racism without an agent.

A discourse on supremacy offers whites and minority students a progressive starting point because it does not cater to white racial thinking. Racial minorities comprise its projected audience, whether or not this is literally the case. As a result, it recognizes the existence of minority subjects and affirms their history. It begins from their starting point, one which needs little convincing about the reality of white domination. Discourses of supremacy acknowledge white privileges, but only as a function of whites' actions toward minority subjects and not as mysterious accumulations of unearned advantages. In our post-September 11 global village, racism reaches into the hearts of more people, into the hearths of their homes and schools. Through discourses of supremacy the racial story unfolds, complete with characters, actions, and conflicts. More important, resolution of the plot transforms into a discreet and pedagogical possibility.

References

Alcoff, L. (2000) Mestizo Identity, in: R. Bernasconi & T. Lott (eds), *The Idea of Race* (Indianapolis and Cambridge, Hackett Publishing Company, Inc).

Apple, M. (2000) *Official Knowledge: Democratic education in a conservative age* (New York, Routledge and Kegan Paul).

Balibar, E. (1990) Paradoxes of Universality, in: D. T. Goldberg (ed.), *Anatomy of Racism* (Minneapolis, University of Minnesota Press).

Bell, D. (1992) *Faces at the Bottom of the Well: The permanence of racism* (New York, Basic Books).

Bonilla-Silva, E. (2003) *Racism without-Racists: Color-blind racism and the persistence of racial inequality in the United States* (Lanham, Rowman & Littlefield).

Davis, A. (1981) *Women, Race, and Class* (New York, Random House).

Davis, A. (1997) *The-Prison-Industrial-Complex* (Audio-CD) (San Francisco and Edinburgh, UK, AK Press Audio).

Davis, F. J. (2001) *Who is Black?: One nation's definition* (University Park, PA, Penn State University Press).

Dog, M. & Erdoes, R. (1999) Civilize Them With a Stick, in: S. Ferguson (ed.), *Mapping the Social Landscape* (Mountain View, CA, London, and Toronto, Mayfield Publishing Company).

Enloe, C. (2001) *Bananas, Bases, and Beaches: Making feminist sense of international politics* (Berkeley and Los Angeles, University of California Press).

Fanon, F. (1963) *The Wretched of the Earth*, trans. C. Farrington (New York, Grove Press).

Fanon, F. (1967) *Black Skin White Masks*, trans. C. Markmann (New York, Grove Weidenfeld).

Feagin, J. (2000) *Racist America: Roots, current realities, and future reparations* (New York, Routledge).

Feagin, J. & Vera, H. (1995) *White Racism: The basics* (New York, Routledge).

Frankenberg, R. (1993) *White Women, Race Matters: The social construction of whiteness* (Minneapolis, University of Minnesota Press).

Frankenberg, R. (ed.) (1997) *Displacing Whiteness* (Durham, NC, and London, Duke University Press).

Hall, S. (1996a) What Is This "Black" in Black Popular Culture?, in: D. Morley & K. Chen (eds), *Stuart Hall* (New York and London, Routledge).

Hall, S. (1996b) On Postmodernism and Articulation: An interview with Stuart Hall, in: D. Morley & K. Chen (eds), *Stuart Hall* (New York and London, Routledge).

Herrnstein, R. & Murray, C. (1994) *The Bell Curve* (New York, Free Press).

Holt, T. (1990) "Knowledge Is Power": The black struggle for literacy, in: A. Lunsford, H. Moglen & J. Slevin (eds), *The Right to Literacy* (New York, Modern Language Association).

hooks, b. (1981) *Ain't I a Woman?: Black women and feminism* (Boston, South End Press).

hooks, b. (1984) *Feminist Theory: From Margin to Center* (Boston, South End Press).

Houston, J.W. & Houston, J. (1973) *Farewell to Manzanar* (New York, Toronto, London, Sydney, Auckland, Bantam Books).

Hunter, M. (2002) "If You're Light You're Alright": Light skin color as social capital for women of color, *Gender & Society*, 16:2, pp. 171–189.

Hurtado, A. (1996) *The Color of Privilege: Three blasphemies on race and feminism* (Ann Arbor, MI, University of Michigan Press).

Hurtado, A. (1999) The Trickster's Play: Whiteness in the subordination and liberation process, in: R. Torres, L. Miron & J. INDA (eds), *Race, Identity, and Citizenship* (Malden, MA, and Oxford, UK, Blackwell).

Ignatiev, N. & Garvey, J. (1996) Abolish the White Race, in: N. Ignatiev & J. Garvey (eds), *Race Traitor* (New York and London, Routledge).

Jordan, W. (1968) *White over Black* (Chapel Hill, University of North Carolina Press).

Kidder, L. (1997) Colonial Remnants: Assumptions of privilege, in: M. Fine, L. Weis, L. Powell & L. Wong (eds), *Off White* (New York and London, Routledge).

Kincheloe, J. & Steinberg, S. (1997) Addressing the Crisis of Whiteness: Reconfiguring white identity in a pedagogy of whiteness, in: J. Kincheloe, S. Steinberg, N. Rodriguez & R. Chennault (eds), *White Reign* (New York, St Martin's Griffin).

Kozol, J. (1991) *Savage Inequalities* (New York, Harper Perennial).

Leonardo, Z. (2000) Betwixt and Between: Introduction to the politics of identity, in: C. Tejeda, C. Martinez & Z. Leonardo (eds), *Charting New Terrains of Chicana(o)/Latina(o) Education* (Cresskill, NJ, Hampton Press).

Leonardo, Z. (2002) The Souls of White Folk: Critical pedagogy, whiteness studies, and globalization discourse, *Race Ethnicity & Education*, 5:1, pp. 29–50.

Lipsitz, G. (1998) *The Possessive Investment in Whiteness* (Philadelphia, Temple University Press).

Marable, M. (1983) *How Capitalism Underdeveloped Black America* (Boston, South End Press).

Massey, D. & Denton, N. (1993) *American Apartheid* (Cambridge, MA, and London, Harvard University Press).

McIntosh, P. (1992) White Privilege and Male Privilege: A personal account of coming to see correspondences through work in women's studies, in: M. Andersen & P. H. Collins (eds), *Race, Class, and Gender: An anthology* (Belmont, CA, Wadsworth Publishing).

Memmi, A. (1965) *The Colonizer and the Colonized* (Boston, Beacon Press).

Miles, R. & Torres, R. (1999) Does "Race" Matter?: Transatlantic perspectives on racism after "race relations", in: R. Torres, L. Miron & J. Inda (eds), *Race, Identity, and Citizenship* (Malden, MA, and Oxford, Blackwell).

Mills, C. (1997) *The Racial Contract* (Ithaca and London, Cornell University Press).

Morris, A. (1984) *The Origins of the Civil Rights Movement* (New York, Free Press).

Neubeck, K. & Cazenave, N. (2001) *Welfare Racism: Playing the race card against America's poor* (New York and London, Routledge).

Nieto, S. (2000) *Affirming Diversity*, 3rd edn (New York, Longman).

Oakes, J. (1985) *Keeping Track* (New Haven, Yale University Press).

Oliver, M. & Shapiro, T. (1997) *Black Wealth, White Wealth: A new perspective on racial inequality* (New York and London, Routledge).

Roberts, D. (1999) *Killing the Black Body: Race, reproduction, and the meaning of liberty* (New York, Vintage Books).

Roediger, D. (1991) *The Wages of Whiteness* (London and New York, Verso).

Rothenberg, P. (ed.) (2002) *White Privilege: Essential readings on the other side of racism* (New York, Worth Publishers).

Said, E. (1979) *Orientalism* (New York, Random House).

Said, E. (1994) *Culture and Imperialism* (New York, Vintage Books).

Small, S. (1999) The Contours of Racialization: Structures, representations and resistance in the United States, in: R. Torres, L. Miron & J. Inda (eds), *Race, Identity, and Citizenship* (Malden, MA, and Oxford, Blackwell).

Spina, S. (2000) The Psychology of Violence and the Violence of Psychology, in: S. Spina (ed.), *Smoke & Mirrors: The hidden context of violence in schools and society* (Lanham, Boulder, New York and Oxford, Rowman & Littlefield).

Spring, J. (2000) *Deculturalization and the Struggle for Equality*, 3rd edn (Boston, McGraw-Hill).

Steinberg, S. (1998) The Liberal Retreat from Race during the Post-Civil Rights Era, in: W. Lubiano (ed.), *The House that Race Built* (New York, Vintage Books).

Stepan, N. (1990) Race and Gender: The role of analogy in science, in: D. T. Goldberg (ed.), *Anatomy of Racism* (Minneapolis and Oxford, University of Minnesota Press).

Takaki, R. (1993) *A Different Mirror* (Boston, New York, and London, Little, Brown and Co.).

Trask, H. (1999) Lovely Hula Hands: Corporate tourism and the prostitution of Hawaiian culture, in: S. Ferguson (ed.), *Mapping the Social Landscape* (Mountain View, CA, London and Toronto, Mayfield Publishing Company).

Walfish, D. (2001) Tracing the Echoes of the Bataan Death March, *The Chronicle of Higher Education*, A56 (11 May 2001).

Washington, B. T. (1986) *Up from Slavery* (New York, Penguin Books).

West, C. (1988) Marxist Theory and the Specificity of Afro-American Oppression, in: C. Nelson & L. Grossberg (eds), *Marxism and the Interpretation of Culture* (Urbana and Chicago, University of Illinois Press).

West, C. (1994) *Race Matters* (New York, Vintage Books).

West, C. (1999a) The Indispensability Yet Insufficiency of Marxist Theory, in: C. West (ed.), *The Cornel West Reader* (New York, Basic Books).

West, C. (1999b) Race and Social Theory, in: C. West (ed.), *The Cornel West Reader* (New York, Basic Books).

Wilson, W. J. (1987) *The Truly Disadvantaged* (Chicago, University of Chicago Press).

Wise, T. (2002) Membership Has Its Privileges: Thoughts on acknowledging and challenging whiteness, in: P. Rothenberg (ed.), *White Privilege: Essential readings on the other side of racism* (New York, Worth Publishers).

16

Teaching White Students About Racism
The Search for White Allies and the Restoration of Hope

Beverly Daniel Tatum

White students can learn about racism without experiencing guilt that can overpower their desire to learn. Janet Helm's model of white racial identity is used as a framework for helping students abandon racism and define a positive white identity.

ERIC

Think of a nationally known white person whom you would describe as a racist. If you are like most of the students in my Psychology of Racism classes and the hundreds of workshop participants I address each year, at least one name comes to mind fairly quickly. The names of past and present Klan leaders and conservative southern politicians are usually the first to be mentioned.

Think now of a nationally known white person you would consider to be an antiracist activist, a white man or woman who is clearly identifiable as an ally to people of color in the struggle against racism. Do you find yourself drawing a blank? Perhaps you thought of Viola Liuzzo, James Reeb, or Michael Schwerner, white civil rights workers who were slain during the years of the civil rights movement. If we add the qualifier "still living," who comes to mind? If you have managed to think of someone who fits this description, notice that it probably took significantly longer to come up with an answer to this question than it did to the first.

The fact is there are white people who can be named in this category. You might have remembered Morris Dees, the executive director of the Southern Poverty Law Center and a vigorous anti-Klan litigator. The name of Anne Braden, a long-time civil rights activist, might have come to mind. Perhaps you knew the name of Virginia Foster Durr, a southern white woman who was actively involved in the struggle for civil rights in the South and who is featured in the first episode of the documentary series Eyes on the Prize. Maybe you have heard Bill Bradley, a senator from New Jersey, speak eloquently about issues of racism in our society and thought of him.

Other people might be named, but the point is that the names are typically retrieved very slowly, if at all. I have had the experience of addressing roomfuls of classroom teachers who have been unable to generate a single name without some prompting from me. If well-educated adults interested in teaching about race and racism in their classrooms have trouble identifying contemporary white men and women who have taken a public stand against racism, it is a reasonable assumption that our students will not be able to identify those names either.

Why is this lack of information of concern? As I have discussed elsewhere, one consequence of addressing the issue of racism (and other forms of oppression) in the classroom is the generation of powerful emotional responses in both white students and students of color.[1] White students, in particular, often struggle with strong feelings of guilt when they become aware of the pervasiveness of racism in our society. Even when they feel their own behavior has been nondiscriminatory, they often experience "guilt by association." These feelings are uncomfortable and can lead white students to resist learning about race and racism. And who can blame them? If learning about racism means seeing oneself as an "oppressor," one of the "bad guys," then of course there will be resistance. Few people would actively embrace such a self-definition.

But what alternatives do we offer to white students? This article is intended to explore this question and its implications for teaching about racism, using Helms's model of white racial identity development as a framework for understanding white students' responses.[2] The perspective I bring to this discussion is that of an African-American female college professor who has been teaching and/or leading workshops on racism in predominantly white settings since 1980. The student voices represented in this article come from journal entries written by students enrolled in my course on the psychology of racism.

Understanding White Identity Development

As Janet Helms explains in her model of white racial identity development, "racial identity development theory concerns the psychological implications of racial group membership, that is belief systems that evolve in reaction to perceived differential racial-group membership."[3] In U.S. society, where racial-group membership is emphasized, it is assumed that the development of a racial identity will occur in some form in everyone. However, the process will unfold in different ways for whites and people of color because of the different social positions they occupy in this society. For whites, there are two major developmental tasks in this process, the abandonment of individual racism and the recognition of and opposition to institutional and cultural racism. Helms writes: "Concurrently, the person must become aware of her or his Whiteness, learn to accept Whiteness as an important part of herself or himself, and to internalize a realistically positive view of what it means to be White."[4] Helms's six-stage model can then be divided into two major phases, the first being the abandonment of racism (a process that begins with the Contact stage and ends with the Reintegration stage). The second phase, defining a positive white identity, begins with the Pseudo-Independent stage and reaches fruition at the Autonomy stage.

Contact Stage

The first stage of racial identity for whites (the Contact stage) is a stage at which there is little attention paid to the significance of one's racial group membership. Individuals at this stage of development rarely describe themselves as white. If they have lived, worked, or gone to school in predominantly white settings, they may simply think of themselves as like the majority of those around them. This view is exemplified by the comment one of my white students made when asked to describe herself in terms of her class and ethnic background. She summed up her middle-class, white European background by saying, "I'm just normal." This sense of being part of the racial norm is taken for granted without conscious consideration of the systematically conferred advantages given to whites simply because of their racial group membership.[5]

While they have been influenced by the prevailing societal stereotypes of people of color, there is typically limited awareness of this socialization process. Often individuals at the Contact stage perceive themselves as completely free of prejudice, unaware of their own assumptions about other racial groups. I would describe the majority of the white men and women I have had in my course over the last twelve years as being in this stage of development at the start of the semester.

Disintegration Stage

However, participating in a classroom where the social consequences of racial group membership are explicitly discussed as part of the course content typically propels white students from the first stage to the next, referred to by Helms as the Disintegration Stage.[6] At this stage, white students begin to see how much their lives and the lives of people of color have been affected by racism in our society. The societal inequities they now notice are in direct contradiction to the idea of an American meritocracy, a concept that has typically been an integral part of their earlier socialization. The cognitive dissonance that results is part of the discomfort experienced at this stage. One response to this discomfort is to deny the validity of the information that is being presented to them, or to withdraw from the class psychologically, if not physically.[7] However, if they remain engaged, white students at the disintegration stage typically want to deal with the guilt and other uncomfortable feelings by doing something, by taking action of some sort to interrupt the racism they now see around them. If students have learned (as I hope they have) that racism can take both active forms (e.g., verbal harassment, physical violence, intentional acts of discrimination) and passive forms (e.g., silence in the presence of another's racist remarks, unexamined policies and practices that disproportionately impact people of color, the failure to acknowledge the contributions of people of color), then they recognize that an active response to racism is required to interrupt its perpetuation in our society.

"But what action can I take?" is a common question at this point in their development. Jerri, a white woman from an upper-middle-class family, expressed this sentiment clearly in her journal.

> Another thing I realized when I got to college was the privileges attached to being white. My family had brought me up trying to make me aware of other people and their differences—but they never explained the power I had. I do not take advantage of my power—at least I try not to, but it seems inevitable. I feel helpless. There is so much I want to do—to help. What can I do? I do not want to help perpetuate racism, sexism and stereotypes.

Helping students think this question through for themselves is part of our responsibility as educators who have accepted the challenge of teaching about racism. Heightening student awareness about racism without also providing some hope for social change is a prescription for despair. We all have a sphere of influence, some domain in which we exercise some level of power and control. For students, the task may be to identify what their own sphere of influence is (however large or small) and to consider how it might be used to interrupt the cycle of racism.[8]

However, once again, students find that they can think of many more examples of racist behavior than they can think of examples of antiracist behavior. Many white students have experienced their most influential adult role models, their parents, as having been the source of overtly expressed racial prejudices. The following excerpts from the journals of two students illustrate this point:

> Today was the first class on racism. . . . Before today I didn't think I was exposed to any form of racism. Well, except for my father. He is about as prejudiced as they come. [Sally, a white female]
>
>   It really bothers me that stereotypes exist because it is from them that I originally became uninformed. My grandmother makes all kinds of decisions based on stereotypes—who to hire, who to help out. When I was growing up, the only black people that I knew were adults [household help], but I admired them just as much as any other adult. When I expressed these feelings to my parents, I was always told that the black people that I knew were the exceptions and that the rest of the race were different. I, too, was taught to be afraid. [Barbara, a white woman]

Others experienced their parents as passively silent on the subject of racism, simply accepting the status quo. As one young man from a very privileged background wrote:

> It is easy to simply fade into the woodwork, run with the rest of society, and never have to deal directly with these problems. So many people I know from home . . . have simply accepted what society has taught them with little if any question. My father is a prime example of this. His overriding preaching throughout my childhood dealt with simply accepting reality. [Carl, a white male]

Those white students whose parents actively espoused antiracist values still felt unprepared for addressing racism outside of the family circle, a point highlighted by the following journal entry, written by Annette, a white female college senior:

> Talking with other class members, I realized how exceptional my parents were. Not only were they not overtly racist but they also tried to keep society's subtle racism from reaching me. Basically I grew up believing that racism was no longer an issue and all people should be treated as equals. Unfortunately, my parents were not being very realistic as society's racism did begin to reach me. They did not teach me how to support and defend their views once I was interacting in a society without them as a buffer.

How do they learn how to interrupt someone else's racist (or sexist/anti-Semitic/homophobic) joke or challenge someone's stereotype if they have never seen anyone else do it? Despite the lack of examples, many students will begin to speak up about racism to their friends and family members. They often find that their efforts to share their new knowledge and heightened awareness with others are perceived negatively. Alice, a white woman, wrote:

I never realized how much sexism and racism there still is on TV. I don't know if I'll ever be able to watch TV in the same way again. I used to just watch TV shows, laugh at the funny jokes, and not think about sexism or racism. . . . I know my friends and family probably don't think I'm as much fun as I used to be because I can't watch TV without making an issue of how racist and sexist most shows are.

The fear of being alienated from these friends and family members is real, and is part of the social pressure experienced by those at the Disintegration stage of development to back away from this new awareness of racism. The dilemma of noticing racism and yet feeling the societal pressure not to notice, or at least not to speak up, is resolved for some at the Reintegration stage.

Reintegration Stage

At the Reintegration stage, whites may turn to explanations for racism that put the burden of change on those who are the targets of racism.

Race-related negative conditions are assumed to result from Black people's inferior social, moral, and intellectual qualities, and thus it is not unusual to find persons in the Reintegration stage selectively attending to and/or reinterpreting information to conform to societal stereotypes of Black people.[9]

As Wellman clearly illustrates, such thinking allows the white individual to relieve himself or herself of guilt as well as responsibility for working toward social change.[10]

Because the pressure to ignore racism and to accept the socially sanctioned stereotypes is so great, unless we talk about the interpersonal challenges that often confront students at this point in their understanding, we place them at risk of getting stuck in the Reintegration stage. Identifying these challenges for students does not solve the problem for them, but it does help them to recognize the source of some of the discomfort they may experience. It is hoped that this recognition allows them to respond in ways that will allow for continued growth in their own racial identity development.

Pseudo-Independent Stage

Continued, ongoing dialogue about race-related issues is one way to promote such growth. As the students' understanding of the complexity of institutional racism in our society deepens, the likelihood of resorting to "blame-the-victim" explanations lessens. Such deepening awareness is associated with the commitment to unlearn one's own racism, and marks the movement into the next stage of development in Helms's model, the Pseudo-independent stage. This stage marks the beginning of the second phase of this developmental process, creating a positive definition of whiteness.

At the Pseudo-independent stage, the individual may try to deal with some of the social pressures experienced at earlier stages by actively seeking friendships with those who share an antiracist perspective. In particular, some white students may want to distance themselves psychologically from their own racial group by seeking out relationships with people of color. An example of this can be seen in the following journal entry:

> One of the major and probably most difficult steps in identity development is obtaining or finding the consciousness of what it means to be white. I definitely remember many a time that I wished I was not white, ashamed of what I and others have done to the other racial groups in the world. . . . I wanted to pretend I was black, live with them, celebrate their culture, and deny my whiteness completely. Basically, I wanted to escape the responsibility that came with identifying myself as "white." [Lisa, a white female]

How successful these efforts to escape whiteness via people of color are will depend in part on the racial-identity development of the people of color involved.[11] However, even if these efforts to build interracial relationships are successful, the individual must eventually confront the reality of his or her own whiteness.

We all must be able to embrace who we are in terms of our racial cultural heritage, not in terms of assumed superiority or inferiority, but as an integral part of our daily experience in which we can take pride. But for many white students who have come to understand the reality of racism in all of our lives, whiteness is still at this stage experienced as a source of shame rather than a source of pride. Efforts to define a positive white identity are still tentative. The confusion experienced at this stage is clearly expressed by Bob, a white male struggling with these issues. Five weeks into the semester, he wrote:

> There have been many talk shows on in the past week that have focused on race. Along with the readings I'm finding that I'm looking at the people and topics in very different ways than I had in the past. I'm finding that this idea of white identity is more important than I thought. Yet white identity seems very hard to pin hole. I seem to have an idea and feel myself understanding what I need to do and why and then something presents itself that throws me into mass confusion. I feel that I need some resource that will help me through the process of finding white identity.

Immersion/Emersion

The next stage of white racial identity development, Immersion/Emersion, is a stage at which individuals intensify their efforts to create a positive self-definition as a white person. Helms writes, "The person in this stage is searching for the answers to the questions: 'Who am I racially?' and 'Who do I want to be?' and 'Who are you really?' "[12] Students at this stage actively seek white role models who might provide examples for nonoppressive ways of being white. Such examples might be found in the form of biographies or autobiographies of white individuals who have been engaged in a similar process. Unfortunately, these materials are not easily found because the lives of white antiracists or "allies" have not generally been subjects of study, a topic I will return to shortly.

Participation in white consciousness-raising groups organized specifically for the purpose of examining one's own racism is often helpful in this process. At Mount Holyoke College, where I currently teach, such a group was formed (White Women Against Racism) following the 1992 acquittal of the Los Angeles police officers involved in the beating of Rodney King. Support groups of this nature help to combat the social isolation antiracist whites often experience, and provide encouragement for continued development of a self-definition as a white ally.

It is at this stage that the feelings of guilt and shame are replaced with feelings of pride and excitement. Helms writes,

> The person may begin to feel a euphoria perhaps akin to a religious rebirth. These positive feelings not only help to buttress the newly developing White identity, but provide the fuel by which the person can truly begin to tackle racism and oppression in its various forms.[13]

Mary, a senior writing her last journal entry of the semester, reflected this excitement at the changes she was observing in herself:

> This past weekend I went to New York. . . . As always we drove through Harlem on our way downtown. For the first time in four years I didn't automatically feel nervous when we turned that corner. For the first time I took an active interest in what was going on in the neighborhood and in the neighborhood itself. When the bus driver pointed out some points of interest like the Apollo, I actually recognized the names and was truly appreciative that the driver had pointed them out. I know this doesn't sound like much to get excited about, and in all honesty it doesn't really excite me either. In a way though, I guess this serves as an object lesson of sorts for me; I CAN unlearn the racism that I've been taught. It required some thought beforehand, but it certainly wasn't difficult by any means. Clearly, the next step is to identify something new to focus on and unlearn THAT as well. I can't help feeling like this is how a toddler must feel—each step is a challenge and although sometimes you fall, you don't usually hurt yourself. But overwhelmingly, each step is exciting and an accomplishment. This metaphor has at least one flaw, however. I really can't believe that this ever becomes as unconscious and unthinking as walking is for us all. Maybe it will become as effortless, but I think that if it becomes unthinking then an essential building block of unlearning racism will have been taken away.

Autonomy Stage

The last stage, the Autonomy stage, represents the culmination of the previous stages. The newly defined view of one's whiteness is internalized, and incorporated as part of one's own personal self-definition. This new sense of oneself must continue to be nurtured and supported, but as it is internalized, the individual may begin to expand his or her focus to awareness of other "isms."

Thus one finds the Autonomous person actively seeking opportunities to learn from other cultural groups. One also finds him or her actively becoming increasingly aware of how other forms of oppression (e.g., sexism, ageism) are related to racism and acting to eliminate them as well.[14]

Though this is descibed as the "last stage," it is important to understand that this process is not a static or a linear one. In the process of moving through these stages, there may be back-and-forth-movement, revisiting earlier stages and then moving forward again. I find the image of a spiral staircase is a helpful one in explaining this concept to students. As a person ascends a spiral staircase, he may stop and look down at the pattern on the floor below. When he reaches the next level, he may look down again and see the same pattern, but the vantage point has changed.

Educational Implications

Each of these stages has implications for classroom interaction and student responsiveness to race-related content. The denial and resistance to the recognition of racism are characteristic of the first phase of white racial identity development. Strategies for responding to student resistance have been discussed in an earlier paper.[15] Here we will explore the particular challenges presented to the instructor and the student once the shift has been made to the second phase of development, the creation of a positive white identity.

Three Models of Whiteness

The process of developing a positive white identity, described in the later stages of Helms's model, is hindered by the fact that there are really only three major models of whiteness readily available with which students might identify. The first model, that of the actively racist white supremacist, is familiar to many students. They have seen Klan leaders on the news and on television talk shows. As was illustrated earlier, they may have grown up in homes with parents who, though not Klan supporters, actively embraced the notion of the superiority of whites and the inferiority of people of color. The "white supremacist" model, however, is one that is clearly rejected at this phase of development.

The second model of whiteness might be described as the "what whiteness?" view. As described in the Contact stage, many whites simply do not acknowledge their racial category as personally significant. This failure to acknowledge the salience of skin color in U.S. society is associated with the failure to acknowledge the reality of racism. However, once racism has been acknowledged as a system of advantage based on race, the heightened awareness of white privilege eliminates this model as a personal option.[16] The individual can no longer ignore the fact that whiteness matters.

The third major model of whiteness might be described as the "guilty white" model. This style is characterized by the heightened awareness of racism and the accompanying shame and embarrassment about being white that so many of my students describe. Experiencing oneself as guilty is an uncomfortable state of being, and therefore is not a particularly appealing model for whites. In addition, the internal focus on one's own "guilt by association" can be immobilizing, and therefore interferes with one's ability to take effective action to interrupt expressions of racism. It is for this reason that people of color will often express impatience at what might be viewed as self-indulgent expressions of white guilt.

None of these three models of whiteness is attractive to the white individual struggling to define a positive sense of whiteness. Such an individual may feel that he or she is "re-inventing the wheel," and may retreat in frustration to an earlier stage of racial identity development. However, this frustration might be avoided if another, more positive model were readily available.

The Model of the White Ally

In fact, another model does exist. There is a history of white protest against racism, a history of whites who have resisted the role of oppressor and who have been allies to people of color. Unfortunately these whites are often invisible to students; their names are unknown.

Think back to the beginning of this article. How many names of white antiracists were on the tip of your tongue? If students have studied the civil rights era (many of my students are poorly informed about this period of history), they may know about Viola Liuzzo and Michael Schwerner and other whites killed for their antiracist efforts. But who wants to be a martyr? Do they know about white allies who spoke up, who worked for social change, who resisted racism and lived to tell about it? How did these white allies break free from the confines of the racist socialization they surely experienced to redefine themselves in this way? These are the voices that many white students are hungry to hear.

This information needs to be provided in order to help white students construct a pro-active white identity. In my class I try to provide concrete examples of such people. White professors teaching about racism who see themselves as allies may be able to share examples from their own lives and in this way might be role models for their white students. As an African-American professor, I am limited in this regard.[17] My strategy has been to invite a well-known white antiracist activist, Andrea Ayvazian, to my class to speak about her own personal journey toward an awareness of racism and her development as a white ally.[18] Students typically ask questions that reflect their fears about social isolation at this phase of development. "Did you lose friends when you started to speak up?" "My boyfriend makes a lot of racist comments. What can I do?" "What do you say to your father at Thanksgiving when he tells those jokes?"

White students, who often comment about how depressing it is to study about racism, typically say that the opportunity to talk with this ally gave them renewed hope.

> Today's class began with a visit from . . . a white woman who has made dismantling white privilege a way of life. . . . Her personal story gave me a feeling of hope in the struggle against racism. [Terri, a white woman]
>
> Now that we have learned about the severity of all of the horrible oppression in the world, it is comforting to know how I can become an ally. [Barbara, a white woman]
>
> What a POWERFUL speaker! Andrea was so upbeat and energetic. I think that her talk really boosted the spirits in our class. I personally have become quite disillusioned with some of our small group discussions of late, and having her talk brought some deep reflection and positive insight on the future—especially ideas and revelations concerning my role as perhaps a white ally. . . . Her presentation was overall very well received, and I enjoyed it very much. There is hope! [Robin, a white female]

One point that the speaker discussed at length was the idea that "allies need allies," others who will support their efforts to swim against the tide of cultural and institutional racism. This point was especially helpful for one young woman who had been struggling with the feelings of isolation often experienced by whites in the Disintegration stage. She wrote:

About being an ally, a positive role model:

> . . . it enhanced my positive feelings about the difference each individual (me!) can make. I don't need to feel helpless when there is so much I can do. I still can see how easily things can back-up and start getting depressing, but I can also see how it is possible to keep going strong and powerful. One of the most important points she made was the necessity of a support group/system; people to remind me of what I have done, why I should keep going, of why I'm making a difference, why I shouldn't feel helpless. I think our class started to help me with those issues, as soon as I started to let it, and now I've found similar supports in friends and family. They're out there, it's just finding and establishing them—it really is a necessity. Without support, it would be too easy to give up, burn out, become helpless again. In any endeavor support is important, but when the forces against you are so prevalent and deep-rooted as racism is in this society, it is the only way to keep moving forward. [Joanne, a white woman]

In my view, the restoration of hope is an essential part of the learning process. Otherwise, students, both white and of color, become immobilized by their own despair.

Though the focus of this article is clearly on the process of white racial identity development, it should be pointed out that students of color also need to know that whites can be allies. For some students of color, the idea that there are white people who have moved beyond guilt to a position of claiming responsibility for the dismantling of institutional racism is a novel one. They too find hope in the possibility. Writing in response to the activist's visit, Sonia, a Latina, commented:

> I don't know when I have been more impressed by anyone. She filled me with hope for the future. She made me believe that there are good people in the world and that whites suffer too and want to change things.

In addition to inviting Andrea Ayvazian to my class, I try to provide written materials about white people who have been engaged in examining their own white identity and who have made a commitment to antiracist activity in their own lives. However, this information is not easily located. One of the consequences of racism in our society is that those who oppose it are often marginalized. As Colman McCarthy writes in the foreword to The Universe Bends toward Justice, "students know warmakers, not peacemakers."[19] As with other marginalized groups, the stories of peacemakers, of white allies, are not readily accessed. Yet having access to these stories makes a difference to students who are looking for ways to be agents of change. A resource list of materials I have been able to identify is included at the conclusion of this article.

Students, motivated by their own need for such information, can be quite resourceful in the generation of this knowledge. Recently, a white woman who had taken my Psychology of Racism course conducted an independent study project investigating the phenomenological experience of being a white ally on a college campus. Interviewing other white women, ranging in age from nineteen to forty-seven, she was able to generate valuable information about the daily implications of being an antiracist? It was apparent that her research was more than an academic exercise—indeed a way to strengthen her own commitment to antiracist action. More of this kind of research needs to be done so that the fourth model of whiteness, that of the white ally, becomes a more visible option for white students.

Though the focus here has been on the provision of white role models for students trying to construct a positive white racial identity, it is important to acknowledge that there is a parallel need for both white students and students of color to see and read about clear examples of empowered people of color. Teaching about racism should not be only a litany of the ways people of color have been victimized by oppression. It must also include examples of the resistance of people of color to victimization. Just as white students are not eager to see themselves as oppressors, students of color do not want to be characterized as victims.[21] In addition, white students should not be led to believe that the role of the ally is to "help" victims of racism. The role of the ally is to speak up against systems of oppression, and to challenge other whites to do the same. Teaching about racism needs to shift from an exploration of the experiences of victims and victimizers to that of empowered people of color and their white allies, creating the possibility of working together as partners in the establishment of a more just society.

Notes

1. See Beverly Daniel Tatum, "Talking about Race, Learning about Racism: An Application of Racial Identity Development Theory in the Classroom," Harvard Educational Review 62 (February 1992): 1–24.
2. Janet E. Helms, Black and White Racial Identity: Theory, Research and Practice (Westport, Conn.: Greenwood Press, 1990).
3. Ibid., p. 3.
4. Ibid., p. 55.
5. For further discussion of the concept of white privilege and the advantages systematically conferred on whites, see Peggy McIntosh's working paper, White Privilege and Male Privilege: A Personal Account of Coming to See Correspondences through Work in Women's Studies (Wellesley, Mass.: Wellesley College Center for Research on Women).
6. Helms, Black and White Racial Identity, chap. 4, p. 58.
7. Tatum, "Talking about Race, Learning about Racism."
8. For a discussion of the use of action-planning projects in a course on racism, see ibid.
9. Helms, Black and White Racial Identity, p. 60.
10. David Wellman, Portraits of White Racism (New York: Cambridge University Press, 1977).
11. For further discussion of the interaction effect of stages of racial-identity development for people of color and for whites, see Tatum, "Talking about Race, Learning about Racism."
12. Helms, Black and White Racial Identity, p. 62.
13. Ibid.
14. Ibid., p. 66.
15. Tatum, "Talking about Race, Learning about Racism."
16. Wellman, Portraits of White Racism.
17. Though I cannot speak from experience as a white ally, I do use examples of being an ally in those areas in which I am a member of the dominant group. For example, as a Christian, I can give examples of being an ally to Jews by interrupting anti-Semitism. Similarly, as a heterosexual, I can give examples of interrupting homophobic and heterosexist behavior.
18. I am fortunate that Andrea Ayvazian lives in my local community, For those interested in more information about her work, she can be contacted at Communitas, Inc., 245 Main St., Suite 207, Northampton, MA 01060.
19. Angie O'Gorman, The Universe Bends towards Justice: A Reader on Christian Non-Violence in the U.S. (Philadelphia: New Society Publishers, 1990).
20. Stacy K. Chandler, "White Allies in a College Community: An Exploratory Study of the Subjective Meaning of Being an Anti-Racist" (Paper presented at the 46th Annual Mount Holyoke Undergraduate Psychology Conference, May 1, 1993). Copies available from B. D. Tatum, Department of Psychology and Education, Mount Holyoke College, South Hadley, MA 01075.
21. See Beverly Daniel Tatum, "African-American Identity, Achievement Motivation, and Missing History," Social Education 56 (1992): 331–34.

Suggested Resources

The following resource list includes materials that examine the meaning of whiteness and/or provide biographical information about the lives of white allies. This list should not be considered an exhaustive one. It does represent the most useful materials I have been able to locate to date.

Barnard, H. F., ed. Outside the Magic Circle: The Autobiography of Virginia Foster Durr. Tuscaloosa: University of Alabama Press, 1985.

Barndt, J. Dismantling Racism: The Continuing Challenge to White America. Minneapolis: Augsburg Press, 1991.

Barndt, J., and C. Ruechle. "Rediscovering a Heritage Lost: A European-American Anti-Racist Identity." In America's Original Sin, 73–77. Washington, D.C.: Sojourner, 1992.

Berry, W. The Hidden Wound. Boston: Houghton Mifflin, 1970.

Blauner, B. Black Lives, White Lives: Three Decades of Race Relations in America. Berkeley: University of California Press, 1990.

Boyle, S. P. The Desegregated Heart. New York: William Morrow, 1962.

Braden, A. "An Unfinished Revolution: The Vision of a Common Destiny." In America's Original Sin, edited by Jim Wallis, 690. Washington, D.C.: Sojourners, 1992.

Colby, A., and W. Damon, Some Do Care: Contemporary Lives of Moral Commitment. New York: Free Press, 1992.

Dees, M., with S. Fiffer, A Season of Justice: A Lawyer's Own Story of Victory over America's Hate Groups. New York: Touchstone Books, 1991.

Dennis, R. M. "Socialization and Racism: The White Experience." In Impacts of Racism on White Americans, edited by B. Bowser and R. G. Hunt, 71–85. Beverly Hills: Sage, 1981.

Derman-Sparks, L., C. L. Higa, and B. Sparks. "Suggestions for developing positive racial attitudes." Interracial Books for Children Bulletin 11, no. 3–4 (1980): 10–15.

Hampton, H., and S. Fayer, Voices of Freedom: An Oral History of the Civil Rights Movement from the 1950s–1980s. New York: Bantam Books, 1990.

Helms, J. E. A Race Is a Nice Thing to Have: A Guide to Being a White Person or Understanding the White Persons in Your Life. Topeka: Content Communications, 1992.

Johnson, R. E. "Making a Stand for Change: A Strategy for Empowering Individuals." In Opening Doors: Perspectives on Race Relations in Contemporary America, edited by H. J. Knopke, R. J. Norrell, and R. W. Roger, 151–164. Tuscaloosa: University of Alabama Press, 1991.

Katz, J. White Awareness: Handbook for Anti-Racism Training. Norman: University of Oklahoma Press, 1978.

King, L. Confessions of a White Racist. New York: Viking, 1971.

Lester, J., "What Happens to the Mythmakers when the Myths Are Found to be Untrue?" Unpublished paper available from Equity Institute, Emeryville, Calif., 1987.

Levy, D. S. "The Cantor and the Klansman (an interview with Michael Weisser and Larry Trapp)." Time, February 17, 1992, pp. 14–16.

Mizell, L., S. Benett, B. Bowman, and L. Morin. "Different Ways of Seeing: Teaching in an Anti-racist School." In Freedom's Plow: Teaching in the Multicultural Classroom, edited by T. Perry and J. W. Fraser. New York: Routledge, 1993.

Nieto, S. "Vanessa Mattison: A Case Study." In her Affirming Diversity: The Sociopolitical Context of Multicultural Education, 60–68. New York: Longman, 1992.

Pratt, M. B. "Identity: Skin, Blood, Heart." In Yours in Struggle: Three Feminist Perspectives on Anti-Semitism and Racism, edited by E. Bulkin, M. B. Pratt, and B. Smith, 11–63. Ithaca, N.Y.: Firebrand, 1984.

Smith, L. Killers of the Dream (rev. and enl.; originally published 1949). New York: Norton, 1978.

Stalvey, L. M. Education of a WASP (originally published 1970). Madison: University of Wisconsin Press, 1989.

Terkel, S. "Beyond Hatred: The Education of C. P. Ellis." Quest, 1980, pp. 23–26, 100–101.

Terkel, S. Race: How Blacks and Whites Think about the American Obsession. New York: Anchor Books, 1992.

Terry, R. W. For Whites Only. Grand Rapids, Mich.: William B. Eerdmans Publishing, 1970.

Wallis, J. "By Accident of Birth: Growing Up White in Detroit." In America's Original Sin, 64–68. Washington, D.C.: Sojourner, 1992.

Ware, V. Beyond the Pale: White Women, Racism and History. London: Verso, 1992.

I would like to gratefully acknowledge the assistance of Stacy Chandler in the compilation of this resource list.

Part Eight

Critiques of Critical Race Theory

17

Some Critical Thoughts on Critical Race Theory

Douglas E. Litowitz

Critical Race Theory (CRT) is perhaps the fastest growing and most controversial movement in recent legal scholarship, stirring up debate in much the same manner Critical Legal Studies (CLS) did fifteen or twenty years ago. Although CRT was inspired in part by the failure of CLS to focus sufficiently on racial issues, it remains indebted in style and substance to CLS; it also draws from such diverse sources as Continental philosophy (especially postmodernism and poststructuralism), radical feminism, Marxism, cultural studies, and the black power movement. CRT is still a young movement: it emerged in the 1980s and held its first official conference in 1989. Judging by the sheer volume of recent articles and symposia on CRT, the movement is here to stay.[1] Several months ago, Temple University Press published a comprehensive anthology of writings by CRT scholars under the title *Critical Race Theory: The Cutting Edge*,[2] and I will use this text as a springboard for my assessment and critique of CRT as an intellectual movement.

Writings that fall under the CRT rubric are diverse and cannot be easily categorized or summarized, except to say that they all address, however directly or obliquely, the various ways in which assumptions about race affect the players within the legal system (judges, lawyers, and lay people) and have a determining effect on substantive legal doctrines. To be sure, a previous generation of scholars (most of whom were white males) had written about the intersection of race and law, but their work followed the traditional method of legal scholarship and was nowhere as confessional or interdisciplinary as the current scholarship in CRT. The last several years have seen an explosion in CRT-style articles, giving rise to the need for a collection of core texts that are representative of CRT as a movement.

Critical race theorist Richard Delgado has assembled just such a collection of pivotal writings in *Critical Race Theory*. This multifaceted anthology was assembled from an impressive range of articles in leading law journals. Some fifty wide-ranging articles appear under twelve separate headings, including "critique of liberalism," "storytelling," "revisionist interpretations of history," and other CRT focal points. Many of the major CRT players are represented, including Derrick Bell, Patricia Williams, Regina Austin, and Delgado himself. Conspicuously absent are founding CRT scholars Mari Matsuda, Charles Lawrence, and Kimberlè Crenshaw, whose work can be found in the other widely-available anthology on CRT, the influential *Words That Wound*.[3] In the introduction to *Critical Race Theory*, Delgado mentions the importance of these thinkers and directs the reader to their essays elsewhere. Surely the anthology would have been more thorough had it included works by Matsuda, Lawrence, and Crenshaw (who, according to Delgado, "declined to participate"), but *Critical Race Theory* can nonetheless stand on its own as the most comprehensive introduction to CRT currently available. So I recommend the anthology for legal scholars who are interested in exploring CRT either on their own or through a law school seminar. Those who are thinking about using the anthology as a textbook will be thankful for Delgado's introductory essay on CRT, his brief statements introducing the various sections, and his suggestions for further reading (all of which, however, are somewhat abbreviated).

At nearly six hundred pages, the anthology is perhaps too lengthy, yet one gets the impression that more than a few of the contributions have been cut abruptly, as is the case with Delgado's own seminal article proposing a tort action for racial epithets,[4] which ends before Delgado can present and defend his proposed statute. Still, in cases like this it is useful to treat the anthology as a path to the complete articles, which are available in any law library. I have only two remaining qualms about the formal aspects of the volume. First, Delgado is perhaps over-represented here, appearing in a full nine of the fifty selections. He is doubtless a pivotal figure in CRT, but the book makes him appear more central than he might in fact be. Second, although the book contains a few selections that are critical of CRT, one might have preferred a chapter devoted exclusively to authors who are critical of CRT. Delgado has included the important critical work of African-American law professor Randall Kennedy, but the anthology would have benefitted from other critical selections, perhaps from Stephen Carter[5] and Richard Posner.[6] Still, these are minor flaws; overall the book is clearly organized and the essays are engaging.

Now for the bad news. After a thorough reading, and even rereading, I cannot shake the feeling that there are some systematic problems with CRT. I use the term *systematic* to indicate my contention that much of the work in CRT is problematic at the level of deep structure; that in many cases CRT takes an approach that embodies fundamental errors or confusions about the proper role of argumentation within the law and the proper methodology of legal scholarship. In what follows I will present five problems that CRT scholars should address. I offer these points as a somewhat sympathetic and interested critic who finds much value in CRT, but who also recognizes that a great deal needs clarification. Let me begin by presenting the basic theoretical underpinning of CRT and by looking at two representative articles from the anthology. I will then offer my critique of the movement.

I. The Basic Themes of CRT

Prior to editing this anthology, Delgado co-authored the introductory essay to *Words That Wound*, collaborating with high-profile CRT thinkers Mari Matsuda, Charles Lawrence, and Kimberlè Crenshaw. In that essay, CRT was introduced as a new movement centered around six "defining elements," which can be paraphrased as follows:

  1. Racism is endemic to American life. Race has a hand in all decisions by courts

and legislatures, if only because judges and legislators go about their business from a particular "raced" perspective (not simply as judges or legislators per se, but as blacks or whites, men or women). Legal scholarship as well is racially situated, such that there is a "black" and a "white" view on legal issues.

2. The existing legal system (and mainstream legal scholarship as well) are not color-blind although they pretend to be. Despite the pretense of neutrality, the system has always worked to the disadvantage of people of color and it continues to do so. People of color are more likely to be convicted, to serve more time, to suffer arbitrary arrest and deprivation of liberty and property. A pervasive but unconscious racism infects the legal system.

3. The law must be understood historically and contextually. A court which is hearing a case involving women or people of color must take into account the context and history of our legal system as one that has marginalized these "out-groups."

4. The subjective experiences of women and people of color render them especially well-suited for analyzing race relations law and discrimination law. Women and minorities see the world differently—they see sexism and racism where dominant groups cannot. Minorities make better race-relations scholars (and law professors) because they have experienced racism first-hand.

5. CRT scholarship borrows from diverse intellectual traditions, including the political activism of the 1960s, nationalism, postmodernism, Marxism, and pragmatism.

6. CRT works toward the elimination of oppression in all forms (race, class, gender) and issues a challenge to hierarchy itself.[7]

In the introductory essay to *Critical Race Theory*, Delgado has narrowed these six features into four defining elements, which might be paraphrased as follows:

1. Racism is "normal" in our society. Racist assumptions about minorities pervade our mind-set and are reinforced in the media and popular culture. Race is encoded not merely in our laws, but in our cultural symbols such as movies, clothes, language, and music. Our commonsense assumptions about people of color are biased—"we are all racists."

2. Liberalism has failed to bring about parity between the races, for the simple reason that formal equality cannot eliminate deeply entrenched types of racism (sometimes called "microaggressions") which are encountered by minorities on a daily basis. Liberal solutions to affirmative action and free speech are *white* compromises which fail to significantly advance minority interests. Although liberalism professes to value equality, it actually prevents the radical reforms necessary to achieve true equality between the races.

3. CRT posits an "interest-convergence theory" which holds that the dominant white culture can tolerate minority successes only when these successes also serve the larger interests of whites. Major civil rights advances occur rarely, and only in situations where whites stand to benefit as well. Every movement toward change is a struggle against the dominant white culture. People of color can only achieve limited success under the current system.

4. CRT issues a "call to context" which rejects the formal perspective taken by white male scholars who subscribe to the "dominant narrative" of the law, whereby the law is seen as clear and neutral. CRT advocates a situated perspective which brings out the nuances of life as experienced by historically oppressed minorities. The dominant type of legal scholarship should be countered with techniques such as storytelling, science fiction, sarcasm, and parody.[8]

These lists differ slightly, but each captures the basic themes of CRT, and when read together they provide a fairly comprehensive and accurate blueprint for the work being done by critical race theorists. To be sure, not every article in Delgado's anthology hits these points on all fours, but each article focuses on at least one of the elements listed above. To get a feel for how CRT operates, we should examine two articles chosen more or less at random from the anthology: Thomas Ross's piece on the Supreme Court's decision in *City of Richmond v. J.A. Croson Co.,*[9] and Patricia Williams's autobiographical essay.[10] These articles are representative of CRT and will provide a suitable backdrop for my subsequent discussion.

The first essay discusses the *Richmond* case, in which the Supreme Court held a minority set-aside ordinance enacted by the City of Richmond unconstitutional. The ordinance required thirty percent of the subcontracting work for the City to be assigned to minority-owned firms; the law was designed to level the playing field after centuries of racism in the Richmond construction industry. The Court's majority ruled that the ordinance denied white contractors equal protection under the law (as required by the 14th Amendment) because the ordinance required the City to use race as a consideration in the awarding of city contracts.

The *Richmond* case is highly controversial, and it is not surprising to find a law professor like Thomas Ross arguing that it was wrongly decided. But one might expect his analysis to take place on doctrinal grounds, perhaps by advancing the argument that the 14th Amendment was intended to block laws which discriminated against blacks, and therefore does not bar an arrangement which provides reparation for past discrimination. That would be an argument about *doctrine*, because it would look to the Constitution and its history for a proper solution to the case. But CRT often eschews doctrine in favor of a different type of analysis, and so we find Professor Ross looking at the opinion in *Richmond* in terms of *narrative* and *rhetoric*. He argues that the concurring opinion by Justice Scalia focuses obsessively on the racial set-aside language of the ordinance without attempting to understand the racist context which it was designed to remedy. As Scalia describes the ordinance, one could get the false impression that it was enacted out of thin air by black City Council members as a way of hurting whites. In contrast, Justice Marshall's dissenting opinion takes history and context into account by providing a historical narrative about racism in the City of Richmond, seeing the ordinance as an overdue response to the legacy of racism in Richmond. Ross favors Marshall's account because it leads to "empathy," which might convince whites to favor the type of set-aside program enacted by the City. In a subtle and intriguing series of passages, Ross shows how Scalia turns the affirmative action debate on its head by portraying the white contractors as victims of the black councilmen, thereby distracting our attention from the centuries of racism in which whites oppressed blacks. According to Ross, Marshall's opinion subverts Scalia's maneuver and "invites the white reader to imagine the hurt and insult of racism."[11]

Several things are worth noting about the article. First, Ross does not set forth a doctrinal argument which proves (or attempts to convince his audience) that set-asides of the sort at issue are constitutional. Instead, it *begins* from the position that set-asides are legitimate, and then ferrets out the devious rhetorical devices (such as the avoidance of history and context) which Justice Scalia uses to reach a different conclusion. Second, notice the supposition that different Justices have different perspectives on the law simply because of their race: not only do Justices Scalia and Marshall think differently about the law, they also speak differently and have different narratives of the Constitution. Finally, note the implication that abstract, formal reasoning is less valuable than empathy and context.

Turning to the second article, Professor Williams's contribution is striking in that it does not discuss any recent cases, nor does it even address legal theory in the abstract. She begins with a fictional story about a power struggle in Celestial City, which is her way of telling a friend what the CLS movement is "really all about."[12] She eventually turns to an account of her attempt to rent an apartment in New York City so that she could team-teach a contracts course with Professor Peter Gabel, who was also looking for an apartment. It turns out that Gabel, who is white, was able to reach an oral lease agreement sealed by a handshake, whereas Williams felt compelled to draw up a formal lease agreement. Williams speculates that her need for a formal contract was motivated by the historical marginalization of black females: the formal agreement empowers her with the legal status which black females have been denied. After discussing this event at length, she recalls a childhood memory of riding in the family car and arguing with her sister about whether the road ahead was purple or black. Williams eventually bullied her sister into an admission that the road was black, but her father pointed out that her sister still saw the road as purple. From this event, Williams concludes that people have deeply entrenched viewpoints and that we should try to become good listeners to hear "the uncensored voices of others."[13] Williams recounts the feelings aroused by the knowledge that her great-great grandfather was a white slave owner and a lawyer. She talks about how this legacy has affected her and how she was driven at times by the "false idol of the white-man-within-me," and finally, she imagines a scenario in which she is asked to defend her great-great grandmother in court from being sold under a slave contract. She concludes the article with a somewhat kinetic passage which advocates giving rights to trees, cows, rivers, rocks, and even to "history."[14]

Notice the classic features of CRT embodied in Williams's article. First, the emphasis on storytelling and the subjective experience of race. Second, the notion that law must be understood by looking at the past treatment of women and minorities (in the slave-holding era) because the attitudes of this era affect our present perceptions of race. Third, the notion that race affects every aspect of our lives, from the way we wear our hair to the way we search for an apartment. Notice finally, the supposition that viewpoints are deeply entrenched and difficult to change. As with Professor Ross's article, there is little discussion of doctrine and no legal argument in the strict sense. Instead, the author's goal is to use a story or narrative to bring about a psychological shift in how we view the world. Professor Williams writes, "It is my hope that in redescribing the historical alchemy of rights in black lives, the reader will experience some reconnection with that part of the self and of society whose story unfolds beyond the neatly staked bounds of theoretical legal understanding."[15] Delgado and the other CRT founders praise this method in *Words That Wound*: "Critical race theorists embrace subjectivity of perspective and are avowedly political. . . . We use [   ] personal histories, parables, chronicles, dreams, stories, poetry, fiction, and revisionist histories to convey our message."[16]

Traditionally, law review articles have attempted to explain what the law is or should be on a particular subject by expounding theory, reviewing applicable precedents, or examining legislative histories. By eschewing traditional legal scholarship in favor of an avowedly politicized stance, critical race theorists hope to engage in a program of "challenging racial orthodoxy, shaking up the legal academy, questioning comfortable liberal premises, and leading the search for new ways of thinking about our nation's most intractable, and insoluable, problem—race."[17] No one should expect the traditional trappings of legal scholarship from CRT, and indeed CRT questions the very standards of the scholarship that hold sway in legal academia.

II. Two Good Points and Five Problems

Before I present five problem areas for CRT, I want to briefly mention two important points raised by the movement: the pervasiveness of racism, and the need to consider multiple perspectives in legal scholarship. To begin with, CRT is doubtless correct that racism is endemic in American society. Racism is deeply ingrained, not merely in certain aspects of our legal system, but in our collective unconscious and our everyday attitudes toward people of color.[18] And because racism is typically unconscious, it is notoriously difficult to bring into a light in which people can see it; everyday acts of racism are subtle and very difficult to regulate by law. This point is brought out nicely by Peggy Davis in her contribution, *Law as Microaggression*,[19] which documents the dozens of individual slights which affect minorities on a day-to-day basis. As Margaret Russell points out in her fine piece on law and popular narratives,[20] the dominant media (movies, TV) perpetuate denigrating and condescending images of minorities, images which find their way into the courtroom. This concern with racism at the level of ordinary experience has driven CRT toward the recent "cultural studies movement" in which popular images are dissected and examined for bias in race, class, and gender. This is an important line of research because it exposes racism where it is most intractable: at the core of our everyday assumptions and practices. And of course it follows that formal equality cannot eradicate *all* racism, because even when formal equality is mandated by law, the seemingly color-blind standards of law (reasonable doubt, legitimate force, due process) are applied differently to blacks and whites because of unconscious racism. There is a danger not only of racist laws (which are becoming less common), but also a danger of the racist application of neutral laws.

I also agree with CRT that legal scholarship should incorporate the perspectives of those who are denied a voice under the current legal system, people such as minorities, women, criminals, jurors, and the poor. For too long, legal scholarship has focused on the perspective of judges and lawyers, and if we get too wrapped up in this viewpoint we can become insensitive to the ways in which our practices affect everyday people who must live with the laws we enact and the cases we decide. There is much to be learned by comparing how black and white people see legal issues, and there is a good deal of research presented in this anthology which shows that perceptions of the legal system differ by race. For example, Delgado and Jean Stefancic point out that whites tend to favor an absolute position on freedom of speech because they see free speech as a safeguard for the maximum flow of information, whereas blacks are dubious of absolute freedom of speech because they bear the brunt of offensive speech.[21] Similarly, Peggy Davis points out that black jurors are more likely to see the criminal justice system as biased according to race and class,[22] and Sheri Lynn Johnson shows that this perception of bias is rooted in a legacy of racism at the hands of white judges and juries.[23] It stands to reason that if judges and lawyers see minorities in stereotypical and distorted ways (for example, that blacks are violent and overly sexual), then they will misjudge, for example, the degree of force that is "reasonable" when the police arrest a black male. CRT is correct to point out that if we want to determine if the legal system is biased against women and people of color, we should probably ask *them* for *their* impressions, rather than rest content with the accepted wisdom that the system is color-blind.

A. The Critique of Liberalism Needs to Be Focused

In *Critical Race Theory* we are informed that CRT is "discontent with liberalism," which is not uncommon nowadays, but "liberalism" is being understood as "a system of civil rights litigation and activism characterized by incrementalism, faith in the legal system, and hope for progress, among other things."[24] This is an unusual characterization of liberalism, which raises the question whether CRT is properly critiquing liberalism at all. According to most thinkers, the classic tenet of liberalism is that the right precedes the good: the state should be neutral between competing conceptions of the good life.[25] For liberals, the main purpose of the law is to protect citizens from harm by others (including the government and its agents), so that individuals can be free to pursue their own plans in free agreement with others. In exchange for state protection, the individual agrees to obey the law and not harm other people. This is the classical liberal position which runs through the work of John Stuart Mill, John Rawls, and Ronald Dworkin.[26] Typically, liberals endorse representative democracy and a limited welfare state, organized under a republic which follows the rule of law and guarantees the equality, liberty, and property interests of its citizens. Certainly liberals can disagree over political questions such as the proper extent of taxation or conscription, and they can also disagree on whether a liberal society should support affirmative action, euthanasia, or boxing. But liberalism is characterized by a core commitment to equal rights, autonomy, and due process. And so it is puzzling to see liberalism defined by Delgado (and others in CRT) as a movement distinguished by a belief in progress and a faith in the legal system.

This confusion is compounded by the readings under the heading "Critique of

Liberalism."[27] Nowhere in these readings is there any mention of Rawls, Dworkin, Mill, Kant, Locke, or any other classic or contemporary liberal. Instead, the first selection is a science fiction story by Derrick Bell in which aliens visit America to offer an economic and environmental bail-out in exchange for turning over all of the black people, who will then be taken up into space and never seen again.[28] Bell sketches a situation in which the dominant white society accepts this trade and imposes it on the black citizens by amending the Constitution so that the trade is rendered constitutional. Bell says that the hypothetical trade would probably be accepted by white Americans, and he argues (without much evidence) that middle and lower-class whites seem to accept the income gap which separates them from upper-class whites because they retain a "property right in their whiteness" which elevates them above blacks. He concludes with the pessimistic claim that minorities cannot continue in a cycle of "progress and reform" because "[p]olitics, the courts, and self-help have failed or proved to be inadequate,"[29] which (I suppose) means that black progress requires some sort of revolution.

It is difficult to see what Bell's article has to do with liberalism, and the subsequent selection takes us even farther afield. Michael Olivas tells us that Bell's figurative trade with space aliens has already occurred in American history, in the antebellum South, for example, when the lives of blacks were sacrificed to benefit whites, and in the forced westward march of Native Americans so that whites could take Indian land, and in the exclusion of the Chinese under draconian immigration laws.[30] These historical accounts are intertwined with reminiscences about Olivas's grandfather and the stories he told, but there is nothing on liberalism as a doctrine. In the final article offered as a critique of liberalism, Girardeau Spann argues that the Supreme Court has become a majoritarian force (read: a *white* force) aligned against minority interests, such that a "rational minority response . . . would be to abandon efforts to influence the Court and to concentrate minority political activities on the representative branches."[31] In other words, minorities should give up trying to seek legal reforms on the ground that they are required by justice, and instead should seek empowerment in other branches (hence Spann's appeal to "pure politics," as opposed to the impure politics of the judiciary).

All of this is interesting in terms of strategy and legal history but it gets us nowhere as a critique of liberalism. And indeed, none of these selections challenge liberalism as a theoretical approach, except to say that the civil rights movement advanced by liberalism has not brought about perfect equality between the races, and that the liberal legal reforms of the 1960s have been a hollow hope, a failure. But I doubt that liberals ever believed that legal reform alone would magically eliminate all vestiges of racism. Liberals, I think, felt that the battle against racism should be fought on all fronts, including legal reform, and that we should do our best to eliminate discrimination in as many contexts as possible (housing, education, employment), and enact affirmative action schemes in the hope that they withstand constitutional muster. Liberals hope for a better, fairer society, and while it is true that our society has made only modest gains in this direction, this is not the fault of liberalism as a doctrine. It is due rather to the inequalities in wealth and political power which predated liberal reform and which liberals are trying to remedy. To fault liberalism for the oppression and inequality of blacks or for the mistreatment of Native Americans and Chinese immigrants is to lay blame with the wrong party. Further, Spann's and Bell's rejection of attempts to work within the legal system bespeaks a kind of fatalism that one wouldn't expect to find in law professors who are concerned with civil rights. The deeper problem, however, is that none of these articles deals with liberalism as a *theory*.

Perhaps a more subtle critique of liberalism can be found in the work of critical race theorist Mari Matsuda, who, in another context, has made the argument that when the liberal state tolerates racial epithets under the guise of free speech, the state is actually *promoting* racist speech. That is, by remaining neutral, the state authorizes hate speech:

> [T]olerance and protection of hate group activity by the government is a form of state action.... To allow an organization known for violence, persecution, race hatred, and commitment to racial supremacy to exist openly and to provide police protection [for such groups] means that the state is promoting racist speech.... *State silence . . . is public action. . . .*[32]

The argument here is that the state cannot be neutral, so it should not try to be. Since the state must promote a particular view, it should take the high road and come out against racist speech.

The error here, I think, is to conflate state tolerance of hate speech with state promotion of such speech. Matsuda's analysis cannot account for cases in which the state allows speech on both sides of an issue. For example, the State of Illinois recently allowed a demonstration by the KKK and a simultaneous counter-demonstration for ethnic diversity to take place side-by-side: would Matsuda have us believe that Illinois was simultaneously promoting racism *and* ethnic diversity? Matsuda's argument that state tolerance of speech is equal to promotion of such speech would also require the absurd result that the government encourages violent revolution against itself because it allows Maoists and Anarchists to hold rallies. Isn't it simply more accurate in these cases to say that the state is providing a neutral forum for speech, that the state *can* be neutral when it wants to be?

Matsuda is upset that the state permits racist speech because she thinks that "the state is the official embodiment of the society we live in,"[33] and since our society should not be racist, neither should it tolerate racist speech. This essay overlooks the fact that the state itself can be neutral or even anti-racist in its own actions and speech while simultaneously tolerating racist speech by private parties. A deeper concern is that Matsuda's claim smacks of the far-right notion that the state should advance a particular moral agenda rather than allow its citizens to choose their own agenda (however noxious) through public debate; far from being radical, this is a view which sits comfortably with conservatives. It was precisely under dubious appeals to the state as the embodiment of "moral fiber" and "blood and soil" that past governments were given too much power to regulate speech and conduct. If Matsuda got her wish and the state were magically transformed so that it "embodies the society we live in," then minorities would suffer, not gain, because our society can be quite racist.

I am not persuaded by those sections of the anthology that set out CRT's critique of liberalism. Given liberalism's emphasis on individual dignity, fairness, and due process, it would seem that CRT should embrace the fundamental tenets of liberalism, especially because liberals have been active supporters of minority rights since the early 1960s. If indeed CRT finds it necessary to critique liberalism as a doctrine, then it must do so in the proper way, by looking at key liberal theorists and pointing out their errors. This requires an engagement with Rawls, Dworkin, and Feinberg, an engagement which CRT has yet to initiate. Finally, if liberalism is to be rejected, we must find a replacement approach and understand how this new approach will preserve individual rights. Solving this problem would be a worthwhile project for a critical race scholar.

B. The Danger of Narcissism

Sigmund Freud once used the expression "narcissism of minor differences" to denote how various ethnic groups proclaim their uniqueness and superiority over other ethnicities based upon a handful of idiosyncratic traits, when in fact they are not very different from the other groups.[34] Freud's terminology seems to fit much of the work being done in CRT to the extent that many critical race theorists end up writing about themselves on the ground that their personal experience is unique and that there is something special that they can contribute because they are black, Latino, Asian, and so on. So instead of writing an article on why a particular law is wrong or unconstitutional, the critical race scholar provides a "raced" or "situated" analysis along the lines of: The Black View of Case *X*, or The Latino Perspective on Statute *Y*. Inevitably the authors of these types of articles write about the perspective of those who share their ethnicity. I must admit some reservations about the ultimate value of this scholarship.

In *Critical Race Theory* we find Jennifer Russell writing about what it is like to be a black woman law professor;[35] Margaret Montoya (a Latina law professor) writing about what it is like to grow up Latina and to attend Harvard Law School;[36] Robert Chang writing about what it is like to be an Asian-American legal writing instructor;[37] and Alan Freeman (a white law professor) writing about how his whiteness is an "inescapable feature" and an "uncrossable gap" which might render him incapable of truly contributing to CRT.[38]

Many of these writers are writing about themselves, and not just about how this or that event has influenced them (for example, how growing up black has motivated someone to be a civil rights lawyer), but writing about deeply personal events that are seemingly unrelated to legal questions. For example, two authors in this collection discuss in detail how they wear their hair, one article starting with the refrain, "I want to know my hair again, to own it, to delight in it again."[39] Generally speaking, articles in this vein have a similar format: first a series of personal stories and memoirs, then a discussion of cases and statutes from 1750 to 1950 in which courts have been insensitive to the target group, and then a conclusion which states that prejudice is still alive and well today. In most articles there is little discussion of the law as it is now, although abominations like *Dred Scott v. Sandford*,[40] *Plessy v. Ferguson*,[41] and *Korematsu v. United States*[42] are repeatedly mentioned. And when recent cases are mentioned, they are often discussed without an effort by the author to see both sides of the issue—to see how the court could have reached its decision.

CRT's message about the legacy of racism is important, but one gets the impression that writing these pieces is a relatively easy game to play, that all one needs is an angle, a personal trait which can serve as an entrance into the game; and if one possesses several angles, she can write about how these facets intersect, that is, what it is like to lie at the "intersectionality" of blackness and femininity,[43] or to be Latino and gay.

I am not a critical race scholar but I could probably produce a manuscript in this vein in a relatively short time by following the standard format. I would begin with a story about what it was like to grow up Jewish, how I went to temple, celebrated Passover, got ridiculed by kids at school, heard people refer to Jews as "kikes," went to Germany and became depressed about the Holocaust, how I see swastikas in the bathrooms at the school where I teach, and so on. I could then discuss how Jews were discriminated against here in America, how we couldn't attend certain schools, couldn't vacation in certain places. And I could conclude by saying that anti-Semitism still exists today and that we should be on the lookout for it.

But we need to ask where these stories and narratives lead in the law, especially constitutional law. The answer is nowhere. The reason for this is that in most cases the law does not turn on my private story about growing up Jewish, nor does it turn on anybody's personal account of being black, Hispanic, and so on: these are *private* issues; the law turns on *public* issues.

To see this, consider what would happen if I (or any other Jew) were asked to determine, first as a Jew, then as a judge, the infamous case *Village of Skokie v. National Socialist Party of America*.[44] How would my situated perspective as a Jew differ from my perspective as a judge in reaching an answer to the question whether the Nazis have the right to march in a predominantly Jewish suburb? Would my raised consciousness as a Jew somehow transform my judicial opinion from a generic opinion into a Jewish opinion?

Perhaps I am naïve, but it seems that my status as a Jew really doesn't matter when it comes time to rule on the constitutionality of the ordinance in *Skokie*, because that issue turns on a public question about the Constitution as it affects all Americans, not on the private question about what it is like for me to be a Jew. Certainly, as a Jew I have some insights into the horrors of Nazism, but this, standing alone, does not give me a privileged interpretation of the Constitution as it affects Jews and Nazis. If anything, it might distort my view of the Constitution, making me a poor judge of the law. My "raised consciousness" is useful in the sense that I will be unlikely to hold mistaken beliefs about Jews, but my decision in this case will come down to constitutional doctrine, and the right decision in *Skokie* is the right decision for us all—black, white, Jew, Asian, and, I suppose, Nazi.

Much CRT scholarship seems to be infused with the mistaken notion that blacks have a unique ability to write about how the law affects blacks, that only Hispanics can really see how the law affects Hispanics, that white judges can't act as good judges in cases involving these "out-groups." So the movement can easily fracture into a composite of diverse people who write about themselves and their out-group; each person claims a scholarship interest in his own ethnicity or gender or both. The notion that each race has a unique view of the law is common in CRT, as we can see from the following reading of *Plessy* and *Brown v. Board of Education*[45] by a black

CRT scholar: "From a white perspective, it is unclear what is wrong with separate but equal, but when one takes a black perspective, it is easy to see why *Plessy* was wrong and why *Brown* was constitutionally right."[46] This passage ignores the point that the Constitution (and other laws) are public documents that affect all of us regardless of our race—so *Plessy* was wrong from *any* decent perspective, and *Brown* was right from *any* perspective; it is not a question of black and white, but a question of right and wrong.

Part of the problem here is that CRT seems to fall victim to balkanization, a splintering effect in which each racial, ethnic, or gender category becomes a unitary focus, to the neglect of the fragile overlapping consensus which binds us. Thus Paulette Caldwell contributes *A Hair Piece*[47] which goes into great detail about her own hair as a way of exploring the issues raised in a federal case which upheld the right of American Airlines to prohibit a black employee from wearing her hair in braids.[48] The court found that the company's rule against braided hair applied neutrally to both blacks and whites (at the time, the movie "10" had popularized braided hair for white women), and the court also pointed out that the rule did not discriminate against an immutable racial characteristic of blacks, such as bushy hair or dark skin. This was a controversial decision, and, like Caldwell, I disagree with the court's ruling; but the wrongfulness of the decision is not really affected in any way (nor is any light shed on the decision) by finding out how Caldwell wears her own hair. The implication from Caldwell's discussion of her hair is that she has special knowledge of this case because she is black, a special ability to see that the court was wrong. But we don't need an argument against a bad decision from a *black* perspective; we need an argument that works from *all* reasonable perspectives, especially if we want to convince people who are outside our race and ethnicity.

C. The Trouble with Storytelling

Much of CRT revolves around personal stories which are drawn from the experiences of minority law professors, detailing not only negative experiences such as name calling and ostracism, but also positive aspects of their heritage, such as racial solidarity, the importance of tradition and honor, and the struggle against oppression. In a useful contribution to the anthology, Daniel Farber and Suzanna Sherry identify three features of the new storytelling:

> First, the storytellers view narratives as central to scholarship, while de-emphasizing conventional analytic methods. Second, they particularly value "stories from the bottom"—stories by women and people of color about their oppression. Third, they are less concerned than conventional scholars about whether stories are either typical or descriptively accurate, and they place more emphasis on the aesthetic and emotional dimensions of narration.[49]

This approach is borne out in many selections from the anthology, including Patricia Williams's story about renting an apartment in New York City,[50] Margaret Montoya's reminiscences of braiding her hair in the Latina style,[51] and Jennifer Russell's explanation of how she feels like a "gorilla in your midst" as a black female in the legal academy (in a nauseating act of racism, a photograph of a gorilla was placed in her mailbox).[52] In a representative article on the power of narratives, Richard Delgado describes the hiring procedure at a law school which rejects a candidate of color, recasting the story from three different perspectives—the "stock story" of the white professor on the hiring committee, and two "counterstories" from a radical activist of color and an anonymous commentator.[53]

All of this storytelling is interesting, even fascinating, but I think it can be dangerous as well. As lawyers, we seek doctrinal solutions to problems, and indeed this is precisely what distinguishes us from the public at large. For example, the general public is free to see a criminal trial (O.J. Simpson's, say) as a story about good and evil, black and white, or love and hate, whereas lawyers see it through the filter of the law—in terms of probable cause, hearsay exceptions, burdens of proof, permissible jury instructions, rights to suppress evidence, and so on. *We are lawyers precisely because we do something more than listen to stories: we filter stories through the framework of legal doctrine.* While it may be useful for lawyers to see the facts of a case as a narrative construction, or even to think of the law itself as a work of fiction,[54] lawyers must look beyond stories to questions of doctrine, policy, and argument.

There is a danger in storytelling precisely because it can lead in any and every direction, politically speaking. It is true that narratives about oppressed groups often lead to left-leaning social reform for the simple reason that narratives tend to humanize people whom we would otherwise consider outsiders. For example, when we read in the anthology about the experiences of minority CRT scholars struggling against racism, we begin to identify with them, and, frankly, we start rooting for them. Of course, if one identifies with people of color or with women, it is possible that one will be more likely to understand their side of an issue.

But this cuts both ways. If one set of narratives can make us *more* sympathetic to people of color, it stands to reason that a different set of narratives can make us *less* sensitive. Indeed, Delgado contributes an article[55] to the collection which recognizes that black thinkers like Shelby Steele and Stephen Carter make use of stories, irony, and humor to send a conservative message that contrasts with the narratives offered by CRT scholars Derrick Bell and Patricia Williams. We can easily imagine the emergence of narratives and stories in which white authors describe the experience of being denied entry into professional schools when they would have been accepted had they been black or female. In extreme cases it might be imagined that such authors would use storytelling to glorify a white utopian society without minorities. The error by CRT is to think that storytelling is inherently liberating when in fact it is inherently neutral—neither liberal nor conservative, neither constraining nor freeing.

Another danger of legal storytelling is that it plays upon emotion, instead of reason, and therefore it can convince people to adopt a position without giving them a doctrinal basis for it. Suppose you were uncommitted in the last presidential election, and I wanted to persuade you to vote for Bill Clinton. One method that I might use would be to cite Clinton's accomplishments, his attempt to balance the budget, his health-care proposal, or his record of judicial appointments. These are all relevant points because they bear directly on his ability to serve the country. But now suppose that I suddenly realize that these arguments, while relevant, may not work; in fact, you stand ready to present some counter-evidence against my points. In that case, I might switch tactics and try to convince you by telling a story. I might tell you about what it was like for Clinton to grow up as a poor child in the rural South, how he struggled from humble beginnings to realize the American dream of becoming President. My goal would be to move you emotionally so that you undergo a psychological conversion in which you find yourself voting for him even though you remain unconvinced of his qualifications. The problem with convincing people in this way is that it is circuitous and skirts the real issues; it is a way of convincing people at any cost, in order to serve a higher cause. CRT sometimes works similarly, where issues that should be decided on doctrinal grounds by looking at federal law (issues like affirmative action, free speech, and criminal sentencing) are determined by stories, personal accounts, and other miscellanea.

It is somewhat difficult to make sense of CRT's turn away from doctrine. In this anthology we find Alan Freeman praising Derrick Bell for his lack of doctrinal argument:

> Bell's approach to legal doctrine is unabashedly instrumental. The only important question is whether doctrinal developments have improved, worsened, or left unchanged the actual lives of American blacks. . . . Bell eschews the realm of abstract, ahistorical, normative debate; he focuses instead on the relationships between doctrine and concrete change, and the extent to which doctrine can be manipulated to produce more change.[56]

I am disturbed by the notion that doctrine (constitutional doctrine, no less) is understood by Bell to be merely "instrumental" and something to be "manipulated" to satisfy the all-important test of black empowerment. After all, if the law is to be judged simply as an instrument for black empowerment, then the best legal system would be one which helps blacks at any cost, for example, by "manipulating" legal doctrine through "instrumental" measures like exempting blacks from income tax, requiring whites to give a tithe to the NAACP, redistributing white pensions to blacks, and appointing only blacks to the judiciary. But these changes in the law would violate deeply held notions of fairness, property, and due process. Bell's self-professed "racial realism" seems to be radical and tough-minded, but it sanctions some irresponsible legal reforms.

As a final point about storytelling, I am concerned about the potential for self-stereotyping that occurs when minority law professors write stories instead of producing exhaustively researched law review articles. The idea that minorities are specially endowed with story-telling abilities but not with analytical skills is precisely the type of stereotype that should be countered.

D. The Fatalistic Pseudoscience of Interest Convergence

It was once (and perhaps remains) a tenet of ultra-orthodox Marxism that the bourgeoisie tolerates advances by the proletariat only when such advances also benefit the bourgeoisie to an even greater extent. This was not called an interest-convergence theory at the time, but it might as well have been. The Marxist formula was designed to advance the party line about the intractability of class warfare and the impossibility of progress without full-scale communist revolution. After all, there is no point in pursuing piecemeal reform when every step forward for the workers is an even greater step for the owners.

The problem with the Marxist formula was that it was a piece of pseudoscience incapable of demonstration or refutation. For example, if one pointed out to the ultra-Marxist that the New Deal of the 1930s was an advance for the proletariat, the Marxist could respond by saying that the New Deal was really motivated by the need for capitalists to keep the economy going, so the real beneficiaries were the bourgeoisie. The Marxist claim was pseudoscience because the Marxist refused to specify the evidence that would refute his claim: indeed, no evidence could disprove the claim, because any evidence against the claim was simply reinterpreted as evidence in favor of it.

Philosophers can recall a similar situation with the position known as "psychological egoism," which in its strongest version holds that everybody always acts self-interestedly. When the person who holds this view is asked to explain why people give anonymous gifts to charity and risk their lives fighting for others, she responds by redescribing these selfless acts as really egotistical, saying that if we really understood the person's true motivations, we would see that they were acting egotistically. There is certainly no way to prove or disprove psychological egoism as a doctrine; the best we can do is to say that it fails to describe the facts of life as we experience them, that it is a poor interpretation of human behavior.

The same can be said for the much-vaunted interest convergence thesis, which finds its way into a fair amount of CRT scholarship. The interest-convergence thesis originated with Derrick Bell, whose view is paraphrased by Delgado as follows: "whites will advance the cause of racial justice only when doing so coincides with their own self-interest."[57] According to some critical race theorists, "civil rights law was never designed to help blacks,"[58] and decisions like *Brown* were decided not on the basis of racial justice, but as a mechanism for whites to win the Cold War.[59]

On its face, the interest-convergence thesis is a strange claim. After all, the whole point of the desegregation cases, the Voting Rights Act, Title VII, and so on, was to advance black interests by eradicating racism. The Court's decision in *Brown* makes no mention of the Cold War or the interests of the dominant white culture in desegregation. There have indeed been cases in which the Court was motivated by alleged interests of national security, as in the disastrous *Korematsu* decision, but in that case the Court told us what it was doing, for better or worse. All of this goes to show that there is little direct evidence that the decision in *Brown* was meant to help whites more than blacks. Furthermore, if desegregation and affirmative action benefitted whites, why were whites so resistant to them?[60]

According to Delgado's interpretation, the interest-convergence theory is confirmed by our experience with affirmative action, which he describes as a "majoritarian device" designed to benefit whites.[61] According to Delgado, affirmative action is not intended to help blacks, but to assuage white guilt and to absolve whites from taking further steps toward racial justice:

> Crits [critical race theorists] point out that periodic victories—*Brown v. Board of Education*, the 1964 Civil Rights Act—are trumpeted as proof that our system is fair and just, but are then quickly stolen away by narrow judicial construction, foot-dragging, and delay. The celebrations

assure everyone that persons of color are now treated fairly in virtually every area of life. . . .
With all that, if blacks are still not achieving, well, what can be done?[62]

The implication here is that whites benefit from affirmative action more than blacks, hence the convergence of interests in which the modest gains by blacks are outweighed by gains for whites. This comment seems to confuse cause and effect, however. The "periodic victories" to which Delgado refers were caused by a concern for black equality as a matter of justice; it makes little sense to recharacterize these victories as "allowed by whites." With regard to affirmative action schemes, Delgado is probably correct that some whites have become complacent about advancing black interests, or that some whites have had their guilt assuaged since these programs became popular, but this is hardly what one would call a "benefit" that whites receive from affirmative action. In any event, there is no evidence that whites allow affirmative action because it benefits them, and in fact the opposite is true—most whites who endorse affirmative action (myself included) believe that it will work to their personal detriment, but nevertheless feel that it is required by justice.

The interest-convergence thesis seems to hold that blacks can advance *only* when whites also advance, or in other words, that in every case where blacks advance, whites also advance. This blanket statement can be refuted by a single instance (a single piece of legislation or a single court decision) in which blacks gained and whites did not. Examples of this abound—affirmative action, Title VII, fair housing laws, and prohibitions on red-lining. To say that these much-needed reforms were really an advancement for whites is to reinterpret the facts in a way that is highly implausible.

But even if the interest-convergence theory were true, what would follow from it? How would it alter the project of reforming the law to achieve greater racial justice? As far as I can tell, it would have absolutely no effect on the effort to defend affirmative action, to push for redistricting of congressional seats, and to advocate greater minority representation in the judiciary. The only effect of the interest-convergence thesis is one of fatalism, to paint a picture of heroic struggle against impossible odds. I can't see how this attitude advances people of color, and I don't see what CRT has to lose by abandoning the interest-convergence thesis.

E. "Outsiders" and "Insiders"

Much of the cachet of CRT is purchased on the notion that it fosters a new type of "outsider jurisprudence" which subverts the "dominant narrative" of the law in favor of accounts which are highly personal and grounded in the social reality and unique experience of the author.[63] According to Mari Matsuda, this is part of an attempt to "know history from the bottom" and to reject views of the world which are "androcentric, Eurocentric, and falsely universalist."[64] Delgado echoes this theme by saying that mainstream scholars have erred by endorsing universalism over particularity, by favoring abstract principles and the rule of law over multiple perspectives.[65] The subtext of these messages is that outsiders (read: women and people of color) have a unique view of the legal system that cannot be fully understood by white male insiders. Matsuda says that minorities have a "special voice,"[66] and Delgado suggests that "[t]he time has come for white liberal authors . . . to redirect their efforts [and make way for] talented and innovative minority writers and commentators."[67] He reports:

> [N]early three-fourths of articles on equality or civil rights published in the leading journals during the last five years were written by women or minorities. Ten years ago, the situation was reversed: minorities were beginning to publish, but their work was largely ignored. The same is true in other areas as well. Critical legal studies and other modernist and postmodern approaches to law are virtually the norm in the top reviews. Formalism has run its course.[68]

Now it is somewhat ironic that so many self-titled "outsiders" are sitting on the faculties at top law schools and publishing in the best law journals. When seventy-five percent of the articles on civil rights are written by "outsiders," then the term is no longer meaningfully applied. The problem here is not only that the term "outsider" is being misused, but more broadly that it is increasingly hard to find an outside to the "outsider" view. This is an obscure way of saying that many of the CRT articles focus so heavily on the outsider view that they totally neglect any other vantage point. The outside perspective is valuable in the first place because it provides check and balance against the views of the insiders; so that what results is an overall balance between inside and outside. And that is our goal—a balanced view.

When a majority of scholars claim to be outsiders, it is hard to find an insider viewpoint to balance the outsider viewpoint. This may sound like an overly academic concern, but it is a very real problem owing to CRT's rejection of the notion that scholarship should consider all sides of an issue. In discussing the First Amendment concerns raised by speech codes on college campuses, the editors of *Words That Wound* admit that: "We do not attempt to present all sides to this debate. Rather we present a dissenting view grounded in our experiences as people of color. . . ."[69] Similarly, when Delgado discusses a decision by a law school hiring committee to reject a candidate of color, he does not present the school's position in its best light, but rather assumes that the school's explanation is bogus and proceeds to examine how the school's decision can be attacked by counter-stories and demonstrations.[70] What is lacking here is balance, nuance, and a weighing of competing interests and accounts, not to mention the principle of charity whereby one criticizes an argument by first placing it in its best light. In Delgado's hypothetical case, the law school's hiring committee was concerned that the black candidate had not published anything and was unable to teach a course in commerical law; these are real lacunae that would hold back any candidate, white or black, but Delgado dismisses the committee's concerns as "deeply coercive."[71] In a separate article, Thomas Ross criticizes the notion that there are "innocent whites" who are harmed by affirmative action,[72] yet he fails to consider the perspectives of, for example, poor Appalachian males or recent immigrants who are denied spots in professional schools to make way for blacks who were raised in wealthy families. It simply will not do to say that *all* whites are equally complicitous in this country's legacy of racism and that *all* blacks are innocent victims; what results is a somewhat simplistic universe of oppressors and oppressed, sketched in black and white. What is missing here, I think, is what is missing in much of CRT work: balance, nuance, and a weighing of insider and outsider perspectives.

III. CRT as Consciousness Raising

I think we can put CRT in its best light by seeing it as a form of what Marxists and feminists refer to as consciousness raising. That is, CRT elevates our sensitivity to racial issues and gives us a heightened awareness of what it is like to experience the sting of racism. And there is no question that it accomplishes this goal. One emerges from reading this anthology (and from reading other CRT articles) with a new sensibility, as if one is seeing the world through a new set of eyes. This alone is worthwhile for at least three reasons: it clarifies and brings to the fore the racist stereotypes and assumptions which pervade our psyches; it reminds us of our brutal history of racial prejudice and exclusion; and it humanizes people of color so they do not seem so Other, and instead appear as living, breathing people who deserve equal treatment.

But there is a problematic assumption running through much CRT scholarship to the effect that once our consciousness has been raised through narratives and stories, the correct legal decision will immediately become clear to us. That is, judges and lawyers who genuinely understand the experiences of people of color will start making decisions that will benefit these "out-groups." But is this a correct assumption? I think not, for the simple reason that a raised consciousness is no guarantee that a particular decision will be chosen. This can be seen by the rise of African-American intellectuals who have experienced stinging acts of racism yet remain staunchly opposed to affirmative action and set-asides, on doctrinal grounds. The very existence of neoconservative black intellectuals like Stephen Carter and Shelby Steele (not to mention Justice Clarence Thomas and law professor Randall Kennedy) militates against the idea that the subjective experience of racism will automatically lead to some sort of psychological conversion in which judges and lawyers will know how to "do the right thing."

CRT acts as a sort of disinfectant which dispels some widely-held misconceptions about people of color, assumptions which are often held unconsciously by judges and lawyers. A judge who has read the works of Patricia Williams and Derrick Bell may be less likely to hold stereotypical, denigrating views of black people, and while this may not affect every decision that she makes, it can have a certain salutary effect. And the importance of this gestalt switch, this psychological conversion in how one sees minorities, should not be minimized, because many judges and lawyers carry around distorted beliefs on racial matters.

But even when CRT has raised our consciousness to the point where it is clear of racism (or at least relatively clear of it), there remains a separate debate which must take place at the level of legal doctrine, where we discuss theoretical questions of equality, fairness, due process, and desert. Assuming that CRT wants to contribute something more than consciousness raising, it needs to address this doctrinal, theoretical level, and to make the constitutional arguments that appeal to all of us (black, white, Asian), because we are splintered enough as it is.

Notes

1. *See* Richard Delgado & Jean Stefancic, *Critical Race Theory: An Annotated Bibliography*, 79 Va. L. Rev. 461 (1993); Richard Delgado & Jean Stefancic, *Critical Race Theory: An Annotated Bibliography: 1993, A Year of*

Transition, 66 U. Colo. L. Rev. 159 (1994); *see also* Symposium, *Critical Race Theory*, 82 Cal. L. Rev. 741 (1994); Symposium, *Race Consciousness and Legal Scholarship*, 1992 U. Ill. L. Rev. 945 (1992).

2. Critical Race Theory: The Cutting Edge (Richard Delgado ed., 1995) [hereinafter Critical Race Theory].

3. Mari J. Matsuda et al., Words That Wound: Critical Race Theory, Assaultive Speech, and the First Amendment (1993).

4. Critical Race Theory, *supra* note 2, at 159–69. Richard Delgado's *Words That Wound: A Tort Action for Racial Insults, Epithets, and Name Calling*, 17 Harv. C.R.-C.L. L. Rev. 133 (1982), is reproduced more fully in Matsuda et al., *supra* note 3, at 89, 89–110.

5. *See, e.g.*, Stephen L. Carter, *Academic Tenure and "White Male" Standards: Some Lessons from the Patent Law*, 100 Yale L.J. 2065 (1991).

6. *See, e.g.*, Richard A. Posner, *Nuance, Narrative, and Empathy in Critical Race Theory, in* Overcoming Law 368, 368–84 (1995).

7. This is paraphrased from Charles R. Lawrence III et al., *Introduction to* Matsuda et al., *supra* note 3, at 1, 6–7.

8. This is paraphrased from Richard Delgado, *Introduction to* Critical Race Theory, *supra* note 2, at xiii, xiii–xvi. For contrast, see Delgado's eight-point list of CRT themes in Richard Delgado, *When a Story Is Just a Story: Does Voice Really Matter?*, 76 Va. L. Rev. 95, 95 n.1 (1990).

9. 488 U.S. 469 (1989); *see* Thomas Ross, *The Richmond Narratives, in* Critical Race Theory, *supra* note 2, at 38, 38–47.

10. Patricia J. Williams, *Alchemical Notes: Reconstructing Ideals from Deconstructed Rights, in* Critical Race Theory, *supra* note 2, at 84, 84–94.

11. Ross, *supra* note 9, at 45.

12. Williams, *supra* note 10, at 85.

13. *Id.* at 89.

14. *Id.* at 92–93.

15. *Id.* at 86.

16. Lawrence et al., *supra* note 7, at 3–5.

17. Richard Delgado, *Introduction to* Critical Race Theory, *supra* note 2, at xiii, xiii.

18. On this point, see Charles R. Lawrence III, *The Id, the Ego, and Equal Protection: Reckoning with Unconscious Racism*, 39 Stan. L. Rev. 317 (1987).

19. Peggy C. Davis, *Law as Microagression, in* Critical Race Theory, *supra* note 2, at 169, 169–79.

20. Margaret M. Russell, *Race and the Dominant Gaze: Narratives of Law and Inequality in Popular Film, in* Critical Race Theory, *supra* note 2, at 56, 56–63.

21. Richard Delgado & Jean Stefancic, *Images of the Outsider In American Law and Culture: Can Free Expression Remedy Systemic Social Ills?, in* Critical Race Theory, *supra* note 2, at 217, 217–27.

22. Davis, *supra* note 19, at 174–77.

23. Sheri Lynn Johnson, *Black Innocence and the White Jury, in* Critical Race Theory, *supra* note 2, at 180, 180–90.

24. Critical Race Theory, *supra* note 2, at 1.

25. According to Michael Sandel:

> [Liberalism's] core thesis can be stated as follows: society, being composed of a plurality of persons, each with his own aims, interests and conception of the good, is best arranged when it is governed by principles that do not *themselves* presuppose any particular conception of the good . . . but rather that they conform to the concept of *right*, a moral category given prior to the good and independent of it.

Michael J. Sandel, Liberalism and the Limits of Justice 1 (1982).

26. *See* Ronald Dworkin, *Liberalism, in* Liberalism and Its Critics 64 (Michael Sandel ed., 1985) ("[For the liberal,] political decisions must be, so far as is possible, independent of any particular conception of the good life, or of what gives value to life.").

27. Critical Race Theory, *supra* note 2, at 1–36.

28. Derrick Bell, *Racial Realism—After We're Gone: Prudent Speculations on America in a Post-Racial Epoch, in* Critical Race Theory, *supra* note 2, at 2, 2–8.

29. *Id.* at 8.

30. Michael A. Olivas, *The Chronicles, My Grandfather's Stories, and Immigration Law: The Slave Traders Chronicle as Racial History, in* Critical Race Theory, *supra* note 2, at 9, 9–20.

31. Girardeau A. Spann, *Pure Politics, in* Critical Race Theory, *supra* note 2, at 21, 31.

32. Mari J. Matsuda, *Public Response to Racist Speech: Considering the Victim's Story, in* Matsuda et al., *supra* note 3, at 19, 48–49 (emphasis added).

33. *Id.* at 49.

34. Sigmund Freud, Civilization and Its Discontents 68 (James Strachey trans. & ed., W.W. Norton 1961).

35. Jennifer M. Russell, *On Being a Gorilla in Your Midst, or, The Life of One Black Woman in the Legal Academy, in* Critical Race Theory, *supra* note 2, at 498, 498–50.

36. Margaret E. Montoya, Máscaras, Trenzas, y Greñas: *Un/masking the Self While Un/braiding Latina Stories and Legal Discourse, in* Critical Race Theory, *supra* note 2, at 529, 529–39.

37. Robert S. Chang, *Toward an Asian American Legal Scholarship: Critical Race Theory, Post Structuralism, and Narrative Space, in* Critical Race Theory, *supra* note 2, at 322, 322–36.

38. Alan D. Freeman, *Racism, Rights, and the Quest for Equality of Opportunity,* Harv. C.R.-C.L. L. Rev. 295, 299 (1988).

39. Paulette M. Caldwell, *A Hair Piece: Perspectives on the Intersection of Race and Gender, in* Critical Race Theory, *supra* note 2, at 267, 267–77.

40. 60 U.S. (19 How.) 393 (1857).

41. 163 U.S. 537 (1896).

42. 323 U.S. 214 (1944).

43. For example, see Kimberlè Crenshaw's discussion of her "intersectionality" as black and female, in Kimberlè Crenshaw, *Beyond Racism and Misogyny: Black Feminism and 2 Live Crew, in* Matsuda et al., *supra* note 3, at 111, 113.

44. 373 N.E.2d 21 (Ill. 1978).

45. 347 U.S. 483 (1954).

46. Jerome McCristal Culp, Jr., *Toward a Black Legal Scholarship: Race and Original Understandings,* 1991 Duke L.J. 39, 57 (1991).

47. Caldwell, *supra* note 39, at 267–77.

48. *See* Rogers v. American Airlines, 527 F. Supp. 229 (S.D.N.Y. 1981).

49. Daniel A. Farber & Suzanna Sherry, *Telling Stories Out of School: An Essay on Legal Narratives, in* Critical Race Theory, *supra* note 2, at 283, 283.

50. Williams, *supra* note 10, at 86–87.

51. Montoya, *supra* note 36, at 529–39.

52. Russell, *supra* note 35, at 498–501.

53. Richard Delgado, *Legal Storytelling: Storytelling for Oppositionists and Others: A Plea for Narrative, in* Critical Race Theory, *supra* note 2, at 64, 64–74.

54. *See e.g.,* Ronald Dworkin, *How Law Is Like Literature, in* A Matter of Principle 146, 146–66 (1985).

55. Richard Delgado, *Beyond Criticism—Synthesis? Left-Right Parallels in Recent Writing About Race, in* Critical Race Theory, *supra* note 2, at 464, 464–73.

56. Alan D. Freeman, *Derrick Bell—Race and Class: The Dilemma of Liberal Reform, in* Critical Race Theory, *supra* note 2, at 458, 458–59.

57. Delgado, *supra* note 55, at 466 (paraphrasing Derrick Bell from Derrick A. Bell, Jr., Brown v. Board of Education and the Interest-Convergence Dilemma, 93 Harv. L. Rev. 518 (1980)).

58. *Id.*

59. Mary L. Dudziak, *Desegregation as Cold War Imperative, in* Critical Race Theory, *supra* note 2, at 110, 110–21.

60. A leading textbook on constitutional law asks a similar question about Bell's reading of *Brown:* "If desegregation was really in the interest of the white majority, why did it have to be judicially imposed?" Geoffrey R. Stone et al., Constitutional Law 466 (1986).

61. Richard Delgado, *Affirmative Action as a Majoritarian Device: Or, Do You Really Want to Be a Role Model?, in* Critical Race Theory, *supra* note 2, at 355.

62. Delgado, *supra* note 55, at 466 (footnote omitted).

63. Delgado, *supra* note 17, at xiii.

64. Matsuda, *supra* note 32, at 19.

65. Delgado, *supra* note 17, at xv.

66. Mari J. Matsuda, *Looking to the Bottom: Critical Legal Studies and Reparations,* 22 Harv. C.R.-C.L. L. Rev. 323, 324 (1987).

67. Richard Delgado, *The Imperial Scholar: Reflections on a Review of Civil Rights Literature,* 132 U. Pa. L. Rev. 561, 577 (1984).

68. Richard Delgado, *Rodrigo's Chronicle, in* Critical Race Theory, *supra* note 2, at 346, 347 (footnotes omitted).

69. Lawrence et al., *supra* note 7, at 2.

70. Delgado, *supra* note 53, at 64–74.

71. *Id.* at 68.

72. Thomas Ross, *Innocence and Affirmative Action, in* Critical Race Theory, *supra* note 2, at 551, 551–63.

18

Telling Stories out of School
An Essay on Legal Narratives
Daniel A. Farber and Suzanna Sherry

Introduction

Once upon a time, the law and literature movement taught us that stories have much to say to lawyers, and Robert Cover taught us that law is itself a story. Instead of living happily ever after with that knowledge, some feminists and critical race theorists have taken the next logical step: telling stories, often about personal experiences, on the pages of the law reviews. By 1989, legal storytelling had risen to such prominence that it warranted a symposium in a major law review. Thus far, however, little or no systematic appraisal of this movement has been offered. We agree with the story-tellers that taking the movement seriously requires engaging its ideas, and that it is time for a "sustained, *public* examination of this new form of legal scholarship."

Before we begin, it may be helpful to say a few words about what we mean by legal storytelling. Reliance on case studies and other narratives is hardly new to legal scholarship. Based on our reading of the literature, however, we have identified three general differences between the new storytellers and conventional legal scholars. First, the storytellers view narratives as central to scholarship, while de-emphasizing conventional analytic methods. Second, they particularly value "stories from the bottom"—stories by women and people of color about their oppression. Third, they are less concerned than conventional scholars about whether stories are either typical or descriptively accurate, and they place more emphasis on the aesthetic and emotional dimensions of narration. These three differences combine to create a distinctive mode of legal scholarship.

As with many intellectual movements, it is easier to point to examples of legal storytelling than to provide a crisp definition. Although legal storytelling takes many forms, Patricia Williams' "Benetton" story might be considered a classic example of the genre. In this story, she describes at length how she was refused admission to a Benetton store, and how she encountered difficulties in persuading a law review to publish a full account of this episode. It is not extraordinary that this narrative would be published; what is new and noteworthy is that a book consisting of a series of such autobiographical narratives would be hailed as a major work of legal scholarship.

In this article, we will provide an overview of the legal storytelling movement and evaluate its claims. Rather than asking whether storytelling is, generally speaking, a beneficial activity, we will focus on the appropriate role of storytelling in legal scholarship. That task, however, requires consideration of some subsidiary questions. In Part I, we will consider the connection between storytelling and the thesis that women and people of color write in a different voice. In Part II, we will examine legal storytelling from the perspective of practical reasoning by exploring the ways in which concrete situations function in legal thought. After concluding that stories can contribute significantly to our understanding of the law, we will suggest that although storytelling has no necessary gender-based, racial, or ideological connection, some special benefits may flow from stories "from the bottom." Having established that at least some storytelling is a legitimate form of legal scholarship, we will turn in Part III to the question of how to evaluate scholarly efforts of this kind. How do we determine the validity of these stories? How do we assess the quality of this form of scholarship? And what do "validity" and "quality" mean in this setting?

Advocates of storytelling have questioned the traditional standards for evaluating scholarship. A constructive response to this challenge cannot simply reassert those traditional standards. Instead, it should explore the fundamental purposes of legal scholarship. Here, we suggest that *legal* scholarship should help the reader understand law, and that legal *scholarship* should comport with the goals and attributes of the academy rather than mimic other forms of communication. The question, then, is how well a scholarly work serves these goals. In general, we conclude that legal storytelling can contribute to legal scholarship. We also believe, however, that storytellers need to take greater steps to ensure that their stories are accurate and typical, to articulate the legal relevance of the stories, and to include an analytic dimension in their work.

I. Storytelling in a "Different Voice"

The body of literature asserting that women and people of color have unique perspectives to contribute to legal scholarship is vast and growing rapidly. Feminist legal scholars who embrace this view often speak of women's "different voice," harkening back to Carol Gilligan's groundbreaking book, *In a Different Voice*. Prominent scholars of color who believe that there is a distinctive "voice of color" have often denominated their own scholarship "critical race theory." Because different voice feminists and critical race theorists have much in common, we will refer to both groups collectively as "different voice" scholars, differentiating among them as necessary.

At this point, it may be helpful to explain our understanding of the concept of different voices. So far as we are aware, there is no serious disagreement that some differences exist between the average life experiences of white males and those of other groups. It is plausible to assume that these differences in experiences cause some variations in attitudes and beliefs, particularly in those areas most closely connected with the differences in experience. Thus, for example, it would not be surprising to discover that blacks and whites have different attitudes about school busing, or that men and women tend to disagree about what constitutes sexual harassment. Our understanding of the different voice thesis, however, is that it goes beyond assuming differences only in the average attitudes and beliefs of different

groups. Instead, it also postulates that members of different groups have different methods of understanding their experiences and communicating their understandings to others. This becomes relevant to storytelling through the claim that
abstract analysis and formal empirical research are less appropriate than stories for
communicating the understandings of women and people of color.

It is sometimes difficult to sort out the various claims that different voice scholars
make. They all seem to agree that women and people of color speak in distinct voices,
and many claim further that the minority or female voice is best heard in, and
uniquely suited to, legal storytelling. We find disagreement, however, on the source of
the different voices. Some theorists suggest that gender and minority heritage in
themselves create a unique perspective or different voice that would persist even in a
completely egalitarian society. Others argue that it is the experience of oppression
that creates the different perspective. Whatever the source, however, many different
voice scholars also argue that traditional academic standards reflect a white male
voice and therefore undervalue the work of women and people of color. In this
section, we will explore the nature and source of the different voice, deferring until
Part III our discussion of evaluative standards.

A. Feminism

In 1982, Carol Gilligan published *In a Different Voice*, which asserted that men and
women may approach moral questions differently. Since then, scholars in a variety
of disciplines, including law, have suggested that women have a general world-view
that differs in significant respects from that of men. Although the details differ,
these scholars share a common description of the differences between male and
female perspectives: Women are inherently both more connected to others and more
contextual than men.

Feminist legal scholars who have adopted the different voice perspective contrast
women's contextual voice with the male voice of the law. For example, Lucinda
Finley argues that law and legal reasoning reflect a male voice by emphasizing
"rationality, abstraction, a preference for statistical and empirical proofs over experiential or anecdotal evidence," and "universal and objective thinking." Martha
Fineman describes how feminist legal theory can become "an exercise in the concrete." Margaret Jane Radin suggests that feminism shares with pragmatism "a commitment against abstract idealism, transcendence, foundationalism, and atemporal
universality; and in favor of immanence, historicity, concreteness, situatedness, contextuality, embeddedness, [and] narrativity of meaning." The feminine voice is also
portrayed as more empathic and emotional. It is important to note the breadth of
these claims: Feminist "different voice" scholars do not suggest simply that women
might have a different perspective on issues directly involving gender relations, but
rather that women's unique perspective casts a different light on virtually all legal
issues. These feminist scholars, including one of the authors of this article, have
examined the implications of contextuality and connection in the context of a great
variety of legal questions.

Although rarely made explicit, the connection between this description of women's voice and the methodology of storytelling is obvious. If legal reasoning, especially "grand theory," is overly abstract, objective, and empirical, then the antidote is legal storytelling, which usually focuses on the narrator's experience of events. Stories supply both the individualized context and the emotional aspect missing from most legal scholarship. Thus "personal narrative" is described as a "feminist method."

Despite the widespread invocation of different voice theories, the existence of such a voice and its connection to legal storytelling are matters of dispute even within the feminist legal community. Gilligan's work is highly controversial within her own discipline, and Gilligan herself rejects extreme claims of differences between men and women. Her later work suggests that the moral approaches of men and women form overlapping bell curves, and that fully mature individuals of either sex should be able to use both "voices." Other researchers in the field have been unable to duplicate Gilligan's original findings, and many have criticized her methodology. If male and female styles of thought were radically different, one would expect more consistent empirical evidence of gender differences.

Some feminist legal scholars have condemned suggestions about women's different voice as both unsound and unwise, because they are likely to lead to further marginalization of women in economic and political spheres. Others, whom Robin West describes as "radical" as opposed to "cultural" feminists, attribute women's different voice to the male foot on women's throats, suggesting that "women's connection to others is the source of women's misery, not a source of value worth celebrating." And any claim that women think differently is subject to a charge of "gender essentialism," which ascribes a unitary voice to women.

Other scholars deny that the "voice" of context and connection is uniquely female. Joan Williams, for example, points out that the "feminine voice" is simply another in a long line of epistemological critiques of liberalism, and therefore hardly unique to women. Margaret Jane Radin suggests that feminist jurisprudence shares much with pragmatism. Male and female scholars alike have lamented the lack of a "human voice" in the law, describing such a missing voice in terms very similar to those used by feminists. Thus Julius Getman praises Charles Black's use of the human voice in Black's article on segregation, which (unlike traditional scholarship) used real experiences of real people to illuminate legal theory. Without recourse to feminism, Lynne Henderson observes that legal decisions are too frequently isolated from both experience and empathy. Both Carol Rose and Robert Cover, among others, have eloquently described storytelling by other cultures and other voices, including those of white males.

Finally, there is a great deal of uncertainty about the source of women's unique perspective, if it does indeed exist. The earliest discussions of women's voice suggested that differences were based on biology or on childrearing practices, and some scholars still adhere to this view. Several of them have taken this view to extremes; one even relies on a contrast between women's lunar biological cycles and the historical importance of the solar calendar to suggest that the latter was a method for consolidating male power. Recently, however, many feminist legal scholars have attributed women's different perspective to experiences of exclusion, discrimination, and marginalization. We will discuss this claim and its relationship to critical race theory later in the article.

Thus, although some evidence exists that men and women possess different perspectives on the law, the weight of the evidence does not support either of the strong versions of the different voice thesis: i) that the voices of men and women are so different that the former normally can neither understand nor evaluate the work of the latter, or ii) that women are in a unique position to transform legal scholarship. At most, the empirical evidence suggests that women may write about or emphasize different aspects of the law than men, potentially providing a more complete vision of the legal system.

B. Critical Race Theory

Because the feminist version of different voice theory is older and therefore better developed than the critical race theory version, we found arguments regarding the voice of color particularly difficult to evaluate. However debatable Gilligan's conclusions regarding women's different voice may be, critical race theory has not yet established a comparable empirical foundation. We know of no work on critical race theory that discusses psychological or other social science studies supporting the existence of a voice of color. Most critical race theorists simply postulate the existence of a difference, often citing feminist scholarship for support, and thus implicitly equating a male voice with a white voice. One scholar denies that the existence of a distinct voice of color can or need be proven, as it is solely a matter of authorial intent: Those who intend to speak in the voice of color do so. The best evidence supporting the existence of a voice of color is said to be that minority "scholarship raises new perspectives—the perspectives of [minority] groups." Thus far, however, there has been no demonstration of how those new perspectives differ from the various perspectives underlying traditional scholarship.

Related to the lack of evidence for the existence of a distinct voice of color, we have found little exploration of the content of such a voice. Although descriptions of how women focus on context and connection may be vague, laden with impenetrable jargon, and sometimes even inaccurate, they are often detailed and rich with examples. In contrast, descriptions of the voice of color are less common in the literature, and again often piggyback on feminist scholarship. The voice of color is described as contextualized, opposed to abstraction and detachment, and "grounded in the particulars of . . . social reality and experience." The most concrete description we could find is that the voice of color "rejects narrow evidentiary concepts of relevance and credibility."

These rather vague descriptions fail to identify the content of a distinct voice of color. Because the few examples offered focus on racially charged issues such as affirmative action and hate speech regulations, they provide little insight into any broad differences between voices of color and supportive white voices. Indeed, Mari Matsuda suggests that "multiple consciousness," her term for the perspective of women of color, is accessible to everyone. And Patricia Williams, a feminist often cited as one of the foremost voices of color, seemingly implies that the voice of color has at least entered into that of western humanity generally, when she argues that "people of color have always been part of Western Civilization." A recent book by an

African scholar suggests that the commonality of African cultures is a white myth invented to dominate blacks. Of course, the difficulty in describing the voice of color does not disprove its existence, but it does make analysis more difficult.

Finally, although many critical race theorists claim a special affinity between storytelling and the voice of color, the connection is unclear. Two separate links have been suggested. First, several critical race scholars note that minority cultures have a strong tradition of storytelling, as opposed to more formal types of literature. Second, storytelling is said to be a method of communication that can convey new truths that "just cannot be said by using the legal voice." Thus, Richard Delgado suggests that "counterhegemonic" storytelling is one cure for the prevailing racist mentality. Indeed, Alex Johnson contends that white men do not tell stories because they would have to tell of their own dominance.

These efforts to link stories with the voice of color are problematic. White men clearly *do* tell stories. In fact, many European cultures have rich storytelling traditions. Moreover, a number of critical race theorists themselves assert that dominant groups, as well as conservative members of minority groups, tell their own stories, and that the difference between their stories and those of outsiders is simply that the former are more readily accepted.

The problem, then, is to identify the distinctiveness of stories told in the voice of color. Like many recent feminist voices, the voice of color sometimes seems to be defined on the basis of content: It embodies a certain view of race or gender relations (and occasionally other hot political topics). This becomes most apparent when we examine critical race scholars' attempts to explain the source of the voice of color. While an occasional statement suggests that culturally ingrained differences account for the distinct voice, most critical race theorists attribute the voice of color to the "experience of domination" and "marginal status." Like the feminists who attribute women's distinctive voice to gender oppression, these scholars define the voice in political terms. Matsuda notes that outsider scholarship concerns itself with such issues as affirmative action, pornography, and hate speech regulation because those with a different voice "recognize that this has always been a nation of dominant and dominated, and that changing that pattern will require affirmative, non-neutral measures designed to make the least the most." She also suggests that the purpose of storytelling is to demonstrate how the pain caused by racism outweighs the pain of ending it. Alex Johnson characterizes the voice of color as any voice that addresses "the plight of people of color." Jerome Culp describes the voice of color as "based not on color, but on opposition to racial oppression." And Richard Delgado asserts that the purpose of storytelling is to "subvert" the status quo. Finally, Toni Massaro characterizes the goal of the new storytellers, including critical race theorists, as "a hope that certain specific, different, and previously disenfranchised voices . . . *will prevail.*" According to this view, then, the true voice of color belongs only to a subgroup of people of color who have certain political views.

In addition, it would be helpful to have a more complete explanation of how black law school professors—whose occupation confers social and economic privilege, and who may come from privileged backgrounds similar to their white counterparts'—have a special claim to represent the view of poor blacks in urban ghettos.

Indeed, there is evidence that they do not fully share the views of most African Americans. Stephen Carter points out that while most critical race theorists are politically to the left of their academic colleagues, most studies show African Americans to be considerably more conservative than whites on many issues. This suggests that perhaps only a minority of African Americans truly speak with a political voice of color. As Alex Johnson notes, critical race theorists may conflate race and socioeconomic class: "If one substitutes the word 'poor' or 'oppressed' for 'color' in much of the literature advocating the existence of the voice of color, or claiming to speak in that voice of color, the content of that literature would be, by and large, unchanged." Ideology, then, may be as important as race or class in defining the speaker's "voice." For instance, many of the stories that feminists and critical race theorists tell about the hiring and promotion practices of law schools are similar to those told by white male critical legal scholars.

Because critical race theorists have not articulated their claims as fully as feminists have, their theories are more difficult to evaluate. Without a clearer conception of the "voice of color," it is difficult to assess the arguments on behalf of its existence. If those who argue the existence of fundamental cognitive differences between races or genders have the burden of proof, they clearly have failed to carry that burden. Even if they do not bear the burden of proof, we think there are sound reasons to reject such claims. If radical differences did exist, we would expect that empirical studies or at least everyday observations would consistently reveal some differences, even if the results were not all of the magnitude predicted by the theory. Moreover, the most clearly articulated claim of the proponents, that different voices are characterized by contextuality and concreteness, may well be true as a description of overlapping bell curves, but is clearly false if those traits are claimed to be the sole property of any single group. Finally, the argument for a unique voice of color is undermined by the inability of the proponents to agree on its attributes or on paradigm cases. For these reasons, the claim for fundamental group differences is not only unproven but implausible.

As we have seen, there is some evidence for a weaker form of the feminine voice thesis, which claims that women are more likely than men to exhibit certain cognitive traits. A similar case for the existence of a voice of color has yet to be made, but we are reluctant to dismiss such claims out of hand for three reasons. First, there is substantial (though hardly ironclad) evidence to support some version of the "different voice" thesis regarding women. If such a voice exists, it may be a product of social subordination, something that people of color have also experienced. Second, some minority groups, such as Native Americans, reflect cultures that are clearly quite different from the dominant American culture. It seems plausible that these cultural differences would lead to different perspectives on the legal system. Other groups, such as African Americans and Hispanics, may manifest less fundamental but nevertheless significant cultural differences; to the extent these differences exist, they too might result in distinctive perspectives on law. Third, we give some weight to the unified insistence of so many minority scholars that there is indeed a different voice; where there is so much consensus, it would be rash to dismiss completely the possible existence of some intergroup differences.

In the remainder of this article, we will examine the contribution that stories—especially those "from the bottom"—can make to legal scholarship. We will then consider how traditional standards of evaluating scholarship might apply to storytelling. Our analysis is based on a somewhat agnostic view of the different voice theory. While we reject the strongest version of the theory, which postulates radical distinctions that would make the scholarship of women and men, whites and people of color, almost unintelligible to one another, we accept as a working hypothesis a weaker version—that women and people of color can sometimes provide a perspective that is not as easily accessible to white men. The new voice is not an entirely new hue, but simply a different shade.

II. The Virtues of Narratives

Our next task is to consider whether stories, as concrete depictions of events, can contribute to understanding law. Because we have concluded that there is no radical distinction between the forms of reasoning used by different groups, we must phrase our question in terms of how concreteness and contextuality function in human reasoning (rather than in specifically "feminine" or "African American" reasoning). Having established some of the functions that stories serve in human reasoning, we can then ask whether the particular stories told by members of oppressed groups have any distinctive contribution to make. Our mission in this section is to construct an argument on behalf of narrative in general (and "stories from the bottom" in particular), without relying on any radical differences in the voices or world-views of different groups.

A. Practical Reasoning and Storytelling

1. An Introduction to Practical Reason

The strongest arguments in favor of legal storytelling are best understood within the context of the current intellectual reaction against formalism and grand theory. A broad array of recent legal commentary has suggested a movement away from these dominant forms of legal analysis, which focus on abstract, deductive reasoning from high-level principles or general rules, toward something new, sometimes called practical reason or pragmatism. This movement is often associated with the emerging interest in republicanism and often feminist legal theory. Here, we will use "pragmatism" as the generic name for this movement and will refer to the forms of thought endorsed by pragmatists as "practical reason." Storytelling is allied with pragmatism in its rejection of formalism, and with practical reason in its regard for concreteness. Pragmatist theories of practical reason, we believe, illuminate both the uses and limitations of storytelling.

As Frank Michelman observes, practical reason "seems always to involve a combination of something general with something specific," so that judgment "mediates between the general standard and the specific case." In applying a standard, we must interpret it, he says, thereby reconstructing "the standard's meaning and rightness." Michelman also notes that "[t]his process, in which the meaning of the rule emerges, develops, and changes in the course of applying it to cases is one that every common law practitioner will immediately recognize." The search, then, is for contextual justification for the best legal answer among the potential alternatives. Or, to use an image common in discussions of practical reasoning, justification is thought to be more of a web than a tower, drawing on the coherence of many sources, rather than building on a single unified foundation.

It is easier to give examples of practical reason and to distinguish it from other forms of thought than to describe its operation. As Michelman indicates, practical reason does not mean, as is sometimes thought, replacing rules or principles with ad hoc decisionmaking or raw intuition. Rather, pragmatism rejects the view that rules in and of themselves dictate particular outcomes.

The work of cognitive psychologists has provided some insight into the nature of practical reason. Studies of expert decisionmaking confirm the widespread use of the kind of reasoning described by Michelman, which moves between the concrete and general. This body of literature provides three major conclusions about how experts make decisions. First, expertise does not simply consist of knowing a greater number of facts or rules. Instead, it involves the skill of picking out the key features of a new situation. Second, this skill is learned primarily through experience with large numbers of past situations. Third, expertise is not merely an act of intuitive perception. Radiologists, for instance, do not merely perceive x-rays more accurately than lay people; they give better reasons for their interpretations and are better able to test those interpretations against additional information.

Moreover, the acquisition of expertise may be linked with the use of stories. For instance, an anthropological study of Xerox repair technicians concluded that they acquired expertise not through formal training programs but through examining actual problems. In particular, they learned from "the stories tech-reps tell each other —around the coffee pot, in the lunchroom, or while working together on a particularly difficult problem." These stories are crucial to the technician's acquisition and application of expertise:

> In a sense, these stories are the real "expert systems" used by tech-reps on the job. They are a storehouse of past problems and diagnoses, a template for constructing a theory about the current problem, and the basis for making an educated stab at a solution. By creating such stories and constantly refining them through conversation with each other, tech-reps are creating a powerful "organization memory" that is a valuable resource for the company.

The literature of cognitive psychology thus seems to support the existence of practical reason and suggests that it is linked with storytelling. Pragmatism accommodates storytelling by stressing that "reason" can include informal and nonalgorithmic forms of thought, and by viewing concrete situations as useful for understanding more general rules or principles. In contrast, foundationalism and formalism leave little room for "stories" as a useful intellectual exercise, emphasizing instead abstract theory and highly rigorous empirical research. But while practical reason involves the interplay between the general and concrete, it may require greater connections with general theories and standards than some legal storytellers wish to make. We will return to that question in Part III.

2. The Role of Stories in Practical Reasoning

Before we turn specifically to stories "from the bottom," it is worth briefly noting several general benefits that flow from attention to the kind of concrete examples found in narratives. First, consideration of concrete situations provides a method of testing and refining normative principles. A classic explanation of this method appears in John Rawls' discussion of reflective equilibrium. According to Rawls, the best available method of moral reasoning involves moving between general theories and intuitions about specific moral judgments. General theories are tested for their fit with specific intuitions, which are themselves subject to rejection if they cannot be reconciled with some coherent theory. This approach should seem particularly familiar to lawyers, given its close resemblance to common law reasoning. In fact, the process of testing proposed rules against concrete intuitions is the core of the "Socratic method" in law school teaching.

Second, concrete situations—particularly those in which the participants make normative judgments—may also demonstrate the appropriate exercise of practical reasoning. Richard Eldridge argues that reading literature allows us to reconcile the particular with the universal. He denies that either particular circumstances or universal moral principles alone can define what it means to be a moral person, and suggests instead that both inform human deliberation about morality and the good life. Narratives, then, as "the fullest reflective accounts there are of deliberation and action in specific circumstances," help us understand both the universal and particular aspects of moral personhood.

Similarly, Martha Nussbaum suggests that stories involving difficult moral decisions help us understand the process of moral reasoning. On this neo-Aristotelian account, stories can augment personal experience in developing the kind of background necessary to make sound moral judgments. The process Nussbaum describes is not unlike that by which experts—ranging from chess masters to radiologists—learn to make good judgments. That process involves both personal practice and careful study of case histories (or, in the case of chess masters, past games). One of us has likewise suggested that some judicial decisions function as models, providing lawyers with examples of how best to analyze problems in a given area of the law.

Finally, on an empirical level, study of concrete situations provides an obvious source of information. Case histories and fieldwork have long been used in such disciplines as psychoanalysis, anthropology, political science, and medicine. As we will discuss in Part III, there are familiar methodological risks to relying on these techniques. Nevertheless, even the social scientists who consider these techniques less reliable than more formalized statistical and experimental methods would be hard-pressed to dismiss them as useful starting points, which can then be subjected to more rigorous testing procedures. For example, by closely examining the record in a leading case, lawyers may formulate general theories about an area of the law.

These uses of concrete examples are not necessarily tied to any ideological position, nor are they the unique domain of a particular race or gender. The Aristotelian lineage of practical reason is itself proof that European males are quite capable of utilizing concreteness as well as abstract analysis. The affinities between practical reason and the best of the common law tradition illustrate the same point. Justiciability doctrine, which is based on the assumption that legal issues are best decided in the context of concrete cases, was the invention of white males. As Part I indicates, although concreteness and contextuality may be more frequently found in the thought of some groups, such as women or people of color, they are not the exclusive province of any single group.

The uniqueness of legal storytelling thus does not lie in its focus on the concrete rather than the abstract. That focus is characteristic of the much broader movement away from formalism and grand theory in contemporary scholarship. Rather, legal storytelling's most distinctive claim is that particular types of concrete examples—those drawn from the experiences of the downtrodden—have a special claim on our attention. We explore this claim in the next section.

B. Stories from the "Bottom"

1. Stories and Ideological Transformation

The core of the storytelling movement is the claim that stories told by the oppressed have special value. The broadest claims credit stories with substantial ideological power through which they either "constitute" a community of outsiders or transform the viewpoints of insiders.

One frequent claim on behalf of storytelling is that stories build solidarity among the members of an oppressed group, thereby providing psychological support and strengthening community. We have no reason to question these effects, or to dismiss them as negligible. Nevertheless, we do not believe that these effects in themselves are sufficient to validate the stories *as scholarship*. As Kathryn Abrams says, "It seems reasonable to ask of narrators who are, in fact, legal scholars that their stories be framed in such a way as to shed light on legal questions." The crucial test of scholarly writing must be whether it provides an increased understanding of some issue relating to law. Community-building may be valuable, but it is an enterprise quite distinct from increasing understanding of the law.

Supporters of storytelling also maintain that stories by the oppressed can transform the consciousness of "dominant" readers by introducing them to a radically different world-view. For example, Richard Delgado has suggested that "[s]tories, parables, chronicles, and narratives are powerful means for destorying mindset—the bundle of presuppositions, received wisdoms, and shared understandings against a background of which legal and political discourse takes place." Delgado argues that the mindset of the dominant group is the "principal instrument" of subordination, and for this reason concludes that storytelling has greater potential to produce radical social change than other techniques like litigation:

> Stories attack and subvert the very "institutional logic" of the system. On the rare occasions when law-reform litigation is effective for blacks, the hard-won new "rights" are quietly stolen away by narrow interpretation, foot dragging, delay, and outright obstruction. Stories' success is not so easily circumvented; a telling point is registered instantaneously and the stock story it wounds will never be the same.

Delgado's argument presupposes that members of dominant groups share a coherent "mindset" which underlies the "institutional logic" of the system, while members of subordinated groups have a different and incompatible mindset. Although Delgado is not entirely clear on the meaning of "mindset," he seems to be referring to something more fundamental than a mere set of empirical presuppositions; for example, he also refers in similar terms to the "thought structure by which we create our world." One possible interpretation of Delgado's statements is that groups have radically different ways of thinking about the world, which can be effectively bridged through stories. This is a strong claim, possibly stronger than he intends to make. In any event, it is a position that we find untenable. In Part I, we called into question the assumption that the "different voices" of subordinated groups reflect radically different ways of thought. Moreover, if whites did inhabit a socially constructed reality wholly distinct from people of color, it would be difficult to understand how communication across this gulf could take place. Any sentence uttered by a person of color, under this assumption, would be connected with one coherent world-view in the mind of the speaker, but a white listener could only understand the sentence within her own, equally coherent but quite different, world-view. In essence, the speaker would be using one language and the hearer would be listening to a completely different one, even though the words of both languages would sound identical. Thus this view calls into question the enterprise of storytelling itself as a means of communication.

It may be that Delgado, as well as other storytelling advocates, employs a more narrow definition of "mindset" that directly concerns only race or gender issues. According to this interpretation, the differences in perceptions among the various groups are limited to certain areas of life. Consequently, all groups possess similar thought processes in general, and common ground exists as a basis for communication on most subject matters. The claim, then, is only that racial or gender attitudes of "insiders" can be powerfully transformed by exposure to stories. However, even this limited claim about the effect of stories seems implausible. Some advocates of storytelling place excessive confidence in the ability of language to change fundamental beliefs; one scholar goes so far as to call rhetoric "a magical thing . . . [that] transforms things into their opposites" and makes "[d]ifficult choices become obvious." Although we agree that stories can sometimes significantly affect their audiences, these writers seem to have markedly unrealistic expectations about the magnitude of the effects.

Despite the many general assertions about how narratives can transform the political perspective of "insiders," conversion stories are notably scarce. As storytelling advocates admit—and as cognitive psychologists would predict—responses by "insiders" are typically defensive or dismissive. Stories undoubtedly can have beneficial effects, at least at the margin, on public attitudes, yet current storytelling seems ill-conceived for creating such an effect. Effective communication requires bridging the gap between the viewpoints of speaker and listener, rather than simply presenting the speaker's views without regard to the standpoint of the listener. But in our extensive reading of the storytelling literature, we have found few efforts to connect the events in the stories with the experiences of white or male readers. Thus, whatever potential storytelling might have to change attitudes is unlikely to be realized by the current generation of efforts.

2. Stories, Cases, and Legal Scholarship

Although current storytelling efforts are unlikely to have a major impact on public attitudes, stories from the bottom may still provide some benefits by helping to identify and eliminate biases in the legal system. The storytelling literature contains a good deal of rhetoric, such as the following eloquent statement by David Luban, suggesting that the legal system "silences" certain stories:

> Equally important is the parallel power over local narratives, the power of the victor to build whatever facts he or she wishes into the fabric of legal decisions by (re)interpreting the record. Just as in the case of political narratives, losers endure not only the material burdens of defeat, but also the ignominy of helplessly witnessing their own past edited, their own voices silenced in the attempt to tell that past. And thus the fight of those voices that have been silenced by the law—and those obviously include not only the voices of miscreants and justifiably unsuccessful litigants, but also the voices of racial minorities, of women, of homosexuals, of the poor—is, as Benjamin put it, "the fight for the oppressed past."

The metaphor of "silencing" is powerful but elusive. In what respect, for instance, is losing a lawsuit the same as being gagged? Losers are in fact often very vocal, perhaps more so than victors (who seem just as likely to enjoy their victory in smug silence). In part, the "silencing" metaphor invokes some broader concepts about the relationship between power and truth, but it does not elucidate that relationship. The basic idea seems to be that we fail to receive information about the experiences of outsiders because the legal system itself filters out these stories. Or, turning to social science jargon, the claim is that our present sample of stories is biased. Although the claims are perhaps exaggerated, they do have some substance. To evaluate this substance, we must examine the sources of the bias and ascertain what the value of the missing information would be.

One source of bias is simply that people tend to associate with those similar to themselves and, consequently, possess few informal methods of tracking the experience of other groups. A related problem is that our perceptions of the frequency of a problem may depend on vantage point. For example, if relatively few men engage in sexual harassment, men might think sexual harassment occurs relatively infrequently. Women, on the other hand, may view it as a widespread problem if, for instance, a small number of men each harasses many women. Moreover, behavior that is widespread may seem trivial to members of a dominant group but quite significant to members of subordinated groups. Because legal analysis is often based on informal experience and folk wisdom rather than rigorous social science, these problems may lead to mistaken policy recommendations.

Legal storytelling is unlikely to correct these forms of bias because the problems themselves stem from broader social conditions. More effective solutions include integration and affirmative action, both of which attack the problem directly by broadening the personal contacts of the individuals involved. And to the extent that vicarious contacts through stories can be used to supplement these direct solutions, there is little reason to think that the publication of stories in law reviews is the best solution. For example, novels can provide much more textured versions of individual experiences, while movies and television have greater dramatic impact and reach far larger audiences than law review prose. Moreover, there is reason to question whether the personal stories of middle-class law professors can accurately convey the perspectives of the truly disadvantaged.

The more interesting sources of bias stem directly from the legal system itself. First, as several advocates of storytelling have pointed out, the facts in appellate opinions are usually stated in terms most favorable to the victor. As a result, stories told in appellate opinions are likely to be biased in favor of a group consisting of successful litigants. This group will therefore systematically exclude individuals whose problems are not yet addressed by existing legal rules, since they will have lost the litigation. For example, if the legal system provides no remedy for victims of hate speech, they will not win lawsuits, and their version of the facts will not be reflected in appellate opinions. Although most legal scholars recognize that appellate opinions are highly unreliable and biased sources of empirical evidence, we are all prone to rely on them nonetheless, given that they are so easily accessible.

Second, some facts are filtered out even before the opinion-writing stage. For example, if the legal system disallows damages for emotional distress, evidence of these damages will be considered irrelevant. Cases involving certain fact patterns will simply not be brought if the law clearly offers no remedy. Hence, lawyers, judges, and scholars may be unaware of widespread problems. For instance, before sexual harassment became a potential cause of action, a victim of harassment would have had no reason to bring a clearly futile lawsuit. Therefore, male legal observers would be unaware that this was a widespread problem. Similarly, prosecutors may be reluctant to bring acquaintance rape cases, which may lead criminal law specialists to assume that this form of rape is uncommon.

Some cases may not be brought because they fail to fit existing legal categories. For example, allegations about heterosexual abuse often surface in divorce cases. But because the law does not recognize lesbian marriages and thus cannot recognize lesbian divorces, information about physical abuse between lesbians is less likely to come to the attention of the legal system. More subtly, in the effort to force grievances into existing legal categories, lawyers may strip away crucial aspects of the victim's experience.

A third source of bias emerges from the impact of legal rules on conduct. When legal rules disfavor certain kinds of conduct, we may rarely observe such conduct and conclude that few people are motivated to engage in it. For example, if the legal system generally disfavors altruism, it may produce a self-confirmatory body of evidence about the weakness of altruistic motivations. This evidence might then mislead legal theorists into rejecting altruism as a potentially powerful social force. An even clearer case involves intentional racism. Given the existence of Title VII, only a very poorly informed employer will ever explicitly state that he is firing an employee out of racial animus. In the absence of such cases, lawyers and scholars may conclude that racial animosity has vanished from the workplace.

There are certainly ways of correcting such biases apart from storytelling. Survey research, for example, may document the existence of behavior that is overlooked by the legal system. Still, storytelling can at least suggest areas where more formal social science research might be helpful. The use of narratives can also provide several other special benefits.

To begin with, careful study of a case history may provide important insights that are missing from statistical analysis. Social science data may be crude or unreliable, and formalized research often says more about what is happening than why it is happening. It takes considerable skill to identify causal relationships from cross-sectional or even the less commonly available longitudinal data. Often, these relations are elusive despite use of the best available statistical techniques.

Moreover, even if we are able to describe or predict behavior, our understanding may be incomplete without some awareness of how the person in question experiences the situation. Stories can be a source of empathetic understanding about members of outsider groups. This type of understanding may be particularly important for some kinds of legal policy analysis. Much of legal analysis involves balancing trade-offs of various kinds. Our ability to engage in such balancing is heavily dependent on our ability to assimilate the emotional experiences of those affected by a legal rule.

Finally, stories may be useful to counteract weaknesses in the ways in which we process information. Vivid examples often influence us more than statistical evidence, which explains, for example, why many people are more afraid of airplane crashes (which are statistically rare) than car crashes (which are statistically more common but less horrifying). Also, statistical information is subject to "framing" effects: A treatment with an eighty-percent survival rate sounds better than one with a twenty-percent mortality rate, even though the two are equivalent. If used carefully, stories can help counter these distortions. As we will discuss in the next section, however, stories can also make these problems worse.

III. Standards for Evaluating Stories as Scholarship

We have seen that stories can make a legitimate contribution to legal scholarship, defined broadly as writing that increases our understanding of the legal system. This says nothing, however, about the validity or quality of any particular exercise in storytelling. We now turn to the question of how to assess scholarship in this genre.

Evaluating scholarship, particularly scholarship of a new type, raises two separate issues. The first is the question of validity: When should a story be considered a valid source of insight? One might view this as the question of whether the raw "data" of the stories themselves are sufficiently reliable that they can be put to further use, regardless of whether the information is new or important. Just because a text contains valid material, however, does not necessarily mean that it is good scholarship. Thus, the second issue involves determining the standards for evaluating quality.

A. Validity Issues

1. The Problem of Fiction

Legal scholars use the fictional form in a variety of ways. Sometimes, it serves simply as the framework for developing an argument, as in Plato's *Republic*. In this form, the author does not claim to be narrating true events, but merely claims to be presenting true ideas. The work must stand or fall on its conceptual merits. Similarly, a story may be an extended hypothetical, used to work out in detail the consequences of a given position. These forms of scholarship pose no inherent challenge to conventional intellectual standards.

The fictional form might also be used for some of the purposes discussed in Part II: for example, to suggest a new hypothesis to test or to provide an empathetic understanding of a situation. A story may still serve these functions well even if it is a composite of many people or episodes, rather than a precise depiction of particular events. The more fictionalized the story, however, the more troublesome its use as empirical evidence becomes. Relying on fiction as evidence is rather like an episode recounted by Patricia Williams: "An image that comes to mind is that of movie star Jessica Lange, who testified to Congress about the condition of farms in the United States because she had *played* a farmer's wife. What on earth does 'testimony' mean in that context?" As this example suggests, a convincing fictional portrayal risks creating a spurious aura of empirical authority. This risk is compounded when the author of the fiction is a scholar, publishing in a scholarly journal, because the audience is unsure whether the author is speaking as a scholar or solely as an artist.

2. Truthfulness in Nonfiction

Relatively little legal storytelling is presented as fiction. Rather, the majority of stories are presented as descriptions of specific experiences, whether of the author or of someone else. Thus, the author is claiming that the stories are true. Some advocates of storytelling, however, question whether empirical accuracy is an important aspect of these stories. While we acknowledge that the meaning of "truth" is itself contested, we do not believe it necessary to explore philosophical disputes over the nature of truth in order to resolve the standards for assessing non-fictional stories. In particular, we need not subscribe to any form of positivist or correspondence theory of truth. The real question here is not objective "truth," but honesty: Is the author's account what it purports to be?

We can distinguish three different statements about the perception of an event:

(1) "If you had been watching, this is what you would have seen";
(2) "The situation might not have looked this way if you had been watching, but this is how it felt to me"; and
(3) "The situation didn't feel this way to me at the time, but this is how it seems to me now."

The first standard is the customary test for the truth of a description of events. The argument that, unlike white men, women and people of color use only the second or third standards for truth is a version of the "strong" different voices position, which we rejected in Part I. In any event, since the first standard is the ordinary understanding of truth, it would be dishonest to present statements that are only true under the second or third standards without an explicit disclaimer. Whether or not those standards are as valid as the conventional standard, the reader is entitled to notice of when they are in use. Saying, "if you had been there, especially if you were a male observer, you probably would not have seen anything that appeared to be violence, but I felt exactly as if he had slapped me," is entirely different from saying, "he slapped me," without notifying the reader that your statements should be given an unconventional interpretation. Again, the issue is one of honesty and fair dealing. Just as it is a basic principle of contract law that a party may not knowingly take advantage of a mistaken understanding by the other party, it would be similarly wrong for a scholar to take advantage of an audience that he knows will believe a story to be literally true unless told otherwise. Misleading the reader on this crucial point amounts to intellectual deception.

It would be especially undesirable to foster doubts about whether statements by women or people of color imply the same notions of truth as those of white males. One of the staples of feminist literature is that women's assertions are treated as presumptively unreliable and lacking in credibility. Patricia Williams has made the same point about African Americans. It would be disastrous to reinforce the idea that women and people of color do not adhere to the same standards of "truthfulness" as white men.

Because the issue is one of honesty, we also reject Kathryn Abrams' argument that it would be untroubling, at least with respect to narratives that are presented as factual, if they were to turn out "not to track the life experiences of their narrators in all particulars" or to be composites. As a general matter, we do not believe that deliberate, material changes in the factual content of narratives should be acceptable. In a narrative that purports to be a rendition of actual events, misrepresentation of these events can come perilously close to what is known in other fields as research fraud: doctoring data to fit your thesis.

Professor Abrams also makes another, more nuanced argument concerning honesty and truth: "Creating any narrative involves a process of mediation, of muting and amplification, of selection among details. What sorts of modifications 'insider' narrators should be required to disclose to their readers is a difficult question. . . ." There is clearly some validity to this argument. Just as journalists modify even direct quotes to increase intelligibility, any narrative necessarily involves selectivity. Specifying the bounds of permissible behavior may be less a matter of adherence to a clear rule than the responsible exercise of practical reason to avoid the problems identified above. Because we believe that using analytic arguments together with stories adds a type of "quality control" that minimizes these dangers, we will return to questions of selectivity in our discussion of quality issues in Part III.B.

We do not mean to imply that any of the new storytellers are engaging in deliberate falsehoods. The question of honesty or truth is primarily important for preventing *unintentional* distortion. All of us—insiders and outsiders alike—have faulty memories and a limited perspective of events. When making statements that claim to represent more than our current feelings about past events, we should recognize and guard against the pitfalls of our partiality. The safeguards we discuss in the remainder of this article are designed to counter those lapses.

3. Methods of Judging Truthfulness

A major difficulty with storytelling is verifying the truthfulness of the stories told. One genre of storytelling for which challenging accuracy is particularly troublesome is the "first-person agony narrative" in which the author's experience of pain is used to criticize a social practice. Just as lawyers normally are not allowed to offer testimony at trial, or to vouch for witnesses, scholars should not be readily allowed to offer their own experiences as evidence. The norms of academic civility hamper readers from challenging the accuracy of the researcher's account; it would be rather difficult, for example, to criticize a law review article by questioning the author's emotional stability or veracity.

Even third-party accounts of victimhood raise serious problems. In criticizing conservative stories about "political correctness," Mark Tushnet has quite aptly pointed out these problems in connection with a particular story:

> The *Christian Science Monitor*'s off-hand summary of [the story] is unfortunately typical of the reporting on political correctness. Its most characteristic feature, in fact, is that it relies on no reporting whatsoever. The victim's account of the incident is the only source of evidence. The reports never note that victims have a perfectly understandable desire to present what happened to them in a way that makes them appear best. When the reports are offered by people with a political ax to grind, one can fairly wonder exactly what happened. The proper conclusion, I think, is that accounts offered by politically interested people drawn almost entirely from the victim's side of the story almost certainly overstate the extent to which something called political correctness came into play.

The point is well taken, and applies to stories about discrimination just as much as to stories about political correctness.

Assessments of truth are made more difficult by the impracticability of independent investigation. Kathryn Abrams argues that stories may carry their own indicia of truth by providing "a complex, highly particularized account of an experience unfamiliar to many readers" or by creating a "flash of recognition." She is not alone in believing that a high level of detail provides internal evidence of veracity: The Supreme Court has said exactly the same thing in holding that detailed but unverified accounts by anonymous informants may constitute probable cause. The argument is no more convincing when offered by feminists than it is from Chief Justice Rehnquist. The "flash of recognition" argument is also troubling, creating the risk that the author gains credibility by appealing to the reader's preconceptions and biases.

The ultimate problem with Abrams' argument, however, is that it relies on our intuitive ability to determine whether a person is telling the truth. Unfortunately, the substantial body of social psychology research on this subject has very discomfiting conclusions. Human beings are actually extremely poor at determining whether a person is lying, even in face-to-face contexts. For this very reason, disciplines such as anthropology and history that rely on informants or documents have evolved rigorous methodological standards for the use of such evidence. It is an error to think that skepticism of witnesses is typical of "white male thinking." On the contrary, these standards are a relatively late development in intellectual history. Like other groups, white males are all too willing to credit stories without critical examination. Individuals overcome this proclivity only through rigorous training.

One aspect of the rejection of "objectivity" deserves further consideration. Doubts about "truth" and "objectivity" as white male standards may be based on a not-unreasonable fear that these standards have a disparate impact. Dominant groups such as governments and corporations have the resources to maintain massive record-keeping systems, organizational structures to facilitate systematic observation, and funds to procure formal social science expertise. Those "on the bottom" may have only their own voices in which to offer their conflicting experiences. For example, a tribe may find that it has only oral history to offer against the formal land records of the dominant culture. To make matters worse, members of subordinated groups sometimes may lack the kinds of middle-class life histories on which our culture tends to base credibility. This disparity is another source of bias in our access to stories. The solution is not, however, to sweep the problem under the rug by simply accepting all "stories from the bottom" as gospel. Rather, it is to take whatever steps we can to test the credibility of *both* the "official" and the "counterhegemonic" versions of events.

We do not mean to assert that legal scholars should consider only evidence meeting formal social science standards. We cannot always afford the luxury of waiting for definitive findings. Furthermore, practical reasoning allows other forms of experience to supplement formalized research. Nevertheless, we need to be aware of the risks in relying on unverified narratives, and take whatever steps are possible to guard against those risks.

4. Typicality

Even if a story is true, it may be atypical of real world experiences. The importance of typicality depends partly on the use of a particular story. If the story is being used to suggest a hypothesis or a possible causal mechanism, then a prior showing of typicality is unnecessary. On the other hand, if the story is being used as the basis for recommending policy changes, it should be typical of the experiences of those affected by the policy. Owen Fiss has cogently argued that when the Supreme Court "lays down a rule for a nation . . . [it] necessarily must concern itself with the fate of millions of people. . . . Accordingly, the Court's perspective must be systematic, not anecdotal. . . ."

Studies by cognitive psychologists demonstrate that humans tend to overrely on atypical examples. Because individuals assume that dramatic or easily remembered events are typical, they often overestimate the likelihood of such events. Even when they correctly appraise a trait as typical, they overestimate its prevalence, assuming that more members of the group possess the trait than really do. In other words, people frequently engage in what we commonly call stereotyping. Finally, people are too quick to assume the presence of a pattern from a small number of cases.

Like the careful treatment of narrative sources, the use of modern empirical techniques to correct for these misperceptions and distortions is not the natural outgrowth of "white male thinking." If formal empirical techniques were inherent in white male culture, they would have developed much earlier, and would be much easier to teach to white men than they actually are. Instead, such techniques are painfully developed methods of avoiding genuine errors. We have already made clear our view that these methods can be significantly supplemented by individual case studies, but we must always be vigilant when doing so.

It bears repeating that typicality is unrelated to any commitment to "objectivity" as a philosophical position. Instead, we are merely asking, "If we checked with more people in the same situation, how many of them would tell similar stories?" If most of their stories would be different, then the informational value of the particular story selected by the author is limited. Moreover, to ignore the typicality concern would be to allow an unrepresentative individual to speak for a group, in effect silencing other members.

Stories that are presented without minimum safeguards for truthfulness and typicality do not even qualify as scholarship, much less good scholarship. Although some of the stories currently appearing in law reviews seem shaky when measured by these criteria, we are confident that other stories will meet the threshold requirements. We therefore turn to issues of quality.

B. Assessing Quality

Questions about the quality of academic scholarship arise in many different situations. When we discuss the latest scholarship with colleagues, we make judgments about what we have read. When we write, we choose which works to cite or to build on, and which to ignore. On occasion, we may be asked to make judgments about the quality of a candidate's scholarship in connection with personnel decisions. And when we teach, we must decide which scholarship can best contribute to the education of our students.

Within the profession, what constitutes poor, competent, or outstanding legal scholarship is disputed. Much of the dispute stems from disagreements about the purposes of legal scholarship: Are we writing for each other or for legal decision-makers outside academia? Is doctrinal analysis the core of legal scholarship, or is it too pedestrian and practice-oriented? Should we engage in "internal" critiques of legal rules, or "external" critiques of legal practice (including the practice of scholarship)? Must our work be prescriptive, or ought it to be mainly descriptive?

Although most of this debate concerns the distinctive nature and purposes of legal scholarship, our concern here is with the more basic question of what qualifies as good scholarship in general, in any academic discipline. Most academics would agree that traditional standards of merit do exist. And most would concede that the standards can often be applied unevenly, or too leniently. We are not suggesting that all extant scholarship *does* meet the standards we propose, only that it aspires to.

Different voice theorists argue, however, that those traditional standards operate unfairly against the scholarship of women and people of color generally, and against storytelling in particular. They are thus claiming to be exempt from conventional standards, which differentiates their work from other scholarship (including traditional but substandard scholarship). Before discussing the specific standards that might be applied to stories, we need to consider the attack on the general standards of the academy.

The issue of evaluating scholarship often arises in personnel decisions. Attacks on faculty hiring and promotion practices have, by and large, moved away from claims of intentional discrimination, and most critics now concede that the same standards are usually applied to everyone, at least superficially. The more common argument is that the universal standard of "merit" is ideologically and culturally defined in a way that excludes the unconventional voices of women and people of color. To remedy this problem, different voice scholars, especially critical race theorists, argue that traditional standards should not be applied to the work of minority scholars.

Alex Johnson, for example, argues that "the meritocratic evaluative standard . . . embodies white, majoritarian norms," and that that standard is "inappropriate when applied to scholarship written in a distinct voice of color," because it is "culturally biased against the inclusion of a voice of color." Similarly, Richard Delgado states that the meritocratic standard "measures the black candidate through the prism of pre-existing, well-agreed-upon criteria of conventional scholarship and teaching. Given those standards, it purports to be scrupulously meritocratic and fair." Despite this purported fairness, however, Delgado suggests that "[m]erit criteria may be the source of bias, rather than neutral instruments by which we determine whether or not that bias exists." Indeed, according to Delgado, merit is "potentially hostile to the idea of voice," has "a special affinity for procedural racism," and is "the perfect excluder of 'deviant' or culturally stigmatized groups." Likewise, Derrick Bell suggests that the refusal to recognize even outstanding nontraditional scholarship disproportionately harms blacks, "whose approach, voice, or conclusions may depart radically from traditional forms." And Jerome Culp implies that ordinary scholarly standards impose a "herculean task" on black legal scholars.

These arguments assume that the work of women and minority scholars *is* different—so different that it cannot be judged by conventional standards of merit. As noted earlier, available evidence does not support such a strong claim about "different voices." The critique of traditional standards as biased appears to be based largely on the fact that the works of some outsider scholars have not fared well under those standards. As Randall Kennedy points out, however, this might be because those specific works lacked merit. The arguments also assume that people of color cannot meet the traditional standards of merit, a suggestion that many scholars of color naturally find demeaning, and for which no evidence exists.

Thus, we find little support for the general claim that traditional standards are inherently unfair to work by women and minorities. A narrower, and more interesting, claim is that these standards are inappropriate for assessing legal storytelling as a particular genre of scholarship. In examining this claim, we first reject the alternate standards proposed by some different voice scholars to evaluate legal stories. We then return to a consideration of the traditional standards, attempting both to articulate them more fully and to reply to attacks on specific aspects of those standards. In particular, we will address the question of whether some analytical component is a requirement of good scholarship.

1. Different Standards

Little has been written about what standards ought to apply to different voice scholarship in place of traditional standards. Richard Delgado argues that it is too soon to apply *any* standards, leaving one to wonder how the work of these scholars ought to be evaluated for purposes of promotion and tenure, or even for purposes of deciding what readings to recommend to others.

Mary Coombs has proposed a pragmatic standard: The scholarship should be judged "in terms of its ability to advance the interests of the outsider community," with the caveat that any criteria for evaluating new articles must "definitionally give high marks to the works of" the movement's own heroes, Patricia Williams, Catharine MacKinnon, Martha Fineman, Mari Matsuda, Derrick Bell, and Richard Delgado. Judging scholarship by its political effect suffers from two independent flaws. First, it is questionable whether academic work, however sharply directed at shaping external decisions, should be judged solely by its influence. As others—including those sympathetic to different voices—have noted, scholarship that is only indirectly geared toward outside decisionmakers is often of great value to other scholars. Moreover, to the extent that success depends on the actions of the established legal hierarchy of judges and legislators, Coombs is proposing a standard that very few academic lawyers—of any sex, color, or political persuasion—will be able to meet. Coombs apparently recognizes this, and makes this standard aspirational rather than absolute. Even so, the focus on outside decisionmakers detracts from the basic question of whether the work is good scholarship as opposed to good advocacy.

The second flaw in Coombs' proposal is that it imposes a single ideological veneer on a broad spectrum of scholarship. Only those who agree both on the problems facing the outsider community and on the policies that count as solutions will have their work evaluated positively. Thus, a person of color whose scholarship attacks the notion of a voice of color (or affirmative action) as dangerous to the community of color is likely to be judged harshly by Coombs' standard.

Potentially more useful is the suggestion that standards of quality take certain individual scholars as their benchmark. Unfortunately, Coombs does not defend her choice of particular heroes except to say that each is central to the enterprise of storytelling and that each has "transformed the way we think about law and legal culture." But transformations can occur by means and in directions that might not entitle their authors to adulation. Articles based on inaccuracies, for example, or which rely on deception or other illegitimate means, should not be considered great scholarship, no matter how noble their goals.

Another problem is that Coombs implies that "we"—those whose views have been transformed—includes only the outsider community, which itself seems to be limited to individuals whose views have been transformed by these scholars. This tautological analysis effectively renders the choice of benchmarks immune from criticism. Especially in light of both Coombs' explicit criterion of political impact and the tendency, noted earlier, to equate different voices with radical ideology, it is too likely that the benchmarks were chosen (whether by Coombs or by her informants) for their ideological positions rather than for the excellence of their scholarship. Consequently, a storyteller who tells a more conservative story, however skilled in the techniques exemplified by the benchmark scholars, is not likely to be rated highly. For example, how many of the outsider scholars would support the recent Supreme Court decision to allow introduction of victim impact statements in criminal trials, which surely can be as poignant and well-crafted as the stories in law reviews? Moreover, to the extent that only outsider scholarship is transformed by the specified scholars, the use of benchmarks seems to undermine Coombs' general requirement that the work be useful. For example, scholarship that persuades only such a limited audience may be therapeutic for outside scholars, but is unlikely to help outsider communities substantially. A more useful approach might be to analyze why bench-mark scholars' work is particularly meritorious, rather than defining merit by its presence in their work. This would force Coombs (or her informants) to defend the choice of benchmarks, and thus to confront directly the potential for bias.

Several scholars have suggested that stories ought to be judged by aesthetic standards, perhaps similar to those we apply to works of fiction (whatever those might be). This standard coincides nicely with viewing legal storytelling as serving a transformative purpose. In this regard, storytelling might serve the same functions as novels or plays in helping us to understand our lives. Martha Nussbaum argues that great works of fiction can develop philosophical positions that cannot be articulated as well in conventional discursive prose. For example, she finds deep insights on some issues of moral philosophy in the novels of Henry James.

Whether or not stories about the law, written by lawyers, can serve this function is somewhat beside the point. Nussbaum is not arguing, after all, that Henry James should have published his short stories in philosophy journals, or that he should have been given tenure in a philosophy department. Thus, such work might fail to be good legal scholarship, not because it falls short of particular criteria, but because it transcends the scholarly enterprise. While *Crime and Punishment* may increase our knowledge of the legal system, so too do the Federalist Papers have a narrative structure. But to call Dostoevsky a legal scholar may be just as misleading as calling James Madison a novelist. Without denigrating the abilities of legal storytellers, we see no reason to expect them to produce great literary works of the caliber of a Dostoevsky (or a Virginia Woolf or a Toni Morrison, for that matter).

In rejecting the creation of literature as a form of legal scholarship, we are admit-tedly indulging a mild presumption in favor of institutional specialization. While works of literature may well be a source of important insights for lawyers, we contend that creating literature has little nexus with the specific institutional traits of law schools, and seems far more congenial to other settings such as creative writing departments or traditional communities of writers and artists. Thus, we do not believe that the production of literature ought to be considered part of the mission of law schools. Just because something is worthwhile does not mean that it should take place under a law school umbrella. Indeed, to the extent that fictional or fic-tionalized accounts purport to be scholarship, they jeopardize the credibility of legal scholarship.

Finally, both Mary Coombs and Kathryn Abrams suggest general criteria of good scholarship that are essentially weak versions of traditional standards of quality, including that it "facilitate further discussion within the legal academic community," and that it not be badly written or "simply repeat what has already been stated or shown to be invalid." Both scholars, however, reject the notion that good legal scholarship must necessarily convey some analysis or reasoned arguments; narrative alone can apparently be sufficient.

Reason and analysis, in fact, seem to be prime targets of those who criticize traditional criteria of merit. For example, Bell says that traditional standards unjusti-fiably require "analytical [and] historical scholarship." Delgado makes a similar point in a fictional portrayal of an attack on a candidate of color: "The faculty had disliked his colloquium, finding it devoid of history, economics, or theory. It struck them as the talk of 'just a practicing lawyer'; it was 'too much like a brief.' " Mary Coombs has given the most detailed description of the traditional standards to be rejected: "Scholarly" work is "analytic, tightly reasoned, elegantly anticipating and effectively refuting counter-arguments." These, then, are the standards that critics say are inappropriately applied to storytelling in a different voice.

Unlike these critics, we believe that storytelling—and outsider scholarship in general—can and should be judged by standards that include the requirement of an analytic component. The remainder of this article will attempt to define those standards and explore how they might be applied to legal stories.

2. Application of Conventional Standards

Despite their differences, outsider scholars and traditional scholars agree that the criteria for evaluating scholarship can only come from the practices of those within the academic community. Here, we will explore some overarching requirements shared by all academic communities—the standards that distinguish scholars from politicians, novelists, newsgatherers, clergy, demagogues, lovers, and other assorted communicators. Although feminists and critical race theorists may be a community distinct from traditional legal scholars, they are still part of the academic community in general. Thus, their stories should be evaluated by the same standards as traditional scholarship to whatever extent those standards reflect the goals and methods of "scholarship" as a distinct form of communication.

We emphasize that we are not proposing rigid formal characteristics for good legal scholarship. Nor do we suggest that, in speaking of "good scholarship," all other writing by law professors is lacking in value. Other types of writing may be worthwhile ways of laying a foundation for later researchers, educating lawyers and judges about complex areas of the law, or increasing public awareness of legal issues. Instead, we are suggesting that the lack of certain formal attributes makes it difficult for a work to function as scholarship. While it might be a mistake to say *a priori* that an airplane must have wings on both sides of the body, it is probably hard to design a plane that works well otherwise. Similarly, although it is conceivable for a work that is, for example, poorly written or lacking in reasoned analysis to be good scholarship, we believe that it is unlikely.

Therefore, our aim is to identify the core goals of legal scholarship. To that end, we propose to divide the traditional standards of scholarship into three categories: (1) consensus standards, which provoke little controversy even among the new scholars; (2) reason and analysis, which many outside scholars label as a source of bias and explicitly reject as necessary for scholarship; and (3) methods of evaluating the importance of a work, the task that is the most difficult and potentially fraught with prejudice.

Almost everyone would agree that a work of scholarship should be comprehensible to its audience, say something new, and demonstrate familiarity with the relevant literature. Despite their vagueness, these standards can still help expose some stories as not very good scholarship. For example, a much-cited article by Marie Ashe exemplifies one form of feminist narrative that would not constitute good scholarship under our definition. It contains a "torrent of physical detail" about her own reproductive experiences (including graphic descriptions of the births of her children), with some brief and cryptic suggestions about law interspersed among the stories. Even Kathryn Abrams, who praises storytelling in general and some aspects of Ashe's piece in particular, notes that "[g]rasping the relation between her narratives and her prescriptions is . . . truly strenuous." In fact, Abrams had to read the article three times before she even "began to suspect" that the point of the article was to urge the deregulation of reproduction. Clearly, an article whose thesis a knowledgeable and sympathetic reader can barely understand on the third try fails the requirement of comprehensibility.

The Ashe article also implicates a broader question about comprehensibility. Part of the problem for Abrams, and presumably for most readers, is that Ashe does not effectively link her narratives to her legal analysis. What, then, of articles that contain virtually no legal analysis at all? While the stories themselves may be comprehensible, the reason for publishing them in law journals is not. The criterion of comprehensibility, which is simple and uncontroversial when limited to questions about misuse of the English language, becomes much more difficult as it shades into questions about how readers understand the law-related point of the story. Thus, although we treat the need for analysis as a separate issue because of its controversial nature, it might also be considered a more nuanced aspect of comprehensibility.

The criterion of originality poses similar hurdles for storytellers. The first problem is determining what it means for a piece of scholarship to be original. William Nelson argues that a work cannot be new merely to the author or to some readers; rather, it should be "knowledge that no one had possessed before," knowledge that is new to the community of legal academics. Whether it consists of new facts or new ideas, Mary Coombs agrees that scholarship should not "simply repeat what has already been stated."

Beyond this minimum, Stephen Carter suggests that the idea be "nonobvious": Good scholarship should contain ideas that "would [not] have been obvious to the ordinary scholar in the field." Coombs rejects this standard as too strict, and, in any event, it would almost certainly exclude much of existing traditional scholarship. The nonobviousness criterion is also flawed for two other reasons. First, the best scholarship often makes its conclusions *seem* obvious: We all want our readers to respond by exclaiming "Of course! Why didn't I think of that?" Second, not all good scholarship contributes nonobvious ideas. Sometimes, especially in critiques, it is necessary to state the obvious, especially if no one else will. Thus Carter's suggestion of nonobviousness, though intriguing, is unworkable in practice.

Even if we limit our inquiry to the minimal standard of "add[ing] to the totality of knowledge," it will still prove difficult to determine whether a particular narrative has had an additive effect. For example, the tenth story documenting how it feels to be discriminated against is not as original as the first, and does not contribute to knowledge unless it either proposes a new legal solution or describes as discriminatory something that might not ordinarily strike us as particularly hurtful. Moreover, it is unclear how much the *first* story contributes to our knowledge. Many of us know that discrimination hurts because we have experienced at least some form of arbitrary treatment, and can extrapolate how it might feel to suffer the same arbitrary treatment over and over again. And, to the extent that we do not know what it feels like to be discriminated against, these stories are unlikely to teach us. As noted earlier, research has shown that we are most likely to believe and understand stories that resonate with something we *have* experienced. The irony is that if the pain of discrimination is similar to what we have experienced, the stories may teach us little we do not already know; if it is dissimilar, stories that simply describe the pain can't teach us about it. A more effective format for outsider scholars would be a combination of narrative and more traditional scholarship that draws analogies among different legal problems, or scholarship that proposes new legal solutions to the problems of discrimination. As with the criterion of comprehensibility, then, requiring scholarship to contribute to knowledge becomes problematic when applied to stories that convey no analysis or reasoned arguments.

Similar problems beset the superficially uncontroversial criterion that scholars be knowledgeable in their fields. The difficulty here is identifying the relevant body of literature with which storytellers should be cognizant. Only other stories? Other outsider scholarship? Traditional scholarship in civil rights? If we limit the relevant literature to outsider scholarship, then we are admitting that traditional scholarship and outsider scholarship have little to say to one another. And however we define the relevant literature, how are we to know whether a pure narrative containing no legal analysis reflects a familiarity with other legal scholarship? The story might be the same whether or not the author had even attended law school, much less kept up in her field.

Any attempt to evaluate scholarship that goes beyond the superficial agreement on the noncontroversial standards thus raises the thorny question of whether good scholarship should be expected to convey some degree of analysis or reasoned argument. In other words, can an unadorned account of personal experiences, standing alone, constitute good scholarship? Unlike many current legal storytellers, we conclude that it cannot.

Reason and analysis are the traditional hallmarks not only of legal scholarship, but of scholarship in general. According to one scholar, neither the exercise of power nor "strategic arguments designed to persuade by their emotional effect on the listener" are acceptable scholarly techniques. The new storytellers, however, challenge this view of scholarship as overly narrow and culturally biased. Consequently, the standards they propose for evaluating stories do not consider analysis or reasoned arguments essential to good scholarship. Rather, the emotive force of the stories is seen as their primary appeal. In our view, however, emotive appeal is not enough to qualify as good scholarship.

The point of all scholarship—including the nontraditional forms—is to increase the reader's understanding (here, of law). The goal of conveying ideas helps distinguish scholarship from other forms of communication, which might be designed primarily to give pleasure or to influence action. A second distinguishing feature of scholarship is that it invites reply. Whether it purports to describe the world or to prescribe human action, scholarship is addressed, at least in part, to other scholars engaged in the same activity. Because articles are part of an ongoing scholarly dialogue, even biting criticism is preferable to silence from other scholars. A third feature distinguishes scholarship from what George Fletcher has called "declarations": Scholarship, in our opinion, takes as its subject "matters about which no one has the authority to make declarations. No one has the authority to declare what is historically true, morally right, beautiful, or even efficient."

Because scholarship is an interactive activity, the reader must be able to disagree with the author and dispute her ideas. What we propose here is a weaker version of the scientific doctrine of falsifiability—something cannot be scholarship if it cannot be disputed. Persuasion, the ultimate goal of all scholarship, requires the active participation of the reader and thus must admit some form of counter-argument. Personal narratives devoid of analysis generally do not satisfy this requirement because it will often be impossible to make counter-arguments to them. Requiring the author to justify the claim that a story deepens or advances our understanding of some aspect of the legal system enables us to assess the validity and persuasiveness of that claim.

The best scholarship not only adds to the reader's knowledge directly but inspires further thought beyond the text. This reflection may take the form of elaboration or disagreement, but ultimately those engaged in scholarship will enter into an ongoing dialogue about their common project. Without reasoned arguments, neither understanding nor dialogue are likely to flourish. Robin West refers to the "unequivocal shock of recognition" upon reading certain articles, and Kathryn Abrams believes Patricia Williams' stories because they "resonate" with her experiences. But for those readers who neither resonate nor recognize, and for those who passionately disagree, there is no way to enter the dialogue. Thus, as Gerald Torres says, unless augmented by analysis, storytelling may "function as an authoritarian conversation-ending move."

Reasoned argument also helps to counteract the peculiar dangers of anecdotal evidence. The value of grappling with concrete examples is lost if we allow ourselves to move away from rigorous standards of honesty and completeness. Maintenance of those standards requires that the author not only present the story but explain why it was selected and how it was verified. Early in this article, we defined legal scholarship as an effort to improve our understanding of the law. Although a story that merely dramatizes some preconceived theory of law may be a useful rhetorical device, it does not teach the reader anything new. It is specifically the risk that the example may *not* fit our preconceived theories that opens up the possibility of learning something new. A scholar who refuses to take that risk is not engaged in genuine research. In particular, a failure to confront available contrary evidence, or at least to present that evidence to the reader, is dishonest. One form of dishonesty is for the narrator to apply unconventional principles to select examples without notifying the reader. A related form of intellectual dishonesty is to delete facts that undermine the scholar's thesis. Inclusion of such facts will often indicate good scholarship, for it demonstrates that the author has grappled seriously with contrary arguments. If a story is presented without any methodological discussion or effort to connect it to a thesis, both the author and the reader are more likely to allow it to slide by without rigorous questioning.

Stories can also be deceptive in subtler ways. As a form of rhetoric, stories can "tak[e] the other in, deflecting her on unacknowledged, perhaps deliberately hidden grounds." Often this is the unintentional result of using first-person narratives. Gordon Wood recognizes that "participants [do not] have a privileged access to knowledge of the events they are involved in." Thus, the accounts may be mistaken or distorted. Stories also tend to "favor those who are near at hand," ignoring more distant voices. Sometimes the deception, whether intentional or not, is the result of treating complex human dramas as morality plays. Occasionally, it stems from willful ignorance. Reasoned argument and critical analysis might evoke more awareness of the limitations of the genre. As we argued earlier, a valid exercise in storytelling must involve efforts to assure the truthfulness and typicality of the story. Because these attributes are not self-documenting, the author must present some analysis to show that the story is credible and representative. This is similar to how a historian must defend her credibility judgments about historical sources and the inferences she has made from the historical record.

To the extent that a narrative merely conveys a concrete experience, it only partially achieves the purposes of legal scholarship. This conclusion flows from our belief in practical reason as a mediation between the concrete and the abstract; the purely concrete narrative remains fixated at one of these poles rather than mediating between them. Stories are best suited, in our view, for enriching legal scholarship with concreteness, but they need to be supplemented with reason and analysis. It is possible, at least in theory, that a narrative could be effectively used not only to convey concrete experiences, but also to encode abstract arguments which the reader could then analyze. On the whole, we are dubious about how successfully this encoding can be achieved. In any event, while such narrative would not explicitly provide analysis, it would effectively meet our requirement that analysis be conveyed to the reader. In one form or another, good scholarship must include but also move beyond the concrete.

The last criterion for evaluating scholarship, and perhaps the most difficult to articulate, is significance, which involves judging the importance of a piece of scholarship. Responsible storytellers should aspire to tell stories that are not merely meaningful but significant as well. As Thomas Ross aptly notes:

> "The fact that a story is true is never by itself sufficient reason to tell the story." If I tell a story that I cannot imagine has any purpose, or meaning, or use, and if it has no meaning for you, however true the assertions, perhaps I have violated the central ethical responsibility of the storyteller.

Importance cannot be measured purely by breadth or by actual influence. A scholar who successfully grapples with a narrow but intractable problem, or who crafts an elegant and persuasive argument that encounters a brick wall of ideological opposition, cannot be faulted. How, then, can we measure importance and thus distinguish the competent from the good and the good from the outstanding? It is here that practical reason may provide the best technique. Evaluating the importance of a work requires judgment, not application of wooden standards. It is ultimately a judgment about how the scholarship will stand the test of time. Every imaginative and critical faculty must be brought to bear, and, in the end, it is still a judgment.

Conclusion

In this article, we have tried to take legal storytelling seriously, yet without simply acceding to the storytellers' views about scholarship. Although we have not found sufficient evidence to support strong versions of the "different voice" thesis, we do find weaker versions credible; we also conclude that legal stories, particularly those "from the bottom," can play a useful role in legal scholarship. Unlike some advocates of storytelling, however, we see no reason to retreat from conventional standards of truthfulness and typicality in assessing stories. Nor do we see any reason to abandon the expectation that legal scholarship contain reason and analysis, as well as narrative. A legal story without analysis is much like a judicial opinion with "Findings of Fact" but no "Conclusions of Law."

We suspect that these conclusions will please no one. Arch-traditionalists will believe that, in the name of "practical reason," we have jettisoned intellectual rigor by giving any credence at all to legal storytelling. Advocates of legal storytelling will find us guilty of an illicit attempt to apply white male standards to their outsider jurisprudence: yet another effort by the establishment to domesticate and thereby neutralize a new radical movement. And scholars in the middle—those who like us believe in being open-minded but not empty-headed in response to new ideas—may have the most wounding critique of all: that we have merely stated the obvious. Our consolation is that, serious as these criticisms may be, they cannot *all* be correct.

19

On Telling Stories in School
A Reply to Farber and Sherry
Richard Delgado

I. Introduction

It is difficult to evaluate someone who at the same time is evaluating *you*—putting you under the glass, dissecting your culture, laws, profession, and norms of political fairness.[1] The outsider's task is formidable enough: first seeing, then addressing, defects in the culture in which all of us, including the outsider, are immersed.[2] But when one sets out, as Daniel Farber and Suzanna Sherry do in a recent article, to come to terms with outsider scholarship fairly and sympathetically, the task's difficulty increases by an order of magnitude.[3]

Empowered groups long ago established a host of stories, narratives, conventions, and understandings that today, through repetition, seem natural and true.[4] Among these are criteria of judgment—the terms and categories by which we decide which things are good, valid, worthy, and true.[5] Today, newcomers are telling their own versions, including *counterstories*, whose purpose is to reveal the contingency, partiality, and self-serving quality of the stories on which we have been relying to order our world.[6] These new stories naturally strike us as challenging—as indeed they often are designed to be. Some within the mainstream have dismissed the new stories as false, manipulative, "political"—or not law.[7] More moderate critics like Farber and Sherry urge that we take the newcomers seriously, identify when their workproduct is valid and when it is not, and lay down standards for evaluating it when it is.[8]

What both types of critics tend to overlook is that majoritarians tell stories too. But the ones they tell—about merit, causation, blame, responsibility, and racial justice—do not seem to them like stories at all, but the truth.[9] In a series of articles, I have pointed out the difficulty confronting an outsider—one writing an abolitionist essay, for example, or a novel argument for law reform.[10] New stories are always interpreted and judged in terms of the old.[11] One that differs too drastically from the standard account will strike the listener as extreme, false, or unworthy of belief.[12] Unless the storyteller is exceptionally ingenious, the scope for change through remonstrance, argument, and other verbal means is much more limited than we like to think. Jean Stefancic and I invented the term "empathic fallacy"[13] to describe this limitation. The difficulty it highlights confronts the reformist storyteller with a formidable task. What about the mainstream scholar who wishes to understand, empathize, and evaluate the outsider? As Pierre Schlag has put it, evaluation is very hard to do.[14]

Farber and Sherry have written easily the most sustained treatment of outsider scholarship.[15] Their argument is detailed and scholarly; they cite us chapter and verse. Yet, a number of lapses, large and small, mar an otherwise commendable effort. Part II of this Article identifies a number of these lapses. Part III explains in greater detail why evaluation of outsider scholarship is so hard—and so easy. The Parts work together as follows: The mistakes and failures I highlight in Farber's and Sherry's treatment of outsider jurisprudence illustrate a more general difficulty, which I set out in Part III. My conclusion is that the near impossibility of fairly treating new scholarly movements counsels against laying down evaluative criteria during those movements' early stages.

II. Errors and Misstatements

The footnotes of the Farber-Sherry article disclose a broad familiarity with outsider scholarship; they quote or cite many of the major writers and themes.[16] Yet the sections of their article concerned with describing[17] and identifying a range of valid functions for the new genres[18] contain a number of curious lapses. These errors, committed by serious and careful commentators, cast doubt on the entire evaluative enterprise. For, if observers as well-intentioned as these two go astray, how will others less generously inclined apply the criteria they end up proposing? I point out some of the more notable errors and misinterpretations for two reasons. First, it is important to clear up the errors in themselves; I have noticed that mainstream writers frequently accept their colleagues' descriptions of outsider jurisprudence as true without troubling to consult the original sources.[19] Second, the deficiencies in the Farber-Sherry article cast doubt on the entire enterprise of evaluating outsider scholarship by insider standards. In Part III, I offer a theoretical explanation for that difficulty and a suggestion for what we ought to do in the meantime. The oversights and omissions noted in Part II, then, supply the evidence for the theory in Part III.

A. Thematic Errors and Misconceptions

1. Equation of Outsider Jurisprudence With Narrative Scholarship

I love stories and narratives; indeed, I have written frequently in this mode myself.[20] Indeed, four years ago I wrote a letter to the *Michigan Law Review* that resulted in a symposium issue on legal storytelling.[21] Yet, not all outsider scholarship takes the form of stories or chronicles. Many classics of the critical race theory (CRT) genre,[22] such as Derrick Bell's *Serving Two Masters*[23] or Kimberle Crenshaw's article on transformation and legitimation,[24] are written in the standard casespolicies-arguments mode. Stefancic and I recently completed an extensive annotated bibliography of CRT, in the course of which we read every article and book that arguably fell within the corpus.[25] At most, one-quarter of the works could be described as written in the storytelling or narrative mode. This is not a minor quibble: Farber and Sherry focus on the alleged defects of narrative jurisprudence, yet often impute them to CRT as a whole.

2. Narrative Scholarship and the "Different Voices" Debate

Farber and Sherry write that the case for stories rests on showing that minority scholars write in a different voice, something that has not yet been done.[26] Unlike with women, where the work of Carol Gilligan established an empirical basis for the claim of differentness,[27] with the voice of color, distinctness has not yet been shown. Farber and Sherry reason that there may be a political (leftist) voice, or one of the poor, but aside from these commonalities, minority scholars share little.[28] Some scholars of color are leftist activists, others moderate, still others conservative. What common voice could all of them have, Farber and Sherry ask—and why cannot a white progressive write in the "voice of color?"[29]

Voice is a false issue. The best evidence of storytelling's usefulness lies in the stories themselves. One could argue as well that wolves do not howl, since some howl in a high key, others in a low one, and still others not at all, while some creatures that are not wolves howl as well. The point is not to impose some requirement (of dubious relevance) of uniqueness with respect to howling or legal storytelling, but to learn something about or from the behavior itself.

3. Stories Are Useless Without Analysis and Reasoned Argument

In oral presentations of their paper, Farber and Sherry illustrated one of their reservations about stories by telling one themselves—an anecdote about the young daughter of one of them who crayoned on an upholstered chair and, when scolded, generalized the wrong lesson.[30] Their point is that stories in themselves teach little unless supplemented with analysis and commentary that will enable the reader to connect the story with a more general rule or principle.[31]

True, but irrelevant[32]—most of us already follow this counsel. In perhaps the most notable example of legal storytelling, Derrick Bell and his interlocutor, Geneva, agree that their conversations must include statistics, case authority, and doctrinal analysis lest their colleagues reject their work as nonrigorous.[33] Most of us instinctively follow Bell's example; only a handful of the articles we reviewed consisted of unadorned narratives. Narratives, standing alone, of the sort Farber and Sherry condemn, are rare.

4. Overlooking the Deconstructionalist Tale, or "Counterstory"

When Farber and Sherry write of outsider stories, they seem to be thinking of just one kind—the personal account or description of the author's experience. They speak of "agony tales,"[34] of "unadorned" narratives[35] and the virtues of *concretness* in legal scholarship.[36] They conclude by finding a narrow place for storytelling, but only as an adjunct to traditional analysis and commentary.

This approach neglects a second, much more important type of narrative, namely the counterstory.[37] Majoritarians tell stories, as I noted earlier, but with the conviction that they are not stories at all, but the truth.[38] Accordingly, many CRT writers employ the "counterstory" to jar, mock, or displace a tenet of the majoritarian faith.[39] These tales are not so much aimed at setting forth a minority view, or how the writer felt about a given experience (e.g., experiencing discrimination while shopping). Rather, they are aimed at challenging one of the inscribed and blithely repeated accounts by which majoritarians make sense of their world; stories such as: without intent, no discrimination; outright racism is rare and sporadic; we have all the civil rights legislation and case law we need—any more would disadvantage innocent whites; some cultures unfortunately have less ambition and ability than others; and so on.[40]

It is curious that Farber and Sherry neglected this genre, focusing instead on the poetic *cri de coeur*. Yet, as I and others have pointed out, destruction of contingent, comforting myths is often a necessary prelude to constructing a better, fairer world.[41] The counterstory focuses not on helping a white understand a black, but on helping a white understand a *white*.

5. The Question of Audience

Some stories, Farber and Sherry write, do not ring true[42]; others leave the reader asking, "What am I to make of this?"[43] Still others make the reader wonder if the story is typical—how often can such a terrible thing happen?[44]

Stories, of course, may be told poorly, may leave their audience guessing. But some outsider narratives may puzzle Farber and Sherry simply because they require work on the reader's part,[45] or are not written with him or her in mind at all. The intended audience may be progressive scholars, other crits, or the minority community itself.[46] In the words of a black filmmaker, "[W]e get raves from the Black community . . . [but] snarls from white male critics who insist that the film is not about anything because it's not about anything that concerns them . . . 'How dare you make a film we don't understand?' "[47]

6. Stories' Purpose and Efficacy

Finally, Farber and Sherry try to ascertain the functions of outsider stories in order to evaluate how well the stories fulfill these functions.[48] Here, Farber and Sherry carry out a great deal of armchair analysis—stories might be good for this or that— concluding, naturally, that none of these functions is served, except the narrow, color-neutral one of illustrating practical reasoning.[49]

But it is not necessary to speculate on storytelling's purposes. Minority narrativists have not been shy about meta-analysis, about telling our readers what we think we are doing.[50] And, as for judging stories' impact, why speculate in a vacuum? Book sales, reviews, and placement of articles in top-tier journals[51] might enable us to gauge stories' efficacy without the guesswork.

B. Other Qualms and Reservations

Other inaccuracies in the Farber-Sherry article, while less serious, nevertheless are worth noting for the reasons mentioned earlier. They write that outsider juris-prudence has no particular content,[52] yet writers have had no difficulty in identifying a set of characteristic themes.[53] They write that the new CRT scholars disdain analysis and empirical research in favor of a good yarn,[54] when their work probably contains as much writing of these harder-edged types as does a similar sample of mainstream writing.[55] They write that minority storytelling can have little impact on the reader, since the writer and reader will either share a common world or not. If not, the story will be incomprehensible; if so, it will say little new.[56] (This argument could be used to justify throwing away one's umbrella.)[57] They argue that better ways exist to correct prejudice, such as science[58] (ignoring evidence that science and prejudice have often seemed to coexist quite easily).[59] They write that stories—especially those in the first person—may be unfair, since there is no way to refute them,[60] while others may be "conversation-ending move[s]."[61] (What about majoritarian stories, such as "We have looked everywhere for a minority professor, but the pool is so small?")[62] Stories may deceive the reader by leaving out relevant facts, or by failing to be typical of the situation described.[63] (Every narrative, however, leaves out something; their very point is to make sense out of the welter of phenomena that besiege us every moment.)[64]

III. Farber and Sherry on Evaluating Outsider Scholarship

The outsider storyteller's task, as I mentioned earlier, is formidable indeed.[65] Speech is paradigm-dependent. If racism is deeply imbedded in the very paradigm we rely on to describe and order our world, any story that challenges that paradigm too frontally will strike the reader as incoherent.[66] The task of the *insider* who sets out to understand and order the *outsider's* world is even more difficult—witness the above-noted lapses that Farber and Sherry commit in simply describing and analyzing outsider scholarship.[67] Consider next what they propose in the way of standards for evaluating that scholarship.

The purpose of all legal scholarship, they write, is to help the reader understand the law.[68] How does it do that? They reason that legal scholarship helps the reader by employing reason (especially practical reason) and analysis, by offering suggestions that are generalizable and testable.[69] Scholarship that takes the form of storytelling may be useful, then, but only if the stories are typical,[70] true,[71] and supported by analysis and reason.[72]

We should hesitate to adopt these criteria for outsider scholars. Consider the first criterion, that scholarship helps the reader understand the law. Outsider scholarship is often aimed not at understanding the law, but at changing it.[73] Or consider the requirement of typicality. Outsiders and their experiences by definition will not be typical. Of course, Farber and Sherry may be saying only that outsider stories should be typical of outsider experience. But who is to decide that—surely not one situated outside that experience.[74] Or, take the requirement of truth. Apart from mathematics and the physical sciences, truth is largely socially constructed.[75] If I pronounce society unjust, and you think it is fair and just, which of us has truth on his or her side? If, as I argued earlier, many of the dominant narratives incorporate a majoritarian perspective,[76] the requirement that outsider storytellers adhere to these versions on penalty of being labelled untruthful comes perilously close to requiring them to reject their own culture.

Finally, take the requirement of *generalizability*, which stories are said to achieve only through argument and abstraction. Whom does such a requirement benefit? Naturally, those whose experience is the norm, whose versions of the way things are

are inscribed in all the cultural rules and practices.[77] Empowered groups do not need particularity, context, a focus on the individual.[78] All the general rules, presumptions, and interpretations reflect them and their understandings.[79] Stories that too forcefully call attention to injustice, particularly of novel sorts, will strike them as anecdotal, unprincipled, or unfair. They will give them pejorative labels, like "agony stories,"[80] deem them conversation-closers[81]—all the while overlooking that cheerful majoritarian stories, for example about how much racial progress has been made, strike us the same way.

Consider how these requirements might converge in the case of Patricia Williams' famous Benetton story.[82] A casual or unsympathetic reviewer easily could criticize Professor Williams for making too much of an atypical experience. Most retail stores with which he is familiar are happy to sell to blacks. The unsympathetic reviewer may reason that Williams invites us to see her experience as common—which it is not, thereby violating the criterion of truthfulness. Moreover, she offers little in the way of reasoned argument, thereby missing an opportunity to connect her anecdote with legal doctrine and thereby aid the reader's understanding of the law. For example, she might have drawn a lesson about the public-private distinction, inviting the reader to question the way various spaces in our society are relegated to the private sphere, from which one may exclude others without giving a reason.

But this interpretation would miss Professor Williams' point. The Benetton story is intended to prompt consideration of a new legal category, namely spirit-murder. Spirit-murder is a kind of crime; like most crimes one may not commit it with impunity even on one's own property.[83] Spirit-murder occurs frequently in the lives of minority people—that is why her story rings true. Her point in telling it was not to urge a small, incremental change in the locus of the public-private line. Rather, she intended to call attention to the law's inadequacy in a recurring situation. Focusing on the Farber-Sherry requirements—truth, typicality, and conventional reasoned argument—might easily lead the reader to miss the deeper truth at the heart of Professor Williams' story.

IV. Conclusion

All this counsels caution in evaluating outsiders. Empathy and understanding are difficult across large gaps of culture and experience. Even careful observation is in short supply—slaves observed their masters far more carefully, and with more reason, than the latter did them. Majoritarian tools of analysis, themselves only stories, inevitably will pronounce outsider versions lacking in typicality, rigor, generalizability, and truth. The purpose of many outsider narratives is to put our very ordering principles, including these, in question. Empowered groups long ago inscribed their favorite narratives—ones that reflected their sense of the way things ought to be—into myth and culture. Now they profess to consult that culture, meekly and humbly, in search of standards for judging challenges to that culture.

Neat, but circular. A better approach would be to postpone efforts to evaluate new scholarly movements. There is little urgency; most of the voices have tenure.[84] And, while the scholars may not all be young, the movements are. Critical race theory, for example, held its first national workshop in the summer of 1989. As I pointed out on another occasion, there are many things one can do with an infant—nurture it, get to know it, observe and interact with it.[85] But should we rush in with evaluative criteria to rank its eyes, teeth, limbs, and brain? Sometimes it may be better to live with uncertainty a little longer, tolerate a degree of experimentation, rather than shut off a world-crossing experiment that may one day benefit us all.[86]

Notes

1. On the general difficulty of evaluating non-mainstream legal scholarship, see Pierre Schlag, *Prefiguration and Evaluation*, 80 Cal. L. Rev. 965 (1992). On "outsider" scholarship in general, see, for example, Derrick A. Bell, *Faces at the Bottom of the Well* (Basic Books, 1992); Richard Delgado, *The Imperial Scholar: Reflections on a Review of Civil Rights Literature*, 132 U. Pa. L. Rev. 561 (1984).
2. Immersion in the culture causes even the marginalized to internalize its precepts. See, for example, Richard Delgado and Jean Stefancic, *Images of the Outsider in American Law and Culture: Can Free Expression Remedy Systemic Social Ills?*, 77 Cornell L. Rev. 1258, 1288–91 (1992).
3. See Daniel Farber and Suzanna Sherry, *Telling Stories Out of School: An Essay on Legal Narratives*, 45 Stan L. Rev. 807 (1993). Farber and Sherry set out their own version of what outsider scholarship is, focusing mainly on critical race theory and feminism; identify the role and functions of narratives in outsider scholarship; address the relationship between "voice" and narrative scholarship; and offer an approach to evaluating scholarship employing the narrative, or "storytelling," mode. For other critiques of outsider and narrative jurisprudence, see Randall Kennedy, *Minority Critiques of Legal Academia*, 102 Harv. L. Rev. 1745 (1989); Mark Tushnet, *The Degradation of Constitutional Discourse*, 81 Georgetown L. J. 251 (1992).
4. See Catharine MacKinnon, *Feminism Unmodified: Discourses on Life and Law* (Harvard, 1987); Richard Delgado, *Shadowboxing: An Essay on Power*, 77 Cornell L. Rev. 813, 818 (1992); Richard Delgado, *Mindset and Metaphor*, 103 Harv. L. Rev. 1872, 1874–75 (1990); Elizabeth Spellman, *Inessential Woman: Problems of Exclusion in Feminist Thought* 159 (Beacon, 1988).
5. Delgado, 103 Harv. L. Rev. at 1874–77 (cited in note 4).
6. On the role and function of counterstories, see Derrick A. Bell, *And We Are Not Saved: The Elusive Quest for Racial Justice* 1–10 (Basic Books, 1987) (using myth and fiction to probe America's racial history and consciousness); Richard Delgado, *Storytelling for Oppositionists and Others: A Plea for Narrative*, 87 Mich. L. Rev. 2411 (1989) (discussing storytelling and counterstorytelling as means of oppositional reform).
7. See the authorities cited in note 3. On the "not law" criticism levelled at critical legal studies, see Paul D. Carrington, *Of Law and the River*, 34 J. Legal Ed. 222 (1984).
8. Farber and Sherry, 45 Stan. L. Rev. at 824–30 (cited in note 3) (Part III.B, *Stories from the "Bottom"*); id. at 830–54 (Part IV, *Standards for Evaluating Stories as Scholarship*).
9. Delgado, 77 Cornell L. Rev. at 818 (cited in note 4) (reasoning that majoritarian concepts and practices come to seem unexceptionable, i.e., true "the way things are").
10. See Richard Delgado and Jean Stefancic, *Why Do We Tell the Same Stories?: Law Reform, Critical Librarianship, and the Triple Helix Dilemma*, 42 Stan. L. Rev. 207 (1989); Richard Delgado and Jean Stefancic, *Norms and Narratives: Can Judges Avoid Serious Moral Error?*, 69 Tex. L. Rev. 1929 (1991); Delgado and Stefancic, 77 Cornell L. Rev. at 1258 (cited in note 2).
11. See, for example, Delgado and Stefancic, 77 Cornell L. Rev. at 1279; Delgado and Stefancic, 69 Tex. L. Rev. at 1957.
12. See Delgado and Stefancic, 77 Cornell L. Rev. at 1279. On the many ways in which some writers in the legal mainstream continue to marginalize new scholarship, see Richard Delgado, *The Imperial Scholar Revisited: How to Marginalize Outsider Writing, Ten Years Later*, 140 U. Pa. L. Rev. 1349 (1992).
13. See Delgado and Stefancic, 77 Cornell L. Rev. at 1261. See also id. at 1278–79 (reasoning that new stories always are screened and interpreted through the medium of the old and that ones that are radical departures always are rejected); id. at 1280–82 (designating the belief that we may somehow escape this limitation the "empathic fallacy").
14. Schlag, 80 Cal. L. Rev. at 965 (cited in note 1).
15. Other treatments, such as Mark Tushnet, *The Degradation of Constitutional Discourse*, 80 Georgetown L. J. 251; Mary Coombs, *Outsider Scholarship: The Law Review Stories*, 63 U. Colo. L. Rev. 683 (1992); or Edward Rubin, *On Beyond Truth*, 80 Cal. L. Rev. 889 (1992), in my opinion are less successful than that of Farber and Sherry.

16. For example, Farber and Sherry, 45 Stan. L. Rev. at 814–19 (cited in note 3) (Part II.B) (citing, among others, Alex Johnson, Sharon Rush, Jerome Culp, Randall Kennedy, Richard Delgado, Mari Matsuda, Patricia Williams, Derrick Bell, Lucinda Finley, Robin Barnes, Robert Williams, Stephanie Wildman, Martha Fineman, Catharine MacKinnon, Toni Massaro, Stephen Carter, Duncan Kennedy, and Gary Peller).

17. Id. at 809–19 (Part II).

18. Id. at 819–30 (Part III).

19. For a discussion of this phenomenon, see Delgado, 140 U. Pa. L. Rev. at 1364–65 (cited in note 12).

20. See, for example, Richard Delgado, *Rodrigo's Chronicle*, 101 Yale L. J. 1357 (1992); Richard Delgado, *Derrick Bell and the Ideology of Law Reform: Will We Ever Be Saved?*, 97 Yale L. J. 923 (1988) (book review); Richard Delgado, *Storytelling for Oppositionists and Others: A Plea for Narrative*, 87 Mich. L. Rev. 2411 (1989).

21. Letter from Richard Delgado to Kevin Kennedy, editor in chief, *Michigan Law Review*, June 1, 1988 (on file with author). See *Symposium, Legal Storytelling*, 87 Mich. L. Rev. 2073 (1989).

22. Farber and Sherry use two examples of outsider jurisprudence to illustrate their thesis about storytelling—feminism, Farber and Sherry, 45 Stan. L. Rev. at 810–14 (Part II.A), and CRT, id. at 814–19 (Part II.B). I shall be concerned mainly with their treatment of CRT.

23. Derrick Bell, *Serving Two Masters*, 85 Yale L. J. 470 (1974).

24. Kimberle Crenshaw, *Race, Reform and Retrenchment: Transformation and Legitimation in Antidiscrimination*, 101 Harv. L. Rev. 1331 (1988).

25. Richard Delgado and Jean Stefancic, *Critical Race Theory: An Annotated Bibliography*, 79 Va. L. Rev. 461 (1993).

26. Farber and Sherry, 45 Stan. L. Rev. at 809–19 (Part II).

27. See Carol Gilligan, *In a Different Voice* 69–105 (1982); Carol Gilligan and Jane Attanuci, *Two Moral Orientations*, in Carol Gilligan, Janie Ward, and Jill Taylor, eds., *Mapping the Moral Domain: A Contribution of Women's Thinking to Psychological Theory and Education* 73 (Harvard, 1988).

28. Farber and Sherry, 45 Stan. L. Rev. at 815–18.

29. Id. at 818–19.

30. See, for example, Address by Daniel Farber and Suzanna Sherry, Yale Law School, Oct: 1992. The same story also appeared in an earlier draft of their article (manuscript on file with author).

31. Farber and Sherry, 45 Stan. L. Rev. at 846–53 (Part IV).

32. See text accompanying notes 77–84 (discussing the connection between practical reason and storytelling).

33. For example, Derrick Bell, *Foreward: The Civil Rights Chronicles*, 99 Harv. L. Rev. 4, 14–36 (1985) (cited in note 6); Delgado, 87 Mich. L. Rev. at 2418–22 (cited in note 6). But see Bell, *And We Are Not Saved* at 43 (observing that even dazzling analysis may fail to persuade skeptical white readers).

34. Farber and Sherry, 45 Stan. L. Rev. at 835–38.

35. Id. at 848–51.

36. Id. at 822–24.

37. See Delgado, 87 Mich. L. Rev. at 2413–18, 2429–35.

38. See text accompanying notes 2–5, 9–12; Delgado, 77 Cornell L. Rev. at 818 (cited in note 4).

39. See, for example, Delgado, 87 Mich. L. Rev. at 2438; Bell, *And We Are Not Saved* (illustrating the use of chronicles and counterstories aimed at challenging the dominant stories of race).

40. See sources cited in notes 4 and 6 (identifying and analyzing some of these stories about women and blacks).

41. See, for example, Delgado, 87 Mich. L. Rev. at 2412–18, 2429–35.

42. Farber and Sherry, 45 Stan. L. Rev. at 822–24 (Part III.A.2).

43. Id. at 825–26, 830–31.

44. Id. at 838–40.

45. See text accompanying notes 82–84.

46. On the question of audience, see Regina Austin, *Sapphire Bound!*, 1989 Wis. L. Rev. 539.

47. Patricia Smith, *Voices Struggling to be Heard*, Boston Globe A-5 (Sept. 1, 1991) (interview with Black filmaker Julie Dash).

48. See Farber and Sherry, 45 Stan. L. Rev. at 830–31 (Part III).

49. Id. at 820–24 (Part III.A.1., 2.).

50. See text accompanying notes 38–40; Delgado, 87 Mich. L. Rev. at 2412–15, 2435–40 (identifying the functions of narratives as (i) challenging majoritarian mindset; (ii) making easy issues harder; (iii) introducing formerly excluded perspectives; and (iv) arguing for a re-definition and new understanding of social reform).

51. On the relatively favorable reception of critical and radical-feminist scholars by the law reviews but the more guarded one by mainstream scholars, see Delgado, 140 U. Pa. L. Rev. at 1350–51 (cited in note 12).

52. Farber and Sherry, 45 Stan. L. Rev. at 809–10 (Part I) (no distinctive voice or tenets).

53. See, for example, Delgado and Stefancic, 79 Va. L. Rev. at 462–63 (cited in note 25) (identifying ten such themes); Stephanie Goldberg, *The Law, A New Theory Holds, Has a White Voice*, N.Y. Times B8 (July 17, 1992).

54. Farber and Sherry, 45 Stan. L. Rev. at 808–09.

55. See Delgado and Stefancic, 79 Va. L. Rev. 461.

56. Farber and Sherry, 45 Stan. L. Rev. at 824–26, 847–50.

57. *Viz.*, if a wild storm is blowing, an umbrella won't keep me dry; and if the rain is extremely light, I won't need one at all.

58. Farber and Sherry, 45 Stan. L. Rev. at 830, 835–37.

59. See, for example, Stephen J. Gould, *The Mismeasure of Man* (Norton, 1983).

60. Farber and Sherry, 45 Stan. L. Rev. at 835–38.

61. Id. at 851.

62. For a discussion of this standard argument, see Delgado, 103 Harv. L. Rev. at 1875–76 (cited in note 4).

63. Farber and Sherry, 45 Stan. L. Rev. at 852–53.

64. See Delgado and Stefancic, 69 Tex. L. Rev. at 1932–33, 1956–57 (cited in note 10); Delgado and Stefancic, 77 Cornell L. Rev. at 1279–81 (cited in note 2).

65. See text accompanying note 10 and sources cited therein.

66. Delgado and Stefancic, 77 Cornell L. Rev. at 1279. See Delgado, 87 Mich. L. Rev. at 2413.

67. See notes 26–64 and accompanying text.

68. Farber and Sherry, 45 Stan. L. Rev. at 809.

69. Id. at 846–51.

70. Id. at 838–40.

71. Id. at 832–35.

72. Id. at 850–54.

73. See, for example, Delgado, 87 Mich. L. Rev. at 2415. See also sources cited in Delgado and Stefancic, 79 Va. L. Rev. 461 (cited in note 25) (listing CRT articles, most of which deal with social or legal transformation).

74. For works questioning that such an "essential" unitary experience even exists, see generally Stephen L. Carter, *Reflections of an Affirmative Action Baby* (Basic Books, 1991). See also Kennedy, 102 Harv. L. Rev. 1745 (cited in note 3).

75. On the construction of the social world, see generally Peter L. Berger and Thomas Luckmann, *The Social Construction of Reality* (Doubleday, 1966). For law's role, see Delgado, 77 Cornell L. Rev. 813 (cited in note 4); Catharine MacKinnon, *Toward A Feminist Theory of the State* (Harvard, 1989); MacKinnon, *Feminism Unmodified* (cited in note 4) (discussing law's role in constructing women's reality):

76. See notes 3–6 and accompanying text.

77. Delgado, 77 Cornell L. Rev. at 818. See generally MacKinnon, *Toward a Feminist Theory*; MacKinnon, *Feminism Unmodified*.

78. See Delgado, 77 Cornell L. Rev. at 818–22. See generally Spellman, *Inessential Woman* (cited in note 4).

79. See sources cited in notes 77–78.

80. Farber and Sherry, 145 Stan. L. Rev. at 835–38.

81. Id. at 851.

82. In the story, the author goes to Benetton to buy Christmas presents for her mother. She presses the buzzer, the only way to gain entrance. But the young sales clerk, after scrutinizing her face, denies her entry, even though other customers are present and it is not yet closing time. Patricia Williams, *The Alchemy of Race and Rights* 44–45 (Harvard, 1991). For Farber's and Sherry's doubts about this story, see Farber and Sherry, 45 Stan. L. Rev. at 835 & n. 146.

83. Patricia Williams, *The Obliging Shell: An Informal Essay on Formal Equal Opportunity*, 87 Mich. L. Rev. 2128, 2139–43 (1989); Patricia Williams, *Spirit-Murdering the Messenger: The Discourse of Fingerpointing as the Law's Response to Racism*, 42 U. Miami L. Rev. 127, 129, 135–36, 147–54 (1987).

84. For the manner in which well-meaning senior professors often counsel young scholars of color to postpone writing about race until they have first demonstrated their skills at mainstream doctrinal analyses, see Delgado, 132 U. Pa. L. Rev. at 561–62 (cited in note 1).

85. Richard Delgado, Comment on Mary Coombs, University of Colorado Law Review Symposium on Legal Scholarship, Boulder, Col., Feb. 1992, reprinted in part, 63 Colo. L. Rev. 721 (1992).

86. Richard Delgado, *When a Story Is Just a Story: Does Voice Really Matter?*, 76 Va. L. Rev. 95, 103–05 (1990).

Permissions

Index

CPSIA information can be obtained at www.ICGtesting.com
Printed in the USA
LVOW052027040112

262433LV00002B/8/P